Advance praise for Organization Theory

'Few books so successfully communicate the spirit and possibility of enquiry that draws on the rich resources now available to the non-doctrinaire organization theorist as does Mary Jo Hatch's *Organization Theory*. Here students will learn, and learn to use for themselves, modernist, symbolic, and postmodern perspectives as approaches that can be drawn on, conversed with, and used to add value to either their own research and writing or their practical activity as managers and members of organizations. Especially valuable are the treatments of symbolic culture and physical structure, both relatively neglected topics in most texts.

If you want to recommend a current text that is broad, coherent, and reader-friendly, then look no further!'

STEWART CLEGG, University of Technology,
Sydney, Australia

'When the world was innocent and predictable, and knowledge accumulated from one year to the next, writing a textbook on organization theory was a simple matter of chronological compilation. When the worlds are multiple, fragmented, and in constant kaleidoscopic movement, it takes courage and skill to attempt it. Mary Jo Hatch confronts the plurality of contemporary organization theories with bravura and respect, creatively and critically, representing and reconstructing at once. *Organization Theory* is both a historical testimony and a peek into the future, and it will be the main guide to organization studies well into the 2000s.'

BARBARA CZARNIAWSKA-JOERGES
Gothenburg University, Sweden

'I don't like textbooks as a rule. They are usually rather dull and tend to distort as much as they inform. This book is refreshingly different. It is a model of clarity, it makes rather abstract material accessible without trivializing it. It provides critical, historical, and postmodern perspectives on organization theory that are missing from most texts on the topic. It is an intelligent and balanced treatment that brings in voices of many, often neglected organizational participants who need to be heard if we are to better understand the subject matter. The author's treatment of postmodernism will enlighten both students and teachers and her applications of theory to practice reveal the complexity of dealing with organizational change and the value of adopting a multiple perspective approach to its study. It is at times playful, whilst always being thoughtful and respectful of the importance of the material. I learned a great deal from reading it and I believe others will too. It is a very good textbook and I hope it is widely used.'

PETER FROST, University of British Columbia, Canada

'This book is a vivid example of a true conversation between the author and the reader, who is gradually empowered to think reflexively and to make his/her own picture of this complex and diversified field of study. As with any good textbook, this work defines broad analytical categories, explores basic issues and offers a variety of

theoretical perspectives, in a language that is both simple and comprehensible. What is quite unusual for a textbook is the author's ability to bring the reader — sweetly but tenaciously — to a growing level of epistemological awareness.'

PASQUALE GAGLIARDI, ISTUD and the
Catholic University of Milan, Italy

'For once, a textbook that does justice to the richness of organizational analysis. By employing multiple perspectives, Hatch succeeds in stimulating the imagination and broadening our intellectual horizons. Required reading for everyone interested in the growing irrationality of organizations.'

JOHN HASSARD, University of Keele, UK

'This textbook systematically surveys international organization theory from the three perspectives that currently inform most management theorists' work. It is personal and engaging, without simplifying or mystifying a complex subject matter. I believe academics as well as students will find it a useful, contemporary review of the field. More important, the book provides a needed template for exploring diverse perspectives on how organizations influence modern life and can themselves be influenced and changed.'

ANNE S. HUFF, University of Colorado, USA and
Cranfield University, UK

'This lucid, tolerant textbook covers the usual topics with an unusual range of approaches to organizational theory and research, including the rational and the symbolic, quantitative and ethnographic, critical and postmodern views—a truly international tour de force.'

JOANNE MARTIN, Stanford University, USA

'Mary Jo Hatch's book belongs in the select company of Scott, Perrow, and Morgan as a definitive rendering of organizational theory. This is a careful, informed, and meaningful extension of organizational concepts using symbolic–interpretive and postmodern perspectives. Hatch loves ideas almost as much as she loves choosing the right words to enliven them. The field of organizational studies needs this book as do those who want to position themselves for the 21st century.'

KARL E. WEICK, University of Michigan, USA

'A text that is simultaneously far-reaching and innovative, drawing in US and European sources in an authoritative way. Hatch's enthusiasm and scholarship sustains a stimulating overview of a wide range of contemporary debates and perspectives in organization theory.'

HUGH WILLMOTT, Manchester School of
Management, UMIST, UK

Organization Theory

Modern, Symbolic, and Postmodern Perspectives

MARY JO HATCH

OXFORD

UNIVERSITY PRESS

Great Clarendon Street, Oxford OX2 6DP

Oxford University Press is a department of the University of Oxford.
It furthers the University's objective of excellence in research, scholarship,
and education by publishing worldwide in

Oxford New York

Athens Auckland Bangkok Bogotá Buenos Aires Calcutta
Cape Town Chennai Dar es Salaam Delhi Florence Hong Kong Istanbul
Karachi Kuala Lumpur Madrid Melbourne Mexico City Mumbai
Nairobi Paris São Paulo Singapore Taipei Tokyo Toronto Warsaw

with associated companies in Berlin Ibadan

Oxford is a registered trade mark of Oxford University Press
in the UK and in certain other countries

Published in the United States
by Oxford University Press Inc., New York

British Library Cataloguing in Publication Data

Data available

Library of Congress Cataloging in Publication Data

Data available

ISBN 0-19-877491-5
ISBN 0-19-877490-7 (pbk)

10 9 8 7 6 5

Printed in Great Britain
on acid-free paper by
Bookcraft (Bath) Ltd,
Midsomer Norton, Somerset

For Mom and Dad, who encouraged me to get out in the world

About the author

Mary Jo Hatch is Professor of Organization Theory at Cranfield School of Management in England. She is an American organization theorist who has taught management and organization theory, and published research on organizations, in both the U.S. and Europe during the 1980s and 1990s. Her formal education took place at the University of Colorado, where she studied architecture as an undergraduate; Indiana University where she studied English literature and creative writing as an undergraduate, and later earned an MBA in finance; and Stanford University, where she earned her Ph.D. in organizational behavior with an emphasis on organization theory. She has held teaching posts at San Diego State University and UCLA in the U.S., and the Copenhagen Business School in Denmark. She is an active participant in the American Academy of Management, the British Academy of Management, the Standing Conference on Organizational Symbolism (SCOS), and the European Group for Organization Studies (EGOS). Her research publications appear in *Academy of Management Review*, *Advances in Strategic Management*, *Administrative Science Quarterly*, *Journal of Business Ethics*, *Journal of Management Inquiry*, *Organization Science*, *Organization Studies*, and *Studies in Cultures, Organizations and Societies*. She is European Editor for the *Journal of Management Inquiry* and has done guest editing for *Studies in Cultures, Organizations and Societies* and *Organization Science*.

Preface

A NY narrative depends upon the perspective and location of its author. My perspective is as an American organization theorist, trained and employed in business schools, who has taught management and organization theory, and published research on organizations, in both the U.S. and Europe during the 1980s and 1990s. My formal education took place at the University of Colorado, where I studied architecture as an undergraduate; Indiana University where I studied English literature and creative writing as an undergraduate, and later earned an MBA in finance; and Stanford University, where I earned my Ph.D. in organizational behavior with an emphasis on organization theory. My learning then continued in the context of my teaching posts—at San Diego State University and UCLA in the U.S., the Copenhagen Business School in Denmark, and now at the Cranfield School of Management in England—as well as through memberships in professional associations, including the American Academy of Management, the British Academy of Management, the Standing Conference on Organizational Symbolism (SCOS), and the European Group for Organization Studies (EGOS).

These days I live in a rural English village, in a thatched cottage built in the late 16th century, with beautiful countryside views. I spend my time doing research, reading, writing, travelling to conferences, giving lectures and seminars at a wide variety of universities, and doing a little oil painting. My research interests involve: organizational culture; identity and image; symbolic understanding in and of organizations; managerial humor as an indicator of organizational paradox, ambiguity and contradiction; and aesthetic (especially narrative and metaphoric) aspects of organizing. I consider myself to be a symbolic-interpretive researcher whose methodology shifts between interpretive ethnography and discourse analysis. It is upon all of these experiences that I draw in presenting organization theory. Unavoidable biases with regard to organization theory and its history are created by these particular experiences, and thus the book you are holding is influenced in ways that are difficult for me to specify. Other accounts of organization theory are available and will provide other versions of its story.

I came to write this book because, as a symbolic-interpretive researcher teaching organization theory, I was frustrated by the limited choices of textbooks for my classes. There seemed to be only two alternatives: either a modernist exposition on the content of organization theory with an expressly control-centered, rationalistic orientation; or a radical alternative that focused on criticising the modernist approach and displayed little or no sympathy for the substantial contributions modernist organization theory has made. I wanted a book that paid due respect to the modernist perspective, but that went beyond mere recitation of the findings of modernist research to explore the contributions of ethnographic studies that often challenge modernist notions, and that would give voice not only to the criticisms raised against organization theory as a tool of managerialism, but also to alternatives emerging from interdisciplinary research in the social sciences. I found that if I wanted such a book, I was either going to have to wait for someone else to get around to it, or I was going to have to write it myself. Being impatient, I chose the latter course.

Impatience, however, does not write books. It has taken me ten years to accomplish the task I first imagined in the mid-1980s. The process through which it materialized has been a labor of enthusiasm for the field of organization theory, and of determination to find a way to present material that is commonly believed to be difficult, dry, and boring in the extreme. To translate my vague image into this book required that I delve into my own subjective experience, to draw out the reasons for my enthusiasm and to develop the means of communicating them to others. These tasks I undertook in the classroom, and it is my students who deserve the lion's share of credit for this product—it is they who have been my teachers.

Each chapter of the book was developed through an iterative and interactive process of presenting ideas to my classes, followed by discussions in which I listened and responded to what the students chose to focus on, which generally involved application of the ideas to some aspect of their personal, professional, or anticipated managerial lives. In this way, I was able to observe how students handled the material I presented to them, what they found most interesting in it, and what they thought they might use it for. Along the way I discovered that the best way to present material in anticipation of discussion was to reflect upon what I found interesting in the topic, to press myself to learn something new about it just before going into class (which caused me to be in an active learning mode), and to share through open reflection what I found inspiring and what I was even now learning about it. The students responded well to this approach and appreciated the effort I took, because, as they told me, the enthusiasm I demonstrated for the material was contagious.

As I developed my learning-based style of teaching, I found that the students mimicked me in our discussions. A few would begin to focus on what was pertinent or attractive to them, would have insight based on their own experience in combination with the new material, and their unsuppressed enthusiasm diffused to other students who became engaged with the material until eventually (toward the end of our term of study together), most in the room had had the experience of finding organization theory interesting and useful—at least once in their lives. The effect overall was that, as we spent time together in these endeavors, the students became more and more active in their own education, taking an increasing share of the responsibility for their learning onto their own shoulders. This, of course, was not universally true, as in any classroom there were the perennial plodders, but by and large I was pleased that by focusing on the interesting, by following our collective intuition in the exploration of organization theory, we together carved out what I believe is a fair representation of the knowledge organization theory offers. While it is true that I polished the product through many rounds of review with both students and colleagues (who are experts in the subjects the book develops), on the whole the book was produced in dialogue with my students, and its contents reflect what they have been willing to take on board and use in their efforts to become educated future managers. The book is, in a way, a description of what we did together in the classroom.

A key element in my teaching/learning style is to allow students to explore in the directions their own curiosity takes them. The influence I exercise is then directed at developing their natural curiosity into genuine interest and mature engagement with the subject matter. Getting this process started is half the battle, and I see this book as a collection of stimulations for discussions of various aspects of organizing that have proven of lasting interest to the wide variety of students with whom I have shared the learning experience. This material has been developed over my years of teaching undergraduates, post-graduates (MBA and Ph.D.), and executives. Because I have not simplified the complex understandings that Organization Theory offers, but rather have clarified the language in which these ideas were originally (and often subsequently) presented, I find that the material in this book is useful, attractive, and accessible to a wide range of audiences.

There is another aspect to this book that bears mentioning here. At about the time that I concluded my Ph.D. training and took my first job as a faculty member, the push to internationalize business schools reached peak levels in the U.S. At the time, I observed that attempts to internationalize the business school curriculum often consisted of simply using examples of companies headquartered or operating in foreign countries. As a culture researcher, I was suspicious of this approach to internationalization because I realized that examples will always be presented using concepts and perspectives that are rooted in the experiences of their author. Thus, if an author has only made brief (or no) visits to other cultures, then his or her analysis is unlikely to invoke anything like an international perspective. My opportunity to live and work in Denmark presented itself at just the moment these ideas were forming and provided me with an alternative.

Preface

Moving to Denmark (I lived there three and one-half years all told) afforded me the chance to internationalize myself, along with the content of my course. My experiences taught me that internationalization goes way beyond the examples and knowledge that you offer, it is about profound changes in the ways you understand that affect your approach to description, analysis, and explanation—in other words, how you theorize.

My internationalization took root at about the same time that I was writing up the first version of this textbook. This coincidence had several important effects on what I was to produce. First, since I was teaching Danes who were fluent in English, but were not native speakers, I found that I had to restrict my vocabulary. While Danish students could easily follow complex and abstract arguments, and were, from my experience as an American, remarkably and delightfully fond of such arguments, they appreciated my keeping the language simple when I explained complex ideas. I obliged them and became intrigued by the puzzle of retaining the complexity of ideas, while reducing the complexity of how the ideas were presented. As I was teaching and writing at the same time, the language I used with my students slipped naturally onto the pages of my textbook. This turned out to be a real blessing, as it provided the means to write a demanding book about a complex subject that is accessible to anyone with a reasonable proficiency in the English language, a proficiency that has become practically essential in the international world of business. When I returned to the U.S. two years later and began using my manuscript as a text in my American MBA classes, I was startled at the strength of the positive response it received. In retrospect, I suppose it is not surprising that accessibility to complex ideas was appreciated by native as well as by non-native English speakers.

A second effect of my time in Denmark was the profound appreciation for multiple perspectives that it provided. I had already been introduced to the idea of multiple perspectives through my research training which involved struggling with debates over whether qualitative or quantitative methods provided a better means of addressing the problems of organizing—a debate that was raging at the time of my Ph.D. training. After moving to Denmark, the idea of accepting multiple perspectives began to take on new meaning. First of all, I became aware of the differences between European academic traditions of social science that focused on ontology and epistemology, and American academic traditions that were far more concerned with the issues of theory and method. At first I simply substituted my preferred set of terms (theory and method) for theirs (ontology and epistemology), but slowly I began to discern the differences. Eventually I came to an understanding of just how much slips between the cracks of translations of any sort, and on this foundation built my concern to preserve differences even while acknowledging the importance of crossing between different views which highlights their similarities. Out of these experiences, my views about organization theory as offering a fundamentally multiplicitous approach to understanding began to take shape. It is this theme that, as my Scandinavian friends would say, provides "the red thread" that holds this book together.

The particular perspectives that I identify as critical to grasping what organization theory has to offer I label modernist, symbolic (or, to be more accurate, symbolic-interpretive), and postmodern, after current fashion in the field today. At other times and in other places, these perspectives have been labelled differently. The **modernist perspective** has also been known as the rational perspective, the open systems view, the positivist school, and the quantitative approach. The **symbolic-interpretive perspective** has been known as the qualitative approach and is sometimes equated with the organizational culture school. The **postmodern perspective** has links to critical organization theory, the labor process school and radical feminism as well as to poststructuralist philosophy and literary theory. While these three perspectives will be distinguished throughout the book, in the end it must be admitted that the contours of these and other perspectives constantly shift and change so that there can be no final categorizing of ideas.

Still, there is value in making, for the moment at least, distinctions between several perspectives. For one thing, this practice broadens intellectual horizons and stimulates the imagination, both of which help to build knowledge and feed creativity. For another, learning to appreciate and rely upon multiple perspectives increases tolerance for the views of others and the capacity to make positive uses of the diversity multiple perspectives bring to organizations and to life in general. It is my belief that, if we are ever to realize the value of theory for practice, then we must master the use of multiple perspectives, for it is in bringing a variety of issues and ideas to the intellectual table that we will learn how to be both effective and innovative in our organizational practices.

Please be aware that I am not attempting integration of the multiple perspectives of organization theory. Each perspective has contributed something of value to my understanding of organizations and I want to relate that understanding to new students of the subject of organization theory, whether they be undergraduates, postgraduates, or practicing managers. I have attempted to communicate my enthusiasm for these ideas and to bring them to life for the reader. The structure I offer, such as it is, is provided by the chronology of the ideas, which typically progresses from modernist, through symbolic-interpretive to postmodernist ideas. I am not trying to privilege any particular viewpoint, I just want to let students vicariously experience the ideas in the rough order of their influence on the field (which was not always their order of appearance in the larger world).

Preface

Above all, I want students to feel free to play with ideas, but also to accept the discipline of focused study. To learn through their own experience that the hard work of studying other peoples' ideas can liberate their own thinking. The book is demanding—students who have used the book say they feel they have to underline *everything* because it all seems important. They report that they must (and do!) read the chapters multiple times. What is most important, they start talking about these ideas in class, and by their reports, outside of it as well. The book seems to stimulate interest in organization theory, and that, I think, is its greatest strength.

I do not, however, suffer under the illusion that the book has no faults. I am sure it has plenty. Most of all, it is incomplete—a work in progress as any book on a dynamic field of study must be. I know also that it inspires contradictory opinions—postmodernists complain that it isn't postmodern enough, modernists have said that it goes too far. My view is that organization theory is an open field, filled with controversy and contradiction. I want this book to reflect the many aspects of the discipline and to grow along with the field. In this I rely upon your support and feedback; together we can make this a book that gets better rather than worse with each successive edition. But I get ahead of myself here. First let me thank those who have already provided volumes of feedback and who have shaped the book you have in your hand.

The most important group to thank for inspiring this project, and for providing feedback on its progress, are the many students whose company I have enjoyed in the classroom as well as in private discussions outside of class. The learning experiences we have shared are what made writing this book possible and enjoyable. I have had enormous help from colleagues and friends who, along the way to finishing this version, have offered their expertise as advisors on various chapters. They checked and corrected the content, offered suggestions about the flow and structure of the arguments, and without their sound criticism, guidance, and encouragement, I would not have the confidence necessary to publish this material. I offer my deep gratitude to Ria Andersen, David Boje, Finn Borum, Frank Dobbin, Eigil Fivelsdahl, Joe Harder, Gerry Johnson, Kristian Kreiner, Livia Markoczy, Bert Overlaet, Susan Schneider, Ellen O'Connor, Jesper Strandgaard Pedersen, Mary Teagarden, Carol Venable, Dvora Yanow, and several anonymous reviewers. I am also indebted to Majken Schultz and Michael Owen Jones with whom I have worked closely in developing related classroom material and on numerous research projects.

In addition to those already mentioned I would like to single out two people whose extraordinary contributions have improved the quality of this book enormously: my husband Doug Conner and OUP editor David Musson. Both of these individuals read every chapter start to finish on multiple occasions and made many helpful suggestions as to both style and substance. Thanks also to Ann Davies of Cranfield University, and to Donald Strachan and Brendan Lambon of OUP for their efforts in bringing this project from manuscript to published work. San Diego State University, the Copenhagen Business School and Cranfield University each supported my work on this project during its various critical stages. The friendship, support, and inspiration of my close friends Kirsten and Jacob Branner helped to sustain me during the long hours that this project has filled. Last, but certainly not least, I would like to thank my daughter, Jennifer Cron, whose consternation at my confusion about her ways of viewing the world initially inspired me to open my mind to the myriad possibilities of exploring multiple interpretations.

M.J.H.

Cranfield
September 1996

Brief Contents

Detailed Contents

Detailed Contents

Detailed Contents

Detailed Contents

PART III. KEY ISSUES AND THEMES IN ORGANIZATION THEORY

9. Organizational Decision Making, Power, and Politics

Detailed Contents

List of Figures

List of Figures

List of Tables

Part I
What is Organization Theory?

theorist /ˈθɪərɪst/ *n.* a holder or inventor of a theory or theories.

theorize /ˈθɪəraɪz/ *v.intr.* (also **-ise**) evolve or indulge in theories. □□ **theorizer** *n.*

theory /ˈθɪərɪ/ *n.* (*pl.* **-ies**) **1** a supposition or system of ideas explaining something, esp. one based on general principles independent of the particular things to be explained (opp. HYPO-THESIS) (*atomic theory; theory of evolution*). **2** a speculative (esp. fanciful) view (*one of my pet theories*). **3** the sphere of abstract knowledge or speculative thought (*this is all very well in theory, but how will it work in practice?*). **4** the exposition of the principles of a science etc. (*the theory of music*). **5** *Math.* a collection of propositions to illustrate the principles of a subject (*probability theory; theory of equations*). [LL *theoria* f. Gk *theōria* f. *theōros* spectator f. *theōreō* look at]

Oxford Encyclopedic English Dictionary

1 | Why Study Organization Theory?

I WANT to admit something to you right up front: most people are predisposed to dislike organization theory. Some think that theory is impractical and overly academic. Others, especially those who have never studied social science before, find it extremely difficult. The very word "theory" sounds pretentious or intimidating to many people, and "organization" is another horribly abstract sounding term. Why not business or firm or company? Put them together and "organization theory" sounds unbearably dry and not the least bit inviting—unless you are one of the extremely rare people who come naturally to this subject matter. I wasn't one of those and, to tell the truth, I didn't like organization theory when I began my studies.

In a way, my initial disaffection with organization theory inspired this book. Once I began using organization theory in organizations and life in general, my experiences convinced me that this field of study opens up powerful ways of thinking. Organization theory has helped me time and again to analyze complicated situations and discover effective means of dealing with them. It has also opened my mind to many aspects of life, both inside and outside organizations, that I previously took for granted. My amazement at how relevant and valuable this subject matter is caused me to reverse completely my initial opinion of organization theory and find enthusiasm for it. The contrast between my initial opinion and my experience using organization theory made me want to write this book. Through it I hope to share my enthusiasm with you by helping you to discover the benefits and attractions of organization theory for yourself.

There are a few more things I should mention while we are at it. One is that it is somewhat ironic to call this field of study organization theory. While the name organization theory suggests that there is only one—a singular, integrated, overarching truth about organizations—in fact there are many organization theories and they do not always fit neatly together. Some people see this diversity as a stumbling block for an academic discipline because, in their view, if there is no agreement on what we have to offer, then we have nothing to offer at all. Others try to excuse the situation, arguing that organization theory is a very young field that will eventually work out its differences and come around to the singular perspective that (they believe) defines a mature academic discipline. I take an altogether different view. Along with a number of other organization theorists, I believe that organization theory always has been and always will be multiplicitous because of the variety of other fields of study that it draws on for inspiration and because organizations cannot be explained by any single theory.

Some of the influences from which organization theory draws inspiration are displayed in Figure 1.1. The top part of the figure shows the academic disciplines that have contributed to organization theory and the bottom part shows the names of some of the major thinkers from these disciplines. Notice that these influences range from the natural and social sciences to the arts and humanities. Now, I acknowledge that it is a stretch to contemplate contributions from all these different fields of knowledge, but I ask you, where else will you grapple with so many ideas? If, like me, you are fascinated by ideas, then I don't know any other field of study that will present you with greater variety. Even if you aren't particularly taken with ideas, the diversity of organization theory will teach you flexibility and adaptiveness which can't hurt you in times of complexity and rapid change like those we face as we enter the twenty-first century.

I should also explain the middle part of Figure 1.1. The four boxes labelled classical, modern, symbolic-interpretive, and postmodern represent one way of sorting out some of the diversity that organization theory offers. These boxes represent different perspectives on organizations, each with distinguishable assumptions, vocabularies, and, to some extent, theorists. In a way, the boxes give a sense of change over time as new influences on the field invite new theories which become aligned into groups of ideas that seem to belong together. Although there is a sequence to the development of these perspectives, it would be a mistake to think that newer perspectives replace older ones. In organization theory, perspectives accumulate, and over time they influence one another as organization theorists take in more and more of the ideas this field of study offers. This interaction among perspectives produces continuous change which is one reason why it is so difficult to make a case for any particular way of sorting through the ideas and perspectives of organization theory, including the one I presented to you in Figure 1.1. However, as a newcomer to the field, you will probably appreciate a little order; most people find it useful to hear about how others have come to terms with the diversity. This book is built around the theme

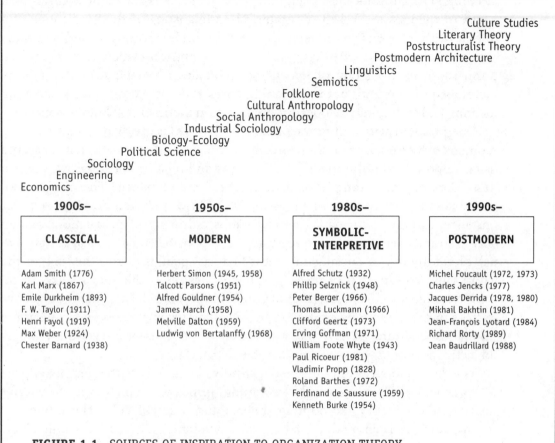

Culture Studies
Literary Theory
Poststructuralist Theory
Postmodern Architecture
Linguistics
Semiotics
Folklore
Cultural Anthropology
Social Anthropology
Industrial Sociology
Biology-Ecology
Political Science
Sociology
Engineering
Economics

1900s–	1950s–	1980s–	1990s–
CLASSICAL	**MODERN**	**SYMBOLIC-INTERPRETIVE**	**POSTMODERN**

Adam Smith (1776)	Herbert Simon (1945, 1958)	Alfred Schutz (1932)	Michel Foucault (1972, 1973)
Karl Marx (1867)	Talcott Parsons (1951)	Phillip Selznick (1948)	Charles Jencks (1977)
Emile Durkheim (1893)	Alfred Gouldner (1954)	Peter Berger (1966)	Jacques Derrida (1978, 1980)
F. W. Taylor (1911)	James March (1958)	Thomas Luckmann (1966)	Mikhail Bakhtin (1981)
Henri Fayol (1919)	Melville Dalton (1959)	Clifford Geertz (1973)	Jean-François Lyotard (1984)
Max Weber (1924)	Ludwig von Bertalanffy (1968)	Erving Goffman (1971)	Richard Rorty (1989)
Chester Barnard (1938)		William Foote Whyte (1943)	Jean Baudrillard (1988)
		Paul Ricoeur (1981)	
		Vladimir Propp (1828)	
		Roland Barthes (1972)	
		Ferdinand de Saussure (1959)	
		Kenneth Burke (1954)	

FIGURE 1.1. SOURCES OF INSPIRATION TO ORGANIZATION THEORY

The boxes indicate four major perspectives on organizations used as a framework for this book. The dates above the boxes indicate the decade when the perspective became recognizable within the field. Contributing disciplines are indicated above the boxes and some of their influential thinkers are indicated below. Notice that some contributions predate their influence on organization theory indicating the lag in communications between disciplines.

of multiple perspectives, and what I call modern, symbolic-interpretive, and post-modern perspectives will, in particular, frame our discussion as we work through the variety of theories and metaphoric appreciations of organizations that constitute the field of organization theory and the chapters of this book.

One last issue of introduction. Until very recently most organization theorists took the view that theories represent truth, that some do a better job than others, and that science is in the business of determining which theories are the most accurate. From this modernist point of view, judgments about the accuracy and truth of theories are based on empirical comparisons of the predictions of a theory with relevant facts collected about the world. Incorrect or deficient theories can be identified when compared to this empirical evidence, and removed from the collective body of knowledge. This describes the scientific method developed to its zenith in the natural sciences and applied disciplines like engineering and technology. Modernist organization theorists still hold this view.[1]

One problem with testing organization theories in this way is that the phenomena of interest are not often directly verifiable. That is, what can be observed is far removed from the theoretical concepts and relationships that we want to test. Consider the example of organizational performance. Theorists cannot agree about what constitutes performance or how it should be measured. For instance, should performance be defined as efficiency in production, market share, strategic effectiveness, quality, social responsibility, ecological sustainability, or is it merely financial gain? If it is financial gain, is it over the long or the short run? Within each of these possibilities lies other dilemmas. Take profit. Profit seems objective enough until you begin to consider the many subjective factors that enter into its computation—deciding what is a cost versus what is a capital expenditure, to give just one example. Thus, even a fact so seemingly objective as profit is open to considerable debate.

The debate about profit is ultimately resolved, but only with reference to a set of practices such as general accounting principles which are themselves influenced by theory (accounting theory) and a set of culturally influenced norms (such as listening to the advice of accountants). There is very little objectivity in management, when you get right down to it. And it is difficult to imagine how any theory of organizational performance can ever be proved right or wrong by a comparison with empirical evidence when the evidence is itself the product of other theories (in this case the theory of how to compute the profits of a firm) and of social practices that are developed by other organizations (government regulations concerning accountability to shareholders and to tax authorities). This is the symbolic-interpretive view, and according to symbolic-interpretivists, these are matters of social convention, not natural law.

Today it is increasingly common to find organization theorists who regard social theories as perspectives on a reality that is as much constructed by theories as it is represented by them. That is, social scientists work with realities created by social forces that are themselves the subject of study. This circularity sets social sciences, like organization theory, apart from the traditions of natural science and presents complicated issues for social theorists to consider. It also helps to explain why you should study organization theory. If theories are implicated in the production of knowledge and thus in our constructions of reality (e.g., organization, performance, profit, management), then you will want to know the theories that others are using and how to create your own so that you can more consciously (and conscientiously) participate in these processes.

This book is about organization theory and in it you will read about many different ways in which organizations are understood. These different theories of **organization** can guide your actions by giving you abstract images of what an organization is, how it functions, and how its members and other interested parties interact with and within it. But this book will do more than introduce you to theories of organization, it will offer you insight into the ways that theorists develop their theories and will help you to develop your own **theorizing** skills of abstraction, analysis, and reasoning. If you master these skills, you will be able to make significant contributions to any organization in which you take membership. Knowing organization theories will help you to understand how the organization works and to diagnose its problems. Knowing how to theorize will help you to develop, maintain, and change your understandings of organizations and what you are doing with and within them.

MULTIPLE PERSPECTIVES

Organization theorists often justify the diversity of organization theory and its multiple perspectives by pointing out the complexity of organization.[2] Organizational complexity can be colorfully illustrated by the Hindu parable of the blind men and the elephant. Six blind men of Hindustan, so the parable goes, met with an elephant one day. And, after their meeting, each described what he had encountered. The first said that an elephant was like a leaf. The second adamantly disagreed, claiming that it was certainly like a wall. The third described the elephant as a mighty tree, the fourth a spear, the fifth a rope, and the last one thought it was really a snake. Each of them had gotten hold of a different part of the elephant and so had come away with remarkably different understandings of this creature.

The point of retelling the story here is that organization theorists are a lot like those blind men, and organizations are their elephant. Like the blind men, organization theorists encounter a large and complex phenomenon with perceptual equipment that handicaps them with respect to knowing in a holistic or total way. Thus, they develop perspectives that have some bearing on organizations, but that are each inadequate in their own way. Only when viewing these numerous perspectives all at once do you get any sense of the magnitude of the problem you face when confronting the study of organization.

What is Organization Theory?

The complexity and multiplicity of organizations further suggests that the perspectives you use will affect your perceptions of organizational reality. Focusing attention on particular aspects of organization means ignoring other aspects. Although adopting multiple perspectives does not remove the problem of ignored aspects, it does expose you to more aspects than would a single point of view. This reduces the chances that you are ignoring something important and encourages you to become comfortable with a new type of understanding, one that holds the promise of new sources of inspiration and innovation.

Of course, multiple perspectives come with their own problems. For instance, because theories may be built on a variety of assumptions, concepts and perspectives can compete or conflict with each other. As a result, you may experience organization theory as uncertain, ambiguous, contradictory, and paradoxical. Prepare to be confused. At first the study of organization theory may seem easy. A few concepts, a few theories—big deal. But as you progress in your development of concepts and understanding, and particularly as you attempt to reconcile your growing theoretical knowledge with your personal experience, you will discover that the task is as complex as organization itself.

To give you a taste of the contentious nature of organization theory, I should point out that the view that multiple perspectives will map more of the territory and therefore provide you with greater and better knowledge is a strictly modernist interpretation of the blind men and the elephant parable. The modernist view is based on the belief that there is an objective, physical reality in question and thus any perspective is but a different view of the same thing (whether that be an elephant or an organization). In contrast, many symbolic-interpretivists and postmodernists assert that knowledge cannot be tested against the real world because the real world is constructed from our experiences, ideas, and statements (e.g., our theories about the world). That is, reality is subjectively defined, therefore different views construct different realities and these realities may be complementary, conflicting, or contradictory. Multiple perspectives may provide you with diverse possibilities for constructing your world and for understanding the constructions of others, but there is no guarantee of greater and better knowledge because there is no universal standard against which greater and better can be measured.

We will return to this and other differences between perspectives in the next chapter, but before we begin to explore organization theory, it will be helpful to explain what a theory is, and to define two important terms—"concept" and "abstraction"—both of which are basic to theorizing. Following this, I will briefly describe the plan of the rest of the book. The chapter will conclude with a conceptual model of organization that will help you to remember the structure of the book and at the same time remind you of the core concepts of organization theory: environment, technology, social structure, organizational culture, and physical structure.

THEORY AND CONCEPTS

Theory rests on a set of assumptions that forms the foundation for a series of logically interrelated claims. For instance, some theories assume that reality is objective (out there) whereas others assume that it is subjective (in here). Many objectivists reason that since reality is out there it can be studied by observers who are independent of their subject of interest. Subjectivists argue that since reality is in here it is personal and relative, and, therefore, independent observation is impossible. They reason instead that knowledge is mediated and thus altered in significant ways by the act of observation. Different assumptions lead to different theories.

Because of these differences, it is important to identify the assumptions on which a particular theory rests. In organization theory when a set of basic assumptions underlies multiple theories, the theories come to be recognized as a distinctive perspective or paradigm.[3] Familiarity with these different perspectives will help you to comprehend the multiple ways of theorizing about organizations. Furthermore, because the assumptions underlying a given perspective or paradigm were typically introduced into organization theory at different times, perspectives often have historical associations. In the next chapter I will discuss several different views of the history of organization theory and of the three major perspectives that form the framework for this book: modern, symbolic-interpretive, and postmodern.

Theory

A **theory** is an explanation, that is, it is an attempt to explain a segment of experience in the world. The particular thing that a theory explains is called the **phenomenon of interest**. In organization theory the primary phenomenon of interest is the organization. However, organization can be defined in many different ways, for instance, as a social structure, a technology, a culture, a physical structure, or as a part of an environment. Organization can also be studied in terms of the central issues and recurring themes of organizing including control, conflict, decision making, power and politics, and change. This book will introduce you to theories concerning each of these topics.

What is Organization Theory?

A theory consists of a set of concepts and the relationships that tie them together into an explanation of the phenomenon of interest. For example, organization can be theorized as a social structure created through conflict over power relations that is expressed in physical structure, technology, and culture. Alternatively, it might be theorized as a technology constructed through decisions that demand certain structural, cultural, and physical arrangements. However, before you can be expected to tackle theorizing, you will need to develop your understanding of the basic concepts. In this book we will start with basic concepts and build up to the larger abstractions that form organizational theories.

Concepts and the Process of Abstraction

Concepts provide categories for sorting, organizing, and storing experience. They are ideas formed by the process of abstraction. Webster's *New World Dictionary* defines **abstraction** as the "formation of an idea by mental separation from particular instances." This means that you build concepts in your mind on the basis of your acquaintance with instances that are familiar to you, either as the result of personal experience, or on the basis of what others have told you. For example, your concept of "dog" is built upon your personal encounters with representatives of this class of animal such as dogs you have owned or that have bitten you; upon stories you have heard others tell; and upon encounters with non-dogs that, when you were a young child, helped you to understand what a dog was by knowing what a dog was not ("No, that's a cat").

Concepts are like empty baskets to be filled with experience. If you first encounter a concept through academic study, it is empty. You must fill it with meaning by relating personal experiences to it so that the concept becomes enriched in much the same manner as occurred when you learned the concept of dog as a young child. That is, you must gather specific examples that fit the concept until it is more or less fully formed. Of course you can continue enriching your concepts for the remainder of your life. This is what experts do. For example, a person who trains dogs learns more about them all the time, and so their concept of dog is continually enriched and expanded. There is no end to the subtlety you can develop in your understanding by enriching your concepts and, of course, by adding new concepts to your knowledge base. The trick is to get the process of abstraction started.

In this book you will encounter other peoples' concepts and their general descriptions and definitions based on their experiences of, and within, organizations. Your task will be to make these concepts your own by relating them to your own experience; any concepts that you develop using only other peoples' experiences will never be entirely yours. To make a concept your own requires that you build it upon a foundation of your own experiences and meanings. Later in this chapter I will describe a strategy for using the examples in this book to help you with this part of your learning process.

Although concepts are associated with specific cases, a concept is not a simple aggregation of all the information you remember about specific examples. A concept is much more compact than this. Concepts are formed by removing some of the detail of particular instances so that what remains is only the essence of the thing, trimmed of non-essential information. In forming a concept, unique elements or features of specific examples are ignored; only those features that are common to all examples of a concept are included. Thus, the concept dog is associated with four legs, a tail, a cold nose when it is healthy, and two ears, but not black spots, big paws, or a habit of jumping on strangers, which are features of particular dogs, but not all dogs. The process of removing unique details so that essential qualities remain is called the process of abstraction. Of course this does not happen in one leap; there is much trial and error learning involved in the abstraction process.

You may wonder why you would want to drop all the interesting details out of your daily experiences in order to build concepts. One reason is that it gives you an increased ability to process information. When you encounter a new example of a well-developed concept, you have numerous bits of information about that object at your fingertips. For instance, if you recognize the object as a dog, you may instantly be aware of the possibility that it will growl if it feels threatened. This information has immediate value. Concepts also make it possible to communicate knowledge. For instance, you can tell your children that some dogs bite and so they should not reach out their hands to strange dogs until they are confident that the dog is friendly.

In addition to giving you the ability to generalize your knowledge and to communicate it to others, concepts give you enormous powers of thought. They allow you to associate volumes of information with a single idea and thereby to process this information rapidly whenever you think of, or with, the concept. You can see the importance of this aspect of concepts in terms of the psychological process known as **chunking**. Cognitive psychologists tell us that humans have the capacity to think about, roughly, seven pieces of information (plus or minus two) at one time. This means that you can think about seven different dogs and nothing else, or, through chunking larger portions of your knowledge structure, you can think about all the dogs in the universe and six other kinds of animal, or you can even think about the entire animal kingdom and six more things besides. Chunking illustrates the power of abstraction—using concepts allows you to consider large blocks of knowledge, a handy capacity to have when your daily activity demands that you understand and stay abreast of developments within a complex entity such as an organization.

Be sure to notice that there is both something gained and something lost when you use concepts. You gain the ability to think about numerous instances or cases of the abstract category, but you lose the rich detail that the individual cases contain. You will want to learn to use concepts because they permit you to communicate and understand general ideas about complex subjects, such as organizations. This will enable you to see day-to-day issues in a larger perspective that expands your thinking and gives you ready access to your accumulated base of knowledge. But you should also remember that abstract reasoning alone will not provide the important details that comprise the situations of daily life that you will be called upon to confront in your role within an organization. Applying theory, which is rooted in abstract reasoning, demands that you be able to add critical details back into your formulations after you have analyzed and understood the general aspects of the situation at hand. You will want to develop both concepts and theorizing skills with a broad base of personal experience and then learn to translate your general knowledge into specific understanding.

I believe the great frustration with organization theory that many students and practitioners report they feel is the result of not understanding that the application of theory is a creative act. A belief that abstract theory can generate instant solutions to specific problems is naive. It is equally naive to reject theory as having little value simply because you have not yet learned how to use it. This book is devoted to helping you learn how to use organization theory as a stimulus to creative problem solving in organizational settings and as a route to developing your organizing and theorizing skills.

PLAN OF THE BOOK

Part I of the book introduces the approach I am taking in presenting organization theory and theorizing to you. Chapter 1 has introduced you to theory and theorizing and presented reasons for studying organization theory. Chapter 2 introduces the multiple perspectives that form the framework of this book—modern, symbolic-interpretive, and postmodern—and presents a historical account of their development in and of organization theory. As explained already, although these perspectives are presented chronologically, this does not mean that earlier perspectives have been abandoned by organization theorists. Organization theory benefits from all of these perspectives. Therefore, Chapter 2 might better be thought of as an archaeology rather than as a history. Instead of attempting to plot the course of events that comprise the past of organization theory, Chapter 2 tries to dig up the ancient life and culture of the ideas that constitute the field.[4]

Part II of the book will present you with the core concepts organization theorists use for understanding and theorizing organizations. In these chapters you will learn to look at organizations in many different ways: as members of the environment that supports and constrains them (Chapter 3); as subjects of human influence through strategic action (Chapter 4); as technologies for producing goods and services for society (Chapter 5); as social structures ordering the activities of their members (Chapter 6); as cultures that produce and are produced by meanings that form a symbolic world (Chapter 7); and as physical structures that support and constrain both activity and meaning (Chapter 8). These different conceptual approaches to understanding organization are related in numerous ways, yet each contributes something unique. As you read and reread these chapters, strive to develop your appreciation for both the similarities and differences between them.

In addition to providing exposure to the core concepts of organization theory, Part II will present several different theories of organization that are built upon the core concepts. Within each chapter these theories will be presented in historical order; in most cases this means beginning with modern and proceeding to symbolic-interpretive and postmodern perspectives (Chapter 8 on organizational culture is the exception). This format should give you a sense of the continuity that contextualized the theorists' efforts at the time that they did their theorizing. It will also help you to experience organization theory as a series of challenges and disagreements among theorists and their ideas about organizations. The theories will not only give you exposure to the various types of explanation offered by this field of study, they will also provide a focus for describing the skills and practices organization theorists use. In discussing how theorists produce theory, I am trying to encourage you to become more actively theoretical in your own treatment of organizations.

There are many practical issues of recurring interest to both managers and organization theorists. I have selected a few of the most central of these as subjects for Part III of the book. Chapter 9 examines organizational decision making, power, and politics. Chapter 10 looks at conflict and contradiction; and Chapter 11 examines issues of control and ideology in organizations. Chapter 12 is focused on organizational change. Each chapter presents some additional new concepts to add to your knowledge base as well as several theories that link these new concepts with the core concepts developed in the second part of the book. These chapters will help you further your mastery and elaboration of basic concepts at the same time that they will push you to practice and improve your theorizing skills. Each of these chapters continues to move from the modern toward interpretive and postmodern conceptions in order to encourage flexibility with respect to understanding and using these different ways of theorizing about organization. Thus, Chapters 9 through 12 will continue the project set out at the start—to help you develop theorizing skills by exposing you to the concepts, models, and methods organization theorists use to understand and theorize organization.

Examples and How to Use Them

The examples provided in this book are designed to trigger associations with experiences you have had so that you can fill your concepts with your own meanings. Try taking each example and imagining what it is that you have personally experienced that might relate to it. Be playful. Do not feel constrained to the obvious associations, but also challenge yourself to consider things you have only a vague notion or a hunch might be applicable. As you do this you will begin to translate the concept into your own experiential terms.

Having identified examples from your own experience, use your examples to practice applying the concept or theory you are trying to understand. Although your theoretical understanding will be limited at this point, trying to describe and analyze the example you have identified from your own experience will help you to build this understanding. As your pool of concepts and theories expands, you will find yourself analyzing your experiences in new ways. For instance, by relating experiences that you never before thought of as related, or by seeing previously hidden or disregarded aspects of a situation in which you were involved, you will reveal aspects of your own personal experience of which you were previously unaware. In other words, use your personal experience to understand concepts and theories, and use your developing concepts and theories to better understand your experiences. This sort of give and take between theoretical understanding and personal experience is essential to the development of your theorizing skills and your knowledge of organization.[5]

A Conceptual Model of Organization as a Starting Point

Throughout this book I will provide many conceptual models such as you see in Figure 1.2. These models visually represent theories as a set of concepts and their relationships, and are frequently used by organization theorists to make abstract understanding seem more tangible. Figure 1.2, for example, is a visual way of communicating the central message of this book: that organizations are usefully conceptualized as technologies, social structures, cultures, and physical structures that overlay and interpenetrate one another within the context of an environment. To depict these relationships, the model shows technology, social structure, culture, and physical structure as interconnected circles (or, even better, as spheres) surrounded and penetrated by an environment that they simultaneously help to constitute.

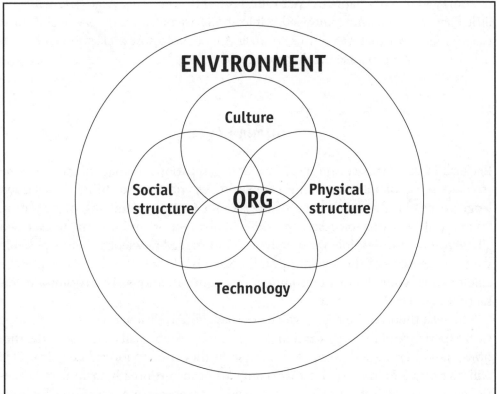

FIGURE 1.2. FIVE CIRCLES MODEL

The organization as an interplay of technology, social structure, culture, and physical structure embedded in and contributing to an environment. The four smaller circles intersect to remind you that these concepts are interrelated. They are enscribed within a fifth, larger circle to indicate the important relationship between all aspects of the organization and its environment.

Diagrams such as Figure 1.2 can help you to remember a great deal about the theories you will be studying. Giving these diagrams close attention will often reveal aspects of the theory that are subtle but important. For example, let the interconnections of the four circles in Figure 1.2 remind you that none of these concepts or theories is complete in itself; each shares some aspects with the others and it is the combination of these different ways of understanding that allows you to produce rich and complex views of organization using organization theory.

I should warn you that, as you move toward understanding each core concept, there will be times when you get caught in these intersections and become confused as to which concept or theory you are using. Expect this, and try not to feel discouraged when it happens. Without passing through this stage, you will have little chance of becoming knowledgeable about organization theory or skillful at theorizing. Trust that out of this confusion will come a new clarity about organization and the processes of theorizing.

SUMMARY

Because of the diversity and pluralism of organizations, managers must be able to make sense of and use multiple perspectives and learn to bring their knowledge to bear on a wide range of decisions every day. Studying organization theory will help you to master the skills of abstraction and theorizing that will allow you to use multiple perspectives to tap more knowledge than is possible without the skills of the organization theorist. But remember that you must be able to apply your abstract reasoning to concrete situations. This means a reversal of the process of abstraction.

The best theories are those which you have found or invented to match your own experience of the organization, and in this book you will learn about the theories that others have developed and the skills they used to formulate them. This will give you a foundation for theorizing. You can use already formulated theories as they stand, if this proves useful to your purposes, or as templates for your own theory building efforts. In any case, organization theory requires both the mastery of existing theories and personal development of the methods and skills of theorizing.

You have your own reasons for studying organization theory. My reason is that organization theory broadens my perspective on organizations and the world in general and opens my mind to new ideas and possibilities for change and transformation. I am constantly renewed by my work in this field and find that the ideas I can trace back to it give me a sense of understanding in which I have great confidence. The confidence comes from discovering that I can apply what I have learned from organization theory with at least two outcomes of great value to me. One of these outcomes is an increased power to create through and with abstract reasoning skills; the other is the enhancement of my ability to learn. Although it may hold other meanings and possibilities for you, I hope that my enthusiasm, which is built on my own particular needs and values, will inspire you to explore organization theory.

KEY TERMS

organization	concept
theorizing	abstraction
theory	chunking
phenomenon of interest	

ENDNOTES

1. For example, read British organization theorist Lex Donaldson (1985).
2. The multiple perspectives approach to organization theory has been explored by a variety of researchers. One of the earliest and most influential of these was American political scientist Graham Allison (1971), who analyzed the Cuban Missile Crisis using several different theoretical perspectives. Gibson Burrell and Gareth Morgan (1979), working within the traditions of organizational sociology, analyzed the philosophical foundations of rational, interpretive, radical structuralist, and radical humanist traditions in organizational analysis. Using Burrell and Morgan's analysis, John Hassard (1988, 1991; Hassard and Pym 1990) has been particularly active in promoting the multiple perspectives approach within organization theory. Also in the sociology of organization, Richard Scott (1992) presented rational, natural, and open systems views of organizations. Joanne Martin (1992) built her analysis of organizational culture theory around a multiple perspectives approach including integration, differentiation, and fragmentation perspectives.
3. The concept of paradigm and its applications within organization theory have been widely debated within organization theory. For example, see Kuhn (1970 [1961]); Burrell and Morgan (1979); Morgan and Smircich (1980); Hassard (1988, 1991); Gioia and Pitre (1990); Jackson and Carter (1991); Willmott (1990, 1993); Weaver and Gioia (1994); Schultz and Hatch (1996).
4. The archaeological approach to social science was suggested and developed by Michel Foucault (1973 [1970], 1972).
5. This technique is an application of the hermeneutic circle (e.g., Ricoeur 1981).

REFERENCES

Allison, Graham (1971). *The essence of decision: Explaining the Cuban missile crisis*. Boston: Little, Brown.

Burrell, Gibson, and Morgan, Gareth (1979). *Sociological paradigms and organizational analysis*. London: Heinemann.

Donaldson, Lex (1985). *In defence of organisation theory*. Cambridge: Cambridge University Press.

Foucault, Michel (1973 [1970]). *The order of things*. New York: Vintage Books.

Foucault, Michel (1972). *The archaeology of knowledge & the discourse on language*. New York: Pantheon Books.

Gioia, Dennis A., and Pitre, Evelyn (1990). Multiparadigm perspectives on theory building. *Academy of Management Review*, 15: 584-602.

Hassard, John (1988). Overcoming hermeticism in organization theory: An alternative to paradigm incommensurability. *Human Relations*, 41/3: 247–59.

Hassard, John (1991). Multiple paradigms and organizational analysis: A case study. *Organization Studies*, 12/2: 275–99.

Hassard, John, and Pym, Denis (1990) (eds.). *The theory and philosophy of organizations: Critical issues and new perspectives*. London: Routledge.

Jackson, Norman, and Carter, Pippa (1991). In defense of paradigm incommensurability. *Organization Studies*, 12/1: 109–28.

Kuhn, Thomas (1970 [1961]). *The structure of scientific revolutions*. Chicago: University of Chicago Press.

Martin, Joanne (1992). *Cultures in organizations: Three perspectives*. Oxford: Oxford University Press.

Morgan, Gareth, and Smircich, Linda (1980). The case of qualitative research. *Academy of Management Review*, 5: 491–500.

Ricoeur, Paul (1981). *Hermeneutics and the Human Sciences* (trans. J. B. Thompson). Cambridge: Cambridge University Press.

Schultz, Majken, and Hatch, Mary Jo (1996). Living with multiple paradigms: The case of paradigm interplay in organizational culture studies. *Academy of Management Review*, 21: 529–57.

Scott, W. Richard (1992). *Organizations: Rational, natural, and open systems* (3rd edition). Englewood Cliffs, NJ: Prentice-Hall.

Weaver, Gary, and Gioia, Dennis (1994). Paradigms lost: Incommensurability, structuration and the restructuring of organizational inquiry. *Organization Studies*, 15: 565–90.

Willmott, Hugh (1990). Beyond paradigmatic closure in organisational enquiry. In J. Hassard and D. Pym (eds.), *The theory and philosophy of organization*. London: Routledge, 44–62.

Willmott, Hugh (1993). Breaking the paradigm mentality. *Organization Studies*, 14/5: 681–719.

FURTHER READING

Classics

Smith, Adam (1957). *Selections from "The Wealth of Nations"* (ed. George J. Stigler). New York: Appleton Century Crofts (originally published in 1776).

Marx, Karl (1954). *Capital*. Moscow: Foreign Languages Publishing House (first published in 1867).

Durkheim, Emile (1949). *The division of labor in society*. Glencoe, Ill.: Free Press (first published in 1893).

Taylor, Frederick W. (1911). *The principles of scientific management*. New York: Harper.

Fayol, Henri (1949). *General and industrial management*. London: Pitman (first published in 1919).

Weber, Max (1947). *The theory of social and economic organization* (ed. A. H. Henderson and Talcott Parsons). Glencoe, Ill.: Free Press (first published in 1924).

Barnard, Chester (1938). *The functions of the executive*. Cambridge, Mass.: Harvard University Press.

Modernist perspective

Simon, Herbert (1957). *Administrative behavior* (2nd edition). New York: Macmillan (first published in 1945).

Parsons, Talcott (1951). *The social system*. Glencoe, Ill.: Free Press.

Gouldner, Alfred (1954). *Patterns of industrial bureaucracy*. Glencoe, Ill.: Free Press.

March, James G., and Simon, Herbert (1958). *Organizations*. New York: John Wiley.

Dalton, Melville (1959). *Men who manage*. New York: John Wiley.

Bertalanffy, Ludwig von (1968). *General systems theory: Foundations, development, applications* (revised edition). New York: George Braziller.

Symbolic-interpretive perspective

Propp, Vladimir (1958). *Morphology of the folktale*. Bloomington: Indiana University Press (first published in 1928).

Schutz, Alfred (1967). *The phenomenology of the social world* (trans. G. Walsh and F. Lehnert). Evanston, Ill.: Northwestern University Press (first published in 1932).

Whyte, William F. (1943). *Street corner society*. Chicago: University of Chicago Press.

Selznick, Philip (1949). *TVA and the grass roots*. Berkeley: University of California Press.

Burke, Kenneth (1984). *Permanence and change: An anatomy of purpose* (3rd edition). Berkeley: University of California Press (second edition originally published in 1954).

Saussure, Ferdinand de (1959). *Course in general linguistics* (trans. Wade Baskin). New York: McGraw-Hill.

Goffman, Erving (1959). *The presentation of self in everyday life*. Garden City, NY: Doubleday Anchor.

Berger, Peter, and Luckmann, Thomas (1966). *The social construction of reality: A treatise in the sociology of knowledge*. Garden City, NY: Doubleday.

Barthes, Roland (1972). *Mythologies* (trans. A. Lavers). New York: Hill & Wang.

Geertz, C. (1973). *Interpretation of cultures*. New York: Basic Books.

Ricoeur, Paul (1981). *Hermeneutics and the Human Sciences* (trans. J. B. Thompson). Cambridge: Cambridge University Press.

Postmodern perspective

Foucault, Michel (1972). *The archeology of knowledge and the discourse on language* (trans. A. M. Sheridan Smith). London: Tavistock Publications.

What is Organization Theory?

Foucault, Michel (1973). *The order of things*. New York: Vintage Books.

Jencks, Charles (1977). *The language of post-modern architecture*. London: Academy.

Derrida, Jacques (1978). *Writing and difference* (trans. Alan Bass). London: Routledge & Kegan Paul.

Derrida, Jacques (1980). *Of grammatology* (trans. Gayatri Chakravorty Spivak). Baltimore: The Johns Hopkins University Press.

Bakhtin, Mikhail (1981). *The dialogic imagination: Four essays* (trans. Chorale Emerson and Michael Holquist). Austin: University of Texas Press.

Lyotard, Jean-François (1984). *The postmodern condition: A report on knowledge*. Minneapolis: University of Minnesota Press.

Baudrillard, Jean (1988). *Selected writings* (ed. M. Poster). Palo Alto, Calif.: Stanford University Press.

Rorty, Richard (1989). *Contingency, irony, and solidarity*. Cambridge: Cambridge University Press.

2 Histories, Metaphors, and Perspectives in Organization Theory

THERE are many ways to talk about the history and development of a field of study. I presented one of them in Chapter 1—the academic genealogy shown in Figure 1.1. The figure identifies theorists from a wide range of academic disciplines who contributed ideas to the modern, symbolic-interpretive, and postmodern perspectives of organization theory. In this chapter we will explore these ideas, but we will also look at the events of industrial history that shaped and were shaped by these ideas.

We begin with a look at the history of industrial development and the changing nature of work and organizations since the introduction of the factory in the late eighteenth century. This historical account will give you some background to the current debate about whether post-industrialism marks the culmination of the industrial era or is just one more phase of industrial development. The first section concludes with discussion of this debate. In the second section, I will briefly present influential ideas put forward during the Classical period and trace some of the ways in which their influence lives on in the modernist, symbolic-interpretive, and postmodern perspectives of organization theory. The third section explores contemporary influences on organization theory, examining the root ideas of modernism and symbolic-interpretivism, and then entertaining a sample of the notions that postmodernism brings to organization theory. I will finish up the chapter by making some comparisons among the three perspectives. The first comparison will be cast in terms of epistemological assumptions, that is, we will consider the different positions each perspective offers on the question: *How* do we know what we know about organizations? In the last section of the chapter we will compare the perspectives in a more artistic way, exploring how root metaphors organize the images and language associated with each perspective and leave lasting impressions of their fundamentally different ways of representing organizations and managers.

THE TIMES THEY ARE A CHANGIN' . . .

In this section we will consider a historical account taken from the sociology of industry provided by British sociologist Tom Burns. This particular version of organizational history reflects the close alignment between modernist developments in organization theory and those in industry. However, Burns's discussion of what he calls the third phase of industrialism resonates with recent ideas about post-industrial society and organization which symbolic-interpretivists and postmodernists increasingly use as a departure point for their theories. We will look at the characteristics of post-industrialism and of post-industrial organizations as a futuristic extension to Burns's historical account of industrial development in the West.

Three Phases of Industrialism

Burns defined the trajectory of Western industrial development in terms of three distinguishable phases. According to Burns, the first phase grew out of the use of machines to extend and enlarge the productivity of work and ushered in the factory system. The factory system offered an alternative to subcontracting which was the way industrial labor was organized before factories appeared. In subcontracting, groups of individuals, typically working under a master craftsman, contracted out for specific jobs. In factories, the subcontractor's role was replaced by that of the foreman who worked under the direction of a general manager or the factory owner. Foremen's responsibilities and freedoms were considerably less than those of subcontractors (e.g., responsibility for hiring and firing, assigning work tasks, and defining the pace of work was taken over by factory owners), but the social status of both groups was roughly equal.

Factories first appeared mainly in the British textile industry. They consisted of collections of machines located in one building and were tended by feeders and by maintenance and repair workers. In phase one, the machines in a factory were typically all of a single type involving only one task or simple, repetitive process. More complex tasks were still carried out using the older system of subcontracting. While the maintenance workers and supervisors in the early factories were nearly always men, most of the operative workers were women, and they, in turn, were often assisted by children.

During the second phase of industrial development, which began roughly in the 1850s and 1860s, the factory system diffused into clothing and food manufacturing, engineering, and chemical, iron, and steel processing, all of which depended upon complex production processes. According to Burns, this growth and the increased technical complexity of manufacturing operations demanded parallel growth in systems of social organization and bureaucracy, with their emphasis on control, routine, and specialization. These changes were reflected in large increases in the ranks of managers and administrative staff (e.g., professional and clerical workers) and were accompanied by improvements in transportation and communication, freer trade, growing public interest in the consumable products of industrialism, and the armaments revolution that followed improvements in steel and chemical technology and the development of machine tools. Developments similar to those in industry were seen in the growth of national armies and governmental administrations. It was changes introduced in the second phase that attracted the attention of the Classical writers of sociology. For instance, Weber and Marx predicted that these changes would lead to the creation of a new middle class of managers, clerical workers, and professionals employed by large, hierarchical organizations. According to Burns, many parts of Western industrial society still operate in phase two.

Burns claimed that the third phase of industrial development is just now emerging. In this phase, production catches up with and overtakes spontaneous domestic demand. In these circumstances, the capitalist organization's dependence on growth leads to enhanced sensitivity to the consumer, to new techniques to stimulate consumption (e.g., advertising, product development, design, consumer research, market research, marketing promotion), to the internationalization of firms in search of new markets, and to new technical developments that increasingly occur within industrial firms (e.g., via research and development). This new relationship with their markets demands greater flexibility of organizations which are required to be customer-oriented, active internationally, and technically innovative. What is more, higher levels of commitment to the economic performance of the firm are demanded of all organizational members which leads to more participative styles of organizing. These ideas, which Burns equated with the third phase of industrial development, have been interpreted by others as indicating a more fundamental change, at least in the West, from industrialism to post-industrialism.

Post-Industrialism and the Post-Industrial Organization

According to futurist Alvin Toffler in his 1970 book *Future Shock*, a good way to envision the extent of the social transformation initiated by computer and telecommunications technology is to compare it to the transformation from agricultural to industrial societies that occurred during the industrial revolution. The American sociologist Daniel Bell gave these new developments the name post-industrialism in his 1973 book *The Coming of Post-Industrial Society*. There he argued that, whereas industrial societies are organized around the control of labor in the production of goods, **post-industrial society** is organized around the creation of knowledge and the uses of information. According to Bell, post-industrial society is shaped and defined by its methods of acquiring, processing, and distributing information, all of which have been revolutionized by the computer. This emphasis on information has led some, Bell among them, to label the current era the information age, and to predict the rise of the service sector and the decline of manufacturing, with technicians and professionals (knowledge workers) replacing capitalists as the most powerful members of society.

Bell and others attribute the emergence of the global economy to the ability to instantaneously share knowledge and information, which is a product of the computer revolution. A further implication of the computer revolution, initially remarked by futurist John Naisbitt in his popular book *Megatrends*, is the abandonment of hierarchies in favor of communication networks with a consequent shift from vertically to horizontally structured organizations. This aspect of the information age provides the departure point for most discussions of the **post-industrial organization**.

Discussion of the post-industrial organization typically involves comparisons of the forms of work and organization that became familiar during phase two of industrialism with those anticipated as a consequence of the recent shifts equated with the information age. Much energy has been devoted to describing what, in particular, is changing. To give a flavor of these changes, Table 2.1 groups some typical ideas in relation to the environment, technology, social structure, culture, physical structure (space-time), space, and the consequences of these changing conditions for the nature of work in organizations.

The prototypical post-industrial organizational form is the network (described in Chapter 6), but other forms associated with post-industrialism include joint

TABLE 2.1. COMPARISON OF CHARACTERISTICS ASSOCIATED WITH INDUSTRIALISM AND POST-INDUSTRIALISM

	Industrial	**Postindustrial**
Environment	• nation states regulate national economies • mass marketing • standardization • the Welfare State	• global competition • de-concentration of capital with respect to nation state • fragmentation of markets and international decentralization of production • rise of consumer choice, demand for customized goods • rise of social movements, single-issue politics, service class • pluralism, diversity, localism
Technology	• mass production along Taylorist/Fordist lines • routine • manufacturing output	• flexible manufacturing, automation • use of computer for design, production, and stock control • just-in-time systems (JIT) • emphasis on speed and innovation • service/information output
Social structure	• bureaucratic • hierarchical with vertical communication emphasized • specialization • vertical and horizontal integration • focused on control	• new organizational forms (e.g., networks, strategic alliances, virtual organization) • flatter hierarchies with horizontal communication and devolved managerial responsibility • outsourcing • informal mechanisms of influence (participation, culture, communication • vertical and horizontal disintegration • loose boundaries between functions, units, organizations
Culture	• celebrates stability, tradition, custom • organizational values: growth, efficiency, standardization, control	• celebrates uncertainty, paradox, fashion • organizational values: quality, customer service, diversity, innovation
Physical structure (space–time)	• concentration of people in industrial towns and cities • local, nationalistic orientation • time is linear	• deconcentration of people • reduction in transportation time links distant spaces and encourages international, global orientation • compression of temporal dimension (e.g., shortening product lifecycles) leads to simultaneity

---

TABLE 2.1. Continued

	Industrial	Postindustrial
Nature of work	• routine • deskilled labor • functional specialization of tasks	• frenetic, complex • knowledge-based skills • cross-functional teamwork • greater emphasis on learning • more outsourcing, subcontracting, self-employment, teleworking

Based on: Clegg (1990); Harvey (1990); Heydebrand (1977); Kumar (1995); Lash and Urry (1987, 1994); Piore and Sabel (1984).

---

ventures, strategic alliances, and virtual organizations. One important distinguishing feature shared by post-industrial organizations is the disappearance of organizational boundaries. This idea inspires views of a future in which organizations are much smaller, more fluid and flexible than they are now, with invisible or no boundaries between the organization and its external environment. Boundaries between internal groups like sales, production, and engineering also collapse in the post-industrial organization. People working in post-industrial organizations will not make distinctions between departments, hierarchical positions, or even jobs the way most of us do now. Instead they will focus on collaborating with others as experts working in temporary teams and will place much greater emphasis on learning in order to keep up with rapid change. Post-industrial organizational life is characterized by uncertainty, contradiction, and paradox, which contrasts sharply with the industrial organization's stability, routine, and tradition.

While most observers agree that something has changed drastically, there is little agreement about whether this change is out there in the real world, or whether it is in here, in our understanding of ourselves and our relationships with the world we construct around us. The post-industrial thesis is that the changes are real in an objective sense. Modernist critics of the post-industrial thesis argue that the so-called changes associated with post-industrialism, although real, have been with us throughout the modern period and so are nothing new and are not nearly as transformative as the post-industrial thesis claims. Meanwhile, many symbolic-interpretivists and postmodernists think that the changes introduced by the computer revolution are not located in the objective world, but rather are to be found in and through our subjective experience (which has been altered by our use of the computer, telecommunications, and rapid forms of transportation). We will return to these differences below when we consider the epistemological assumptions underlying the perspectives of organization theory. But first we will follow up the history of ideas introduced in Chapter 1.

CLASSICAL INFLUENCES ON ORGANIZATION THEORY

There are really two streams contained within what organization theorists now call the Classical School. The sociological stream focused on the changing shapes and roles of formal organizations within society and the broader influences of industrialization on the nature of work and its consequences for workers. This was the interest of Classical scholars such as Emile Durkheim, Max Weber, and Karl Marx. The other stream comprises what organization theorists sometimes call Classical management theory to distinguish it from the more sociological approach. This stream was shaped by Frederick Taylor, Henri Fayol, and Chester Barnard, among others, and focused on the practical problems faced by managers of industrial organizations. In a way, the tension between theory and practice that has been present in organization theory since its inception can be traced to these two influential streams of Classical thought. The ideas of both streams can be traced back even further to the influence of the famous political-economist Adam Smith.

In this section, I will introduce you to some of the ideas of these influential pioneers of social science and suggest links between their ideas and the three perspectives of organization theory. As we go through this material remember that, since organization theory did not emerge as a recognizable field of study until sometime in the 1960s, what is called the Classical period is really part of its prehistory. Furthermore, you should be aware that organization theory is just one of several disciplines inspired by the Classical writers identified in the figure. Other disciplines that trace their origins to these ideas include industrial relations, industrial and organizational psychology, organizational sociology, management theory, and organizational behavior. Some researchers loosely group all of these fields into the more general category of organization studies.

A word of warning—if you have not studied social science before, this section may seem overwhelming at this point. Try rereading it after you have finished Part II of the book; once you are familiar with the basic concepts to which this history relates, this section will make more sense to you. But do not skip over the following sections on contemporary influences and comparisons of the three perspectives, as they will give you necessary background for reading Part II.

Adam Smith, Political-Economist (Scottish)

If you search for the origins of organization theory, you will most likely meet the political-economist Adam Smith, who, in 1776, published *The Wealth of Nations*. In this book, Smith described techniques of pin manufacturing and, in doing so, was the first to record and explain the efficiencies inherent in the **division of labor**. As you will learn in Chapter 6, the division of labor has to do with the differentiation of work tasks and the resulting specialization of labor, ideas that are central to the concept of social structure in organizations. This is why many organization theorists give Smith the place of honor in their intellectual histories.

Karl Marx, Philosopher-Economist (German)

Karl Marx is perhaps best known for his theory of capital and related ideas about alienation. The **theory of capital** is built upon Marx's belief that collective work, or labor, forms the foundation for the social world. He sees labor as emerging from physical needs defined by the fundamental relationship between humans and their physical environment. Society and culture then emerge from the challenges presented by discovering that collective work is more productive than individual work. In other words, the human need to survive, which derives from the dangers and opportunities presented by the physical world, leads to the emergence of the social and cultural world. The particular form taken by the social and cultural world, which then acts back upon the physical world, is subject to the relations of power worked out politically between those who comprise and organize the labor-based collective.

In his theory of capital, Marx argued that capitalism rests upon a fundamental antagonism between the interests of capital (capitalists, e.g., the owners of factories and the means of production) and those of labor (i.e., the workers whose activities form the core of the production process). The antagonism, in part, arises over how to divide the surplus value (i.e., excess profits) generated by the combination of labor and capital produced when products or services are exchanged on a market at a price that is higher than production costs. Each side, naturally, argues that the surplus should belong to them, and therefore the capitalist system is characterized by a struggle between the interests of capital and those of labor.

But antagonism between labor and capital also arises from the necessity to ensure profitability. Without profitability, the survival of the individual firm and the entire capitalist economy would be in jeopardy. Profitability depends upon the organization and control of work activity. This is because competition from other firms puts downward pressure on the prices for a firm's products and services, which translates into a need to reduce the costs of production, of which labor is a large component. This encourages capitalists to pressure labor to work more efficiently, which is accomplished by inventing new forms of managerial control over workers and work processes. The control systems become additional sources of antagonism between management and workers who attempt to resist this control. Marxist theory considers control to be one of the key themes of organization theory, which in Classical management theory and modernist organization theory is interpreted as a primary function of the executive, and in postmodern theories becomes a foundation for critiques of managerialism. The issue of control will be taken up in Chapter 11.

Because capitalists own the means of production (i.e., the plant, equipment, and other necessities of economic enterprise), they often have greater political power to design organizational control systems than do their workers who depend upon them to supply employment, machines, and other resources needed to transform their labor potential into marketable products and services. Capitalists tend to use their greater power to further disempower workers, for example, by replacing worker control over work with managerial control, creating competition among workers via differential pay or through the division of labor. All of these tactics reduce the workers' collective political influence and hence their ability to resist management's efforts to control them. This concern with power can be traced to discussions of organizational power and politics, which we will examine in Chapter 9.

Once labor is defined as a cost of production, rather than as a means to achieve a collective purpose for the good of society, workers are disenfranchised from the product of their own work efforts, a condition that Marx characterized as **alienation**. According to Marx, alienation occurs when labor is transformed into a commodity to be bought and sold on an exchange market, which leaves humans with only an instrumental relationship with one another based on the economic value of their labor potential. Unless the workers organize their resistance (e.g., via unions), managerial exploitation and the disempowerment and alienation of workers will grow unabated. Thus, according to Marx, the result of antagonism between capital and labor is a build up of institutionalized forms of mutual control and resistance (e.g., management vs. unions) temporarily held in place by the dynamics of a capitalist economy. This line of thinking has been a major influence on contemporary discussions in industrial sociology and labor process theory, which we will discuss in Chapter 10.

Emile Durkheim, Sociologist (French)

Over one hundred years after Smith introduced the concept of the division of labor, French sociologist Emile Durkheim wrote his book on the subject. In *The Division of Labor in Society*, published in 1893, Durkheim extended the concept of the division of labor beyond manufacturing organizations to explain the structural shift from agricultural to industrial societies that accompanied the industrial revolution. Durkheim described this shift in terms of increases in specialization, hierarchy, and the interdependence of work tasks. Early modernist organization theorists regarded these concepts as key dimensions for defining and describing complex organizations, as you will see in Chapter 6.

Durkheim also proposed the distinction between formal and informal aspects of organizations and emphasized the need to attend to workers' social needs as well as the demands of formally organizing their work efforts. The theme of social needs is of major interest within the fields of organizational behavior, and industrial and organizational psychology. The distinction between formal and informal aspects of organizing exposed the tension between economic and humanistic aspects of organizing that vex organizers and have traditionally divided organization theorists into opposing camps.[1]

In addition to his work on the division of labor, Durkheim made a major contribution to establishing sociology as a scientific discipline through his work on methodology. Particularly with his books *The Rules of Sociological Method* and *Suicide*, which emphasized objective measurement and statistical description and analysis, Durkheim helped lay positivistic methodological foundations, not only for sociology, but also for modernist organization theory.

Frederick Winslow Taylor, Founder of Scientific Management (American)

At the turn of the century, Frederick W. Taylor proposed applying scientific methods to discover the most efficient working techniques for manual forms of labor. Taylor called his approach **Scientific Management**, and he claimed that its successful application would fully exploit the efficiencies of specialized labor through the close supervision of employees carrying out highly specified physical work. Efficiency was to be encouraged and supported by a piece-rate incentive system in which workers were paid according to the amount of work of a prespecified nature that they performed in a given period of time. The new system permitted management to define the tasks that workers performed, and also to determine how they approached these tasks. Notice also how Taylor's method shifted control of work tasks from craftsworkers to management.

In Taylor's view, Scientific Management was a direct attack on worker soldiering, a practice in which workers limited their output in the interests of maximizing their incomes and assuring job protection for themselves and fellow workers (workers reasoned that a given amount of work done slowly requires more workers). Taylor's system undermined the authority of the workers and their master craftsmen by introducing managerial control and supervision, and by offering differential pay for performance which eroded worker solidarity. These aspects of Scientific Management earned it considerable and lasting ill-repute as being ruinously ignorant of the trust and cooperation between management and workers upon which organizations depend. So much furor was created by Taylor that Scientific Management was the subject of an American Congressional investigation. This controversy has recently re-emerged in postmodern criticism of modernist management practices where Taylorism and its subsequent developments by Henry Ford (involving the mass-production assembly line which some postmodernists refer to as Fordism) are a favorite target along with the Tayloristic practices associated with the total quality management (TQM) movement.[2]

Perhaps the most enduring image of Taylor is as a promoter of rationalization in organizations. His belief in the powers of objective measurement and the discovery of laws governing work efficiency are carried into the modernist perspective in organization theory where Taylor's techniques lay the groundwork for management control systems. Today, postmodern organization theorists reinterpret Taylorism as an early manifestation of the managerial ideology of control (a theme we will explore in Chapter 10). They see Taylor's system, not so much as a means to make organizations more rational, but rather as being justified in terms of the *value* for rationality that was unquestioningly accepted during the early part of the twentieth century. In this view, Taylorism legitimizes management, particularly in its role as control agent, by asserting that the practices of Scientific Management must be accepted because they are rational.

Henri Fayol, Engineer, CEO, and Administrative Theorist (French)

Fayol had been an engineer and manager in the mining industry, and eventually became CEO of an ailing French mining company. His successful turnaround of the company earned him great admiration in France, and upon his retirement he established a center for the study of administration in an effort to codify and pass on the wisdom he had gained. In his book *General and Industrial Management*, first published in 1919, but not available in English translation until 1949, Fayol presented what he believed to be universal principles for the rational administration of organizational activities.

Fayol's efforts laid the groundwork for much discussion among management theorists about the necessary number and precise specification of administrative principles. The principles themselves involved issues such as span-of-control (the number of subordinates that can be overseen by one manager); exceptions (subordinates should deal with routine matters, leaving managers free to handle situations that existing rules do not address); departmentation (the grouping of activities such that similar activities form departments within the organization); unity-of-command (each subordinate should report to only one boss); and hierarchy (the scalar principle linked all organizational members into a control structure that resembled a pyramid). The administrative theorists' view that one best way to administer organizational activities could be identified proved to be too ambitious. Nonetheless, their approach to organizations contributed many of the basic dimensions of organizational social structure that underlie modernist organization theories which we will take up in Chapter 6.

Fayol also emphasized the importance of *esprit de corps* among the members of an organization. He argued that unity of sentiment and harmony can contribute greatly to the smooth functioning of an organization. Similar ideas arose in contemporary organization theory in the early conceptualizations of organizational culture, to be discussed further in Chapter 7. Fayol also specified the responsibilities of the manager. The functions he specified were: planning, organizing, command, coordination, and control. These came to be known as the functions of management and were elaborated and taken by many as the initial definition of the field of management.

Max Weber, Sociologist (German)

Like Durkheim, German sociologist Max Weber was interested in defining the key characteristics of industrial societies, one of which he saw as an unavoidable increase in bureaucracy. In contrast to feudal and other traditional forms of organizing, Weber emphasized the rational virtues of bureaucracy which included formal authority based on precise and generalized rules and procedures (described as legalistic forms of control). In Weber's view, bureaucracy provided the benefits of rationalization. Whereas, in his view, earlier **forms of authority** rested on the personal attractiveness of leaders (charismatic authority) or the traditional rights of dominant groups such as aristocracy or landholders (traditional authority), Weber credited bureaucracy with being objective and impersonal and therefore unbiased and rational (hence his label for this new form was rational-legal authority).

Weber's **theory of bureaucracy**, along with its central themes of authority and rationality, were presented in his book *The Theory of Social and Economic Organization* which was published in German in 1924 and in English translation in 1947. Weber saw bureaucracy as a way to rationalize the social environment in a manner that was similar to technology's rationalizing influence on the physical environment. This led modernist organization theorists of the 1950s and 1960s to equate Weber's ideas about rationalization with their concerns for technical efficiency (the legacy of Taylorism and the engineering roots of industrialism). In any event, the link that is attributed to Weber between bureaucratic rationalization and technical efficiency persists in modernist organizational theory which considers Weber to be one of its founding fathers.

Weber himself, however, apparently recognized that the uses of rationalization rest upon value-based criteria. Evidence for this is found in his distinction between formal and substantive rationality. **Formal rationality** involves techniques of calculation, while **substantive rationality** refers to the *desired ends of action* that direct the uses of calculative techniques. Different desired ends will lead to different uses of formal rationality. Weber warned that formal rationality without conscious consideration of substantive rationality leads, in his colorful phrase, to an "iron cage" capable of imprisoning humanity and making man a "cog in an ever-moving mechanism."[3] Such sentiments position Weber closer to postmodern critics of modernist organization theory, while his interest in values is carried on by symbolic-interpretive researchers.

Chester Barnard, Management Theorist (American)

Chester Barnard extended Durkheim's idea of informal organization to Classical management theory by suggesting that managing this aspect of organizing was a key function of the successful executive. Barnard emphasized the ways in which executives might develop their organizations into cooperative social systems by focusing on the integration of work efforts through communication of goals and attention to worker motivation, ideas that made a more direct contribution to the field of organizational behavior than to organization theory. However, the significance Barnard and his followers attached to the cooperative aspects of organizations is sometimes blamed for having blinded early organization theorists to the importance of conflict as a fundamental aspect of all organizations. Nonetheless, the consideration Barnard gave to issues of value and sentiment in the workplace identified themes that are echoed in contemporary research on organizational culture, meaning, and symbolism which we will take up in Chapter 7.

CONTEMPORARY INFLUENCES ON ORGANIZATION THEORY

Just as Classical ideas formed a backdrop to our discussion of the roots of organization theory in general, there are key ideas and theories that are specifically associated with each of the three perspectives of modernism, symbolic-interpretivism, and postmodernism. In this section these ideas are presented as a means of initiating discussions of the perspectives of organization theory that will continue throughout the book. As in the rest of the book, I will present these ideas more or less in the chronological order of their influence on organization theory so that you can experience for yourself the continuities, as well as the discontinuities, in thought from which the perspectives emerged. But remember that the order of appearance is related to the influence on organization theory; quite often these ideas influenced other disciplines before organization theorists caught wind of them and applied them to the study of organizations.

First, we will look at General Systems Theory, which inspired much of the modern approach to organization theory and helps sustain continued allegiance to modernism among many contemporary organization theorists. Next we will examine enactment theory and the social construction of reality, two related ideas that underpin the symbolic-interpretive perspective. Following this we will give consideration to postmodernism and some of the postmodern concepts that are currently influencing organization theory.

Modernist: General Systems Theory

In the 1950s, German biophysiologist Ludwig von Bertalanffy presented a theory intended to explain all scientific phenomena across both natural and social sciences from the atom and molecule, through the single cell, organ, and organism, all the way up to the level of individuals, groups, and societies. He recognized that all these phenomena were related—societies contain groups, groups contain individuals, individuals are comprised of organs, organs of cells, cells of molecules, and molecules of atoms. To generalize, he referred to all of these phenomena as systems. Bertalanffy then sought the essential laws and principles that would explain all systems. Thus, the theory he envisioned involved generalizations drawn at such a high level of abstraction that the essence of all scientific knowledge would be clarified and integrated. He called his vision General Systems Theory.

Bertalanffy based General Systems Theory on the assumption that the common methodology of the sciences (i.e., the scientific method) implies, or at least permits, theoretical unity. In proposing General Systems Theory he did not expect to do away with the varied branches of science. These, he predicted, would continue to investigate the unique features of their phenomena of interest. Meanwhile, general systems theorists would focus on the similarities underlying and uniting all phenomena. Thus, General Systems Theory knocked down some of the barriers between the sciences, proposing cross-disciplinary research as a revolution in the way science is conducted.

To understand the importance of systems thinking for organization theory, it is first necessary to grasp the concept of a system. A **system** is a thing with inter-related parts. Each part is conceived as affecting the others and each depends upon the whole. The use of the term "thing" shows you just how general General Systems Theory is. This theory can be applied to any *thing* that science can study. The idea of interrelated parts (in systems theory these are called subsystems) emphasizes that, while all systems can be analytically broken down for the purposes of scientific study, their essence can only be identified when the system is confronted as a whole. This is because subsystem interdependence produces features and characteristics that are unique to the system as a whole.

Consider the example of a frog. You may have been asked to dissect a frog in biology class. However, no matter what you came to understand about the relationships among frog parts, there was no way your new understanding would enable you to put it back together again. That difference between the reassembled frog and the living one illustrates the unique aspects of a holistic system. That is, the totality that is referred to as a system must be apprehended in its entirety; a system can never be fully understood merely by analyzing its parts, nor even by reassembling them. Nonetheless, the systems approach does not imply that analyzing the parts of a system is a bad idea, simply that it is inadequate because it misses something essential. The implication is that, to comprehend a system, you must not merely analyze (or synthesize or integrate), you must also be willing to transcend the view of the individual parts to encounter the entire system at its own level of complexity.

Another important feature of subsystems is that they can be highly differentiated. Differentiation provides the system with the benefits of specialization. Of course, specialization at the subsystem level eventually creates a need for integration and coordination at the systems level, or in other words, a need for organization.

What is Organization Theory?

One of Bertalanffy's most ardent supporters, and a major contributor to General Systems Theory in his own right, was Kenneth Boulding. Boulding, an American economist, conceptualized the sciences as an ordered hierarchy of systems.[4] Today, Boulding's **hierarchy of systems** is widely used to explain the major concepts of systems theory (Table 2.2).

TABLE 2.2. BOULDING'S HIERARCHY OF SYSTEMS

Level	Characteristics	Examples
1. Framework	• labels and terminology • classification systems	anatomies, geographies lists, indexes, catalogs
2. Clockwork	• cyclical events • simple with regular (or regulated) motions • equilibria or states of balance	solar system simple machines (clock or pulley) equilibirum system of economics
3. Control	• self-control • feedback • transmission of information	thermostat homeostasis auto pilot
4. Open (living)	• self-maintenance • throughput of material • energetic input • reproduction	cell river flame
5. Genetic	• division of labor (cells) • differentiated and mutually dependent parts • growth follows "blue-print"	plant
6. Animal	• mobility • self-aware • specialized sensory receptors • highly developed nervous system • knowledge structures (image)	dog cat elephant whale or dolphin
7. Human	• self-consciousness • capacity to produce, absorb, and interpret symbols • sense of passing time	you me
8. Social organization	• value system • meaning	businesses governments
9. Transcendental	• "inescapable unknowables"	metaphysics, aesthetics

Based on: Boulding (1956).

The first thing to notice about Boulding's hierarchy is that it is organized by levels of complexity and comprehensiveness. It begins with the simplest system and moves to greater complexity with each successive level in the hierarchy. Within the hierarchy all lower level systems are embedded in systems of a higher order, or, to put it the other way around, each higher order system contains systems of a lower order. Thus, as you move to higher levels in the hierarchy, each level includes the characteristics of lower levels, but higher level systems have unique characteristics that cannot be associated with lower level systems. This implies that theories about lower level systems can be applied to systems of a higher order, but not vice versa. This is why we can use theories produced within the natural sciences to help explain organizations. Remember, however, that theories of organization based solely on models of lower level systems will always be blind to the uniqueness that the higher level system manifests.

Notice that we are systems of level 7 (human) complexity, which means that embedded in us are systems of levels 1 (frameworks) through 6 (animals), while we are embedded in systems located at levels 8 (social organizations) and 9 (transcendental). This means that organizations, our subject of study, are more complex than we ourselves are, and furthermore, that we are embedded in organizations. Most other systems you encounter and attempt to study are at the same or lower levels of complexity, while much of the domain of organization theory is located above your own level of complexity. Your perspective on organizations is, therefore, relatively unique in your experience of the world. It is one of the few subjects that you can study from the perspective of a participant (that is as a subsystem) and whose complexity supersedes, and often overwhelms, your own.

From level 2 on up, all systems are dynamic, that is, they have moving parts and imply change of some sort. Level 1, or framework systems, involve only static systems of understanding, such as categorization schemes and structures that are relatively stable, like a building, anatomy, and geography. Although all systems have a framework, systems from level 2 on up are much more than this. Level 2 represents the simplest dynamic systems. These move in repetitive or routine patterns like the cyclical returning of the seasons which astronomy explains using the conceptual framework of the solar system and a clockwork model of planetary motion. As you move to higher levels of the hierarchy, the concept of system dynamics becomes increasingly complex.

From level 3 in Boulding's hierarchy on up, systems have the capacity for control due to their ability to generate and use feedback to correct deviations from predetermined desired states. The thermostat is a good example of a control system, also known as a cybernetic system. These, and lower level systems, are sometimes referred to as closed systems because, once they are designed and

What is Organization Theory?

built, they do not require additional inputs to operate. They are self-maintaining with respect to the purposes they were built to serve. Organizations use many kinds of cybernetic systems to correct behavior. For instance, analyses of fluctuations in share price, sales volume, and employee turnover are used, respectively, as indicators of investor satisfaction with organizational performance, customer satisfaction with products and services, and employee satisfaction with the organization and with their jobs. This sort of information provides the basis for self-assessment and for planning future courses of action.

 Level 4 in the hierarchy of systems introduces the important idea of an **open system**. Systems at level 4 and above are open in the sense that they depend on their environment for inputs to feed and support their existence. The open system provides a conceptual model that is fundamental to modernist organization theories. In this model, a system takes in inputs from its environment such as sources of energy (e.g., carbon, sunlight, oxygen). These inputs are then transformed into outputs, a process that sustains the life of the system. In the case of the organization, inputs include raw materials, capital, knowledge, labor, and equipment, and the transformation process is the production of goods and/or services which are then output to the environment as inputs for other systems to absorb into their transformation processes. The sales of goods and services produced by the company allow the organization to continue functioning. Figure 2.1 provides a visual representation of the organization as an open system.

At the present time, natural science has not progressed very far beyond open systems understanding. Exciting work is being done on genetic systems using the model of DNA as a self-replicating structure; this work is beginning to suggest models of the fifth level of systems theory such as German sociologist Niklas

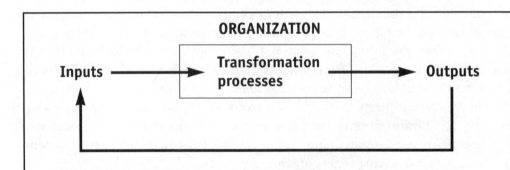

FIGURE 2.1. AN OPEN SYSTEMS VIEW OF THE ORGANIZATION

This model depicts the organization as a mechanism for transforming inputs such as raw materials into outputs such as goods and services.

Luhmann's theory of self-organizing and self-reproducing social systems.[5] But even these developments leave an enormous gap between what science offers and the level of complexity Boulding claimed characterizes organizations. Until the gap is narrowed, organization theorists must use the relatively simplistic theories of lower level systems if they want to continue to follow the path cut by the natural sciences, which is the objective of most modernist organization theorists.

You should be sure to notice that what we have called the parts of the system could also be discussed as systems in their own right. But, systems are not only comprised of other systems, they make up still other systems. That is, the general systems view is one of systems operating within systems operating within systems . . . every system has subsystems, but is also a subsystem of a larger system. Thus, in applying systems theory, it is necessary to approach any phenomenon as a nested system consisting of: the supersystem, the system itself, and its subsystems. This aspect of systems theory is sometimes referred to as **embeddedness**, and it can create all kinds of confusion about levels of analysis. The particular system you wish to focus on defines your **level of analysis** and pinpoints relevant supersystems (those in which the system is embedded that occur at the next higher level of analysis) and appropriate subsystems (those at the next lower level of analysis). To make matters worse, you also need to distinguish levels of analysis from another use of the term "level" with which you may already be familiar—management level in an organizational hierarchy (i.e., executive, manager, supervisor).

Figure 2.2 should help you to visualize these different concepts of level and their relationships. Within modernist organization theory, the first source of confusion is that what is defined as a system shifts with the focus of your discussion or analysis. If you are talking about an organization, for instance, this is defined as the system of interest, which means that units or departments will be regarded as subsystems, while the environment will be considered the supersystem in which it is embedded. But you could define a department within the organization as your system of interest, in which case individuals would be subsystems and the organization would form the supersystem. The terms "system," "subsystem," and "supersystem" provide a way to frame discussions in terms compatible with the abstract concepts of General Systems Theory. This allows you to apply General Systems Theory to any system you choose as your focus. Meanwhile, the specific levels of analysis (in organization theory these include, for example, the organization, its units, and the environment) keep you focused on your definition of the system of interest.

A second source of confusion lies in the differences in perspective that are typical of different levels of management. In modernist organization theory, top management's perspective is usually conceptualized in terms of the

Systems level	Level of analysis	Hierarchical level
Supersystem	Environment	Top management
System	Organization	Middle management
Subsystem	Unit or department	Supervision

FIGURE 2.2. CONCEPTS OF LEVEL

The concept of "level" is used in several different but not entirely unrelated ways in organization theory. For instance, when the organization is the level of analysis, it becomes the system and the environment is the supersystem with departments or other units being the subsystems. Likewise, in traditional forms of organization the major responsibility of top management is managing the organization-environment relationship, while middle managers are generally focused on coordinating and integrating the activities of several subunits within the organization, and lower level managers or supervisors are focused on the subunit for which they have responsibility.

organization's relationship with its environment. Middle management generally is defined in relation to the internal activities of the organization, especially with translating top management's strategic vision into coordinated activity among the organization's units. The perspective of supervision is normally equated with the day-to-day problems of managing workers within one unit. Thus, the perspectives of the different levels of management can be related to the levels of analysis described as environment, organization, and unit. You could imagine that they are equivalent. However, there are many circumstances when this would be inaccurate.

Take the example of a retail sales clerk. This person is typically positioned below the level of management, yet maintains constant contact between the organization and its environment in the process of selling goods to customers. Therefore, the levels depicted in Figure 2.2 (levels of analysis and levels of management) are conceptually related, but not necessarily equivalent. In learning the language of organization theory you will want to be attentive to the concept of level and learn to apply it with great care.

Until you are familiar with conceptualizing in this way, you will probably get lost one or two times. That is, you will begin thinking about an aspect of organization at one level of analysis, with the perspective of a particular level within a hierarchy, and then, without realizing it, you will switch your analytical level or your hierarchical perspective and confuse yourself (and anyone else with whom you are attempting to communicate). This is a normal occurrence when you begin to apply organization theory. Press on; you will eventually come through the haze and discover new powers of conceptualization along with developing your understanding of the modernist perspective.

Symbolic-Interpretive: Enactment and the Social Construction of Reality

American social psychologist Karl Weick introduced **enactment theory** in 1969 in his book *The Social Psychology of Organizing*. According to Weick's theory, when you use concepts like organization, you *create* the phenomenon you are seeking to study. Similarly, in conceptualizing the environment, organizations produce the situations to which they respond. Enactment theory focuses attention on the subjective origin of organizational realities. Weick states that he purposely used the term "en*act*ment to emphasize that managers construct, rearrange, single out, and demolish many 'objective' features of their surroundings. When people act they unrandomize variables, insert vestiges of orderliness, and literally create their own constraints."[6]

According to Weick, by stating an interest in organization and establishing a language for talking about it, we reify the subject of our study, that is, we make the phenomenon *real* by speaking and acting in ways that give it tangibility. The concept of **reification** can be compared to the work of a mime. A mime, by pretending to make contact with a door or a wall, causes us to imagine that a wall or door is present—we can see the absent object through the mime's descriptive attitudes and movements. Reification has a similar power to make us see.

The difference between miming and enactment is that we are aware of the difference between the door the mime creates in our mind and a real door. In the case of enactment, we can make an environment, a culture, a strategy, or an organization appear, but once we have done so there is little difference between our creation and reality. Of course we do not usually enact these realities individually, rather there is often a certain amount of social agreement and cooperation that occurs before such existence is claimed. In fact, when an individual persistently attempts to enact their own reality individually, we may view them as abnormal, not fitting in, or, in some extreme cases, insane. Thus, enactment overlaps with **social construction of reality theory**.

The idea that reality is socially constructed was most forcefully argued by

What is Organization Theory?

Peter Berger and Thomas Luckmann, two German sociologists who wrote an influential book entitled *The Social Construction of Reality*.[7] These theorists argued that human social order is produced through interpersonal negotiations and implicit understandings that are built up via shared history and shared experience. What sustains social order is at least partial consensus about how things are to be perceived and the meanings for which they stand. Through interpretation, members of a society make patterns of meaning out of their activities in the world, and then assume that the patterns they imposed exist apart from the interpretations that produced them.

For instance, Weick argues that the environment of an organization is constructed from the activities of collecting and analyzing information about the environment and from decisions taken on the basis of analysis which lead to various activities, including further constructions of the environment. While the environment is assumed to have generated the analysis, it is actually the analysis that forms the environment to which the organization responds. According to social construction theory, this enacted environment is then presumed to have caused both analysis and decisions as if it were separate from them. Since the decision makers, by collecting and analyzing information, create the environment they respond to, we say they socially construct the reality of their environment and enact what *they* take to be the objective world.

The social constructionist position explicitly recognizes that the categories of language used to understand organizations (such as environment, structure, culture) are not real or natural in an objective sense. Instead, they are the product of beliefs held by members of a society. That is, we invent and sustain the meanings of terms that we then use to understand the world. Thus we act and interpret action within a sociocultural context of our own making. Or, as American cultural anthropologist Clifford Geertz put it: "man is an animal trapped in webs of significance he himself has spun."[8]

The social constructionist perspective is partly modern in the sense that, once reified, the world goes on just as it does for those who take a purely objectivist position. However, the idea that reality is not so much objective as it is **objectified** (i.e., socially constructed in a way that makes it *seem* objective) introduces a new understanding of instability and the potential for organizational change. If organizations are social constructions, then we reconstruct them continuously and could, if we were conscious of these processes, change them in the reconstruction process. Symbolic-interpretive research, in examining the subjective, social foundations of organizational realities, begins to make us conscious of our participation in organizational processes. This dawning realization links symbolic-interpretive perspectives with postmodernists who want to take control of these processes and reconstruct the organizational world along more emancipated lines.

Postmodernism in Organization Theory

It is impossible to choose a core theory, or a typical set of ideas, to exemplify post-modernism—the incredible variety of ideas labelled postmodern defies summarization, and the postmodern value for **diversity** contradicts the very idea of unifying these different understandings into a single, all-encompassing explanation. For these reasons many organization theorists working outside the postmodern perspective regard postmodernism as an anything goes approach. This is inaccurate because, although postmodernism *is* relativistic in the sense that it abandons notions of universal criteria for truth or excellence, it does not sacrifice standards altogether (which is a naive view of relativism). Instead, postmodernists tend to view questions of right and wrong, good and bad, as social constructions that would be usefully redefined as matters for personal reflection and practice.

The critical aspects of postmodern organization theory trace to Marxist and neo-Marxist theorizing, particularly in Europe. However, some of the earliest uses of the term "postmodernism" referred to aspects of architectural style that emerged in the mid- to late twentieth century, as described by American architect Charles Jencks in his 1977 book *The Language of Post-Modern Architecture*.[9] Structures that are postmodern stand in opposition to the functionalist style of modern architecture that was typical of building design in the 1930s through the 1960s. The major critique of functionalist (modernist) architecture by postmodern architects is that it is sterile and lifeless. Postmodern architects seek to renew traditions of making built spaces symbolically rich and meaningful by invoking past styles and reinterpreting them using the marvelous new materials and construction techniques that inspired the functionalist movement. That is, they fuse modern techniques with traditional concerns for the symbolic meanings expressed by built spaces. Furthermore, postmodern architects' use of modern construction methods allows them to juxtapose several period styles in unexpected ways for startling visual effects that often involve disorientation (e.g., in time, when they mix period styles) and evoke laughter or a feeling of playfulness, especially through the use of ironic humor. For instance, the facade of the Chiat-Day advertising agency building in Los Angeles sports a gigantic pair of binoculars, and the Disney headquarters building displays larger-than-life Disney cartoon characters.

As it applies to organization theory, postmodernism evolved most directly out of the poststructuralist movement in French philosophy which is associated with the events of the late 1960s as these unfolded in Europe. It also found its way into organization theory through applications of linguistic, semiotic, and literary theory via the interest in meaning and interpretation introduced by symbolic-interpretive organization theorists. Like postmodern architecture, postmodern philosophy developed in opposition to modernism. In postmodern theory, modernism is generally described as the culmination of the **Enlightenment Project** to rationalize human culture and society, and is criticized for its unquestioned value for rationality and for its efforts to develop an integrated theory of the universe based on scientific principles and methods (e.g., Galileo and Newton's efforts to discover universal laws in astronomy and physics). Modernism in organization theory (e.g., General Systems Theory), which has likewise sought universal explanations that could approach, if not achieve, the status of natural laws, is thus also open to postmodern critique.

Postmodernists challenge the modernist desire for unifying views with their belief that knowledge is fundamentally fragmented, that is, knowledge is produced in so many different bits and pieces that there can be no reasonable expectation that it will ever add up to an integrated and singular view. For instance, French postmodernist Jean-François Lyotard contemptuously labeled efforts at universal understanding as **grand narrative**. Such labels underscore postmodern views of reality as a multiplicitous, fragmented, and contradictory notion that we must learn not to take for granted as we are encouraged to do by the simplifying assumptions that make most forms of science possible.

Fragmentation is a favorite theme among many postmodernists who relate this concept to post-industrial breakdowns in the family, community, and society as well as to the threats to self-identity produced when individuals are called upon to play multiple roles with little temporal and spatial separation between them. For example, teleworking (i.e., work that can be done anywhere and then channelled to the organization through computerized communication links) collapses the distinction between public and private life and, when employees work from their homes, places individuals in the simultaneous and often contradictory roles of employee and family member. This can fragment the identities of family members/workers who are regularly called upon to make rapid transitions between one identity and another. At the same time teleworking produces spatially distributed (or even virtual) organizations in which individual work lives are further fragmented by the spatial distances inserted between co-workers, and between workers and their organization. This fragmented condition is complicated by the variety of types of roles extreme differentiation has wrought upon society (e.g., farm hand to astronaut, priest to hairstylist, creative artist to factory worker) which is one explanation often given for the diversity and multiplicity of post-industrial life.

Postmodernists often challenge modern notions of truth and the search for one best way. For example, postmodernism denies the priority of perception that underlies most of modern science. It challenges the claim that sensory perception is the true and only way to knowledge, arguing that sensory perception is no more truthful, and may even be less valid, than other ways we could know something, such as through intuition or aesthetic experience. And, if sensory perception does not serve as the sole basis for (objective) empirical tests of our theories, then the scientific view of knowledge is opened to debate. As opposed to its self-interpretation as the search for Truth, modernism is reinterpreted by postmodernists as a series of truth *claims*, supported mainly by modernist rhetoric about how scientific and rational modernism is.

Postmodernism also opposes the modern view of human progress. Post-modernists challenge the idea of knowledge as a unified body of thought to be continuously honed and supplemented so that human civilization can progress toward some mutually desirable future—that science and technology lead to a better life. Calling this unexamined assumption the **progress myth**, many post-modernists point to the ways in which those in power use progress as a rationale for maintaining their vested interests in the status quo. They further express belief in the impossibility of defining a mutually desirable future due to human diversity, which is an important value for many postmodernists. A fragmented knowledge of the world resonates with the breakdown of boundaries between nations and their peoples, and the resulting dispersal and mixture of cultures, politics, and religions that were kept bounded and well-apart during the industrial era.

As I mentioned already, one of the most compelling aspects of postmodernism is its striking similarity with post-industrial society and organization, discussed earlier in this chapter. Predictions are that the future will find us occupying smaller, more decentralized, informal, and flexible organizations that will be predominantly service- or information-oriented and will use automated production strategies and computer-based technology.[10] As a result of these changes, we will experience organizations as more eclectic, participative, and loosely coupled than ever before, with the implication that members of organizations will confront more paradox, contradiction, and ambiguity. These themes resonate with the philosophy of postmodernism suggesting that a postmodern perspective will help us adapt to changes already taking place, ironically, as a result of continuing applications of modernist science and technology. The irony is that it is modern science and technology that has produced the means of sharing information so quickly that the moment knowledge is produced it is made available for use. The rapid absorption of knowledge, especially social knowledge, means that organizational and other forms of social change become increasingly unpredictable. Hence science creates the conditions under which science itself becomes less and less useful as a means of prediction and control, which has been its primary value to modernists all along.

What is Organization Theory?

What do postmodernists suggest that you do to prepare yourself for a post-modern future? There are many concrete recommendations about how to be postmodern. First, learn to take nothing for granted. Deconstruct all claims of truth in order to determine whose point of view is benefitted by a particular way of looking at or arguing about the world. In simple terms, the method of **deconstruction** involves reducing an argument to its basic assumptions, denying those assumptions by asserting their negation, and considering what this implies about the original argument.[11] Postmodernists claim that the deconstructions you perform will free you from your former totalizing habits of mind (e.g., searching for one right answer, or believing that everyone thinks or should think as you do) and allow you some critical distance from your socially and culturally defined ways of seeing the world.

One idea critical postmodernists particularly like to problematize and deconstruct is power, which, in most industrial organizations, accumulates at the top of the hierarchy. For instance, modernist organization theorists argue that organizations and society benefit from the greater power of management so long as managers use rational techniques to guide and operate their organizations. Critical postmodernists argue that giving managers greater power on the basis of their claims to rationality actually only works to reproduce the dominance of managers and the capitalists who employ them. Dominance of the capitalistic ruling elite is the objective of modernism, according to these critical postmodernists. Thus, the greater strength of management's voice within organizations and society, while seemingly explained by modernist organization theory, is actually only legitimized by it (e.g., the critiques of Taylorism and Fordism). They further claim that such imbalances of power undermine democratic principles.

One postmodernist idea for redressing the imbalance is to give **voice** to silence. This means seeking greater levels of participation by marginalized members of organizations such as women, racial and ethnic minorities, and the oldest and youngest employees. These postmodernists argue that, by focusing on what is normally not said and thus hidden by entrenched ways of thinking and speaking that support the powerful, you will undermine old concepts and dispute the categories into which people have been placed, so that no one will be disadvantaged or disregarded by the ways in which you conventionally speak or think. This move will allow you to imagine alternatives to your taken-for-granted world. In the process you will find that the boundaries that you assume exist between things are permeable, and the socially constructed foundations of your experience of the world will come under your control (or at least within your conscious experience).

All of these suggestions demand **self-reflexivity**, using your methods of understanding and discovery on yourself as well as on the world around you in order to reveal what it is that you are *assuming* when you produce or use knowledge. You will become opportunistic in the sense of being willing to use many contradictory, paradoxical, and incongruous perspectives in order to avoid the traps of dominance hidden within singular points of view. As a result of your increasing multiplicity, you will destroy your conception of self as a singular identity with a unitary perspective. In the colorful words of one of the major inspirations to postmodernism, the French philosopher Michel Foucault, to be postmodern you must "disappear man."[12] In other words, you will take your long-standing conceptions of yourself and the world and throw them away so that other, profoundly different ways of seeing and being can enter your imagination.[13] As you can see in this short description, postmodernism is a radical perspective with a program to start revolutionary change on a personal level through surfacing and then overturning your own taken-for-granted assumptions about yourself, others, and social organization.

EPISTEMOLOGICAL DIFFERENCES AMONG THE PERSPECTIVES

In order to compare the three perspectives of organization theory, we need to take up the important question of **epistemology**. Epistemology is a branch of philosophy that concerns itself with understanding how we can know the world. Along with ontology, which concerns what can be known (i.e., the kinds of things that exist), it forms the foundation for all philosophical thinking. Thinking about differences in epistemologies is a useful undertaking because epistemology is probably the most profound difference we can draw between the three perspectives of organization theory. Although epistemology is a difficult philosophical issue, giving the matter some attention now will help you considerably in your efforts to understand the perspectives of organization theory.

Epistemology concerns assumptions about how knowledge is obtained or created. It is typical in the social sciences to draw a distinction between objectivist (e.g., positivist, empiricist) and subjectivist (e.g., anti-positivist, idealist) epistemologies, as British sociologist Gibson Burrell and British organization theorist Gareth Morgan do in their book *Sociological Paradigms and Organizational Analysis*, which was published in 1979. Objectivist epistemology is built upon a belief that one can only know something through independent observation. Notice that taking an objectivist position means believing that the world exists independent of our knowledge of it. For the subjectivist, all knowledge of the world, if the world

What is Organization Theory?

exists in an objective sense (subjectivists often make no claims about this what-soever), is filtered through the knower and thereby is powerfully altered by cognitive and/or social and cultural forces. Those who take a subjectivist stand believe that knowledge is relative to the knower and can only be created and understood from the point of view of the individuals who are directly involved. A third position, similar in many ways to the subjectivist, argues further that, because all knowledge is shaped by social and cultural processes, dichotomies such as subject/object and epistemology/ontology are arbitrary and inherently unstable; they are simply the products of one set of social and cultural processes operating at a specific point in time in a particular place. This position argues that all distinctions are semantic in origin, and points to language use as a means to redefine questions of both how (epistemology) and what (ontology) we know.

You can see in the third position the line taken up by postmodernists and the ease with which such a stand resolves into the method of deconstruction in which categories are questioned and concepts undermined. Likewise, you will see the seeds of modernism in the objectivist epistemology, and of symbolic-interpretivism in the subjectivist epistemology. Modernist organization theorists argue that the phenomena they study exist "out there" and thus their theories can be tested against reality to assess their correctness. This epistemology suggests why modernist organization theorists are attracted to methods used in the physical sciences (e.g., measurement, the search for general laws). In taking an interest in meanings and interpretations, symbolic-interpretive and postmodernist researchers are practically forced to take a subjectivist epistemological stand.

In the subjectivist epistemology there is no claim made about whether or not reality exists independent of the observer; it is assumed that this cannot be known since all knowledge is mediated by experience. Thus reality is "in here," that is, reality is defined by the individual's subjective experience, albeit under social and cultural influences. This position is extended by postmodernists who see individual subjectivities as themselves constructed within their social and cultural context. That is, the concept of individual or self is itself considered a construction of social and cultural forces that takes place in the domain of language use, for instance, in labelling or other rhetorical acts.

Table 2.3 summarizes key differences in the multiple perspectives offered by organization theory according to the central issue or subject of concern, the preferred methods for conducting research, and the sort of result produced. In the Classical period, for instance, the subject of organizational study was either the effects of industrialism on society (the sociological approach), or how to make organizations more efficient and effective (the managerial approach). The modernist perspective changed the subject from society and management to the organization itself. This perspective seeks explanations for the various forms that organizations take and the outcomes that they achieve (e.g., performance, profitability, control). The modernist perspective takes an objectivist epistemological position in that the organization is studied as an object with dimensions that can be reliably measured, just as you might measure the height of a table or the weight of an elephant. The symbolic-interpretive perspective focuses on the organization too, but from a predominantly subjectivist epistemological position. That is, instead of treating the organization as an object to be measured and analyzed, it is treated as a subject whose meanings are to be appreciated and understood. The postmodern perspective changes the subject once again, this time from organizations to organization theory and theorizing. That is, the focus of postmodernist perspectives embraces the researcher or practitioner who tries to know the organization, as well as the organization itself, such as it is constructed by attempts to know it.

Classical methods are based on historical analysis and personal reflection with typologies (e.g., Weber's three forms of authority) and prescriptive guidelines (e.g., Fayol's functions of the executive) being the typical result produced. The modernist perspective focuses on the organization itself, relying on statistical description and analysis grounded in objectivity which produce comparative studies of organizations. Symbolic-interpretive research methods often employ

TABLE 2.3. DIFFERENCES IN THE MULTIPLE PERSPECTIVES OF ORGANIZATION THEORY

Perspective	Subject/Focus	Method	Result
Classical	• the effects of organization on society • management of the organization	• observation and historical analysis • personal reflection on experience	• typologies and theoretical frameworks • prescriptions for management practice
Modern	• the organization through "objective" measures	• descriptive measures • correlation among standardized measures	• comparative studies • multivariate statistical analyses
Symbolic-Interpretive	• the organization through "subjective" perceptions	• participant observation • ethnographic interviewing	• narrative texts such as case studies and organizational ethnographies
Postmodern	• organization theory and theorizing practices	• deconstruction • critique of theorizing practices	• reflexivity and reflexive accounts

ethnographic techniques (e.g., participant observation and ethnographic inter-viewing) and result in narrative descriptions and case analyses. The postmodern approach employs methods such as deconstruction and other forms of criticism developed in literary theory alongside the historical and critical approaches of Marxist, neo-Marxist, and feminist theory. One important outcome of postmod-ern research on organizations is an increase in self-reflexive theorizing.

You may wonder whether there is any difference between the Classical man-agement theory method of personal reflection (i.e., among the executives such as Taylor, Fayol, and Barnard, who pioneered this field of study) and postmodern self-reflexivity (the act of turning your critical gaze back on yourself and your own practices). In a way, it looks as though organization theory has come full cir-cle back around to the methods of Classical management theory. However, there is an important difference. In the Classical period, managers felt called upon to share the wisdom they had gained as practitioners; postmodernism calls on the-orists to reflect upon and reveal themselves. In the Classical period it was assumed that those in authority (i.e., owners and managers of organizations) had the right to speak and influence others. Postmodernists believe that those in authority (i.e., authors of organization theories, a category that includes man-agers) have the responsibility to reveal their subjective understandings and moti-vations, and the obligation not to impose them on others. The modernist orientation serves to concentrate authority in the hands of management, while the postmodern orientation tries to diffuse authority by increasing the number of stakeholders whose voices are heard in the organizational decision-making process. Where the modernist perspective concerns itself with creating and sus-taining managerial power and control, the postmodern is marked by concern for the morality of organized action, especially as it is (often negatively) influenced by modernist ways of thinking.

You should recognize, however, that most postmodernists would object to being categorized at all in the ways I do in Table 2.3 and many other similar schemes I use throughout the book. Remember, postmodernism challenges dis-tinctions such as these, seeking to undermine categories, blur boundaries, and expose the motivations that produce them. In the case of Table 2.3, for instance, a postmodernist would probably argue that this type of thinking objectifies orga-nization theory and theorizing in ways that reproduce and legitimize the mod-ernist perspective. That is, such thinking renders organization theory just one more object to be studied and we (modernists) all know that objective methods are the proper way to study objects. To overcome the distinctions, postmod-ernists might deconstruct those that structure the Table 2.3 analysis. For instance, a postmodernist might argue that, what is cast as method and what as result is arbitrary. She could playfully encourage you to reverse their meanings and see what this does to your perspective (e.g., in the Classical period the typologies, frameworks, and prescriptions researchers and managers used produced their observations and experiences rather than the other way around).

Notice also the possibilities for word play concerning the term "object" in the paragraph above. Postmodernists question the subject–object distinction, claiming that in research the two are difficult to keep separate, and anyway are arbitrary distinctions imposed by modernist uses of language. Thus, when we say they *object* to (vs. affirm) something, both distinctions are invoked and create a powerful contrast between being made an object (by the modernist perspective) and resisting objectification (an objective—there is another meaning!—of the postmodernist perspective). Their epistemological position renders postmodernists highly sensitive to language, which may account for their preference for metaphor as a way to imagine the diverse ways of constructing organizations and organization theory.

THE METAPHORS OF ORGANIZATION THEORY

Although theories of organization built upon the models of traditional science continue to be useful, you may find, as symbolic-interpretive and postmodern organization theorists have, that they are not enough to satisfy your curiosity. Many organization theorists also develop understandings built on methods borrowed from the arts and humanities. One of these methods—metaphor—is a particularly useful means of recognizing and understanding the essence of a given phenomenon. For example, organization theorists use different metaphors to communicate different perspectives. You should notice, however, that metaphor has played a significant role in the natural sciences, too. The chemist Friedrich Kekula, for example, claimed that his discovery of the ring structure of benzene was based on a dream of a snake trying to eat its tail. His metaphoric association of the snake image and the problem of the structure of the benzene molecule led to this now famous discovery. The use of metaphor for theory building has a long and respectable tradition in the natural as well as the social sciences.

Metaphor allows you to understand one kind of experience in terms of another by suggesting an identity between two things that you would not normally consider to be equivalent, such as life and a long and winding road; man and a lion. So long as you understand one element of the metaphor, you can learn something about the other. Thus, metaphor encourages you to explore the parallels between an object of interest and something that is better known to you, or at least known in a different way.

What is Organization Theory?

In *Images of Organization*, British organization theorist Gareth Morgan examined many ways in which metaphor has served organization theory as a means to understanding and analyzing organizations.[14] For instance, he explored parallels between organizations and machines, biological organisms, brains, cultures, political systems, and psychic prisons. Other metaphors that have enjoyed popularity among organization theorists include text, discourse, art, jazz, and drama.

Table 2.4 shows how each of the perspectives of organization theory can be equated with a guiding or root metaphor. A **root metaphor** offers a distinctive and fundamental way of seeing, thinking, and talking.[15] It captures the essence of a well-established type of experience that organizes all other experiences of the world into a singular, overpowering perspective. In the remainder of the chapter we will explore these four influential metaphors. As we do so, try to imagine each of the perspectives of organization theory and the Classical period through the interpretive lens of its root metaphor.

TABLE 2.4. THE METAPHORS OF ORGANIZATION THEORY

Perspective	Metaphor	Image of the organization as . . .	Image of the manager as . . .
Classical period	Machine	a machine designed and constructed by management to achieve predefined goals	an engineer who designs builds and operates the organizational machine
Modern	Organism	a living system that performs the functions necessary to survival esp. adaptation to a hostile world	an interdependent part of an adaptive system
Symbolic-interpretive	Culture	a pattern of meanings created and maintained by human association through shared values, traditions, and customs	an artifact who would like to be a symbol of the organization
Postmodern	Collage	An organization theory is a collage made from bits of knowledge and understanding brought together to form a new perspective that has reference to the past	a theorist the theorist is an artist

The Machine Metaphor: Organizations as Tools of Management

Just as you might build a machine for accomplishing certain tasks, such as drilling a hole in wood or affixing a bumper to an automobile, so you can build entire organizations for designated purposes. This is the type of thinking associated with the machine metaphor of organization theory. The machine metaphor arose during the 1800s when many new machines were invented as part of the industrial revolution. This metaphor dominated art and literature in the nineteenth and early twentieth centuries and entered Classical management theory via its concerns for structure and efficiency.

The machine metaphor framed discussions of how to best design the organizational machine as an instrument for accomplishing specific (usually production) tasks, and inspired the image of managers as organizational engineers whose task it is to design and operate an effective and efficient organization. Even today, to a certain extent, all organizations are expected to behave in machine-like ways—they should routinize efficient operations, be predictable, and operate reliably whenever this is feasible. These demands are echoed in the popular metaphor of the computer, which organization theorist Martin Kilduff identified as an updated machine metaphor.[16]

The Organic Metaphor: Organizations as Living Systems

Ideas about biological evolution contributed to von Bertalanffy's General Systems Theory and provided organization theorists with the metaphor of the organism. This biological metaphor implies that, like a living organism, the organization is dependent upon its environment for the resources that support its life. Instead of providing food and shelter, the organization's environment provides raw material, knowledge, labor, and capital—resource inputs to transformation processes that sustain an organization in ways similar to the digestive processes of biological organisms.

The organic metaphor of the organization is also associated with the ideas of organic functioning and adaptation within an ecological system. While organization demands life-sustaining functions just like those of the biological organism (digestion, respiration, circulation), both organism and organization must also adapt to the wider environment on which they depend for their survival. The organic metaphor focuses on organizational processes related to survival, and thus on maintaining exchanges with the environment so that raw materials will be supplied as needed.

The recognition that there are different species of organizations adapted to different environments helped establish contingency thinking among organization theorists. This metaphor should remind you that different types of organizational species will face different demands and respond in different ways. Thus, there can be no one best way of organizing that will work equally well for all organizations.

What is Organization Theory?

The metaphor of the organism frames the modernist approach to organization theory and emphasizes environmental dependence, technology as a transformation process, and structural adaptation, as strategies for organizational survival (themes we will pick up in Chapters 3 through 6).

The Culture Metaphor: Organizations as Cultures

Using culture as a metaphor for organizations is perhaps a little like a dog chasing its tail because, in a conscious way at least, you probably know less about culture than you do about organization. However, if what you know about culture differs from what you know about organization, the culture metaphor can reveal new sources of organizational understanding. This is what the culture metaphor offers to organization theory.

From your point of view, the problem is that you need to learn something about culture before you can adopt the culture metaphor as a way of learning about organization. This we leave until Chapter 7. However, for now, you should know that the culture metaphor emphasizes the customs and traditions, stories and myths, artifacts and symbols of organization (a symbol is a thing that represents some other thing, like a dove represents peace). In the culture metaphor, the manager is a symbol of the organization, a storyteller and a bearer of tradition who is interpreted in multiple ways by the members of the organization.

A Postmodern Metaphor: Collage as a Metaphor for Organization Theory

Collage is an art form in which objects and pieces of objects (often including reproductions of other works of art such as museum postcards) are arranged together to form something new—an art object in its own right. When you use collage as a metaphor for organization theory you are recognizing the value of holding multiple perspectives and using parts of theories to form a new work worthy of display in its own right. The implication is that when organization theorists theorize they act like artists making a collage. They use bits of old theories along with the knowledge and experience they have collected in their lifetimes to create a new theory worthy of use in particular circumstances.

In collage, the artist can stimulate surprise by juxtaposing incongruous images that unleash powerful ideas and feelings capable of provoking the viewer to change his or her accustomed ways of seeing and experiencing the world. In similar fashion, the collage metaphor reintroduces interest in contradiction, ambiguity, and paradox, and redefines issues of power and change (to be taken up in Part III). This metaphor equates the manager with the theorist. It calls on you to recognize that managers and other organizational members create the organization in their hearts and minds as a theory. This means there is a double identity at the heart of the postmodern metaphor—the manager is a theorist, and the theorist is an artist.

As you might have guessed already, postmodernists could never agree to a single metaphor, that would be too much like accepting another grand narrative. Instead, a multiplicity of metaphors has been and probably will continue to be offered. Among the most compelling thus far have been: the organization is a text, a narrative, and a discourse. What metaphors that appeal to postmodernists seem to have in common is a strong aesthetic dimension, that is, they draw out the artistic aspects of the organization by comparing it to forms of artistic representation or discovery. Try imagining an organization that you have participated in as an example of your favorite art form (e.g., a rock concert, a painting, a ballet or an opera, a novel). What aspects of the organization does your metaphor bring to light? What aspects does it hide?

Limitations of Metaphoric Understanding

You should recognize that metaphoric knowledge is partial. That is, a metaphor can reveal only similarities between two things; it remains silent about their differences. When you identify life with a long and winding road you gloss over its brevity and intensity. Similarly, calling a man a lion invokes an image of characteristics such as courage and dominance, but ignores his mouse-like fears and shyness. This implies that the root metaphors of organization theory create blind spots in perception and reasoning.

Because metaphor depends upon identification of the similarities between non-identical things, when you use metaphor to understand one thing in terms of another, you de-emphasize or even ignore the often considerable differences between them. Thus, it is easy to get carried away with a new perspective, overextending the metaphor by taking it to ridiculous extremes. Each of the root metaphors of organization theory either has been, or is capable of being, overextended. Acknowledging the limitations of these metaphors will help you to avoid overextension. For instance, the machine metaphor depends upon the similarities between machines and organizations and underemphasizes the human aspects of organizing, such as emotion and symbolism. Overextension of the machine metaphor leads some people to talk about how to engineer commitment or culture, a use of metaphor that produces a simplistic and misleading understanding of what commitment and culture are and an overestimate of the extent to which managers can control them.

Organism, culture, and collage metaphors can similarly limit organizational understanding. Overextension of the organic metaphor leads to seeing an organization as being much more physically bounded and environmentally determined than it actually is. For instance, organizations have no protective layer, like an organism's skin or shell, to separate them from other organizations or from their environment, nor do they have a biologically determined life span. In like manner, overextension of the culture metaphor leads to an overly symbolic image of organizations, which hides their significant material aspects from view. Finally, overextension of the postmodern metaphors can lead to seeing organizations as much more chaotic and unmanageable than normal everyday experience suggests that they are. But then postmodernism suggests that there is no reality beyond the language we use, thus the metaphor *is* reality within the discourses in which it appears.

The limitations of the metaphors of organization theory suggest that none of them alone provides sufficient understanding on which to base organizational knowledge. Nonetheless, each has inspired partial understandings that have contributed to contemporary organization theory. It is my contention, and the theme of this book, that familiarity with the variety of metaphors, theories, and perspectives offered by organization theory will enhance your knowledge and theorizing skills and enlarge your horizons as organizers in and of the twenty-first century.

SUMMARY

This chapter introduced you to the three perspectives of organization theory that frame this book, and to the historical events and sources of ideas that established, developed, and today help to maintain them. The perspectives were compared on the bases of differences in their epistemological assumptions and their root metaphors. Each of these perspectives of organization theory have contemporary adherents whose research can be found in books and professional journals devoted to the study of organization such as: *Academy of Management Review*, *Administrative Science Quarterly*, *Journal of Management Inquiry*, *Journal of Management Studies*, *Organization Science*, *Organization Studies*, *Organization*, and *Studies of Cultures, Organizations and Society*.

KEY TERMS

three phases of industrialism
post-industrialist society
post-industrial organization
division of labor
theory of capital
alienation
Scientific Management
forms of authority (charismatic,
    traditional, rational-legal)
theory of bureaucracy
formal vs. substantive rationality
system
hierarchy of systems
open system
embeddedness
level of analysis

enactment theory
reification
social construction of reality
objectified (vs. objective)
diversity
Enlightenment Project
grand narrative
fragmentation
progress myth
deconstruction
voice
self-reflexivity
epistemology
metaphor
root metaphor

ENDNOTES

1. For discussions of organization theory as the product of this tension, see Perrow (1973) and Barley and Kunda (1992).
2. Wren (1987); Bernard (1988); Boje and Winsor (1993); Steingard (1993); O'Connor (forthcoming).
3. Quoted in Scott (1992: 44).
4. Boulding (1956).
5. Luhmann (1995). Note that it is difficult to categorize this work as strictly modernist. Luhmann continues to follow the path of natural science, but the level 5 systems he describes push him to consider meaning and interpretation. This pulls him in the direction of symbolic-interpretivism and postmodernism. Nonetheless, his modernist leanings reassert themselves in his systematic attempt to integrate these perspectives into a grand narrative.
6. Weick (1979 [1969]: 243).
7. Berger and Luckmann (1966).
8. Geertz (1973: 5).
9. Jencks traces the term to even earlier uses in the art world.
10. Heydebrand (1989); Johnston (1987); Clegg (1990); Kanter, Stein and Jick (1992).
11. Derrida (1976, 1978); Martin (1990); Calas and Smircich (1991); Kilduff (1993); Linstead (1993).
12. Foucault (1973).
13. Rorty (1989) discusses this position and calls it the ironic disposition.
14. Morgan (1986).
15. Smircich (1983).
16. Kilduff (1993).

REFERENCES

Barley, Stephen, and Kunda, Gideon (1992). Design and devotion: Surges of rational and normative ideologies of control in managerial discourse. *Administrative Science Quarterly*, 37: 363–99.

Bell, Daniel (1973). *The coming of post-industrial society*. New York: Basic Books.

Berger, Peter L., and Luckmann, Thomas (1966). *The social construction of reality: A treatise in the sociology of knowledge*. Garden City, NY: Doubleday.

Bernard, Doray (1988). *From Taylorism to Fordism: A rational madness*. London: Free Association Books.

Boje, David M., and Winsor, R. D. (1993). The resurrection of Taylorism: Total quality management's hidden agenda. *Journal of Organizational Change Management*, 6/4: 58–71.

Boulding, Kenneth E. (1956). General systems theory—The skeleton of science. *Management Science*, 2: 197–208.

Burns, Tom (1962). The sociology of industry. In A. T. Walford, M. Argyle, D. V. Glass, and J. J. Morris (eds.), *Society: Problems and methods of study*. London: Routledge, Kegan and Paul.

Burrell, Gibson, and Morgan, Gareth (1979). *Sociological paradigms and organisational analysis*. London: Heinemann Educational Books.

Calas, Marta, and Smircich, Linda (1991). Voicing seduction to silence leadership. *Organization Studies*, 12: 567–602.

Clegg, Stewart (1990). *Modern organizations: Organization studies in the postmodern world*. London: Sage.

Derrida, Jacques (1976). *Of grammatology*. Baltimore: Johns Hopkins University Press.

Derrida, Jacques (1978). *Writing and difference* (trans. Alan Bass). London: Routledge & Kegan Paul.

Durkheim, Emile (1966). *Suicide: A study in sociology* (trans. John Spaulding and George Simpson). New York: Free Press (first published in 1897).

Durkheim, Emile (1982). *The rules of sociological method* (trans. W. D. Halls). New York: Free Press (first published in 1895).

Durkheim, Emile (1984). *The division of labour in society* (trans. W. D. Halls). New York: Free Press (first published in 1893).

Fayol, Henri (1949). *General and industrial management*. London: Pitman (first published in 1919).

Foucault, Michel (1973). *The order of things: An archaeology of the human sciences* (trans. Alan Sheridan-Smith). New York: Vintage Books.

Foucault, Michel (1977). *Power/knowledge* (ed. Colin Gordon). New York: Pantheon.

Geertz, Clifford (1973). *The interpretation of cultures*. New York: Basic Books.

Harvey, David (1990). *The condition of postmodernity*. Cambridge, Mass: Blackwell.

Heydebrand, Wolf (1977). Organizational contradictions in public bureaucracies: Toward a Marxian theory of organizations. *Sociological Quarterly*, 18 (Winter): 83–107.

Heydebrand, Wolf (1989). New organizational forms. *Work and Occupations*, 16: 323–57.

Jencks, Charles (1977). *The language of post-modern architecture*. London: Academy.

Johnston, W. B. (1987). *Workforce 2000: Work and workers for the 21st century*. Indianapolis: Hudson Institute.

Kanter, Rosabeth Moss, Stein, Barry A., and Jick, Todd D. (1992). *The challenge of organizational change: How companies experience it and leaders guide it*. New York: Free Press.

Kilduff, Martin (1993). Deconstructing organizations. *Academy of Management Review*, 18: 13–31.

Lash, Scott, and Urry, John (1994). *Economies of signs and space*. London: Sage.

Linstead, Steve (1993). Deconstruction in the study of organizations. In John Hassard and Martin Parker (eds.), *Postmodernism and organizations*. London: Sage, 49–70.

Luhmann, Niklas (1995). *Social systems* (trans. John Bednarz, Jr.). Palo Alto, Calif.: Stanford University Press (first published in German in 1984).

Martin, Joanne (1990). Deconstructing organizational taboos: The suppression of gender conflict in organizations. *Organization Science*, 1: 339–59.

Marx, Karl (1973). *Grundrisse: Foundations of the Critique of Political Economy*. Harmondsworth, UK: Penguin (first published in 1839–41).

Marx, Karl (1974). *Capital*, Vol. 1. London: Lawrence and Wishart (first published in 1867).

Marx, Karl (1975). *Early writings* (trans. R. Livingstone and G. Benton). Harmondsworth, UK: Penguin (first published as *Economic and philosophical manuscripts*, 1844).

Morgan, Gareth (1986). *Images of organization*. Newbury Park: Sage.

Naisbitt, John (1984). *Megatrends: Ten new directions transforming our lives*. New York: Warner Books.

O'Connor, Ellen S. (forthcoming). Lines of authority: Readings of foundational texts on the profession of management. *Journal of Management History*.

Perrow, Charles (1973). The short and glorious history of organizational theory. *Organizational Dynamics*, Summer: 2–15.

Rorty, Richard (1989). *Contingency, irony, and solidarity*. Cambridge: Cambridge University Press.

Rosenau, Pauline Marie (1992). *Post-modernism and the social sciences: Insights, inroads, and intrusions*. Princeton: Princeton University Press.

Scott, W. Richard (1992). *Organizations: Rational, natural, and open systems* (3rd edition). Englewood Cliffs, NJ: Prentice-Hall.

Senge, Peter (1992). *The Fifth Discipline*. London: Random House.

Smircich, Linda (1983). Concepts of culture in organizational analysis. *Administrative Science Quarterly*, 28: 339–58.

Steingard, D. S. (1993). A postmodern deconstruction of total quality management (TQM). *Journal of Organizational Change Management*, 6/4: 72–87.

Taylor, Frederick W. (1911). *The principles of scientific management*. New York: Harper.

Toffler, Alvin (1970). *Future shock*. New York: Random House.

Weber, Max (1947). *The theory of social and economic organization* (ed. A. H. Henderson and Talcott Parsons). Glencoe, Ill.: Free Press (first published in 1924).

Weick, Karl E. (1979 [1969]). *The social psychology of organizing*. Reading, Mass.: Addison-Wesley.

Wren, D. (1987). *The evolution of management thought* (3rd edition). New York: Wiley.

FURTHER READING

In addition to the sources cited for further reading in Chapter 1, try the following for post-industrialism and postmodernism in relation to modernism.

Hassard, John, and Parker, Martin (1993) (eds.). *Postmodernism and organizations*. London: Sage, 49–70.

Jencks, Charles (1992) (ed.). *The post-modern reader*. London: St. Martin's Press.

What is Organization Theory?

Kumar, Krishan (1995). *From post-industrial to post-modern society: New theories of the contemporary world*. Oxford: Blackwell.

Lash, Scott, and Urry, John (1987). *The end of organized capitalism*. Cambridge: Polity Press.

Piore, Michael, and Sabel, Charles (1984). *The second industrial divide*. New York: Basic Books.

Reed, Michael I., and Hughes, M. D. (1992) (eds.). *Rethinking organization: New directions in organizational research and analysis*. London: Sage.

Rosenau, Pauline Marie (1992). *Post-modernism and the social sciences: Insights, inroads, and intrusions*. Princeton: Princeton University Press.

On metaphor, see the following sources:

Lakoff, George, and Johnson, Mark (1980). *Metaphors we live by*. Chicago: University of Chicago Press.

Miller, James G. (1978). *Living systems*. New York: McGraw-Hill.

Morgan, Gareth (1986). *Images of organization*. Newbury Park: Sage.

Part II
Core Concepts and Theories

We now begin our study of organization theory and theorizing in detail. In the chapters that make up Part II, you will build your understanding of six core concepts that organization theorists rely upon to construct their theories—organizational environment, strategy, technology, social structure, culture, and physical structure. In each of these chapters I will present theories that relate the core concepts to each other. Thus, as we move through the chapters of this section, we will use the concepts already formed to build more complex theories, so that you will gradually increase the complexity of your theorizing.

In addition, each chapter will continue to build in a chronological sequence, from early notions of the concept in question to later views. Usually this will mean moving from modernist, through symbolic-interpretive to postmodern perspectives. However, this chronology is more rigid for the topics of environment, strategy, technology, and social structure. As we move to the topics of culture and physical structure, the chronology breaks apart and is replaced by something more compatible with postmodernist ideas of fragmentation and collage. In keeping with our theme of multiple perspectives in organization theory, we will explore all of the core concepts of organization theory from modernist, symbolic-interpretive, and postmodern perspectives. However, I should warn you that Chapters 3 through 6 are highly modernist. This is because the concepts discussed in these chapters helped to develop the modernist perspective in organization theory and it is tough to relate their meaning and significance without giving a great deal of attention to this viewpoint. Nonetheless, postmodern perspectives are beginning to appear in research relating to these concepts. For example, ethical concerns about environmental sustainability and the social responsibility of organizations introduce postmodernist critiques into the study of organizational environments. In the study of technology, postmodernism is associated with research into information technology (IT) and its implications for change in the way in which work is done in post-industrial societies. In social structure, postmodernism appears in discussions of new forms of organizing that define the post-industrial organization.

Symbolic-interpretivism plays an important role in organization theory by opening up new discussions such as the topics of organizational culture and symbolism. This perspective challenges modernist views and introduces new ways of thinking. In the areas of organizational culture and physical structures, symbolic-interpretivism presents these concepts as important precisely because of their symbolic potential and role. While postmodernism radicalizes these perspectives, it does not challenge symbolic-interpretivism to the same degree it does modernist views.

3 | The Environment of Organization

I N modernist organization theories, the organizational environment is conceptualized as an entity that lies outside the boundaries of the organization (see Figure 3.1). It influences organizational outcomes by imposing constraints and demanding adaptation as the price of survival. The organization, for its part, faces uncertainty about what the environment demands while it experiences dependence on the multiple and various elements that comprise its environment. It is this dependence and uncertainty that explain organizational structures and action in the environment conceived by modernist organization theorists.

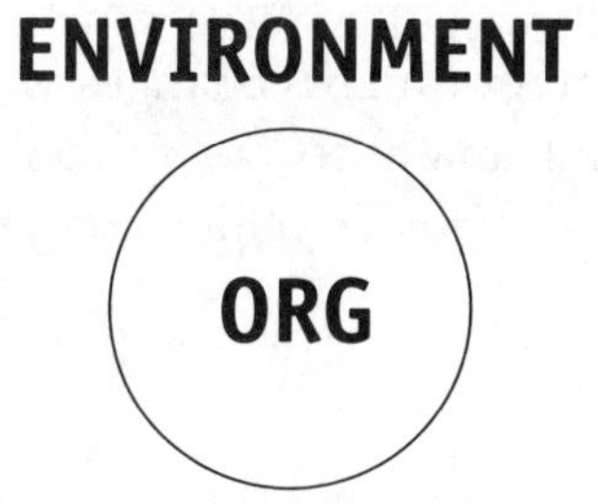

ENVIRONMENT

ORG

FIGURE 3.1. THE ORGANIZATION IN ITS ENVIRONMENT

A simple distinction showing the organization as an entity embedded within a larger system.

Symbolic-interpretivists, in contrast to modernists, view the environment as a social construction. That is, environments are seen as theoretical constructs formed by beliefs about their existence and constituted by expectations that are set in motion by these beliefs. Weick's enactment theory, described in the previous chapter, is an example of this way of conceptualizing the organizational environment. From the symbolic-interpretive perspective environments have material consequences, but they are primarily symbolic; their significance within the organization derives from the interpretations they are given.

Postmodern organization theory offers many approaches to the subject of organizations and environments. One is to problematize the distinction between them, as is suggested by the notion of the boundaryless organization, and introduce new organizational forms such as the network model and the virtual organization. Another is to critique modernist theories of organization–environment relations for being anti-environmental in the sense that they justify exploitation of limited natural resources for competitive advantage while silencing demands for a corporate ethic of environmentally responsible action.

Most organization theorizing about environments up to now has been conducted in a modernist way. However, with institutional theory, the symbolic-interpretive perspective has established itself within this debate. Although postmodern critiques of modernist views of the environment are becoming stronger and more common, they have yet to have much impact on mainstream organization theory. In this chapter we begin with several modernist definitions of environment. Then we will consider four theories of organization-environment relations—contingency theory, resource dependence theory, population ecology, and institutional theory—the last of which represents symbolic-interpretive inroads into the modernist discussion of organizational environments. Next we consider the history of theorizing the issue of environmental uncertainty to illustrate how thinking about environments changes when you move from modern to symbolic-interpretive and finally to postmodern perspectives. The chapter concludes with some practical advice about analyzing organizational environments.

DEFINING THE ORGANIZATIONAL ENVIRONMENT

In modernist perspectives, organizational environments are typically defined by their elements. There are several different ways of sorting out these elements. Three of the most common are: the interorganizational network, the general environment, and the international/global environment.

The Interorganizational Network

Every organization interacts with other members of its environment. The inter-actions allow the organization to acquire raw materials, hire employees, secure capital, obtain knowledge, and build, lease, or buy facilities and equipment. Since the organization produces a product or service for consumption by the environ-ment, it will also interact with its customers. Other environmental actors, who regulate or oversee these exchanges, interact with the organization as well (e.g., distributors, advertising agencies, trade associations, governments of the coun-tries in which business is conducted). Taken as a whole, all of these interacting elements form the **interorganizational network**.

The interorganizational network consists of suppliers, customers, competi-tors, unions, regulatory agencies, and special interests (Figure 3.2).[1] Regulatory agencies have legal control over organizational activities, for example, tax author-ities, licensing agencies, and customs inspectors. Special interests are people, groups, or organizations who attempt to influence the activities of the organiza-tion via political, economic, and/or social pressure. Environmental protection groups like Green Peace, and consumer activists such as the Ralph Nader organ-ization, are examples of special interests.

A network analysis presents the interorganizational network as a complex web of relationships in which a group of organizations is embedded (Figure 3.3). Although one organization may be more central to the network than others, the organization of interest to you may not be the one that is most central. The net-work shows the relative positions of all organizations considered. Centrality is shown by the number of linkages an organization has with other elements of its network. The links in the network represent channels through which resources, information, opportunities, and influence flow. The network perspective pro-motes sensitivity to the variety and complexity of interactions that sustain orga-nized activity within the environment.

For modern organization theorists, the main challenge in performing a net-work analysis is determining a reasonable boundary. Because few networks are closed systems, the decision about which environmental actors to include and which to leave out can be somewhat arbitrary. Managers typically avoid this prob-lem by placing their own organization in the center of the network and then adding organizations with which theirs directly interacts, plus its chief competi-tors. If time, energy, and budget permit, further environmental actors can be added to the analysis.

Notice how the managerial solution to defining the network alters the concept of the network used by organization theorists. The managerial solution places

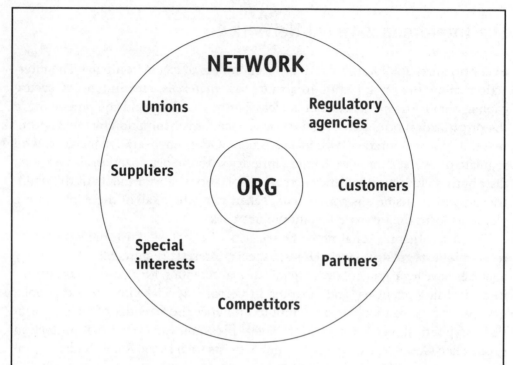

FIGURE 3.2. DIAGRAM SHOWING THE ORGANIZATION IN THE CENTER OF A NETWORK OF INTERACTING AND COMPETING ORGANIZATIONS

Although one's own organization is not always central within its network, managers have a tendency to view the organization in this way.

the organization in the center of the analysis. This can unbalance the analysis, sort of like the problem of a self-centered person. The result of this difference is, first of all, that managers are prone to disregard information that appears outside the periphery of their construction of the network. Some of this information can be highly valuable. Second, the managerial solution tends to slant the reporting of information toward the immediate concerns of the central point in the model—the organization and its top management.

You may think that the arguments just presented overwhelmingly support the theoretical approach to understanding networks. However, the theoretical approach has difficulties as well. The most critical of these from a managerial point of view is that the more balanced view of the network is not immediately translatable into organizational action plans. Because it is formulated at a distance from the concerns of management (its strength in terms of presenting a non-organization centered viewpoint), it is difficult for managers to see the benefit of the analysis (its weakness from the manager's point of view).

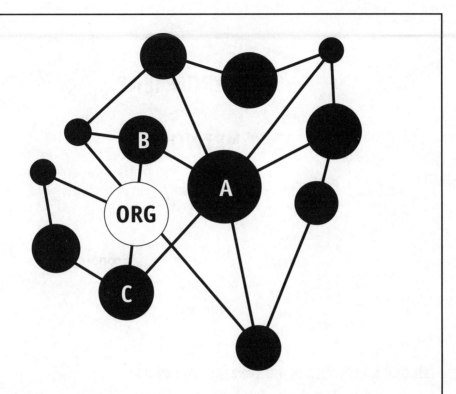

FIGURE 3.3. THE INTERORGANIZATIONAL NETWORK IN A MORE BALANCED PERSPECTIVE

In this view of the network, Organization A, a competitor, is most central. B is a supplier of both ORG and A. C is a customer of both firms.

The General Environment

In addition to significant actors in the organization's network, there are a host of more general forces at work in an environment. These forces will have an effect throughout the network, yet, analysis of the network alone is unlikely to pick them up. For this reason, you will find analysis of general environmental conditions to be useful in more fully appreciating the links between an organization and its environment. To conduct such an analysis, the **general environment** is divided into different sectors including: social, cultural, legal, political, economic, technological, and physical (Figure 3.4).

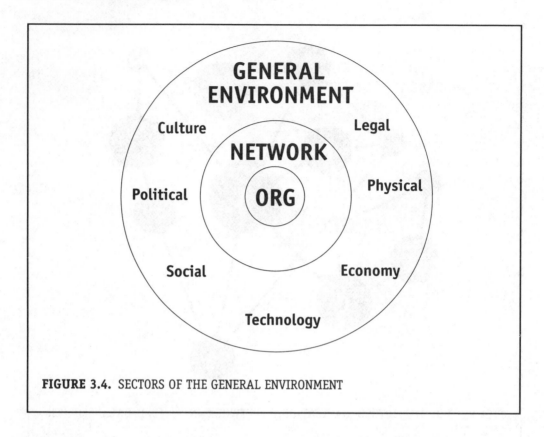

FIGURE 3.4. SECTORS OF THE GENERAL ENVIRONMENT

Social Sector

The social sector of the environment is associated with class structure, demographics, mobility patterns, life styles, and traditional social institutions including educational systems, religious practices, trades, and professions. In the U.S., the aging of the population, an influx of women and ethnic minorities into the workforce, professionalization of many forms of work, and migration out of heavily industrialized areas are all examples of recent trends in the social sector surrounding many American companies. Recent migrations of people from Eastern Europe and North Africa into the wealthier nations of northern Europe are examples of mobility patterns of importance in the general environment of European and African firms.

Cultural Sector

Concern with the cultural sector revolves around issues such as history, traditions, expectations for behavior, and the values of the society or the societies in which the organization operates. Examples of conditions in the cultural sector of many American firms include emphasis on leadership, rationality, and material wealth, while cultural sector trends show a decreasing value for hierarchical authority (especially among the growing ranks of professionals), and increasing value for human rights, quality issues, and protection of the physical environment. Be sure to notice how the social trends and the cultural trends intersect. For instance, the appearance of women and minorities in substantial numbers in the American workforce is showing up as a change in values concerning gender and multi-cultural diversity. These value changes have, in turn, influenced the legal and political sectors of the general environment of organizations operating in the U.S.

Legal Sector

The legal sector is defined by the constitutions and laws of the nations in which the organization conducts its business, as well as legal practices in each of these domains. This sector involves such areas of law and legal practice as corporate, antitrust (anti-monopoly), tax, and foreign investment law. Examples of trends in the legal sector are often difficult to separate from trends in the political and economic sectors. For instance, trends involving both the regulation and the deregulation of certain industries are of major concern to affected organizations in the European Community and in the United States. This sector also bears close links to social and cultural trends such as equal employment opportunity and anti-discrimination legislation in the U.S. aimed at resolving problems associated with the entry of women and minorities into the American workforce. Cross-sector links can also be seen in the aging of the U.S. population with accompanying pressures for corporate support of health care and other retirement benefits.

Political Sector

The political sector is usually described in terms of the distribution and concentration of power and the nature of political systems (e.g., democratic vs. autocratic) in those areas of the world in which the organization operates. The recent renunciation of communist rule in Eastern Europe is an example of significant change in the political (and economic) sector of organizations doing or seeking to do business in this region. The political sector has close ties with the legal sector and both are influenced by trends in other sectors. For example, women and minorities have become more politically active in the U.S. since their entry into the workforce (social sector), and their increased political participation (political sector) has resulted in new legislation for civil rights and affirmative action (legal sector).

Economic Sector

The economic sector is comprised of labor markets, financial markets, and markets for goods and services. The extent to which private versus public ownership is typical, whether or not centralized economic planning is attempted, fiscal policies, consumption patterns, patterns of capital investment, and the banking system all contribute to an analysis of an organization's economic sector. Examples of economic conditions commonly found in an economic sector analysis include: the balance of payments, hard currency issues, economic alliances with other countries, trade agreements, price controls, access to raw materials markets, interest and inflation rates, price indexes, unemployment rates, excess production capacity, and investment risk.

Economic sector trends can have powerful implications for conditions in the other sectors of the general environment. For instance, the shift from communism to capitalism in Eastern Europe (a political as well as an economic sector change) has implications for nearly every other sector in the general environment. Or, to give a more detailed example, in the U.S., concern about gaining access to Chinese markets (economic sector) has driven American politicians to grant China the trading status of "favored nation" (political sector) in spite of convincing evidence of what in the West is considered to be significant human rights violations. However, if the popularity of sanctioning human rights violators continues in the U.S. (cultural sector), firms trading with China will probably experience future difficulties such as product boycotts by American consumers or public outcry leading to political pressure for economic sanctions similar to the situation faced by organizations doing business in South Africa during Apartheid.

Technological Sector

The technological sector provides knowledge and information in the form of scientific developments that the organization can acquire and use to produce output (goods and services). In a sense, the environment possesses the knowledge to produce its desired outputs and contributes this knowledge to various organizations that then carry out production processes for the benefit of others in the environment. Organizations receive knowledge from the environment in such forms as pre-trained and culturally socialized employees, purchases of equipment and software, and the services of consultants and other professionals. A significant recent trend in the technological sector of many organizations has been the availability of computer-based technologies such as personal computers, robots, and video-recording equipment. Applications of multi-media technology loom on the horizon. Advances can also be expected in the fields of genetics, quantum physics and fiber optics; these fields offer other examples of change in this sector.

As we discussed in Chapter 2, there are many, including some leading postmodern thinkers such as Jean-François Lyotard, Daniel Bell, and David Harvey,[2] who believe that recent changes in the technological sector have had such profound influence on the Western world that it is forever changed in all of its aspects. These arguments compare the present historical era to the industrial revolution claiming that this was another time when technology brought great social, cultural, legal, political, and economic change.

Physical Sector

The physical sector includes nature and natural resources. Some organizations have direct and immediate concerns with physical sector elements ranging from coal and oil reserves (e.g., firms operating in the oil industry), accessible harbors (e.g., firms in import/export trades or those operating as shipping companies), viable transportation routes (e.g., trucking companies), and pollution levels (e.g., manufacturing concerns) to severe weather conditions (e.g., firms in the air transportation or construction industries). Examples of general conditions and trends worth watching in the physical sector include possible global warming, changing weather patterns, the disappearance of the rain forests and local disasters such as drought, earthquakes, floods, famines, and volcanic activity.

Except for the case of dwindling natural resources, changes in the physical sector are extremely difficult to predict. Nonetheless, firms that depend on this sector for resources will obviously be economically affected by changes that occur here. Disasters such as the recent earthquakes in San Francisco and Los Angeles in the United States and Kobe, Japan, however, have more than economic impact. For example, changes in attitudes and values toward safety issues (cultural sector) initiate changes in building codes (legal sector) and stimulate the search for new building techniques (technical sector).

Although we separate the general environment into sectors in order to identify and analyze their distinctive influences, the sectors are not really separate as was illustrated above with examples of how the sectors are interrelated. These categories are largely artificial distinctions made by organization theorists to help them address environmental complexity. After you become familiar with these seven categories you may find that you prefer to use only five or six sectors. For instance, collapsing social and cultural, or political and legal categories makes good sense to many people. Or, you may find you need more than seven categories to accommodate all the variety you see in the environment of your organization. The model presented here is merely offered as a starting point for understanding what sort of things modern organization theorists consider when they think about an organization's general environment. It is meant as a stimulus, not a rigid solution. The usefulness of this, or any other organization theory model, will depend upon your elaborating it with specific information based upon your knowledge and experience with organizations. Do not be reluctant to change a theoretical model if the change enables you to better understand your world.

International and Global Environment

The **international and global environment** includes aspects of the environment that cross national boundaries or that are organized on a global scale. Elements of the international environment include institutions such as the United Nations, the International Monetary Fund, GATT (General Agreement on Trade and Tariffs), and international consulting firms. Concern for conditions and trends in the international environment will likewise be part of a total environmental picture. Competition from the East (e.g., Japan, Korea, and China) in markets all over the world is one example of an economic and political trend that is international in its scope and implications.

An example of an international trend that is having effects on political, legal, and economic sectors in many parts of the world is growing concern for the natural environment. The shift in values that promotes saving natural resources and reclaiming polluted regions is encouraging people to organize themselves politically through the Green movement. Since the sentiment underlying the Green movement seems to cross national boundaries, this movement can be interpreted as an example of an international trend with national implications that reach into networks and organizations. For instance, the alliance of shifting cultural values affects national political institutions through establishment of Green parties in various democratic societies and is producing pressures that are affecting international law and cross-national trade relations representing the legal and economic sectors of many nations. These forces may one day become fully organized at the international and even the global level. Consider, for example, the first Earth Summit held in Rio de Janeiro, Brazil, in 1992. Managers need to be aware of the specific ways in which these changes might affect and are already affecting their interorganizational network and their organization.

At this point in time global issues are more image than reality. However, trends in the international environment suggest that markets are moving toward a globally integrated future. Consider, for example, the markets of the Pacific Rim, or the European Community. Further evidence comes from the international success of certain products such as Coca-Cola, Toyota automobiles, Tuborg beer, and McDonald's hamburgers. However, the existence of widely accepted products and growing international markets does not constitute the level of interdependence that is evoked by the image of a global environment. There is still a ways to go before Coca-Cola is available everywhere in the world. Nonetheless, the amount of energy directed at anticipating a global future is clearly creating the very alliances of which that future will be constructed.

In many respects, the international environment can be analyzed using the same distinctions we made under the headings of the interorganizational network and general environment. This is because as soon as an organization begins to expand its activities beyond the boundaries of its home nation, it will interact regularly with representatives of organizations from these other nations—joint venture partners, consumer groups, tariff collecting agencies, tax authorities, licensing agents, to name only a few—and all of these will be part of the organization's network. Even before entering into international operations or exchanges, the organization will be affected by competitors that operate in international markets, and by firms that enter the organization's domestic markets from abroad.

However, the international/global environment is not simply "another layer of things to worry about," as one student put it. It represents a fundamental shift in perspective such as the one shown in Figure 3.5. From this perspective the environment of the organization is seen as one of many interrelated environments. The complexity of this level of environmental analysis is immensely greater than the conceptualizations we considered earlier in the chapter. Thus, once you have learned to take the international environment into account, you will have broadened yourself in a way that changes your orientation toward even the most local aspects of the interorganizational network. This bigger picture is the value of an international perspective and most people now believe that this picture will soon be replaced by a truly global view filled with contradictions and paradoxes such as those evoked by the popular slogan: "Think global, act local."

Environment: The Big Picture

The cross-cutting influences of the different sectors of the general environment and the international and global environments make an important point about theoretical models. We are not dealing with a group of different environments as our language seems to suggest. Rather, we are talking about different aspects of one, highly complex environment. In fact, the organization itself cannot really be separated from its environment because it makes up the environment along with other organizations with which it is involved. This is perhaps most clearly seen with reference to another figure.

In Figure 3.6 the organization is shown within its network which, in turn, is shown within the general environment and subject to its myriad influences, including international and global factors. The influences of conditions and

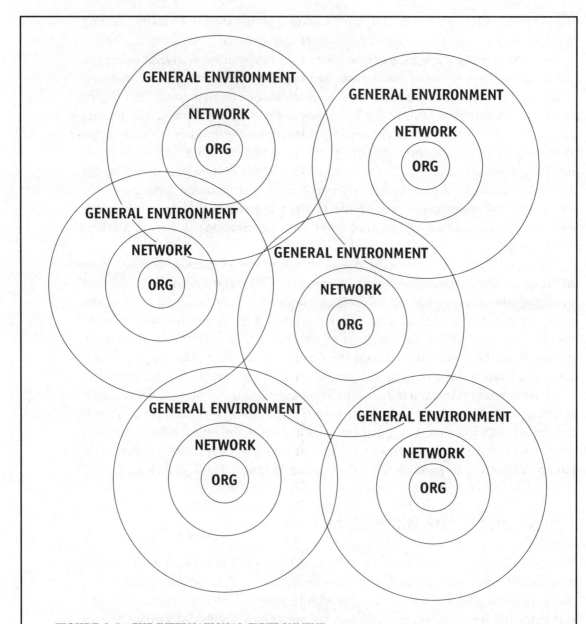

FIGURE 3.5. THE INTERNATIONAL ENVIRONMENT

A complex view of the international environment in which organizations are not central. Organizations are seen as embedded within relational networks that are themselves embedded in even larger networks. Of course, you should remember that many organizations comprise each interorganizational network, instead of the one drawn inside each center circle in the model. Let each organization "circle" shown in this model remind you not only of the organization of interest, but of the interorganizational network in which it operates as was shown in Figure 3.3.

trends in the general environment are separated for purposes of analysis into the seven sectors: cultural, social, political, legal, economic, physical, and technological. These influences can be traced moving through the network and into the organization itself. Thus, the organization is not simply a contributing member of the environment, it is embedded in its environment. Therefore, the distinctions between organization and environment, like those between different environmental sectors, are arbitrary. In general, we make distinctions because without them we might forget to examine aspects of the environment that are critical to our understanding. These particular distinctions are recommended because they are in common use among modernist organization theorists and managers. Later in this chapter we will consider what postmodernists have to say about these and other modernist ideas.

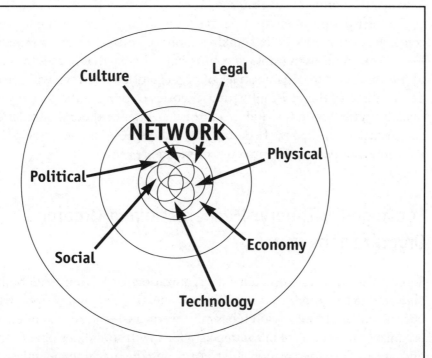

FIGURE 3.6. INTERRELATIONSHIP BETWEEN THE GENERAL ENVIRONMENT, THE INTERORGANIZATIONAL NETWORK, AND THE ORGANIZATION

The general environment penetrates the interorganizational network and the organization even as networks and organizations constitute the environment.

THEORIES OF ORGANIZATION–ENVIRONMENT RELATIONS

There have been two periods of intensive development in the understanding of organization–environment relationships. The first occurred during the late 1950s and early 1960s when the concept of the environment was introduced to organizational analysis by an extension of systems theory. Prior to this, a closed systems view was predominant, especially in Classical management theory where organizations were treated as if their internal operations were the sole concern of management. Systems theorists established the idea that organizations are open to their environments. The first period of study was devoted to conceptualizing the environment and to demonstrating the importance of the new concept. The second period of development began in the late 1970s and continues today. Now, the environment is *assumed* to be influential, and interest is focused on the ways in which this influence operates.

The first period of environmental study in organization theory provided the contingency framework for thinking about organization–environment relations. We will examine an example of contingency theory that relates the environment to mechanistic and organic styles of organization. Then we will turn our attention to three of the most influential theories of organization–environment relations from the second period: resource dependence theory, population ecology, and institutional theory, the latter of which represents the entry point for symbolic-interpretive studies into environmental research.

Contingency Theory: Mechanistic and Organic Organizations

Some of the earliest research on organizational environments built upon the observation that organizations differ considerably depending upon whether they operate in stable or rapidly changing environments. In stable environments, organizations specialize in routine activities with strict lines of authority and distinct areas of assigned responsibility. Applying the machine metaphor, these organizations are called mechanistic. Machines consist of specialized parts engineered into a high-performance system. **Mechanistic organizations** similarly have specialization of parts (the different tasks and jobs that employees do) and these parts are engineered into a high-performance system by management.

In rapidly changing environments, organizations require flexibility and employees are encouraged to apply their skills as needed, fitting into the changing work patterns in whatever way they find to be useful. Modernist organization theorists describe these organizations as organic because, like other living things, they adapt flexibly to changing circumstances. **Organic organizations** have less specialization and are less formalized and hierarchical than mechanistic organizations; they also engage in considerably more lateral communication.

You can discover the difference between mechanistic and organic forms for yourself by comparing some common organizations; college libraries, post offices, and telephone companies have the characteristics of mechanistic organizations while hospital emergency rooms, research laboratories, and family outings are organic. Of course, organizations always combine mechanistic and organic characteristics. For example, most administrative work in universities is done in a mechanistic way, while research activities are more organic. Actually, both of these types of work activity (along with most others) combine elements of mechanistic and organic styles of organization. For instance, university teaching activities are partly mechanistic (e.g., proctoring examinations, reporting grades) and partly organic (e.g., designing curricula, conducting group learning experiences) and within each of these tasks you will discover both mechanistic and organic components as well. Nonetheless, the overall distinction remains useful as a way to characterize the central tendencies of different styles of organizing that appear in two extreme types of environments.

Notice that there is no theoretical reason to consider either organic or mechanistic forms of organization as universally superior; each is appropriate to different environmental conditions. In stable environments, the mechanistic form is advantageous because of the efficiencies it can generate by using standard procedures to perform routine activities. Under these conditions organizations can learn to optimize their activities with respect to minimizing costs and maximizing profits. Under rapidly changing conditions, however, many of the advantages of mechanistic organization are lost. The logic and profitability of routinization breaks down when the organization must constantly alter its activities in order to adapt to rapid changes in the environment. The flexibility that comes with organic forms of organization is preferred in a changing environment because this supports needed innovation and adaptation. The explanation of when to use mechanistic versus organic forms of organization is an example of **contingency theory**.

The contribution early contingency theorists such as British sociologists Tom Burns and George Stalker made to organization theory was to notice that different environmental conditions called for different styles of organizing.[3] That is, the most effective way to organize is *contingent* upon conditions of complexity and change in the environment. This insight may seem trivial because today we accept the importance of the environment almost without question. However, in its time, the theory of mechanistic versus organic organizational forms was insightful and ground-breaking. It continues to offer a foundation for recent discussions of organization–environment relations, like the ones we will consider next.

Resource Dependence Theory

Resource dependence theory was most fully developed by Jeffrey Pfeffer and Gerald Salancik who published their ideas in 1978. Their book was provocatively titled *The External Control of Organizations* to emphasize the point that the environment is a powerful constraint on organizational action. Although resource dependence theory is based on the assumption that organizations are controlled by their environments, these theorists also believe that managers can learn to navigate the harsh seas of environmental domination.

The basic argument of resource dependence theory is that an analysis of interorganizational relations within the network of the organization can help managers to understand the **power/dependence relationships** that exist between their organization and other network actors. Such knowledge allows managers to anticipate likely sources of influence from the environment and suggests ways in which the organization can offset some of this influence by creating counter-dependence.

An organization's vulnerability to its environment is the result of its need for resources such as raw materials, labor, capital, equipment, knowledge, and outlets for its products and services. These resources are controlled by the environment. The dependency these needs produce gives the environment its power. The environment uses this power to make demands on the organization for such things as competitive prices, desirable products and services, and efficient organizational structures and processes. However, the dependency the organization has on its environment is not one single, undifferentiated dependency, it is a complex set of dependencies that exist between an organization and the specific elements of its environment found in the interorganizational network.

A resource dependence analysis begins by identifying an organization's needed resources and then tracing them to their sources. This procedure can be visualized with a combination of the open systems and the interorganizational network models (Figure 3.7). The open systems model helps you to identify resource inputs and the outputs of the organization. You then use the network model to define where the resources and outputs are located. For example, firms that provide raw materials and equipment will be found among the network's suppliers.

Tracing the organization's outputs will identify specific customers in the network. Labor, capital, and knowledge are also brought into the organization and are supplied through other elements of the network (e.g., labor from employment agencies, capital from financial institutions, knowledge from universities).

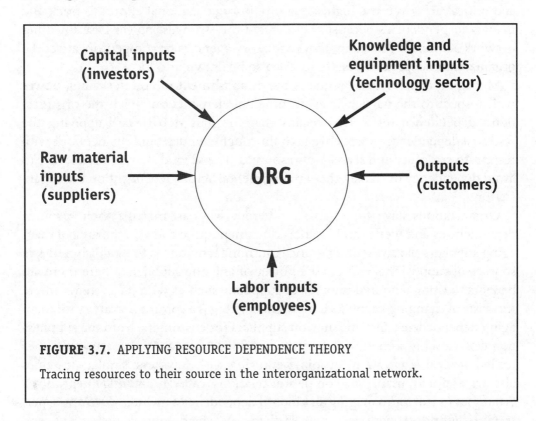

FIGURE 3.7. APPLYING RESOURCE DEPENDENCE THEORY

Tracing resources to their source in the interorganizational network.

After specifying resources and their sources in the network of the organization, the resource dependence perspective moves your attention to those environmental actors who can affect these organization–environment relationships and thereby support or interfere with the organization's resource exchanges. Competition over raw materials and customers is one source of potential influence, and this is where you should bring the firm's competitors into your analysis. Another source is regulatory agencies, and the special interests who compete with the organization for influence over the regulators.

Of course the procedure given above is too ambitious. In practice it will be impossible to consider every source of dependence that an organization has on its environment or every potential competitive or regulatory move. The practical solution is to sort resources according to their criticality and scarcity. **Criticality** is an estimate of the importance of a particular resource. Critical resources are the resources without which the organization cannot function. For instance, beef is a critical resource for McDonalds, whereas drinking straws are not. **Scarcity** is an estimate of the availability of the resource within the environment. Gold and platinum are scarce, air and water are not (yet). Resources that are both scarce and critical are given the highest priority in organizational efforts to track and manage dependencies because these create the strongest power base for other network actors. To the extent that regulatory agencies or competitors affect the organization's dependencies, these will also be drawn into focus.

Managing dependencies requires the establishment of countervailing power with respect to the particular environmental elements on which the organization's dependence rests. This means that the first step toward applying the resource dependence perspective is to thoroughly understand the network with respect to criticality and scarcity of resources. The second step is to seek ways to avoid dependency or make other environmental actors dependent on the organization.

Organizations have found many different ways to manage their resource dependencies and Pfeffer and Salancik document quite a few. In the area of managing suppliers of raw materials, one common technique is to establish multiple sources of supply. This reduces the power of any one supplier. Where there are benefits to using a limited number of suppliers, such as with JIT systems where the costs of changing suppliers is high, contracting is a common strategy for managing dependencies. Dependency on suppliers (or customers, from the suppliers point of view) is sometimes counteracted by acquisition or merger strategies (called vertical integration) or joint venturing with suppliers; similar strategies also are useful for managing competitor relations (called horizontal integration). Strategies useful for managing all kinds of dependencies include: developing personal relationships with members of firms on which yours is dependent, and establishing formal ties such as taking up membership on their board of directors or inviting one of their officers to sit on your board. In the area of managing regulatory dependencies, a common strategy in the U.S. is to send lobbyists to Washington to influence legislators, for example, to work for competitive trade agreements or to vote for favorable corporate tax laws or government funding of research and development. All aspects of marketing—sales, advertising, distribution—can be seen as attempts to manage output dependencies via influence on consumer purchases of company products. Counteracting negative public opinion or the negative influence of special interest groups is sometimes achieved with advertising, for example, using corporate image campaigns.

Labor and knowledge dependencies are sometimes managed with recruitment strategies for attracting executives and other personnel away from competitors. A strategy that can aid in the management of dependency with respect to competitor organizations and regulators is the formation of trade associations. These associations enable their members to share the costs of monitoring conditions and trends in the environment and to pool their influence, for instance by jointly hiring lobbyists to represent their common interests to the government. Of course trade associations are open to criticism and even legal action if they are not careful to monitor themselves with respect to price fixing and other business practices society regards as unfair. In societies in which price fixing is not outlawed, price agreements and cartels are common means of managing environmental dependence between competitors. OPEC is a prime example. Finally, if all else fails, the organization can release itself from unwanted dependencies by changing its environment. For example, an organization can enter or exit a line of business or alter its product/service mix through diversification or retrenchment (e.g., joint ventures, spin offs, mergers, acquisitions). Notice, however, that these strategies merely alter the dependence picture, they do not eliminate the need to manage resource dependence.

Managing resource dependence requires careful definition and monitoring of the environment. It also calls for imagination with respect to balancing the power of others by developing the power of your own organization. As discussed above, Pfeffer and Salancik offer both a model for analyzing dependency in the organizational environment and a set of strategies for managing these dependencies.

Population Ecology

In modernist organization theory, ideas about variation, selection, and retention processes form the basis for **population ecology theory** which has been developed by American organization theorists Michael Hannan, John Freeman, and Howard Aldrich, among others.[4] Like resource dependence theory, population ecology starts from the assumption that organizations depend on their environments for the resources they need to operate. In both views this dependency gives the environment considerable power over the organization. However, whereas the viewpoint of resource dependence theory was clearly the perspective of the organization, population ecology looks at organizations from the perspective of the environment. What interests the population ecologist is not one particular organization seeking its own survival via competition for scarce and critical resources (the resource dependence view), but rather the patterns of success and failure among all the organizations that compete within a given resource pool.[5]

In population ecology the environment of an organization is assumed to have the power to select from a group of competitors those organizations which best serve its needs. You might say that population ecology is an organizational version of Darwin's survival of the fittest principle. The environment is not studied as a whole in population ecology, instead, specific areas within an environment, called ecological niches, are examined. A **niche** consists of the resource pool upon which a group of competitors depends. While similar to the interorganizational network, a niche differs in that its focus is the group of organizations that compete for the resource pool in the niche, rather than the links between a competitor and the organizations that support and regulate it (e.g., suppliers, customers, regulatory agencies, special interests).

Population ecologists assume that organizations sharing a resource pool are competitively interdependent and that the patterns of interdependence that they adopt within the group (called the population) affect the survival and prosperity of individual members. Thus population ecology is based on the assumption that organizations compete for their survival. Population ecology studies have focused, for example, on populations of restaurants, newspapers, small electronics firms, day care centers, and labor unions.[6]

Population ecologists try to predict such things as organizational birth and death rates, and the forms and strategies that successful organizations adopt (e.g., being generalists or specialists that devote their attention to one line of business or a single market). Ecologists are less concerned with particular organizations and more interested with the whole interrelated group of organizations that make up a population. Their main interest is to explain how evolutionary processes result in all the various types of organization we see around us today.[7]

Three evolutionary processes—variation, selection, and retention—explain the dynamics of a population. **Variation** occurs in a population of organizations primarily through entrepreneurial innovation (the birth of organizations), but also through the adaptation of established organizations. The new organizations that are formed through birth or adaptation provide the range of choice the environment has during its **selection** process. The environment selects organizations on the basis of fitness. Fitness means that those organizations that best serve the needs and demands of the environment will be supported with resources and retained. **Retention** equals survival. Non-selected organizations are removed from the population via resource starvation that leads to organizational decline and either death or flight to new resource pools.

Population ecology offers managers a more detached view of organizations than they are normally used to taking. Because this perspective rests in the environmental level of analysis, using it means giving up some seemingly natural identification with the organization. Such detachment is useful for considering alternatives and making decisions (such as which organizations to finance or own, to whom one should extend credit, or with whom one should start a joint venture) because it relaxes the tendency toward over-involvement in the organizational point of view. This perspective also encourages recognition that managers cannot completely control organizational outcomes. Population ecology balances the organization-centered perspective of resource dependence theory and reminds us that, from the manager's point of view, much of what happens to organizations is the result of chance, luck, or fate (i.e., environmental determination). The population ecology viewpoint is also useful for communicating with members of government or regulatory agents whose perspective is normally defined by the environmental level of analysis due to the large numbers of organizations that their policies affect.

There are several constraints on the usefulness of the population ecology view. First, as with Darwin's theory, the definition of fitness is a problem—survival is explained by fitness, but fitness is defined as survival—there is a tautology at the heart of population ecology theory that means we cannot predict survival on the basis of an independent assessment of fit. We only know survival when we see it. Second, the theory applies most readily to populations that are highly competitive. Not all populations fit this description. Populations with significant barriers to entry or exit such as high start-up costs (e.g., automobile manufacturing) or legal regulation (e.g., pharamaceuticals) do not make ideal candidates for population ecology studies. Also, environments that are dominated by a few large organizations, such as the mainframe computer manufacturing industry, are unsuitable populations for ecologists to study. When competitiveness is compromised by the existence of enormously powerful organizations or barriers to entry or exit, the population ecology model loses much of its explanatory power. In these circumstances the institutional view is helpful.

Institutional Theory

Environments can put demands on organizations in two different ways. First, they may make technical and economic demands that require organizations to produce and exchange their goods and services in a market or a quasi-market. Second, they may make social and cultural demands that require organizations to play particular roles in society and to establish and maintain certain outward appearances. Environments dominated by technical or economic demands reward organizations for efficiently and effectively supplying the environment with goods and services. Environments dominated by social demands reward organizations for conforming to the values, norms, rules, and beliefs of society.

American sociologist Philip Selznick, regarded by many as the father of **institutional theory**, observed that organizations adapt, not only to the strivings of their internal groups, but to the values of external society. Recognizing the social and cultural basis of external influence on organizations, however, is only one contribution of institutional theory. Neo-institutionalists attempt to move beyond mere recognition of the social and cultural foundations of institutions to describe the processes by which practices and organizations become institutions. For instance, American neo-institutional theorist Richard Scott defined **institutionalization** as "the process by which actions are repeated and given similar meaning by self and others."[8] Thus, not only organizations, but actions, such as voting and shaking hands, can be conceptualized as institutions of the societies in which they are repeated and given similar meanings. This grounds the definition of institutions in repeated actions and shared conceptions of reality.

Sometimes actions are repeated because explicit rules or laws exist to ensure their repetition (legal and political influences). Sometimes activity patterns are supported by norms, values, and expectations (cultural influences); sometimes by a desire to be or look like another institution (social influences). American sociologists Woody Powell and Paul DiMaggio distinguish between these three different institutional pressures and give them distinctive labels.[9] They argue that when the pressure to conform comes from governmental regulations or laws, then **coercive institutional pressures** are at work. When the pressure comes from cultural expectations, for instance via the professional training of organizational members, then **normative institutional pressures** are at work. DiMaggio and Powell call desires to look like other organizations **mimetic institutional pressures** and explain them as responses to uncertainty that involve copying other organizational structures, practices, or outputs. When an environment becomes organized around social, cultural, political, and legal demands via these institutional pressures, it is said to be institutionalized.[10] According to Scott, the aspects of the environment through which institutional influences operate include: regulatory structures, government agencies, laws and courts, professions, interest groups, and mobilized public opinion.[11] The business press probably also belongs on this list.

The difference between institutionalized and non-institutionalized environments often appears to be simply a matter of rationality. In this view, the technical/economic success factor is viewed as the product of rational decision making, while social conformity is a victory of symbolic management. Conforming to institutional demands wins social support and ensures survival to an organization, not because it makes more money or better products, but because it goes along with accepted conventions.[12] However, rationality alone will not distinguish institutionalized from non-institutionalized environments because rational talk can become institutionalized. That is, the making of decisions that only superficially conform to the norms of rationality can be an effective way to legitimize choices.[13] You have probably made many rational arguments in favor of decisions that were actually emotionally based—to buy a particular car, for example, or to drop a course that was difficult or unappealing. This sort of framing of non-rational logics as rational arguments occurs in organizations just as it does in your private life. John Meyer and Brian Rowan suggest that, in organizations, these rationalized arguments take the form of myths that cannot be objectively tested, but stand as rational on the basis that everyone knows them to be true. **Rationalized myths** are part of the institutional context in which organizations operate and to which they adapt in order to maintain their social legitimacy.

In the institutional perspective, the environment is seen as providing a more or less shared view of what organizations should look like and how they should behave. Often certain structural characteristics, such as bureaucracy in the public domain, or matrix structures in the defense industry, become social standards by which organizations are judged as appropriate and thus granted the social legitimacy required to continue using resources (particularly capital and/or public support). One rather cynical assessment of this perspective is that, once an organization has learned how to look good (e.g., to look like a rational organization), it need do only face work to survive. The actual activities of the firm may be at odds with the outward appearance and the lack of any criteria by which to judge the organization's performance means that institutionalized organizations are not really accountable to society except in a very superficial sense.[14]

One important theoretical contribution of the institutional perspective is the addition of **social legitimacy** to the list of input resources in the open systems model of the organization (Figure 3.8).[15] Not only do organizations require raw materials, capital, labor, knowledge, and equipment, they also depend upon the acceptance of the society in which they operate. Organizations whose environments question their right to survive can be driven out of business. For instance, before the end of Apartheid, the economic embargo of companies doing business in South Africa killed some organizations, threatened the survival of others, and caused still others to terminate their activities in the region. Ralph Nader, Green Peace, and animal rights activists have been similarly involved in attempts to de-legitimate various organizations through the mobilization of public opinion. These examples reveal the importance of social legitimacy by showing what can happen if it is taken away.

In applying institutional theory to an analysis of a particular organization you should consider how the organization is adapting to its institutional context. For instance, analyze the sources (e.g., regulatory agencies, laws, social and cultural expectations) and types of institutional pressure (e.g., coercive, normative, mimetic) exerted by the environment on the organization. Also consider how decision-making processes are being shaped by institutional beliefs versus

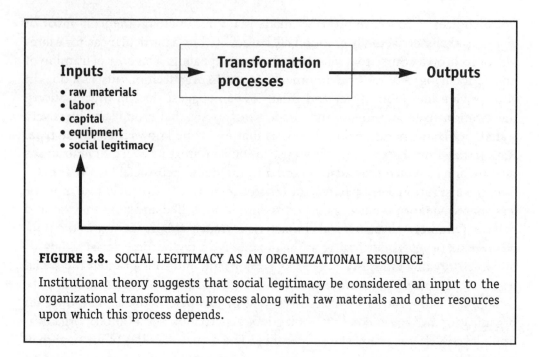

FIGURE 3.8. SOCIAL LEGITIMACY AS AN ORGANIZATIONAL RESOURCE

Institutional theory suggests that social legitimacy be considered an input to the organizational transformation process along with raw materials and other resources upon which this process depends.

rational choice. Finally, try to imagine how the organization might gain greater legitimacy within its institutional context.

Comparing Theories of Organization-Environment Relations

Three distinct points of view are represented in the theories of resource dependence, population ecology, and institutional theory. These viewpoints derive from differing levels of analysis and different assumptions about whether the organization influences, or is simply at the mercy of, its environment.

Resource dependence theory is formulated at the organizational level of analysis and provides the perspective of top management looking outward from the organization to its surrounding environment. Thus, resource dependence theory is distinguished from both population ecology and institutional theory in that the latter two are formulated at the level of the environment. Whereas population ecologists attempt to explain why there are so many different kinds of organizations, institutional theorists try to explain why so many organizations look alike. Nonetheless, both population ecology and institutional theory answer their fundamental questions by referring to the influence of the environment on the organization. This reliance on the environment to explain organizational structures, processes, and outcomes is what all three theories of organization–environment relations hold in common.

In terms of Figure 3.4, population ecology explains the influences generated by the technical, physical, and economic sectors of the general environment, while institutional theory focuses on the influences associated with social, cultural, political, and legal sectors. In spite of their differences, population ecology and institutional theory are similar in that organizations are depicted as relatively passive elements of an environment that shapes them and determines their outcomes. Resource dependence theory, on the other hand, sees organizations as having a more active role through counteraction.

According to American organizational sociologist W. Richard Scott, environments vary in the degrees to which they are institutionalized[16]. When environments have many rules and expectations to which organizations must conform if they are to receive needed social legitimacy, institutional theory is a useful point of departure for explaining the organization's structure and outcomes. When environments are not highly institutionalized, and are influenced more by economic and technical competition, the population ecology perspective is a better starting point. A guide to some of the organizations you might categorize as fitting into these two frameworks is found in Figure 3.9.[17]

Figure 3.9 also shows a distinction between organizations with highly developed technological bases and those with relatively unsophisticated technologies. This distinction captures the extent to which you want to be particularly careful interpreting norms for rationality. In technically sophisticated organizations, rationality is not only a criterion for making decisions, it is also a highly valued form of expression. When technically sophisticated organizations operate in highly institutionalized environments, a rational style of expression becomes as important as rationality itself. As a result, in environments that are both highly institutionalized and technically sophisticated, it is easy to become confused between what is actually rational and what has merely been made to appear so.

Be careful with the typology shown in Figure 3.9. Environments develop institutionally and technically so that the types of organizations that fit into the cells of Figure 3.9 will change with time. At present, for example, retailers are becoming more and more technically sophisticated and biotech companies are coming under increasing institutional (e.g., regulatory) pressure. In the reverse direction, the American defense industry is moving away from a highly institutionalized environment following withdrawal of government funding. This change pushes the industry into an environment for which population ecology provides a more useful model. A similar effect occurs when industries are privatized.

It is important to consider both population ecology and institutional views in

Technical development of environment		Degree of institutionalization: low	Degree of institutionalization: high
	low	**Retail stores**	**Banking**
	high	**Biotechnology**	**Defense industry**

FIGURE 3.9. ENVIRONMENTS VARY BY THEIR DEGREE OF INSTITUTIONALIZATION AND BY THEIR LEVEL OF TECHNICAL DEVELOPMENT

Based on: Scott (1992).

your environmental analyses. The same goes for the inclusion of the resource dependence perspective. Even though one perspective may seem to make more sense than the others, it is good practice to look at the situation through the different lenses provided by the three theories of organization–environment relations. Only after trying the different perspectives are you in a position to evaluate their usefulness to your analysis. In a sense, this is a postmodern strategy of collage, so be sure to open yourself to surprises that may emerge from the juxtaposition of different perspectives.

COMPLEXITY, CHANGE, UNCERTAINTY

In early modernist thinking, **uncertainty** was considered to be a property of the environment resulting from two powerful forces: complexity and rate of change.

Complexity refers to the number and diversity of the elements in an environment. **Rate of change** refers to how rapidly these elements change. Environmental uncertainty, as this perspective came to be known, was defined as an interaction between varying amounts of complexity and change in the environment (Figure 3.10). The problem with the environmental uncertainty perspective was that it assumed that conditions in the environment were experienced in the same way by everyone. Empirical studies of uncertainty, however, found that this was not a good assumption. The same environment might be perceived as certain by one set of managers and uncertain by another. The term "environmental uncertainty" turned out to be quite misleading—environments do not feel uncertain, people do. Furthermore, it became apparent that what affects organizations is not conditions in the environment so much as it is the perceptions of organizational decision makers about how uncertain their environment is.[18] Today organization theorists recognize that uncertainty lies not in the environment, but

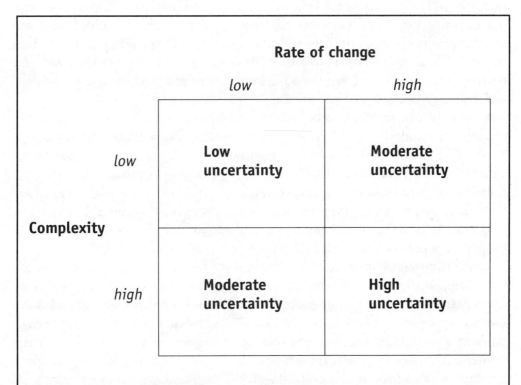

FIGURE 3.10. ENVIRONMENTAL UNCERTAINTY IS DEFINED BY THE AMOUNT OF COMPLEXITY AND THE RATE OF CHANGE IN THE ORGANIZATION'S ENVIRONMENT

Based on: Duncan (1972).

in the individuals who consider the environment when they make organizational decisions. This viewpoint has come to be associated with the information perspective in organization theory.[19]

The **information perspective** argues that managers feel uncertain when they perceive the environment to be unpredictable, and this occurs when they lack the information that they feel they need to make sound decisions. Figure 3.11 helps to visualize the links between perceived environmental conditions, uncertainty, and information. The figure shows that when managers perceive environments as stable and as having minimal complexity, they find that needed information is both known and available, and thus they experience low levels of uncertainty. When environments are perceived to have either high complexity or to be rapidly changing, managers confront either too much information or the challenge of keeping up with changing information, and moderate levels of uncertainty are experienced. In the case of high uncertainty, managers perceive a highly complex and changing environment and will face an overwhelming amount of information, but will not know which information to attend to due to constantly changing circumstances. For instance, advances in computer technology and the internationalization of markets create conditions of increasing diversity that make it difficult for managers to locate and process all the information they need to make sound decisions. But what is more uncertainty provoking is the tension and anxiety produced by not knowing what information they need.

Early efforts to explain how organizations respond to uncertainty relied on the concepts of requisite variety and isomorphism. The **law of requisite variety** was borrowed from General Systems Theory. It states that for one system to deal with another it must be of the same or greater complexity. In organizational terms this means that organizations map perceived environmental complexity with their internal structures and management systems. There is a theoretical limit to this, of course, since if the organization ever realized the full complexity of its environment, it would *be* that environment.

Isomorphism refers to requisite variety—the belief that organizations match the complexity of the environment with internal structures and systems. "Iso" means same and "morph" means form. An organization that is isomorphic with its environment has the same form as that environment. For instance, if the environment is simple, the organization will take a simple form. In a complex environment, the isomorphic organization will be complex too. In changing conditions, of course, the concepts of isomorphism and requisite variety suggest that organizations will change in response.

American organization theorists Paul Lawrence and Jay Lorsch discussed the implications of isomorphism in their book, *Organization and Environment*. They suggested that organizations confront many different conditions and elements in

		Rate of change	
		low	*high*
Complexity	*low*	**Needed information is known and available**	**Constant need for new information**
	high	**Information overload**	**Not known what information is needed**

FIGURE 3.11. LINKS BETWEEN CONDITIONS IN THE PERCEIVED ENVIRONMENT, UNCERTAINTY, AND INFORMATION

their environments. The different environmental demands create pressure for internal differentiation. Put another way, differentiation allows different parts of the organization to specialize in handling responses to different demands from the environment. It is this differentiation of the organization into specialized units for confronting different aspects of the environment that produces the internal complexity of structure and systems referred to by the concept of isomorphism. W. Richard Scott suggested that buffering and boundary spanning are two examples of structural differentiation in response to uncertainty.[20]

Buffering and Boundary Spanning

Buffering involves protecting the internal operations of the organization from interruption by environmental shocks such as material, labor, or capital shortages. This is generally accomplished by assigning some members of the organization responsibility for seeing that the organization's production of goods and services continues uninterrupted. Those who protect the productive capacity of the firm act out the buffering role. For instance, in traditional manufacturing organizations, purchasing agents and sales people buffer production workers from interruptions due to the lack of raw materials from suppliers or orders from customers. Through their efforts, uncertainty associated with a complex or changing environment is absorbed, freeing those in the production centers from concerns that might distract them from their work.

Boundary spanning is the label given to environmental monitoring activities including passing needed information to decision makers. It also describes the activity of representing the organization or its interests to the environment. The difference between boundary spanning and buffering roles is primarily what is transferred between the organization and its environment. In the case of buffering, transfers of material, service, and money between the organization and the environment are of primary concern. Boundary spanners work mainly with the transfer of information across the organization's boundary. Public relations specialists and economic advisors are examples of boundary-spanning roles found in many large organizations.

It is common to find that some organizational members engage in activities that can be described as both buffering and boundary spanning. Sales people, for instance, are responsible for transferring the organization's output to its customers (the buffering role), but they also bring important information about changing customer demands into the organization and represent the organization's capabilities and reputation to the customer (their contribution to boundary spanning). Purchasing agents also combine buffering and boundary-spanning roles. As they transfer raw materials into the organization via purchases of supplies, they also gather information on new supplies and techniques of production from their suppliers.

As a non-manufacturing example, consider your college classroom and the university of which it is a part. Instructors buffer the technical core of your learning process from the uncertainty of knowing what you should learn. Instructors select subjects to be studied, choose material to be presented, and offer texts to be read. At the same time, instructors are boundary spanners in the sense that they read broadly and often conduct research that allows them to bring new information into the classroom. They also engage in boundary spanning when they represent their class to a curriculum committee or the university to prospective students. As a student, you have opportunities to be a boundary spanner too. For example, you can carry ideas from other classes or from your work and other life experiences into the classroom, or by representing the university to someone who might have an interest in becoming a student.

Enactment and the Social Constructionist View of Environments

There is a more radical interpretation of the information perspective you will want to consider. Theorists like Karl Weick, who take an enactment view, argue that conditions in the environment cannot be separated from perceptions of those conditions. This view places both uncertainty and the environment within the decision maker's head. From this subjectivist point of view, the need for information that is experienced by managers causes them to search for and find more information so that the higher the level of uncertainty they feel, the more complex and changing the environment will appear due to the continually expanding search for more information and the growing database that searching generates.

The enactment argument turns the information perspective of Figure 3.11 upside down. Now, instead of arguing that complexity and change challenge organizational decision makers with an increased need for information, the enactment view maintains that demands from uncertain decision makers for more and more information construct a complex and changing environment. In this formulation, people interpret their uncertainty as a lack of information and then attribute their experiences to complexity and change in their environment.[21] While this view is not enough to explain everything we observe in organizations (from where, for instance, does the initial sense of uncertainty come?), it does offer an interesting way to explain the sudden radical shift to greater complexity and change in many of the organizations that have participated in the computer revolution. The computer allows us to process a steadily increasing amount of information which, in turn, permits us to construct an ever more complicated and changing world. The popular film *The Gods Must be Crazy* developed this theme. The point of the film was that we create enormous complexities when we introduce alluring technologies into a society—in the film, the technology was a Coke bottle that was inadvertently dropped into a primitive tribe by someone on an airplane that was passing overhead. In the case of organizations, the alluring new technology is the computer.

In the enactment view, buffering and boundary spanning are two means of creating a complex environment, thus changes in these activities similarly imply changes in the way that environments are constructed. In both the modern and the enactment views, the environment and the organization end up being aligned in terms of complexity and rate of change, but the theories explaining this outcome are radically different. While modernist views see environments controlling organizations, the enactment view sees individuals constructing environments and then responding to their constructions as if the environment they created was forcing them to do so—at which point it is!

One implication of the enactment view not normally taken up by symbolic-interpretivists is that, once we recognize our role as construction workers who build organizational reality, we can free ourselves from situations we do not like and create something else. This is the sort of thinking advocated by postmodernists pushing for radical change.

Postmodernism and Organization–Environment Relations

The social constructionist view suggests exciting possibilities for change. For example, it has been said that this is the type of thinking that brought down the Berlin Wall. However, one might also do well to consider the consequences of a choice to alter an existing social reality—the consequences for Eastern Europe are now emerging as both exciting and terrifying (new relationships with the West, war, genocide). It is one thing to decide you want to deconstruct an undesirable social reality, replacing it with something else is another story. Thus, the postmodern view reminds us that ultimately we bear responsibility for constructing the organizations and other realities that we inhabit.

To see how deconstruction might be applied to theories of organization–environment relations, let's take a close look at one of modernism's central assumptions. Modernist theories assume that uncertainty is undesirable and avoidable, and that it drives organizational action by motivating decision makers to reduce their uncertainty. To deconstruct this theory, first consider ways to oppose its central assumptions. For example, you might argue that, instead of being undesirable, uncertainty is a form of thrill, a state to be sought out as invigorating. Change is not uncomfortable and to be avoided, it is a welcome experience typical of post-industrial life. The final step in the deconstruction is to examine the implications of the new assumptions for the modernist arguments. For instance, arguments proposing to explain organizational action on the basis of aversion to uncertainty make little sense when uncertainty is viewed as invigorating or attractive.

You should realize that postmodernism is unlikely to replace modernist theories of organization with yet more theories. Some postmodernists have a natural distaste for theoretical abstraction based on their conviction that theoretical abstractions are used to disguise hegemonic intentions (e.g., the first world's desire to exploit the third world's resources). As explained in Chapter 2, organization theories proposed by modernists are redefined by postmodernists as grand narratives and their rhetoric deconstructed to reveal the complicity of modernist organization theorists with the capitalist hegemonic order (in Marxist theory, **hegemony** refers to the practice of interpreting the interests of the ruling class as universal). For these postmodernists, it is enough to deconstruct, which is the movement within postmodernism that has earned this perspective a reputation for nihilism.

But there are other postmodernists who move beyond deconstruction. For them, deconstruction is merely an emancipatory move to free oneself from modernist habits of thought (such as assuming uncertainty is undesirable and avoidable). These postmodernists imagine reconstructions of the social order based on alternative, non-modernist conceptions. Sometimes alternative assumptions and values are sought among the indigenous peoples of the world whose voices have not been heard due to the modernist hegemonic practice of using power to silence opposition. For example, the belief of native American Indians that their role in life is to protect the environment (personalized as Mother Earth, provider of the sustenance of life), is contrasted with modern exploitative practices such as strip mining, traditional logging, hunting species to extinction, overgrazing prairies, and burning the rainforests.

A key to understanding and using the postmodern perspective lies in centering your attention on the ways in which language is used to construct reality, and within that reality, identity. For instance, the use of terms like "first world" and "third world" implies a social order with roles of dominance and submission that seem natural once the identifying labels are accepted. Postmodernists often stand behind efforts of marginalized people to redefine their identities by creating their own, more powerful labels and forcing those in positions of dominance to use them. The use of these preferred terms symbolically equalizes the parties to a new discourse that is opened by this change in speaking habits. While such linguistic strategies do not perform miracles, there is reason to believe they unleash transformative powers. Take the cases of women and black minorities in the U.S., whose powers of self-determination greatly increased along with their efforts to substitute identity labels (woman instead of girl or lady, and black or African instead of colored or negro).

According to some postmodernists, similar work needs to be done to reconceptualize the environment. Organization theorist Paul Shrivastava, for example, argues that modernist views of the organizational environment are denatured. He claims that by giving so much attention (voice) to capitalistic concerns with markets, competitors, industry, and regulation, the natural environment is reduced to "a bundle of resources to be used by organizations."[22] Views such as Shrivastava's suggest that the modernist rhetoric of economic necessity has silenced concern for environmental sustainability and justified possibly irreversible abuses to our environment. Conceptions of the environment that marginalize these concerns are provided by the categories and language of modernist theories of organization–environment relations. Postmodernism offers a method for deconstructing these arguments and truth claims and suggesting alternative futures such as Shrivastava's call to place nature at the center of organizational concerns and replace the value for wealth with a value for health.

SUMMARY: HOW TO ANALYZE AN ORGANIZATIONAL ENVIRONMENT

In conducting an environmental analysis from a modern perspective, you must first define the organization whose environment you are interested in analyzing. Then identify the links between this organization and others with which the organization interacts, or that can influence these relationships through competition, regulation, or social pressure. Use the model given in Figure 3.2 to make sure you have not left out any important elements of the network. Following this, consider conditions and trends in the sectors of the general environment and in the international/global environment. Next, assess how the relationships between the organization and its network are likely to be affected by the specific conditions and trends you have identified in the general or international/global environment. In this effort you will find resource dependence theory, population ecology, and institutional theory helpful. Although one or two of these theories will seem most obviously useful for a particular analysis, be sure to try them all to see what insights they offer. Finally, ask yourself what has been left out of your analysis and try to imagine what weaknesses are introduced by the biases you necessarily bring to the effort.

In some ways, the trickiest part of the entire analysis is the first step—defining the organization. This is because the definition implies that you know where the organizational boundary lies. Boundary definition is easier said than done. Take the university as an example and consider the case of students. Are you a member of the university? Are you a customer? A product? Each answer is accurate in some ways and, what is more, each suggests a different definition of what lies inside and what lies outside the organization. Similar analytical choices await you when considering the membership status of faculty (especially visiting and non-tenured faculty), continuing education students, guest lecturers, and alumni. Drawing a boundary around an organization is a difficult exercise and the implications of various definitions for different decision-making situations must be taken into account when you make an analysis.

It is not that one view is correct and the others are wrong; rather boundary definition is determined by your reasons for conducting an analysis. Consider the case of a university. If you are analyzing the environment because the university is considering a tuition increase, then it will be useful to consider students to be customers and, thus, members of the environment rather than of the organization. If you want to analyze the environment because the university wants to apply for outside research funds, then it may be helpful to think of students as members of the organization who will aid in the performance of proposed research activities. If, however, you are interested in discovering how the environment is responding to the university's new general education programs, then viewing students as products of the organization is likely to provide a useful analysis; from this point of view firms recruiting on campus are customers consuming graduating students. If you want to focus on how students can influence the decisions of university administrators, think of students, not just as low status members of the organization, but also as special interest groups, or as regulatory agents (e.g., students sit as voting members on faculty committees) or unions (e.g., students have negotiating rights).

The ways in which the categories were used in the example above illustrates an important point about theorizing. Theoretical categories are not cast in stone, they are ways to think—different categories stimulate different thoughts. Try not to be rigid in your use of categories. When new categories are first encountered nearly everyone feels some anxiety about putting examples in the wrong box, and there is a sense of relief that comes when a box is filled. However, in organization theory it is often the case that a given example will fit more than one category, and it is usually also true that shifting examples from one category to another brings new insight. This shifting around of examples and categories makes some students uncomfortable. What frustrates them is not organization theory, as they generally claim, but their desire to pin everything down. Everything cannot be pinned down in organizations and this is reflected in the ambiguity of concepts. To make effective use of organization theory, managers need to learn to accept some ambiguity in their concepts. This is where postmodern organization theory comes in handy. Postmodernism introduces healthy skepticism about categories and encourages their continual deconstruction. What assumptions lie behind these categories and whose voices are silenced by a particular construction of reality? The message is not to stop categorizing or making distinctions—these are necessary for thought and action. The message of postmodernism is to think, talk, and act in full consciousness—be self-reflexive.

KEY TERMS

interorganizational network
general environment
international and global environment
mechanistic and organic organizations
contingency theory
resource dependence theory
power/dependence relationships
criticality and scarcity of resources
population ecology theory
niche
variation, selection and retention
institutional theory
institutionalization process
coercive, normative, and mimetic
    institutional pressures

rationalized myths
social legitimacy
uncertainty
complexity
rate of change
the information perspective on
    uncertainty
law of requisite variety
isomorphism
buffering
boundary spanning
hegemony

ENDNOTES

1. This formulation can be traced to Dill (1958); Evan (1966); and Thompson (1967).
2. Lyotard (1979); Bell (1973); Harvey (1990).
3. Burns and Stalker (1961).
4. Hawley (1950) is often cited by population ecologists as a source of inspiration. See Weick (1979 [1969]) for a different use of these ideas in an organizational framework.
5. Aldrich and Pfeffer (1976).
6. Caroll (1984); Singh (1990).
7. Hannan and Freeman (1977).
8. Scott (1992: 117).
9. DiMaggio and Powell (1983); Powell and DiMaggio (1991).
10. Selznick (1957).
11. Scott (1987).
12. Zucker (1987, 1988); Powell and DiMaggio (1991).
13. Feldman and March (1981).
14. Meyer and Rowan (1977).
15. DiMaggio and Powell (1983).
16. Scott (1992).
17. Scott (1987).
18. Duncan (1972).
19. Aldrich and Mindlin (1978).
20. Scott (1992: 180–225).
21. Duncan (1972).
22. Boje and Dennehy (1993); Shrivastava (1995: 125).

REFERENCES

Aldrich, Howard E., and Mindlin, Sergio (1978). Uncertainty and dependence: Two perspectives on environment. In Lucien Karpik (ed.), *Organization and environment: Theory, issues and reality.* London: Sage, 149–70.

Aldrich, Howard E., and Pfeffer, Jeffrey (1976). Environments of organizations. In A. Inkeles, J. Coleman, and N. Smelser (eds.), *Annual review of sociology*, Vol. 2. Palo Alto, Calif.: Annual Reviews, 79–105.

Bell, Daniel (1973). *The coming of post-industrial society.* New York: Basic Books.

Boje, David, and Dennehy, Robert (1993). *Managing in the postmodern world: America's revolution against exploitation.* Dubugue, Ia.: Kendall Hunt.

Burns, Tom, and Stalker, George M. (1961). *The management of innovation.* London: Tavistock.

Caroll, Glenn R. (1984). Organizational ecology. *Annual Review of Sociology*, 10: 71–93.

Dill, William R. (1958) Environments as an influence on managerial autonomy. *Administrative Science Quarterly*, 2: 409–43.

DiMaggio, Paul J., and Powell, W. W. (1983). The iron cage revisited: Institutional isomorphism and collective rationality in organizational fields. *American Sociological Review*, 48: 147–60.

Duncan, Robert B. (1972). Characteristics of organizational environments and perceived environmental uncertainty. *Administrative Science Quarterly*, 17: 313–27.

Evan, William (1966). The organization set: Toward a theory of interorganizational relations. In D. Thompson (ed.), *Approaches to organizational design.* Pittsburgh: University of Pittsburgh Press, 175–90.

Feldman, Martha S., and March, James G. (1981). Information in organizations as signal and symbol. *Administrative Science Quarterly*, 26: 171–86.

Hannan, Michael T., and Freeman, John H. (1977) The population ecology of organizations. *American Journal of Sociology*, 82: 929–64.

Harvey, David (1990). *The condition of postmodernity.* Cambridge, Mass.: Blackwell.

Hawley, Amos (1950). *Human ecology.* New York: Ronald Press.

Lawrence, Paul R., and Lorsch, Jay W. (1967). *Organization and environment: Managing differentiation and integration.* Cambridge, Mass.: Harvard University Press.

Lyotard, Jean-François (1979). *The postmodern condition: A report on knowledge.* Minneapolis: University of Minnesota Press.

Meyer, John W., and Rowan, Brian (1977). Institutionalized organizations: Formal structure as myth and ceremony. *American Journal of Sociology*, 83: 340–63.

Pfeffer, Jeffrey, and Salancik, Gerald R. (1978). *The external control of organizations: A resource dependence perspective.* New York: Harper & Row.

Powell, Walter W., and DiMaggio, Paul J. (1991) (eds.). *The new institutionalism in organizational analysis.* Chicago: University of Chicago Press.

Scott, W. Richard (1987). The adolescence of institutional theory. *Administrative Science Quarterly*, 32: 493–511.

Scott, W. Richard (1992) *Organizations: Rational, natural, and open systems* (third ed.). Englewood Cliffs, NJ: Prentice-Hall.

Selznick, Philip (1957). *Leadership in administration.* New York: Harper & Row.

Shrivastava, Paul (1995). Ecocentric management for a risk society. *Academy of Management Review*, 20: 118–37.

Singh, Jitendra V. (1990) (ed.). *Organizational evolution: New Directions*. Beverly Hills, Calif.: Sage.

Thompson, James D. (1967). *Organizations in action*. New York: McGraw-Hill.

Weick, Karl E. (1979 [1969]). *The social psychology of organizing*. Reading, Mass.: Addison-Wesley.

Zucker, Lynn G. (1987). Institutional theories of organization. In W. R. Scott (ed.), *Annual review of sociology*, 13: 443–64.

Zucker, Lynn G. (1988) (ed.). *Institutional patterns and organizations: Culture and environment*. Cambridge, Mass.: Ballinger.

FURTHER READING

Aldrich, Howard E. (1979). *Organizations and environments*. Englewood Cliffs, NJ: Prentice-Hall.

Hannan, Michael T., and Freeman, John H. (1989). *Organizational ecology*. Cambridge, Mass.: Harvard University.

Karpik, Lucien (1978) (ed.). *Organization and environment: Theory, issues and reality*. London: Sage.

Lawrence, Paul R., and Lorsch, Jay W. (1967). *Organization and environment: Managing differentiation and integration*. Cambridge, Mass.: Harvard University Press.

Meyer, John W., and Scott, W. Richard (1992). *Organizational environments: Ritual and rationality*. Beverly Hills, Calif.: Sage.

Oliver, Christine (1991). Strategic responses to institutional processes. *Academy of Management Review*, 16: 145–79.

Pfeffer, Jeffrey, and Salancik, Gerald R. (1978). *The external control of organizations: A resource dependence perspective*. New York: Harper & Row.

Zucker, Lynn G. (1983). Organizations as institutions. In S. B. Bacharach (ed.), *Research in the sociology of organizations*. Greenwich, Conn.: JAI Press, ii. 1–47.

4 | STRATEGY AND GOALS

THE concept of strategy first appeared in organization theory in the late 1950s as a military metaphor. In military organizations, strategy is distinguished from tactics. Military strategy involves the planning and directing of large-scale military operations and is particularly concerned with maneuvering forces into the best possible position prior to engaging the enemy in battle. Tactics, by contrast, involve maneuvering military forces during a battle. In applying the metaphor of strategy to organizations, the enemy is the organization's competition, but other threats from the environment such as special interest groups, technological change, or government regulators must also be kept in mind. The forces to be maneuvered into combat positions are the resources the organization has at its disposal—capital, technology, employees, etc. The battleground is the marketplace. Thus, an organizational strategy is a scheme for competing in the marketplace; tactics are used to carry out planned activities while continuously adjusting to the competitive situation as it unfolds. The objective of military strategy is to overtake enemy territory while protecting your own position. In organizational strategy, the objective is to block or take over competitors' market share without losing any of your own.

The metaphor of organizational strategy has spawned its own discipline, related to, but in many ways separate from, organization theory. While the field of strategic management has strong links with the discipline of marketing, and with industrial organizational economics and its applied fields of finance and accounting, the concept of strategy is usually more restricted within organization theory. In modernist organization theory, the concept of **strategy** refers to top management's planned efforts to influence organizational outcomes by managing the organization's relationship to its environment, while in symbolic-interpretive organization theory, focus shifts to processes of enacting strategies or to the role of strategy in the social construction of organizations.

Core Concepts of Organization Theory

To a considerable extent, the history of the field of strategy parallels that of organization theory. For instance, the modernist influence has been strong in the field of organizational strategy, expressing itself in the concepts of corporate planning and control that dominated corporate strategic thinking in the 1960s and 1970s.[1] There followed in the late 1970s a questioning of the assumptions of rationality upon which planning models were built. This challenge was provoked by observational studies that found that strategists do not act in the ways prescribed by the rational model.[2] This research inspired alternative views of strategy that opened the door to symbolic-interpretive influences seen, for example, in studies that examine how culture affects strategy.[3] However, the symbolic-interpretive perspective has not been as fully developed in the field of strategy as it has been in organization theory. Postmodernists might argue that this is due to strategy researchers' complicity with top management. That is, strategy researchers tend to focus their studies on top managers, thus they effectively ignore the interests and concerns of other organization members and thereby silence their voices. However, postmodern critiques have yet to appear in the strategy literature.

We begin this chapter with discussion of strategic fit, a concept that relates organization and environment through the intentional efforts of top managers and others in the organization. Next we consider the strategy process as an instance of rational decision making, followed by challenges to the rational view (e.g., emergent and symbolic descriptions of the strategy process). The debate about strategy process is then examined in relation to uncertainty using the theoretical framework of contingency theory. The chapter concludes with the concept of goals and its relationship to strategy.

STRATEGIC FIT

In the last chapter we discussed three theories that explain how an organization and its environment are related. In brief review, resource dependence theory presents the organization as having a set of crucial dependencies on its environment, dependencies that must be successfully managed if the organization is to stay in business. Population ecology theory claims that the environment has powers of selection and retention that can overwhelm an organization's best attempts to manage resources. Institutional theory argues that, while economic resources are critical to a firm's operation, organizations should not forget the importance of maintaining social legitimacy—if an organization violates the expectations of its environment, the environment may invalidate it. Each of these theories helps introduce a central concept used by strategists—the concept of **strategic fit**.

The term "fit" (sometimes called congruence or match) defines a successful strategy as one that brings what the organization can do (its competencies) into alignment with the needs and demands of its environment. When the competencies of the organization fit the demands of the environment, then the organization is selected and retained (the population ecology view), provided with resources (the resource dependence view), and legitimized (the institutional view). Strategy is concerned with actively managing fit in order to achieve **competitive advantage** which will ensure the organization's survival, profitability, and reputation.

Notice that this idea—to match the competencies of the organization with the demands of its environment—implies that strategists are expected to be aware of the possibility of fit, and to do something about it. Thus, attention to strategy introduces self-awareness and intentionality into the discussion of organizations. Our three organization–environment theories do not depend upon awareness or intentionality. Their processes work on the organization whether or not anybody has either awareness or intentions. According to resource dependence theory, being dependent upon a customer or supplier leaves an organization vulnerable to its environment, even if management is unaware of its dependence. Likewise, institutional theory does not demand that management deliberately develop the organization's social legitimacy, and population ecology theory claims that environments are indifferent to organizational attempts to strategize because the outcomes of selection and retention processes are largely a matter of chance or luck.

Because of their emphasis on intentionality, strategy researchers develop their own interpretations of organization–environment theories. Their aim is to discover what these and other theories can tell strategists that will improve their chances of developing and maintaining a successful fit between the organization and its environment. This is a difficult assignment with respect to population ecology theory, which can leave you feeling a little helpless. Nonetheless, some strategists insist that, by becoming aware of the patterns of selection and retention processes, they can learn to maneuver their organizations into positions of competitive advantage and thus become more likely to be selected and retained. A few, accepting that survival can be a matter of luck, focus on how some organizations seem to inherit luck[4]—but this is a much less usual view.

The resource dependence perspective is the most natural for the strategist to assume. This is because resource dependence theory is written from the viewpoint of the organization, rather than the environment, and this is the perspective of the strategist. For example, the list of implications of resource dependence theory (e.g., to engage in cooptation, joint ventures, or vertical integration) is a set of alternative corporate strategies for achieving and maintaining fit.

Core Concepts of Organization Theory

The institutional perspective suggests that strategy is a symbolic question. Does the organization look successful? Does it conform to external expectations about its products and its practices? The establishment of public relations (PR) departments is one obvious way in which organizations respond to institutional demands for social legitimacy. But many other, more subtle signs of institutional effects are apparent in organizations, right down to the decor of offices and the style of dress worn by employees. Have you ever wondered why lawyers and investment bankers wear such formal clothing while the employees of engineering firms are much more casual in their style of dress? Institutional theory explains these phenomena as the result of institutionalized expectations.

A strategic interpretation of the institutional perspective suggests that the symbolic aspects of organizations can be managed, for instance, through imitation of successful firms. By using the practices of successful firms as a **benchmark** (a comparison point for judging some aspect of the firm's performance, sometimes referred to as **best practices**), organizations can signal to their environments that they are also successful, thus securing the social legitimacy required to attract resources. From the perspective of population ecology theory, imitating the best practices of other organizations (e.g., Nordstrom's department stores' highly regarded customer service) can also be interpreted as a strategy for enhancing the likelihood of selection and retention through adaptation to environmental demands.

Be sure to notice how the strategist's concern with transforming theoretical knowledge into competitive advantage forces strategy research into a modernist perspective, regardless of the perspective from which the theory was originally developed. The reason for this is that the concept of competitive advantage objectivizes organizations and environments. That is, in order to see firms in competition for scarce resources, you are forced to adopt a view of firms as tangible entities operating in a real world (i.e., the objectivist stance). If social constructionism were adopted instead, the notion of managing fit would be replaced, for instance, by consideration of how organizational meaning is constructed by actors who assume that fit is important, and how the symbols that these actors produce (e.g., corporate mission statements, dress codes, reward and control systems) are read and interpreted by others.

THE STRATEGY PROCESS AS RATIONAL DECISION MAKING

Much of the study of organizational strategy has been conducted within the normative tradition associated with Classical management theory (e.g., the management principles of Henri Fayol). The goal of this line of strategy research has been to develop guidelines that will direct managers to the best possible strategies for the particular situations their organizations face. For instance, Michael Porter offers three **generic strategies** for achieving what he calls sustainable competitive advantage (generic because, theoretically speaking, any organization could use each of these strategies). These are: cost leadership (the organization offers its product at industry prices but makes above average profits by being a low-cost producer); differentiation (the organization commands a premium price for its products or services by maintaining a unique product or corporate image that is of value to its customers); and focus (the organization segments its market and focuses on serving only a particular market segment so effectively that it has virtually no competitors). By and large, this aspect of strategy research is less interesting to organization theorists than are studies that focus on how the strategy process relates the organization to its environment.

The earliest theories of the organizational strategy process typically focused on specification of desired outcomes and the courses of action for achieving them, analysis of the organizational environment and available resources, allocation of those resources and development of organizational structures and control systems. The point of this approach to strategy is to find ways of intentionally and rationally combining selected courses of action with the allocation of resources in order to carry out organizational goals and objectives in order to achieve strategic fit and thereby obtain competitive advantage. This perspective assumes that planning with respect to organizational activities and performance is possible, and equates strategy with a rational decision-making process. A model that portrays **the strategy process** as rational decision making is shown in Figure 4.1 and described below.

Analysis

According to the rational model, the strategy process begins with an analysis of the environment (an external appraisal) and an assessment of the organization (internal appraisal). The **external appraisal** is interpreted to uncover the opportunities and threats that the environment presents to the organization. The

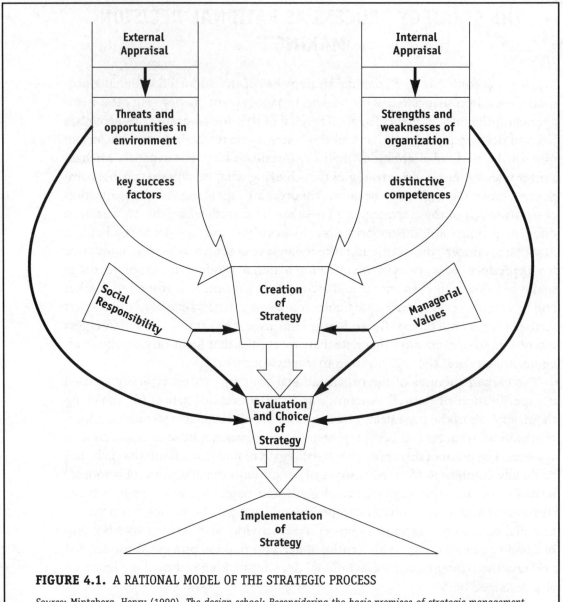

FIGURE 4.1. A RATIONAL MODEL OF THE STRATEGIC PROCESS

Source: Mintzberg, Henry (1990). *The design school: Reconsidering the basic premises of strategic management.* Copyright © 1990 John Wiley and Sons Limited. Reprinted by permission of John Wiley and Sons Limited

internal appraisal reveals the organization's strengths and weaknesses. The combination of external and internal appraisals and their interpretations gives the strategist the basic inputs to the problem of managing fit—definition of the needs and demands of the environment, the assessment of the competencies of the organization, and identification of performance gaps (the difference between potential and actual performance relative to perceived opportunity). Defining the organization in terms of its strengths and weaknesses and the environment in terms of opportunities and threats is referred to as **SWOT analysis**. SWOT is an acronym for Strengths, Weaknesses, Opportunities, and Threats.

External appraisal starts out looking like an environmental analysis. First you give consideration to the elements of the organization's network, and then to conditions and trends in the general environment, including its international and global aspects. Some of the issues to be considered include: the activities of competitors; examination of the organization's relationships with its customers and suppliers; the performance of customers, suppliers and competitors; anticipated changes in customer demand; the possibility of establishing relationships with new suppliers and customers; and the concerns of shareholders, regulators, unions, and other interested parties.[5] In considering conditions, trends and events in the general environment you will want to think about issues such as changing economic conditions, demographic shifts, emerging cultural patterns, legal trends, current political issues, potential scientific discoveries and technical innovations, and changes in the availability of natural resources, just as you would do for an analysis of the general environment of your organization.

What distinguishes external appraisal from environmental analysis is that once you have collected information about the environment, it must be translated into a set of threats and opportunities as seen from the perspective of the organization. The purpose of this focus is to provide you with a sense of how your organization stands in relation to its competitors and other key players in the interorganizational network such as customers and suppliers. For example, external appraisal might suggest that there is potential for entering a new market (opportunity) or it might lead you to anticipate the loss of an important supplier or customer (threat). It can alert you to your competitors' actions, or it can serve as a reminder of future contract negotiations, or of heightened concern by environmentalists with your firm's hazardous waste disposal practices. The appraisal might further reveal that economic indicators are strong, but capital markets are tightening in anticipation of inflationary pressures in the economy; an imminent national election does not look promising for any of the incumbents; technical progress in the industry is slowing; talk of regulation is increasing; or that public sentiment against hostile takeovers is rising. The point of external appraisal is to develop specific implications for the organization you are analyzing. Once you have done this, you shift to the internal appraisal.

The internal appraisal defines the organization's capacity to meet environmental demands. Here you will want to consider such issues as the range of products and services provided by the organization; the distribution network for its products; the geographic distribution of its activities; the ways in which existing structure and technology perform; human resource systems; research and development; procurement systems; characteristics of the organization's culture, its financial position and its technical and managerial capabilities. All known problems and strategic advantages created by these internal conditions are noted and the appraisal is then interpreted in terms of the organizational strengths and weaknesses that it reveals.

On the basis of a comparison between the internal and external appraisals, opportunities found in the environment are matched to organizational strengths, while the weaknesses of the firm and threats within its environment are kept resolutely in mind. If this is done in relation to the organization's competitors, the analysis will typically reveal the organization's **core competencies**—the particular strengths that give the organization its competitive edge in the environment (e.g., outstanding service, product design, brand or organizational image, cost effectiveness, market responsiveness, technical innovation). Subunit evaluations and assessments of technical and managerial talents and limitations relative to various means of exploiting this competitive advantage are then considered.

Formulation

According to the rational model, the formulation stage of the strategy process flows from the analysis. The goals of formulation are to discover ways to leverage opportunities and to close performance gaps. For instance, the organization may face an opportunity to enter a new and growing market, but has little experience with respect to producing for this market, and will face stiff competition if it does enter. On the other hand, it has capital readily available, has successfully completed two acquisitions within the last three years, has a desirable location, enthusiastic employees, and a competitive salary structure so that it can easily attract new talent. Furthermore, the divisional form is already in place so that adding a new line of business would not greatly disrupt current activities. This entire set of circumstances provides the foundation for laying out the alternatives (e.g., do not enter the new market, enter the new market via either a joint venture, a merger, or an acquisition), and for comparing the alternatives that are considered viable.

In general terms, **strategy formulation** involves: (1) consideration of alternative courses of action intended to achieve and/or maintain the fit between environmental needs and organizational abilities, (2) establishing criteria for selection among the alternatives (if these criteria are not already in place), and (3) comparison and choice among the alternatives. However, the focus of strategy formulation for small firms differs from that recommended for large organizations. An organization with only one product, or a single line of business, is mainly concerned with business-level strategy. **Business-level strategy** involves issues that define how the organization will compete in its market. Typical business-level strategies include: expansion into new sales territories, building new plants or offices, cost reduction programs, product or service differentiation, and quality enhancement.

For a large organization with multiple product lines confronting multiple markets, formulation occurs at two levels. The higher level, called **corporate-level strategy**, involves deciding what businesses to be in and, in general, involves determining how to segment the environment and the organization such that different parts of the organization can address different opportunities with maximum overall results. Typical of this level of strategy formulation are decisions to diversify, acquire other firms, engage in joint ventures, reorganize or—when environments present more threats than opportunities—divest, downsize and concentrate on existing lines of business. Large organizations engage in both corporate- and business-level strategy formulation, but business-level strategies in large firms are developed within the units that are responsible for the firm's different lines of business. The major difference is that in larger firms, business strategies are formulated not once, but for each line of business. These multiple business strategies may be coordinated within the corporate strategy formulation process, but some firms prefer to use a hands-off policy, allowing separate business units to operate more or less independently.[6]

Within the rational perspective, strategies are usually equated with measures of organizational performance. Common measures of effectiveness for business-level strategies include market share and profit margin. Corporate strategies are often evaluated in terms of overall financial return on all investments or on shareholders' funds in particular (indicating how effective the management of investment capital has been). Increasingly, organizations are facing pressures to include measures of customer satisfaction and environmental impact, however, these criteria are more difficult to measure and may not be regarded as legitimate by many within the organization. At least today, these tend not to receive the same weight as do financial indicators. Organizations use their criteria as feedback to determine if and when a given strategy should be altered. However, before strategic outcomes can be assessed, the organization must be given time to perform.

Once the strategic objectives are in place at the corporate level in large firms, and at the business level in both large and small firms, then resources are allocated, through the units, to the individuals who will implement the strategy.

Implementation

According to the rational model, **strategy implementation** consists of the mobilization of allocated resources to achieve desired outcomes and involves: (1) resource allocation to support the selected alternative, (2) the development of control systems to measure and assess performance and provide feedback to management, and (3) creating of structures and human resource policies (e.g., with respect to training and rewards) to support the chosen strategy. The tools and techniques of implementation draw upon all of the internal aspects of the organization that we will study in the following chapters of this book: technology, structure (both social and physical), and culture as well as decision making, power and politics, control, and organizational change. From the perspective of the strategist, organization theory is about implementation. However, you should be aware that, in practice, implementation has proven extremely problematic. While strategy researchers and strategists have developed sophisticated approaches to analysis and formulation, models for the implementation of strategy have not kept pace. Some strategy researchers are attempting to solve the problem within the framework of the rational model, but others are questioning the rationalist foundations of the approach and proposing alternatives, which we will consider next.

CHALLENGES TO THE RATIONAL MODEL

The rational model of the strategy process encourages separation between the activities of strategy formulation and implementation. In many organizations this separation occurs through a hierarchical division of labor—some people (typically top managers or formal planning departments) formulate strategy, while others (from middle management on down) are charged with implementing it. Top managers and planners focus on analyzing the threats and opportunities in the environment and on devising strategies for maximizing performance on the basis of the organization's core competencies. Meanwhile the operational level of the organization handles the day-to-day activities involved in realizing the strategic objectives of the firm. Middle managers are charged with translating the

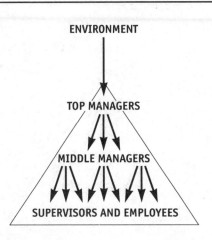

FIGURE 4.2. MIDDLE MANAGERS TRANSLATE THE STRATEGIES OF TOP MANAGERS INTO GOALS AND ACTIVITIES AT THE OPERATIONAL LEVEL

strategies of the top managers into coordinated goals and activities at the operational level (see Figure 4.2).

The separation of duties suggested by the rational model often produces communication problems. Consider what happens when implementors do not understand what formulators intend, or when formulators inaccurately perceive what implementors are able to do, or do not take into account what they prefer to do. The separation can also affect the commitment of implementors to strategic objectives. Numerous psychological studies have shown that when individuals are not involved in establishing their goals, they are much less likely to feel motivated to achieve them than when they are allowed to participate in the process.[7] When this lack of involvement occurs as a result of separation between top managers and their organizations, miscommunication and undercommitment may lead to poorly conceived or misunderstood strategies, or to strategies that are simply ignored or actively undermined. Any of these conditions can turn into a failed attempt to implement strategy.

Participation in the planning process is commonly offered as a curative for the problems of top-down management, however, participation creates problems for the rational model. The rational model is built on a linear process in which ideas flow unidirectionally from the top of the organization to the bottom (see Figure 4.3). When participation is included, the process becomes bottom-up as well as top-down (see Figure 4.4). A view of strategy that explicitly includes bottom-up processes is called emergent strategy. However, this view moves beyond

FIGURE 4.3. STRATEGY LINKS THE ORGANIZATION WITH ITS ENVIRONMENT AND REFLECTS THE INTENTIONS OF THOSE WHO FORMULATE STRATEGY

This figure depicts strategy as a top-down process.

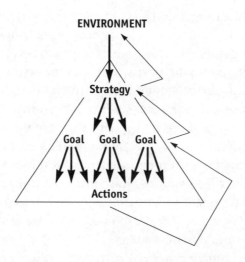

FIGURE 4.4. THE CONCEPT OF EMERGENT STRATEGY ADDS A BOTTOM-UP PROCESS TO THE TOP-DOWN VIEW OF STRATEGY

This model recognizes both planned and unplanned elements as part of the strategy process.

participation, to consider all the ways in which organizational members throughout the organization shape the strategy process.

Emergent Strategies

Some organization theorists define organizational strategy as the direction an organization takes, regardless of whether or not that direction was intentional. According to this view, strategy can be planned, but, even when it is not, it will emerge from the activities of organizational members. **Emergent strategy** evolves from activities taking place throughout the organization and thus *can* be influenced by strategic planning via the rational model, but is shaped by other influences as well.

Strategy researcher James Brian Quinn, in his study of strategists in nine major multinational companies, describes one such view as **logical incrementalism**. "Many a successful executive will initially set only broad goals and policies which can accommodate a variety of specific proposals from below, yet give a sense of guidance to the proposers," Quinn observes. "As events and opportunities emerge," he continues, the executive "can incrementally guide the pattern of escalated or accepted proposals to suit his own purposes without getting prematurely committed to any rigid solution set which unpredictable events might prove wrong or which opponents find sufficiently threatening to coalesce against."[8] Thus, Quinn finds that strategists "constantly reassess the future" and "find new congruencies as events unfurl."[9] In Quinn's view, strategy emerges within the general outline of a strategic plan, but from a foundation of activity taking place throughout the organization and according to a pattern of trial-and-error learning.

Those who favor the rational model tend to take a top-down view, portraying the internal structure and processes of the organization as though they were simply the tools of management. Emergent views provide reasons to believe that existing structures and processes are as likely to influence top management's formulation of a particular strategy as the other way around, thus they challenge the aphorism—structure follows strategy.[10] In the emergent view, structure also influences strategy.

To see why this might happen, consider the distribution of power in organizations. Strategies that maintain the status quo are likely to be favored over those that change the existing distribution of power. This is because the powerful (and do not forget that the *most* powerful are the ones who typically formulate strategy) usually want to maintain or enhance their positions. They are therefore likely to prefer strategies that do not alter existing patterns of resource allocation enough to significantly change the internal power structure. Organizational routines also affect the formulation and implementation of strategies. Existing patterns of activity can blind formulators to new possibilities or frustrate attempts to implement strategies that require breaking down and replacing old habits. For these reasons, the assumption that structure can be easily altered to conform to the requirements of a new strategy is questioned. The image of strategy as emerging from existing internal structures and processes stands in stark contrast to the rational view of strategy as forward looking, planned change in response to environmental demands.

Strategy as Symbolic Action

Some recent work in the strategy field goes beyond the emergent model to question not only the direction of the relationship between strategy and structure, but also the relationship between the analysis, formulation, and implementation phases of the strategy process itself. For example, studies of Japanese organizations suggest that action routinely precedes the public announcement of plans.[11] In these cases the strategy process is the reverse of that depicted by the rational model—implementation precedes rather than follows analysis and formulation. This reverse process, it is argued, legitimates what is already being done and symbolically communicates to others the openness of management to new ideas. However, in the Japanese organization, action itself is usually preceded by both top-down discussion ("ura") and bottom-up consensus building ("nemawashi") such as is described by the emergent view of strategy.

Another view, presented by Karl Weick, suggests that action produces strategy. This more radical view claims that formulation never really occurs at all, instead, a strategy is inferred from successful action that develops through experimentation or is discovered by luck. To illustrate his idea, Weick gives the example of an incident he claims happened during military maneuvers in Switzerland:

The young lieutenant of a small Hungarian detachment in the Alps sent a reconnaissance unit into the icy wilderness. It began to snow immediately, snowed for two days, and the unit did not return. The lieutenant suffered, fearing that he had dispatched his own people to death. But the third day the unit came back. Where had they been? How had they made their way? Yes, they said, we considered ourselves lost and waited for the end. And then one of us found a map in his pocket. That calmed us down. We pitched camp, lasted out the snowstorm, and then with the map we discovered our bearings. And here we are. The lieutenant borrowed this remarkable map and had a good look at it. He discovered to his astonishment that it was not a map of the Alps, but a map of the Pyrenees.[12]

Weick explains that the map of the Pyrenees symbolically oriented and activated the lost soldiers. As they began to act they generated tangible outcomes from which they could gain a clearer understanding of their situation and learn how to solve their problems. Weick concludes: "Managers keep forgetting that it is what they do, not what they plan, that explains their success. They keep giving credit to the wrong thing—namely, the plan—and having made this error, they then spend more time planning and less time acting. They are astonished when more planning improves nothing."[13]

Weick uses his example to help us break free of rationalist assumptions about how strategy works. In his view "execution *is* analysis and implementation *is* formulation."[14] Strategy is a powerful symbol that fulfills rationalistic expectations for leadership. The role of strategists is, therefore, also symbolic; the strategist is a symbol of the culture that looks for leadership in the form of strategy. So long as strategists produce strategy, regardless of whether it precedes or follows action, those who hold expectations are satisfied and life in the organization proceeds along its usual course. Weick does, however, see strategists having some influence on activity. He claims that they can use their symbolic potency to inspire confidence to act and to encourage improvisational activity, both of which he believes enhance the effectiveness of organizing by promoting learning.

Three Alternative Perspectives on Strategy

The rational model and its challengers represent, respectively, Classical management theory and the modernist and symbolic-interpretive perspectives of organization theory. As each perspective sees the organization in different terms, so each presents a different image of strategy.[15] Proponents of the rational model treat the organization like a tool in the hands of top managers and conceive of strategy as a process of designing the organization (as you would design a tool or machine) to achieve a predefined purpose. This image aligns with the machine metaphor of Classical management theory. Those who employ the emergent model see the organization as adaptive and thus they apply the modernist metaphor of the organization as a biological system. In this view, the organization (living organism) is rewarded for successful adaptation or punished for failure to adapt. Here strategy emerges from the organization's struggle to survive. Those who take a symbolic perspective view the organization in terms of the culture metaphor. In this view the organization develops and uses powerful symbols of business culture (e.g., strategy) to mobilize support for its activities. The postmodern perspective, along with its collage metaphor, is so far not included in the field of strategy.[16]

Core Concepts of Organization Theory

The criticisms of the rational model offered above might cause you to want to reject this model out of hand. After all, there is not much evidence that anything like this occurs in real organizations, so why bother with this model at all? The answer to this reasonable question has three parts. First, the rational model develops a historical appreciation of the field of strategy in organizational studies. For instance, the 1970s wave of interest in strategic planning was based on the rational model, and without this historical context, most of the studies produced at that time would likely be misinterpreted. Second, just because it is easy to find evidence that strategy processes are not entirely rational does not mean that the ideal of rationality has been or should be abandoned. Remember, the rational model is normative. This means that its primary purpose is to direct strategic attention in organizations toward the value of rational planning, not to describe what actually goes on in the context of strategic decision making which will probably always be a combination of rational decision making, politics, and organizational culture. Finally, rationality is a powerful symbol of modernity and it will probably not be abandoned anytime soon. What is needed is recognition of its practical limitations. This raises two additional questions: When is the rational model of strategy process likely to be useful? When the rational model is not appropriate, how should you go about making use of the alternatives presented by emergent and symbolic views? To address these questions, we again take our point of departure in the modernist perspective.

UNCERTAINTY AND THE STRATEGY PROCESS

Contingency theory, one of the mainstays of modernist organization theory, is used by organization theorist Henry Mintzberg to provide strategists with a framework for deciding which of the perspectives described above to apply to the strategy process in their organizations. Mintzberg's theory presents links between perceived uncertainty and strategy processes:

[If] the environment is unpredictable—or perhaps more commonly, takes time to figure out after an unexpected shift—then the 'formulator' may have to 'implement' him or herself . . . [alternatively,] . . . Where there is too much information to be comprehended in one brain—for example, in organizations dependent on a great deal of sophisticated expertise, as in high-technology firms, hospitals, and universities—then the strategy may have to be worked out on a collective basis. Here, then, the dichotomy [of formulation versus implementation] collapses in the other direction: the 'implementors' become the 'formulators.'[17]

To visualize the relationship between strategy and uncertainty you can build on the uncertainty matrix presented in Chapter 3 (see Figure 4.5). For instance, in the passage quoted above, Mintzberg is describing the two middle levels of uncertainty shown in the matrix. But before addressing these two cells, first consider the case of low uncertainty.

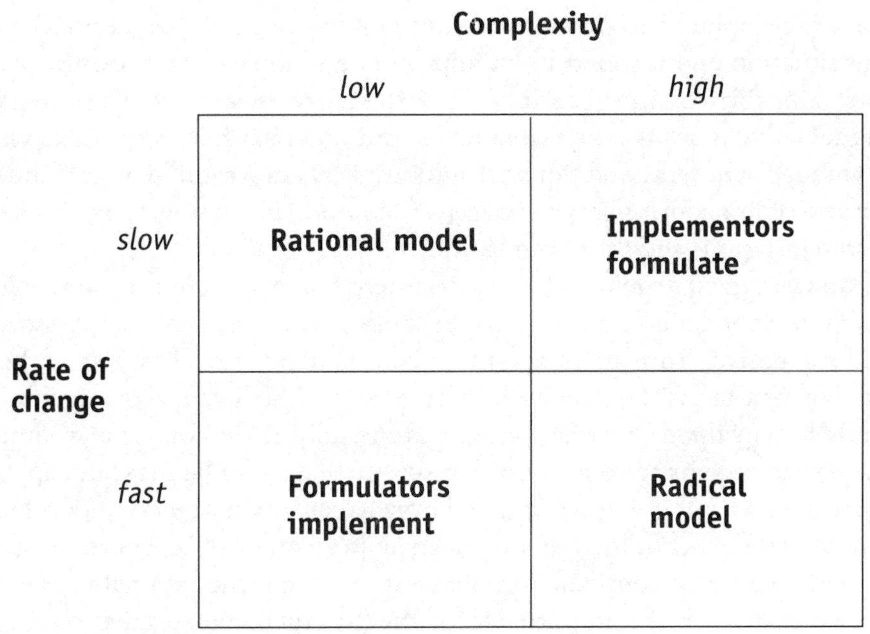

Complexity

	low	*high*
slow	**Rational model**	**Implementors formulate**
fast	**Formulators implement**	**Radical model**

(Rate of change — vertical axis label: slow, fast)

FIGURE 4.5. STRATEGY UNDER VARYING LEVELS OF UNCERTAINTY PRESENTED IN A CONTINGENCY THEORY FRAMEWORK

Based on: Mintzberg (1990).

Imagine that you are an organizational strategist operating in the low uncertainty condition, you easily comprehend the environmental forces that influence the organization because you perceive the environment to be relatively simple. You also face little pressure resulting from change because this environment is stable within your experience. These conditions are the most favorable to the rational model. You will have no great difficulty formulating a strategy and will have ample time to communicate your strategy to the implementors who will carry it out. When conditions do start to change, you can anticipate the changes and reformulate your strategy in plenty of time to avoid disaster. As a low uncertainty strategist, you know what the environment is like, can assess the viability of alternative strategies, and pass responsibility for implementation to others in the organization. As Mintzberg points out, however, strategists often operate under less than certain conditions.

In the case in which low environmental complexity coupled with rapid change is perceived, you will experience a moderate level of uncertainty and a need to move quickly. However, although things seem to be changing very rapidly, they are not so complex as to overwhelm your ability to comprehend critical aspects of the situation and respond in an appropriate manner. The pressure you feel comes in the form of time pressure. The fastest way to implement a strategy is to dispense with communication (that takes time and risks misunderstandings) and do it yourself. Thus, in conditions of low complexity and rapid change, Mintzberg advises combining formulation and implementation into a single role. In this case the strategist (you) and the organization are one.

If you were to confront a stable environment that was complex you would also be likely to experience moderate uncertainty, but in this case the pressure you would feel derives from an incapacity to comprehend critical aspects of the situation that you face. This condition is frequently associated with organizations that rely heavily upon expertise—hospitals and universities for instance. Since the environment is demanding a complex response that overwhelms your capacity to comprehend what is going on, you will have to rely upon others. Under this condition Mintzberg recommends a collective strategy, that is, one that involves those who would be considered implementors within the rational model. Here you can clearly see the importance of the emergent perspective on strategy processes. The advice to follow in these conditions is to work participatively with other members of the organization allowing strategy to emerge from existing structures and processes in the context of continuous interaction.

The most challenging environmental conditions are associated with the category of high uncertainty. These conditions occur in all organizations sometimes (e.g., at the point at which you experience a totally unexpected shift in the environment) and in some organizations much of the time (e.g., organizations heavily involved in new technologies report that these experiences occur regularly). When you confront these conditions, you face the twin problems of incomprehensibility and severe time pressure. You will be unclear about what information you need and will also find that you cannot hope to amass needed information in time to use it. Furthermore, the meaning of the information that is available to you is likely to be ambiguous. To make matters worse, you must take action, with or without a strategy.

Although Mintzberg offers little help (he merely suggests groping and coping until such time as things settle down and permit the re-establishment of more rational strategy processes), symbolic strategy offers an alternative. Here your role is to discover what the organization is doing, and to work to legitimate that activity through the symbolic construction of a rationale to protect the organization from the impossible demands for rationality generated by the environment and by the organization's own members. In other words, use strategy as a sensemaking device to allow organizational members to act and thereby to produce order out of the chaos of their experiences.[18] In this view, the idea of responding to the environment gives a misleading picture of what actually takes place. In the sensemaking view, people in organizations try things out, discover what they are doing as they experience the outcomes of their actions, and then analyze these relationships to make sense of their experience. Their sensemaking becomes codified as strategy when they claim to have intended what they actually did.

A Postmodern Postscript

The sensemaking perspective might be used to imagine a postmodern perspective on strategy. According to postmodern theory, distinctions such as strategist and strategy, organization and environment, are narrative constructions. They are the result of actors attempting to make sense of themselves and their experiences by concocting notions like strategy and organization. You might just as well have created other realities. This view implies that strategists and organizations do not exist as objective realities, but rather are objectivized by our subjective orientations toward them. The value of considering such a bizarre perspective is that it reminds us there are radical alternatives to the strategies, strategists, and organizations that we create and use. It encourages us, on the one hand, not to take ourselves and our organizations so seriously, and, on the other, to take our responsibility for our outcomes more seriously than we ever have before—in short, to consider alternative identities with which we might reform our actions, ourselves, and our organizations.

GOALS

Do goals precede strategy or does strategy precede goals? When viewed as a more or less continuous process involving both strategy and action, the organization appears at times to set goals prior to developing a strategy for achieving those goals, and at times appears to set goals in relation to a well-developed strategy. The problem with making these distinctions is that goals and strategy are interrelated concepts. Strategy can be conceived as a means to, or plan for, achieving goals, and goals can be thought of as one element involved in a strategy process, whether that process is defined as rational, emergent, or symbolic. The difference lies in whether your focus is on designing organizational outcomes (the goals perspective) or on the process by which goals are set and realized (the strategy process view).

Within most complex organizations, strategy is considered to be the responsibility of top management, whereas goals pervade all levels in an organization. This gives rise to an image that places strategy over goals, making it symbolically superior (refer back to Figure 4.3). However, given the inseparability of strategy and goals, this reading of the figure is misleading. Goals have greater reach into the depths of the organization while strategy stretches further into the environment. In these terms, one without the other would render the organization unable to address fit.

From the rational perspective, goals give organizations the direction they need to perform effectively. From the emergent perspective, they help the organization to adapt to changing circumstances, and in the symbolic view, goals give organizations the appearance that they know what they are doing. Effective performance, adaptation to changing circumstances, and the appearance of competence each inspire confidence and commitment which can attract potential employees, investors, and public support.

Official vs. Operative Goals

Modernist organization theorists claim that there are two distinct types of organizational goals—official and operative. **Official goals** tend to be vague and general while **operative goals** are more specific. You will find official goals in corporate charters, annual reports, and public statements by executives and other organizational spokespersons. For example, the official goal of many American universities in the late 1980s and early 1990s was to prepare tomorrow's leaders today, their operative goals often included integrating computers into the classroom and internationalizing course content.

Operative goals designate the ends sought through actual operating policies and procedures. They focus attention on the issues that require effort on the part of specific units and particular employees, thus operative goals define the direction specific units and individuals should take. They can also be used as criteria for evaluating performance. For example, Management by Objectives (MBO) and

Total Quality Management (TQM) programs use pre-determined and agreed upon operative goals as the standard against which an employee's performance is measured.

From the rational perspective, official goals serve as a framework for developing operational goals and thus influence the activities of the organization. An image, referred to as cascading objectives, helps to explain the links between official and operative goals. The official goals stated by top management are divided up and passed down from higher to lower levels in the organization, with each group of subordinates being delegated responsibility for a subset of the goals assigned to his or her unit. The subset is divided again and then again until every member of the organization has been delegated a share of the overall organizational responsibilities (as was shown in Figure 4.2). This is called cascading objectives because the process begins at the top of the hierarchy and flows downward until it reaches the bottom.

Thus you can see why official goals are stated in the broadest possible terms. It is because they must provide a focus for all of the activities of the various units that make up the organization. From the symbolic perspective, official goals have a second purpose, that is to inform and inspire stakeholders in order to ensure organizational commitment and social legitimacy. Since official goals have so many audiences, they must be stated in general terms so that they sound relevant to a large variety of people, as explained in the next section.

Multiple and Conflicting Goals

Organizations have many different stakeholders.[18] **Stakeholders** are individuals, groups, and other organizations that have interests (their stake) in the activities and outcomes of the organization. The prototypical stakeholder is the owner or shareholder. However, there are many other stakeholders including lenders, employees, customers, suppliers, members of the local community, and the local, state, and federal government. Not all stakeholders will agree about how the organization can best serve their interests. For example, imagine that you are the CEO of General Motors. Shareholders are making demands for profitability, while unions pressure you for wage concessions, and environmentalists demand social responsibility with regard to pollution levels at one of the company's plants. Since higher wages and the purchase of effective anti-pollution devices will reduce profits, such demands place you in a contradictory position. Similar conflicts occur between demands for control and flexibility, innovation and risk avoidance, or market share and short-term profits. Pressures coming from the different sectors of the environment cannot be ignored for long, and you and your organization must find a means for satisfying these multiple, conflicting interests.

One way that multiple interests can be served by a single organization is to differentiate so that one part of the organization can address itself to one set of concerns while other parts respond to other environmental demands. In other words, the organization specializes to deal with its multiple conflicting demands. Of course, this does not resolve the conflict in the environment, it merely internalizes it, reproducing the contradictions in the divided interests and concerns of different organizational units. To the extent that these conflicts can be kept separate within the organization, these contradictions may never create major conflicts. When they do, another way to deal with multiple, conflicting goals is through **sequential attention**, now addressing the concerns of one set of interests, later turning attention to the interests of other stakeholders. Although no one set of interests is satisfied all the time, sequential attention does make certain that all interests are satisfied some of the time. A third approach is called **satisficing**. This approach suggests keeping all interests partly satisfied (but never completely so) all of the time.

But the problem of multiple and conflicting goals does not end with the multiple pressures coming from within and outside of the organization. There is also the problem of change in any or all of these sources of conflict and multiplicity. Goals are not fixed for long in most organizations and the changes and introductions of new goals can create additional conflicts and contradictions as the organization struggles to shift its direction with changing conditions in the environment or with organizational change. The situation is really beyond visualization, however, you may get some notion of the level of complexity introduced by multiple and conflicting goals that change over time by comparing Figures 4.3 and 4.6.

The point to be remembered is that organizations typically face numerous demands and pressures from their environments because of their widespread dependence upon resources and legitimacy, and these sources of pressure change over time. When these changing demands and pressures compete for organizational attention and response, as they generally do, they create contradictory situations that must be handled by the organization. No matter how the organization chooses to address these situations, it must in some way or other come to terms with contradiction and this makes organizations themselves contradictory, a theme we will return to in Chapter 10.

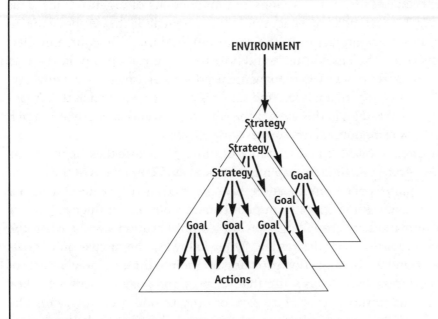

ENVIRONMENT

Strategy

Strategy

Strategy

Goal

Goal

Goal   Goal   Goal

Actions

FIGURE 4.6. MULTIPLE, CONFLICTING GOALS THAT CHANGE OVER TIME INTRODUCE COMPLEXITY INTO AN ORGANIZATION

SUMMARY

Modernist views dominate the study of strategy and strategy researchers most often use the rational decision-making model as their conceptual foundation. Views of strategy compatible with the symbolic-interpretive perspective do exist and have made an impression, particularly in organization theory. The main contribution of this approach so far has been the emergent model which begins by questioning the assumptions of rationality and strategic planning upon which the modernist approach relies. While interest in the role organizational culture plays in the strategy process has been expressed by a few researchers, the field of strategy has not yet fully embraced these efforts.

The view of strategy that organization theorists take is that strategic management provides an important link between the organization and its environment through which information and influence pass. In the modernist view this occurs largely in the direction of the environment influencing the organization. But the environment itself is also influenced through the link between the environment and organization. The concept of emergent strategy provides an explanation for this in that, just as strategy emerges from organizational processes, so the environment emerges from the actions and interactions of organizations. This explanation is then extended by enactment theory to include the symbolic meaning that organizations project onto the environment during the course of their deliberations about the environment and how the organization should respond to it. In the enactment view, top management projects an image of the environment based on a variety of analyses, and it is this projection to which the organization responds. Strategy, in this view, is the label organizational members attach to the process of responding to the projection process.

Goals are often implicated in discussions of strategy because these form points of contact between stakeholders, top management, and employees of the organization. The channels of communication through which goals are developed and responsibility taken guide strategy implementation but also influence further strategy formulation by providing upward communication about what the organization's capacities and desires are. Thus, following the discussion of goals as it travels around the organization provides insight into the emergent aspects of the strategy process. It is in this sense that strategy and goals present a chicken and egg dilemma to those wanting to give priority to one over the other. The issue of goals will be given further consideration in Chapter 11 which takes up the question of how goals fit into organizational control systems and thus provide a link between strategy and everyday work activities as these occur throughout the organization.

KEY TERMS

strategy	strategy formulation
strategic fit	business-level strategy
competitive advantage	corporate-level strategy
benchmark	strategy implementation
best practices	emergent strategy
Porter's generic strategies	logical incrementalism
the strategy process	official goals
external appraisal	operative goals
internal appraisal	stakeholders
SWOT analysis	sequential attention
core competencies	satisficing

ENDNOTES

1. Chandler (1962); Ansoff (1965); Steiner (1979); Argenti (1980).
2. Lindblom (1959); Mintzberg, Raisinghani and Theoret (1976); Quinn (1978).
3. Barney (1986); Johnson (1990, 1992); Fiol (1991).
4. See, for example, Barney (1986).
5. Porter (1985).
6. Goold and Campbell (1987).
7. Locke (1968, 1978); Locke and Latham (1984).
8. Quinn, Mintzberg and James (1991: 103).
9. Ibid. 104.
10. Chandler (1962).
11. Pascale (1979).
12. Weick (1987: 222)
13. Ibid.
14. Ibid. 230.
15. Chaffee (1985).
16. Some strategy researchers, for example Johnson and Scholes (1993: 54), remark that real strategy processes are no doubt some combination of planned, emergent, and symbolic activities. This is not a postmodern position for two reasons. First, such arguments rely upon the objectivizing idea of a "real" strategy process. Second, no insights are provided by the juxtaposition of the alternative views, instead, the possibility of integrating them is suggested.
17. Mintzberg (1990: 186–7).
18. Weick (1987); Huff (1982); Gioia and Chittipeddi (1991).
19. Mitroff (1983); Freeman (1984).

REFERENCES

Ansoff, H. Igor (1965). *Corporate strategy: An analytical approach to business policy for growth and expansion*. New York: McGraw-Hill.

Argenti, J. (1980). *Practical corporate planning*. London: Allen & Unwin.

Barney, Jay B. (1986). Organizational culture: Can it be a source of sustained competitive advantage? *Academy of Management Review*, 11: 656–65.

Chaffee, Ellen Earle (1985). Three models of strategy. *Academy of Management Review*, 10: 89–98.

Chandler, Alfred D., Jr. (1962). *Strategy and structure: Chapters in the history of the American industrial enterprise*. Cambridge, Mass.: MIT Press.

Fiol, Marlena (1991). Managing culture as a competitive resource: An identity-based view of sustainable competitive advantage. *Journal of Management*, 17: 191–211.

Freeman, R. E. (1984). *Strategic management: A stakeholder approach*. Boston: Pitman.

Gioia, Dennis A., and Chittipeddi, K. (1991). Sensemaking and sensegiving in strategic change initiation. *Strategic Management Journal*, 12: 433–48.

Goold, M., and Campbell, A. (1987). *Strategies and styles*. Oxford: Basil Blackwell.

Huff, Anne S. (1982). Industry influence on strategy reformulation. *Strategic Management Journal*, 3: 119–31.

Johnson, Gerry (1990). Managing strategic change: The role of symbolic action. *British Journal of Management*, 1/4: 183–200.

Johnson, Gerry (1992). Managing strategic change: Strategy, culture and action. *Long Range Planning*, 25: 28–36.

Core Concepts of Organization Theory

Johnson, Gerry, and Scholes, Kevan (1993). *Exploring corporate strategy*. New York: Prentice Hall International (UK).

Lindblom, Charles (1959). The science of muddling through. *Public Administration Review*, 19: 79–88.

Locke, Edwin A. (1968). Toward a theory of task motivation and incentives. *Organizational Behavior and Human Performance*, 3: 157–89.

Locke, Edwin A. (1978). The ubiquity of the technique of goal setting in theories of and approaches to employee motivation. *Academy of Management Review*, 3: 594–601.

Locke, Edwin A., and Latham, Gary P. (1984). *Goal setting: A motivational technique that works*. Englewood Cliffs, NJ: Prentice-Hall.

Mintzberg, Henry (1990). The design school: Reconsidering the basic premises of strategic management. *Strategic Management Journal*, 11: 171–95.

Mintzberg, Henry, Raisinghani, Duru, and Theoret, Andre (1976). The structure of unstructured decision processes. *Administrative Science Quarterly*, 21: 246–75.

Mitroff, Ian I. (1983). *Stakeholders of the organizational mind*. San Francisco: Jossey-Bass.

Pascale, Richard T. (1979). Zen and the art of management. *The McKinsey Quarterly*, Summer: 19–35.

Porter, Michael E. (1985). *Competitive advantage: Creating and sustaining superior performance*. New York: Free Press.

Quinn, James Brian (1978). Strategic change: Logical incrementalism. *Sloan Management Review*, no. 20 (Fall): 7–21.

Quinn, James Brian, Mintzberg, Henry, and James, Robert M. (1991). *The strategy process: Concepts, contexts, and cases*. Englewood Cliffs, NJ: Prentice-Hall.

Steiner, G. A. (1979). *Strategic planning: What every manager must know*. New York: Free Press.

Weick, Karl (1987). Substitutes for corporate strategy. In David Teece (ed.), *The Competitive Challenge*. Cambridge, Mass.: Ballinger, 22–33.

FURTHER READING

Chaffee, Ellen Earle (1985). Three models of strategy. *Academy of Management Review*, 10: 89–98.

Child, John (1972). Organizational structure, environment and performance: The role of strategic choice. *Sociology*, 6: 1–22.

Johnson, Gerry, and Scholes, Kevan (1993). *Exploring corporate strategy*. New York: Prentice Hall International (UK).

Miles, Ray E., and Snow, Charles C. (1978). *Organizational strategy: Structure and process*. New York: McGraw-Hill.

Mintzberg, Henry (1990). The design school: Reconsidering the basic premises of strategic management. *Strategic Management Journal*, 11: 171–95.

Stacey, Ralph D. (1996). *Strategic management and organizational dynamics* (2nd edition). London: Pitman.

5 | Technology

E CONOMISTS often describe organizations as black boxes into which resources flow and from which products and services emerge. Such a description is undersocialized according to behavioral economist Mark Granovetter, who argues that the social system in which organizations are embedded is equally important for understanding their contribution to the economy.[1] Both of these views hide the importance of technology. Viewed from within the organization, the economists' black box is actually a system for transforming resource inputs into outputs, at least according to modernist organization theorists who take an open systems approach to organizational technology.

In this chapter we will explore some of the ways in which organizational researchers have opened up the economists' black box and explored its contents. First, we will consider several different uses of the term "technology." Next we consider the typologies of three modernist theorists who described the differences they observed among technologies. Then, keeping Granovetter's point in mind, we look at modernist views of technology in relation to organizational social structure. Not all theoretical approaches to technology and social structure derive from the modernist perspective. Sociotechnical systems theory, which developed from a blend of engineering and organization theory, focuses on both the social and technological aspects of the use of technology in organizations. Recent developments within this field introduce symbolic-interpretive perspectives into technology studies as they explore the social construction of technology. Theorizing about new technologies opens organization theory to ideas from postmodern theory. The chapter concludes with the social construction of technology argument, theories of new technologies, and a look at the role technology plays in postmodern theory.

DEFINING TECHNOLOGY

In modernist organization theory, technology involves the means of achieving something—a desired outcome, goal, or output, usually conceptualized as a product or service. From this perspective technology is typically defined in terms of its:

(1) physical objects or artifacts including products and the tools and equipment used in their production;

(2) activities or processes that comprise the methods of production;

(3) the knowledge needed to develop and apply equipment, tools, and methods to produce a particular output (knowledge refers to know-how, e.g., how to assemble an automobile, design a software program, operate a missile tracking system, or make a sale).[2]

Viewed from outside the organization, as economists generally do, technology is the means by which society provides its members with the things that they need and desire: food, houses, computers, bank loans, medical attention, and education, among others. From this vantage point, an organization is a technology for producing a subset of the objects and artifacts that society demands. For example, electronics firms are a means of designing and manufacturing semiconductors, hospitals are a means of caring for people who are ill, and universities are a means of providing education. This is the black box conception of technology which represents the environmental level of analysis. Viewed from within the organization, however, the technology concept is made more explicit by focusing on how things are actually done, that is, emphasizing the methods and the knowledge with which objects and artifacts are produced. This organizational-level conception of technology derives from the fields of manufacturing, engineering, and operations research.

In addition to environment and organization levels of analysis, the concept of technology can also be applied to other, more micro levels, including the unit (e.g., department) and task levels. For instance, at the unit level, you can locate technologies in the marketing, accounting, personnel, finance, sales, and engineering departments of many organizations, and throughout the ranks of management. From this perspective many technologies operate simultaneously within every organization. The task level of analysis reveals even more diversity of technology; at this level you are focused on the variety of tasks in which organizational members engage. Here you might describe technologies for producing reports, making photocopies, maintaining machinery, assembling products, planning budgets, or giving feedback to subordinates.

Take the example of a university department (unit level). The technology employed to provide instruction to students includes: (1) physical objects such as classrooms, desks and chairs, blackboards, overhead and film projectors, paper, photocopying machines, computers, and video projection systems; (2) activities and processes such as reading, lecture, discussion, experiential exercise, group work, and examinations; and (3) the knowledge of an academic discipline and of how students learn. (Of course, in addition to teaching students, university departments also produce knowledge through research which involves other technologies that can be analyzed at the unit level.) Each activity associated with a unit-level technology can, in turn, be described in terms of the task level of analysis. For example, the technology for writing exams that I use involves: (1) physical objects including a computer, a printer, paper, and a photocopying machine; (2) activities including formulating questions and typing them into the computer, composing and formatting the exam, proofreading, printing, and photocopying; and (3) knowledge of concepts and theories and about how to test for mastery of these, as well as for the extent to which students can apply what they have learned.

At the organizational level, images of technology at lower levels of analysis can be assembled into a conception of the total technology of the organization. In the university example given above, the technology is that of producing knowledge and educating students. A rich image of this technology can be formed from separate analyses of how this is done across the various departments and in each of the classrooms, research laboratories, and administrative offices that make up the university. In this sense, the concept of technology encourages you to imagine the organization as the product of many different objects, activities, and knowledge bases operating and interacting at once. However, modernist organization theorists typically simplify the organizational-level conception by downplaying the diversity of technologies within a given organization and emphasizing the core technology for producing the organization's primary output.

The simplified viewpoint makes it possible to compare organizations with different core technologies by taking note of key similarities and differences between them, such as the differences between providing education or health care, assembling automobiles, and designing computer systems. What is lost in the simplification are the interesting details of technological diversity within the organization. The loss is justified on the grounds of the power of abstractions to make generalized comparisons, but you should not forget what has been given up in the bargain. Recovering this loss lies at the heart of symbolic-interpretive approaches to the study of technology.

A Dynamic View of Technology

Conceptualizing technology as a means to some end leads naturally to a dynamic view. Dynamic models emphasize how things work and studies of technology are similarly oriented. By far the most pervasive dynamic model in modernist organization theory is the open systems model, and this model provides a basic understanding of the organization as technology (see Figure 5.1). From the open systems point of view, an organization is the set of processes by which inputs are transformed into outputs.

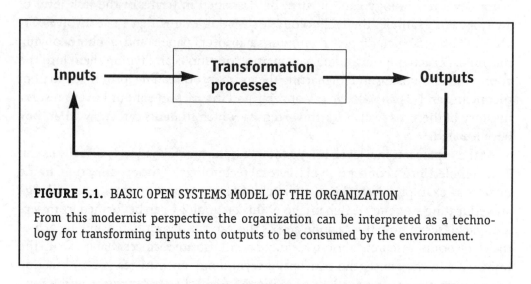

FIGURE 5.1. BASIC OPEN SYSTEMS MODEL OF THE ORGANIZATION

From this modernist perspective the organization can be interpreted as a technology for transforming inputs into outputs to be consumed by the environment.

In using the open systems model it is important that you specify what output the technology produces, for whom, and using what inputs. To analyze technology, first identify the product (or service) of the organization or unit you seek to describe, and then try to discover the inputs necessary to produce that output. Once you have a rough idea of the nature of the output and have identified at least some of the required inputs, begin to describe the process or processes by which the transformation of inputs into outputs is accomplished.

Some organizations employ two or more different core technologies. Many examples of this can be found among conglomerate organizations in which several unrelated businesses are combined, for instance through merger or acquisition. An analysis of multiple-core technology firms requires a separate analysis of each core technology, plus an analysis of the relationships between them (or lack thereof). Notice that, at the unit level of analysis, the descriptions of core technologies within a multiple-core firm are essentially the same analyses that would be undertaken for the organizational level of a firm with a single core technology.

Describing technology in terms of its three primary components—(1) physical objects and artifacts, (2) activities and processes, and (3) the knowledge underlying the development and application of the objects and activities—enables you to place organizational technologies in the context of their resource requirements. A discussion of the sources of these elements traced to the organization's environment will provide insights into some of the organization's dependencies which will contribute to interorganizational network and resource dependence analyses of organization–environment relations described in Chapter 3.

Consider the example of a technology for producing student learning in the university. The output could be defined as elaborated knowledge structures in the heads of students. The input is students who are willing and able to learn. The customer is society, although you might want to consider students themselves, and their future employers, as the direct beneficiaries. In general, the transformation process involves creating opportunities for students to develop their knowledge of academic subjects and their methods and applications. You can further specify the process, of course, by focusing on the technology employed in a particular unit or for a specific task.

Core Technology

Because of the complexity created by different levels of analysis in organization theory, it will be necessary for you to take care to specify what your focus is when you are talking about technology. By now it should be clear that there are many ways of describing organizational technology. In addition to perspectives derived from different levels of analysis, there is the technology that directly produces the products and services that the organization provides to its environment, technologies that indirectly maintain the production processes (e.g., accounting, personnel), and technologies for adapting to the environment (e.g., economic analysis, market research, strategic planning).

To distinguish the organization-level technology for producing goods and services for the environment from these other technologies, organization theorists use the term **core technology**. The core technology of a manufacturing company is its manufacturing process. The core technology of a retail store is buying, displaying, and selling goods; an estate (or real estate) agency's core technology involves brokering the sale and purchase of residential and commercial properties.

The term "core technology" can be confusing because, although the activities that it involves are usually performed by one of the departments of an organization, this same technology is used in an organizational-level analysis to represent the technology of the entire organization. This makes it easy to confuse the organizational and unit levels of analysis. Confusion can only be avoided if you take great care in stating what your level and focus of analysis is. If you find it useful to change levels in order to clarify what is going on in a particular core technology, or if you change your focus to another part of the organization, be certain to note that this is what you are doing so that you do not become lost midway through your analysis.

High Technology

Some people confuse the term "technology" with **high technology**. The latter term is related to, but certainly not identical with, the technology concept as it is used in organization theory. High technology has been used loosely to describe many different aspects of new technologies such as computers, microelectronics, fiber optics, satellite communications, lasers, expert systems, robotics, and multimedia. Sometimes it refers to products embodying these technologies, and sometimes to transformation processes that rely upon one or more of them. At other times high technology merely refers to any business in which technology is changing rapidly or to one that is considered leading edge. High technology has also been defined in terms of the demands for special qualifications that it places on workers, such as demands for computer literacy.

Cyberneticist and technology theorist Milan Zeleny argues for a more theoretically precise definition of high technology, and so he is careful to differentiate technology and high technology. While technology is applied within a given system so that tasks can be performed faster, more reliably, in larger quantities, or more efficiently, high technology changes the organizational system itself. Zeleny states that "high technology changes the nature of tasks and their performance, interconnections and nature of physical, energy and information flows,"[3] and he further claims that "acquisition of high technology implies acquisition of new organizations, new tasks, new styles [or management], new cultures—new ways of doing business."[4]

Service versus Manufacturing Technologies

Another confusion concerning the concept of technology is created by distinguishing manufacturing and **service technologies**. Organization theorists offer three characteristics of service technology outputs; services are:

(1) consumed as they are produced;

(2) intangible;

(3) cannot be stored in inventory.

Consider the example of a news service. The service provided by this type of company is access to information. Information is produced through communication of messages so that it is consumed at the same moment that it is produced. Information has no material form and its news value dissipates so rapidly that, if it is to result in a profit through exchange, it cannot be held for long. The characteristics of providing access to information clearly place this technology into the service classification. But what of the equipment via which the news service relays its messages and which the service supplies to its customers? The paper on which the messages are printed and passed to journalists or newscasters (or the electronic display that carries the messages)? How about the subscription contract for the service? These aspects of the news service technology do not fit as neatly into the definition of service outputs.

Now consider a typical manufacturing technology, for instance, an automobile manufacturing plant. Certainly the products of this technology are tangible, they are not consumed as they are produced, but rather can be stored for months without losing their value and can be resold by customers years after their original purchase. Nonetheless, many aspects of the product of an automobile manufacturing technology are similar to those of a service technology. For example, the style or design of the automobile is intangible, its value dissipates rapidly with the introduction of new models. Another example is the warranty that accompanies newly manufactured automobiles—a warranty is a promise of service that is part of the product sold.

The point made here is that the distinction between service and manufacturing technologies is difficult to maintain beyond a superficial categorization of particular types of businesses into industries (service sector versus manufacturing or other industrial groupings). When you undertake a more detailed analysis of an organization's technology, you will notice that the outputs of most technologies have both service and manufacturing characteristics. It is because of this convergence that manufacturing firms are increasingly turning to the concepts developed for service sector firms, and service firms to manufacturing concepts, in order to improve their performance. Banks, for instance, now conceive of their services as tangible products. This encourages them to focus their attention on "packaging" and other concerns typically associated with the output of manufacturing technologies. For their part, numerous manufacturing firms have become obsessed with the customer, a strategy that arose first in the service sector. The effectiveness of this cross-fertilization of ideas between service and manufacturing sectors indicates that the distinction so often made between them is not a clean one. Nonetheless, it has its place and, when employed with care, can provoke you to consider aspects of technology that you might otherwise overlook.

TYPES OF TECHNOLOGY

In modernist organization theory the study of technology has focused mainly on the variety of technologies in use and the significance of this variety for discovering better ways of organizing. One product of modernist theorizing about organizational technology has been a set of typologies for categorizing and describing technologies. Modernist theorists use typologies to develop and empirically test contingency theories, but typologies are also useful for developing your understanding of the technology concept. You can apply them to a modernist analysis of the organizational technologies that interest you. In this section of the chapter we will examine the typologies of three influential organization theorists: Joan Woodward, James Thompson, and Charles Perrow.

Woodward's Typology

The importance of technology for organization theory was made clear by Joan Woodward, a British organizational sociologist.[5] However, the research question that initially interested Woodward did not concern technology at all, rather it was "What organizational arrangements produce the highest levels of performance?" At the time that Woodward began her study, modernist organization theory was embryonic. The desire to find a single best way to organize—the legacy of the Classical management school—still dominated organization theory. However, since there were differences of opinion over which of the ways proposed by management scholars was actually best, Woodward, being one of the new modernists, decided to design a scientific study to address the question.

Woodward surveyed 100 manufacturing organizations operating in the vicinity of South Essex, England. She measured their relative levels of performance (above average, average, and below average for their industry) and the dimensions of structure underlying what different management theorists had proposed as best ways, such as span of control, the number of management levels, degree of centralization in decision-making practices, and management style. Woodward expected to find that one of the established views was more effective than the others. Thus, she was quite surprised when her analysis of the data revealed no significant relationship between structure and performance.

Such an unexpected result could not be presented without a good explanation. Woodward sought the answer by trying different approaches to her data. At one point she grouped companies according to their level of technical complexity (determined by the type of technology they used to manufacture their products), and this analysis revealed the pattern that made Woodward a famous organization theorist. The typology she had developed revealed that structure was related to performance after all, but only when the types of technology the organizations employed were taken into account. That is, the best structure for an organization (i.e., one associated with high performance) depended upon the type of technology employed. Woodward's typology is shown in Figure 5.2.

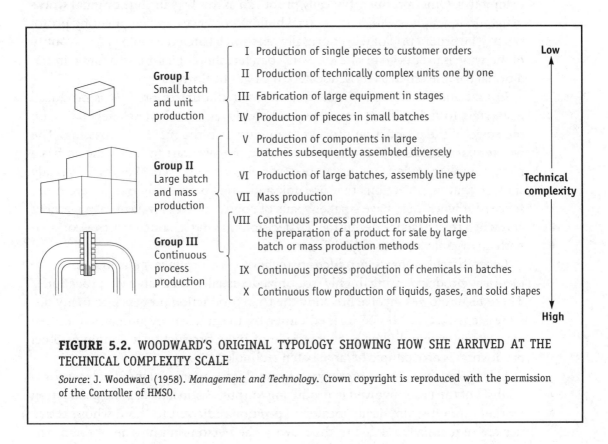

FIGURE 5.2. WOODWARD'S ORIGINAL TYPOLOGY SHOWING HOW SHE ARRIVED AT THE TECHNICAL COMPLEXITY SCALE

Source: J. Woodward (1958). *Management and Technology*. Crown copyright is reproduced with the permission of the Controller of HMSO.

Woodward's typology is usually condensed into three basic technologies:

(1) unit or small batch;

(2) large batch or mass production;

(3) continuous processing.

These three types can be plotted along the single dimension of technical complexity shown at the righthand side of Figure 5.2. **Technical complexity** refers to the degree of mechanization in the manufacturing process. Unit and small batch production anchors the low end of the scale because in these manufacturing processes most of the work is done by hand. As processes move up the technical complexity scale from mass production to continuous processing, more of the work is done by machines.

The **unit and small batch production** category consists of all technologies that produce one item at a time, or a few items all at once. Custom clothing, such as tailored suits or theatrical costumes, is usually the product of unit production techniques. Other products typically produced in this way include original works of art, designer glassware, commercial building projects, and engineering proto-types. The production of wine normally uses small batch technology—a quantity of the wine is produced in one lot. Small batch technologies are also found in traditional bakeries such as those located throughout Europe.

In unit and small batch production, a small amount of product is produced from start to finish. Thus, the individual employee's work varies depending on the stage of the production process through which the material is passing. The worker participates in the whole production process start to finish and so has a fairly complete understanding of the technology being used. Woodward's study showed that organizations that use unit and small batch technologies are more successful when they have smaller spans of control, fewer levels of management and when they practice decentralized decision making (characteristics associated with an organic form of organizing).

Large batch or mass production technologies produce great quantities of identical products using highly routinized, usually mechanized, procedures. These technologies involve breaking the total production process into many discrete steps that can be performed either by machine or by human hands. An automobile assembly line is an example of mass production technology. Steel production is an example of large batch technology.

In large batch and mass production technologies, workers repetitively perform a subset of the tasks involved in producing output. For instance, mass production workers are often physically located in positions adjacent to those whose activities are sequentially related to their own—the person on one side of them performs the task that precedes theirs and the person on their other side performs the task that follows theirs. Woodward's study showed that organizations that use large batch and mass production technologies are more successful when their managers have larger spans of control and when they practice centralized decision making (characteristics associated with mechanistic forms of organizing).

Mass production is a series of discrete tasks performed sequentially, whereas, **continuous processing** is a series of non-discrete transformations occurring in a sequence. Consider the examples of oil refining and waste treatment. In these cases, raw material (crude oil, raw sewage) is fed into one end of the process and, as it flows continuously through the system, unwanted substances (contaminants) are removed or drawn away until the degree of refinement desired is achieved (refined oil, treated sewage). In continuous processing, humans tend equipment that affects the transformation automatically, whereas in mass production, humans directly perform at least some of the tasks by hand. Woodward's study showed that the patterns of organizing in successful continuous processing organizations are similar to those for unit and small batch technologies, they have smaller spans of control and decentralized decision making. However, they have more levels of management than either small batch or mass production technologies.

In general, Woodward found that the highest levels of performance among her firms were achieved when mass production technologies were combined with mechanistic organizational forms, and when small batch or continuous processing technologies were combined with organic forms (findings from her study are summarized in Table 5.1). However, history has shown us that Woodward's typology was limited in two ways. First, her study examined mainly small and medium-sized organizations, and the relationship she found between technology and the structure–performance link proved to be less significant when organizations are larger and more complex. We will return to this issue later in the chapter. For now, let us turn our attention to the second limitation of Woodward's study, namely that it ignored non-manufacturing firms.

TABLE 5.1. FINDINGS FROM WOODWARD'S STUDY LINKING TECHNOLOGY TO SOCIAL STRUCTURE

Structural dimension	Technology		
	Unit production	Mass production	Continuous process
Levels of management	3	4	6
Span of control	23	48	15
Ratio of direct to indirect labor	9:1	4:1	1:1
Administrative ratio	low	medium	high
Formalization (written communication)	low	high	low
Centralization	low	high	low
Verbal communication	high	low	high
Skill level of workers	high	low	high
Overall structure	organic	mechanistic	organic

Source: J. Woodward (1965). *Industrial Organization: Theory and Practice*. By permission of Oxford University Press.

Thompson's Typology

As was discussed earlier, there are important reasons not to push the distinction between manufacturing and service technologies too far. However, in the late 1960s, James Thompson introduced significant advances in theory building efforts by including both manufacturing and service technologies in one typology.[6] Thompson developed his theory of technology around three general types that he labelled:

(1) long-linked;

(2) mediating;

(3) intensive.

Long-linked technologies generally fit into either Woodward's mass production or continuous processing categories. The automobile assembly line is prototypical of long-linked technology. Technologies for producing chemicals and generating electrical power are additional examples. The label "long-linked" was selected because both assembly line and continuous processing plants are linear transformation processes that can be thought of as having inputs entering at one end of a long line of steps from which products emerge at the far end.

Mediating technologies bring clients or customers together in an exchange or transaction. Banks, brokerage firms, and insurance companies all operate using mediating technology. In general, these technologies link partners in a potential exchange by helping them locate one another and conduct their transactions, often without ever having to physically meet. For example, banks use a mediating technology to bring together savers who want to invest money and borrowers who want to take out loans. Banking technology mediates between investors and borrowers by providing a location for both types of customers, and by providing standardized procedures to facilitate their mutual benefit, in this case, interest payments for investors and funds for borrowers. Mediating technologies are so called because firms using these technologies act as go-betweens (i.e., mediators) in bringing together the interests of two or more different parties to a transaction.

Intensive technology occurs in hospital emergency rooms, research laboratories, and in project organizations such as engineering design or construction work. Intensive technologies require coordinating the specialized abilities of two or more experts in the transformation of a usually unique input into a customized output. Each use of an intensive technology requires on-the-spot development and application of specialized knowledge to new problems or different circumstances.

Thompson's ideas about technology were grounded in the process-oriented, open systems model of organization. Thompson recognized that technologies differed substantially depending upon their transformation processes. He noticed that some technologies were characterized by extreme standardization in their processing of inputs into outputs (e.g., automobile assembly workers perform the same tasks repeatedly), while other technologies seemed to have very little standardization of processes (e.g., emergency room personnel must respond to the unique needs of each patient as they come through the door).

Thompson's open systems approach also caused him to be sensitive to the characteristics of the materials that were fed into a technical process and the outputs that the system produced. Some inputs and outputs are highly standardized (e.g., traditional mass production automobile manufacturing assembles nearly identical parts into nearly identical automobiles), while other technologies use unstandardized inputs to produce unstandardized outputs (e.g., hospital emergency rooms transform diseased or injured individuals into stabilized patients ready to be discharged or to accept other hospital services).

Thompson's typology can be easily visualized in terms of the two dimensions shown in Figure 5.3. This two-by-two matrix allows us to consider four possibilities deriving from the combination of Thompson's two conceptual dimensions: (1) standardization of inputs and outputs versus (2) standardization of transformation processes. Using the matrix, you can classify any organization as producing either highly standardized outputs from highly standardized inputs *or* unstandardized outputs from unstandardized inputs, and as either using standardized or unstandardized transformation processes. The four cells of the matrix present four alternative types of organizational technologies: (1) standardized inputs/outputs with standardized transformation processes describe long-linked technologies, (2) unstandardized inputs/outputs with standardized transformation processes describe mediating technologies, (3) unstandardized inputs/outputs with unstandardized transformation processes describe intensive technologies and (4) standardized inputs/outputs with unstandardized transformation processes.

The fourth alternative—standardized inputs/outputs with unstandardized transformation processes—represents an interesting case. The absence of a technology type to fit this category is probably due to the enormous inefficiency associated with such a system. Imagine producing a standard product with standard inputs, and doing so in a different way every time. While such technologies actually exist (e.g., building prototypes for the design of manufacturing processes), Thompson, who was obsessed with discussing what happens under "norms of rationality," ignored this cell in his typology.

		Transformation processes	
		standardized	*non-standardized*
Inputs/ Outputs	*standardized*	**Long-linked**	**?**
	non-standardized	**Mediating**	**Intensive**

FIGURE 5.3. TWO-BY-TWO MATRIX SHOWING THOMPSON'S TYPOLOGY OF TECHNOLOGIES

Based on: Thompson (1967).

Perrow's Typology

Charles Perrow's work corrected a shortcoming in both Woodward's and Thompson's theoretical assumptions. Both Woodward and Thompson treated organizations as if they had only one dominating technology, whereas Perrow picked up the discussion of technology from the unit level of analysis. His greater sensitivity to the number of different technologies that comprise every organization enabled him to recognize the diversity of organizational technologies.[7]

Perrow's approach relied upon two dimensions against which different units of an organization can be measured and compared: task variability and task analyzability. **Task variability** is defined by the number of exceptions to standard procedures encountered in the application of a given technology. **Task analyzability** is defined as the extent to which, when an exception is encountered, there are known analytical methods for dealing with it. Task variability and analyzability can be arrayed in a two-by-two matrix giving four possibilities (see Figure 5.4):

(1) routine;

(2) craft;

(3) engineering;

(4) non-routine.

Task variability

	low	high
high	**Routine**	**Engineering**
low	**Craft**	**Non-routine**

Task analyzability (row label, left side)

FIGURE 5.4. TWO-BY-TWO MATRIX SHOWING PERROW'S TYPOLOGY OF TECHNOLOGIES

Based on: Perrow (1967).

Routine technologies are characterized by low task variability and high task analyzability. The traditional automobile assembly line that fits Thompson's long-linked technology and Woodward's mass production category is also an example of routine technology. Clerical work is another example. Filing clerks, for instance, encounter few exceptions to their standard work practices, and when they do, there is almost always a known method of resolution, such as hierarchical referral (i.e., ask the boss).

Craft technology describes conditions of low task variability and low task analyzability. Construction work is a craft technology. The construction worker encounters few exceptions to standard procedures, but when exceptions are encountered, such as mistakes in planning, or unavailable materials, a way of dealing with the problems that arise must be invented, since pre-determined analytical methods for solving these problems do not exist. Locating water for drilling wells is another example of a craft technology. In this technology, intuition and experience become extremely important when standard geological solutions to finding water fail, thus, although standard procedures usually engender few exceptions, when exceptions do occur (no water is found using all available scientific knowledge), there are few known solutions upon which workers can rely.

Engineering technologies occur where high task variability and high task analyzability are found. The technologies of accountants, most engineers (aerospace engineering better fits the category of non-routine technology), laboratory technicians, and executive secretaries fit the engineering category. In these types of technology many exceptions to standard practices arise, but employees also have known methods for solving these problems, often as the result of advanced and highly specialized training.

Perrow labelled the technologies characterized by high task variability and low task analyzability as **non-routine technologies**. These technologies occur, for instance, in research and development departments, aerospace engineering firms, and prototype laboratories. Thus, Perrow's non-routine category overlaps Woodward's small batch category. It also has commonalities with Thompson's intensive category and his missing category of standardized input/outputs and unstandardized transformation processes. In non-routine technologies, the high number of problems encountered and the lack of known methods for solving them place employees in a more or less constant state of uncertainty.

Using the Three Typologies

Although Woodward and Thompson conceived of technology at the organizational level of analysis, their types are general enough to describe technology at lower levels of analysis. Thus, it is possible to make comparisons among the typologies proposed by all three theorists. You can easily see that there are similarities between the three frameworks presented by Woodward, Thompson, and Perrow, some of which were pointed out above. But there are also important differences. The three typologies do not overlap one another completely even though sometimes they can all be used to describe the same technology, for example, traditional assembly line automobile manufacturing can be described as mass production, long-linked, and routine. In other cases only two of the typologies are useful, for instance, the work done by bank tellers fits routine technology in Perrow's typology, would be categorized as a mediating technology in the Thompson scheme, but would not appear in Woodward's typology because she did not include service organizations (although the work of bank tellers could be described as a unit processing technology in the sense that customers are served one at a time). What is more, technologies can often be described using multiple categories within one typology. For example, training a sports team has aspects of Perrow's routine technology such as doing exercises for strength and agility, and also has aspects of non-routine technology, for instance, specialized coaching for different positions on the team.

Remember not to restrict yourself to one typology, nor to one type within a typology. Work through the entire list and discover how many of the types can be usefully applied to your case. Be sure to consider how your case is similar to each type *and* how it is different, and be as specific as possible. By encouraging you to think multi-dimensionally, this technique will both stretch your imagination and strengthen your ability to perform a modernist analysis. But remember to take great care with levels of analysis; it is easy to switch levels without being aware that you are doing so. Level switching can be very illuminating, but if you lose your bearings, confusion is hard to avoid.

TECHNOLOGY AND SOCIAL STRUCTURE

Several important issues concerning social structure appear in the early studies of technology in organization theory. The first involves a debate about "the technological imperative" which came to be associated with Woodward's theory. The second involves uncertainty, which we also addressed in Chapter 3 in regard to how uncertainty is related to complexity and change in the environment of an organization. In this chapter we examine the relationship between uncertainty and non-routine technology implied by Perrow's theory. The third issue to emerge from technology studies in organization theory is task interdependence, a concept developed by Thompson in relation to his typology. Finally, technical and environmental complexity, uncertainty and task interdependence have been discussed as factors that produce pressure to process information in organizations. We will briefly consider the information processing perspective at the end of this section.

The Technological Imperative

Along with convincing organization theorists of the importance of the techno-logy construct, Woodward's important study ushered in the idea that technology determines which sort of organizational structure is best. Belief in this idea came to be known as **the technological imperative**.

While Thompson and Perrow further developed the technology construct itself, other organization theorists investigated the technological imperative with a variety of replications of Woodward's study. In particular, a group of British researchers from Aston University, known as the Aston Group, found evidence that substantially altered beliefs in the technological imperative.[8] Their studies contained data on a wider range of organizations than did Woodward's research and their analysis showed that the significant correlation between technology and social structure that Woodward reported was itself contingent upon the size of the organization. The Aston studies indicated that technology has greater significance for the structure–performance relationship when organizations are small than when they are large.

The explanation provided by the Aston researchers was that when the organiza-tion consists of little beyond a technical core, as was the case for the relatively small organizations studied by Woodward, then technology has a significant and possibly determining effect on social structure. But, when the organization becomes more complex, this relationship disappears. Another way to interpret the findings of the Aston studies is to recognize that social structures relate to the technology that is being used, which, for some units and their employees, will not be the core tech-nology of the organization. In small organizations most employees are directly involved with the core technology, but in large organizations many employees are involved in technologies that are not directly related to the core. Thus, the overall characteristics of social structures in larger organizations reflect the greater differ-entiation and integration of a wider array of technologies than do social structures in small organizations, because in large organizations the relationship between the core technology and the general characteristics of the complex social structure are diluted. Technology and structure are still significantly related, but the relationship is vastly more complicated in large organizations than it is in small ones.

Technical Complexity, Uncertainty, and Routineness

You will remember that Woodward distinguished technologies by their technical complexity. She measured technical complexity as the extent to which machines perform the core transformation process. In relating technical complexity to structural arrangements, Woodward noticed that technologies at both extremes of her scale (unit and continuous processing technologies) were best served by organic structures, while technologies in the middle range (mass production) performed better with a mechanistic structure. Woodward's explanation for this pattern was the **routineness of work** performed in the various technologies. Both unit and continuous processing technologies involve work that is non-routine, while the work associated with mass production is highly routine. Thus, unit and continuous process technologies are better suited to organic structures because they are more compatible with non-routine work, and mass production technologies are better suited to mechanistic structures because they are compatible with routine work. It may help you to remember the relationship between the routineness of work and technical complexity if you see it as an inverted U-shaped curve (Figure 5.5).

Although Perrow categorized technologies on a different basis than did Woodward, he too noted the importance of routineness. In fact, Perrow's two-by-two matrix is often collapsed onto a one-dimensional scale (see Figure 5.6).

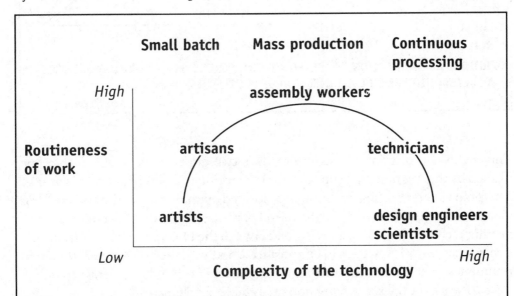

FIGURE 5.5. THE RELATIONSHIP BETWEEN THE ROUTINENESS OF WORK AND TECHNICAL COMPLEXITY

Woodward's findings indicate that both unit and continuous processing technologies are associated with low routineness while mass production technologies have high routineness. Thus, the relationship between routineness of work and technical complexity takes the form of an inverted U.

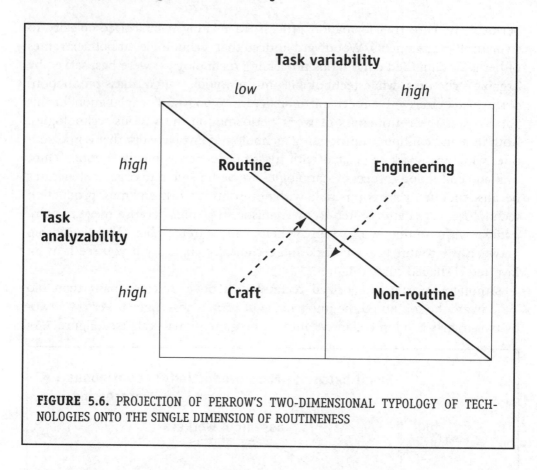

FIGURE 5.6. PROJECTION OF PERROW'S TWO-DIMENSIONAL TYPOLOGY OF TECH-NOLOGIES ONTO THE SINGLE DIMENSION OF ROUTINENESS

This involves projecting points in Perrow's two-dimensional space onto a line formed by the diagonal that runs through the routine and non-routine quadrants. The points, representing technologies located within the quadrants, are thus plotted on this line according to their level of routineness such that craft and engineering technologies will generally fall between the two extremes of routine and non-routine work. However, in contrast to Woodward, Perrow emphasized non-routineness rather than routineness by elaborating on the occurrence of exceptions to work routines involving non-analyzable problems.

Perrow's interest in non-routineness led him to focus on technology as a determinant of uncertainty in organizations. According to Perrow, technology contributes to uncertainty either through variations in the quality or availability of inputs to the transformation process, or through the variable nature of the transformation process itself. When uncertainty is high, it becomes difficult to structure the activities of the organization because the activities that are required are not always known in advance.

Perrow's and Woodward's discussions of the effects of technology are like two sides of a single coin. Both explain the links between technology and social structure in terms of the routineness and non-routineness of work. However, whereas Woodward was the first to propose the relationship between technology and social structure, Perrow sought a more thorough explanation for it. Like Perrow, Thompson also looked for deeper understanding of the links between technology and social structure, but, in contrast to Perrow, did so with greater emphasis on social structure.

Task Interdependence and Mechanisms of Coordination

Thompson recognized that the objects being processed and/or the work processes of a technology may be interrelated so that changes or problems in one part of the technical system affect other parts. He described this situation as task interdependence because those working with such transformation processes are dependent on others for the accomplishment of their tasks. Thompson was particularly interested in the problem of coordination, so he focused on describing the ways in which task interdependence was related to different coordination mechanisms. His work on task interdependence identifies links between the coordination mechanisms and mediating, long-linked and intensive technologies.

In a mediating technology a number of offices or officials perform their work tasks almost independently of one another, as least so far as actual work flow between units is concerned. Therefore, little direct contact is needed between units (or individuals). Cases such as these, where the output of the organization is primarily the sum of the efforts of each unit, are labelled **pooled task interdependence** (see Figure 5.7). Take banking as an example. Banks employ a mediating technology in the sense that they mediate between borrowers and savers or investors. This mediation can be accomplished simultaneously by several bank branches that operate almost independently of one another. Day and night shifts on an assembly line, franchised restaurants, and the different departments of a university or a large retail store are additional examples of units within organizations that typically operate with pooled task interdependence.

According to Thompson, groups operating with pooled task interdependence demand very little in the way of coordination. The coordination required to achieve a coherent organizational identity or to ensure that services are consistent across units can, for the most part, be accomplished through the use of **rules and standard procedures** for routine operations. For example, rules and standard procedures for tasks such as opening bank accounts, investing in certificates of deposit or mutual funds, and applying for and approving loans and lines of credit,

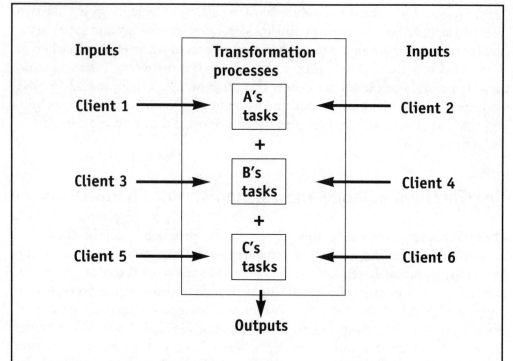

FIGURE 5.7. MEDIATING TECHNOLOGIES GENERATE POOLED INTERDEPENDENCE

Notice that A, B, and C's joint product forms the output of the organization, yet they can operate more or less independently of one another.

produce sufficient coordination for a bank to integrate the activities of its branches.

Long-linked technology involves both pooled and **sequential task interdependence**. For instance, several assembly lines can operate at once in a manner that leaves them practically independent of one another so the different lines are pooled in the sense that their outputs are aggregated into the total output of the organization. However, within each line interdependence is more complex because each worker is dependent on the work of others located at positions prior to theirs on the line. If workers early in the process are not performing their tasks properly, then the work of others further down the line is likely to suffer. This is called sequential task interdependence because the work tasks are performed in a fixed sequence (Figure 5.8).

In long-linked technologies, the sequential nature of task interdependence requires more **planning and scheduling** than does pooled interdependence. Again consider the assembly line as an example. All work tasks must be designed

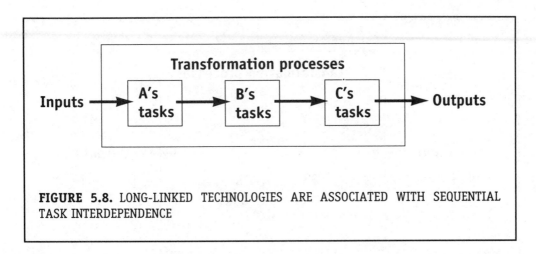

FIGURE 5.8. LONG-LINKED TECHNOLOGIES ARE ASSOCIATED WITH SEQUENTIAL TASK INTERDEPENDENCE

and workers assigned and scheduled to work together in order for the assembly line operation to function properly. Because any break in the line can interrupt production, careful planning of tasks and scheduling of workers is imperative. Of course, in addition to coordination by plans and schedules, rules about coming to work on time and procedures to follow when something on the line has created a problem, are also part of coordinating this type of technology.

The scope of the task within an intensive technology is too large for one individual to perform the transformation alone, so there is need for an exchange of information between workers during the performance of their tasks. Thompson describes this as **reciprocal task interdependence**. In a restaurant, for example, the kitchen staff and the wait staff have reciprocal interdependence because the kitchen is dependent upon the wait staff to provide orders, and the wait staff is dependent upon the kitchen staff to provide meals prepared to the customers' satisfaction. The primary difference between sequential and reciprocal task interdependence is that where long-linked technologies involve work flows that move in one direction only, intensive technologies involve complementary work flows (see Figure 5.9).

To coordinate the tasks central to the operation of an intensive technology requires **mutual adjustment** on the part of the individuals or units involved due to the reciprocal nature of their task interdependence. When intensive technologies involve immediate reciprocal coordination, mutual adjustment takes the extreme form of teamwork. In **teamwork**, work inputs to the transformation process are acted upon simultaneously by members of the work team, rather than passing inputs back and forth as is the case for less intensive forms of reciprocal task interdependence. Take the case of an emergency room surgical operation. The surgeon needs to be able to continuously exchange information with

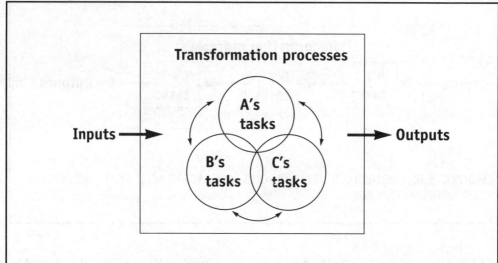

FIGURE 5.9. INTENSIVE TECHNOLOGIES CREATE RECIPROCAL TASK INTERDEPEN-DENCE

A, B, and C are mutually dependent, thus this type of technology generates the highest levels of task interdependence.

the anesthesiologist, assisting doctors and nurses during the performance of the operation. Thus, intensive technologies require joint decision making and either physical co-location or a direct channel of communication such as a satellite link or other instantaneous communication device.

Intensive technology also involves pooled and sequential task interdependence. Mutual adjustment, planning, scheduling, rules and procedures all contribute to the ability of experts to perform when and where their services are required. For example, emergency room doctors have scheduled work hours and rules to follow, ranging from established surgical procedures to wearing a beeper when they are on call. Notice how, as task interdependence increases from pooled to sequential to reciprocal, mechanisms of coordination get added to the organization. Pooled interdependence only requires rules and procedures, but sequential interdependence uses rules, procedures, and scheduling, while reciprocal interdependence uses all these forms of coordination plus mutual adjustment. Such situations are described with a cumulative scale named after Louis Guttman, the sociologist who defined it.[9] In a Guttman scale, each level of a variable implies all the correlates of lower levels of the same variable. Table 5.2 illustrates the Guttman scale for task interdependence and the coordination mechanisms that are related to the three levels of task interdependence discussed by Thompson.

TABLE 5.2. GUTTMAN SCALE OF RELATIONSHIPS BETWEEN TYPES OF TASK INTERDEPENDENCE AND COORDINATION MECHANISMS

Task interdependence	Rules and procedures	Schedules and plans	Mutual adjustment
Pooled	X		
Sequential	X	X	
Reciprocal	X	X	X

Based on: Thompson (1967).

Technology and Information Processing

Jay Galbraith, an American organization theorist primarily interested in the design of organizations, proposes that complexity, uncertainty, and interdependence place demands on an organization to process information in order to coordinate its activities.[10] Galbraith claims that it is demands for communication that shape the structure of the organization. He argues that technical complexity leads to structural complexity, uncertainty promotes organic forms, and interdependence increases demands for coordination, *because* these factors increase the communication load carried by an organization, which, in turn, affects its structural form. Thus, technology is related to social structure through the mediating effects it has on communication.

Notice the similarity between Galbraith's reasoning and Woodward's theory. Just as Woodward identifies technology as a mediating factor in the structure–performance relationship, Galbraith argues communication mediates the relationship between technology and structure (see Figure 5.10). This progressive analysis of finer and finer distinctions and of relationships within relationships is one way that modernist organization theorists develop new theories.

THE SOCIAL CONSTRUCTION OF TECHNOLOGY

A few sociotechnical systems theorists have recently offered a symbolic-interpretive approach to the study of technology which goes by the name **social construction of technology**. These theorists challenge modernist linear models of

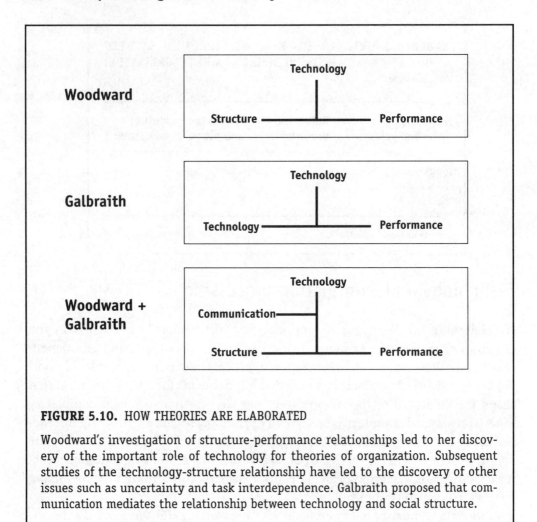

FIGURE 5.10. HOW THEORIES ARE ELABORATED

Woodward's investigation of structure-performance relationships led to her discovery of the important role of technology for theories of organization. Subsequent studies of the technology-structure relationship have led to the discovery of other issues such as uncertainty and task interdependence. Galbraith proposed that communication mediates the relationship between technology and social structure.

technological innovation that depict innovations moving through predictable stages of pure science to applied research, development, production, marketing, and finally to use. In place of these linear models, social constructionists offer detailed examinations of the context surrounding the development of new products and their technologies. You could say that social constructionists turn from the modernist interest in the technology of production to a symbolic-interpretive exploration of the production of technology. In this view, the effects of cultural norms, social relations, and power on knowledge about design and production practices is seen as *socially shaping* products and their technologies. Studies in this tradition attempt to document these social influences and reveal the ways in which technologies are constructed rather than developed as pure applications of scientific findings.

Embedded in the social constructionist view is the belief that the social and the technological mutually constitute one another, for instance, that technological artifacts are socially constructed and interpreted. Thus "both social groups and technologies are generated in the contingent arrangement of the concepts, techniques, and resources brought together in the relevant technological frames. Society itself is being built along with objects and artifacts."[11] Proponents of this perspective argue that there is nothing inevitable about the way that technologies evolve because there is not one best way to design artifacts. Flexibility in how artifacts are designed leaves room for choice based on non-technical criteria such as cultural values, social norms, or power considerations.

Consider the example of Dunlop's innovative air tire, which is provided by social constructionists Trevor Pinch and Wiebe Bijker.[12] The air tire was originally developed as a solution to the vibration problem posed by using hard rubber tires on low-wheeled bicycles (low-wheeled models had been introduced as competitors to the original high-wheeled models). High-wheeled bicycles did not require air tires because their height absorbed much of the shock of uneven roads. Low-wheeled versions, however, gave quite a bumpy ride. But the low-wheeled bicycles, even with the smoother ride provided by air tires, were not readily accepted. For one thing, the air tire was considered by many to be extremely ugly and this lack of aesthetic appeal interfered with its acceptance. But there was another reason for preferring the high-wheeler with its more glamorous hard rubber tires—speed. Bicycle racing had become a popular sport, and when low-wheeled bicycles with air tires began consistently winning races, the air tire earned its place in innovation history. According to Pinch and Bijker, what was required for this innovation to take hold, was that the interpretation of the air tire as a solution to the vibration problem (the interpretation that actually drove the development of the air tire) be reinterpreted as a solution to a speed problem. Without this reinterpretation of the air tire, the air tire would never have enlisted the support of the influential racing cyclists and might well have been abandoned and thus labelled a technological failure.

According to Bijker and John Law, researchers interested in the social construction of technology rely upon two underlying assumptions: that "technologies are shaped by and mirror the complex trade-offs that make up our societies" and that "technologies do not necessarily have to be the way they actually are."[13] Technology is not pure application of science, it is also influenced by social, cultural, economic, and technical relations that precede and shape it, as is indicated by the case of the air tire and its role in the displacement of high-wheelers by low-wheelers in the history of the development of the bicycle.

UNDERSTANDING NEW TECHNOLOGIES

Although theorists who subscribe to the social construction of technology perspective argue that technology influences society as much as society influences
technology, so far their emphasis has been on the latter set of relationships.
Postmodern theorists, however, have picked up the theme of technology's
influence on society, a perspective we will explore in a moment. First, a theory of
new technology will be presented because it provides an entry point for discussing how postmodernism might contribute to organization theory.

Properties of New Technologies

Karl Weick asserts that new technologies made possible by advances in computers and micro-electronics challenge the typologies of modernist organization
theory. He maintains that these new technologies lie on the frontiers of
Woodward's conception of technical complexity and Perrow's concept of non-
routineness. Weick identifies three properties of new technologies, claiming that
what distinguishes them from earlier, less sophisticated, technologies is the
extent to which they consist of stochastic, continuous, and abstract events.[14]

In describing new technologies as **stochastic**, Weick claimed that they perform
in non-determinant ways, mainly due to the dense interactions that arise among
their many components. The result of this complexity is that new technologies
do unexpected things. Thus, they are hard to control and can create incomprehensible failures, such as the Three Mile Island nuclear power plant disaster that
Charles Perrow studied.[15] In his book, *Normal Accidents*, Perrow argues that it was
the simultaneous failure of two fairly minor safety devices embedded in a complex system that misled those involved in their attempts to intervene when the
nuclear reactor began to melt down. The speed with which things went from bad
to worse throughout the system illustrates the effect of an incomprehensible failure due to dense interactions. Although unexpected events also occur with older
technologies (e.g., boilers blow up), new technologies are unique in the sense
that these events cannot be anticipated, will not be repeated, and show up more
or less at random—we can neither learn about them nor from them.

Weick claimed that new technologies are **continuous** in the extent to which
they are automated; the degree of automation places new technologies off the
high end of Woodward's technical complexity scale. New technologies are more
complex than the continuous processes Woodward described in the sense that
they are fully automated rather than merely mechanized or only partially auto-

mated. When systems are fully automated, attention switches from efficiency to reliability because the most important task for operators is to keep the system running. In these systems, efficiency is controlled by equipment settings while operators are charged with seeing that the equipment does not fail to perform.

A related aspect of the continuity of new technologies is that as new problems are encountered and solved, the system is updated and thus the technology is constantly changing. Consider, for example, flexible manufacturing or computerized reservation systems. These systems are regularly updated, not only with new information, but also by alterations to the computer software that controls them. System users are confronted with endless changes in the form of a steady stream of new operating rules and procedures to master. However, learning from these changes is restricted because the focus of system users is so narrow.

Weick argued that, as technical complexity increases, knowledge and labor disappear into machines, therefore new technologies are **abstract**. That is, operators cannot see what they are doing and so must develop and rely on cognitive models of what is going on to understand the processes with which they work. Then, because they are working with symbols of processes as opposed to actual processes, their models expose them to misunderstanding and the possibility of multiple interpretations. When the unexpected occurs, these misunderstandings and multiple interpretations of what is happening create confusion and stress. Weick explains it this way:

New technologies are parallel technologies involving a technology in the head and a technology on the floor. Each is self-contained. Each is coordinated with the other intermittently rather than continuously. Each corrects the other discontinuously. Each can have a sizable effect on the other, and the parallel technologies have a constant amount of mystery that is due to the invisibility of the processes each contains. . . . The gradual decoupling of a mental model of a process from the actual steps that occur in that process allows events to unfold that ramify in their consequences and grow increasingly incomprehensible . . . so that a new technical system and a new set of interactions are created, without any person intending it.[16]

Weick argues that stochastic, continuous, and abstract events associated with new technologies render them substantially more complex and non-routine than was anticipated by Woodward's and Perrow's typologies. Therefore, the original typologies must be updated to reflect the unique demands made by new technologies. Others, however, claim that this is unnecessary because these properties have been part of the concept of technology all along and only appear to be new because they are more concentrated in the new technologies.[17]

Milan Zeleny's definition of high technology as a technology that changes the organizational systems of which it is a part, extends Weick's argument. Zeleny also specifies some of the managerial implications of high technologies. He claims that whereas technology requires the management of performance including concern for productivity improvement, standards and measures, goals and motivation, high technology transforms managers into catalysts for change who encourage and support innovation and self-management through the diffusion of hierarchy and the exercise of organizational and leadership skills.[18]

Postmodernism and New Technology

A critical reading of Zeleny's observation is provided by British organizational researchers Rod Coombs, David Knights, and Hugh Willmott, who equate information technology (IT) with managerial control.[19] These researchers argue that IT is a means to direct thought and action in organization and to discipline members for non-compliance with top management's desires or expectations. They argue that the seeming objectivity of performance data conceals the fact that the categories into which data are collected and from which they are reported impose values on those who work within the control system defined by top management. For example, data reporting the number of patients served per day in a hospital impose a value of speedy processing as opposed to a value for quality of care on the doctors, nurses, and administrators who are pressured by the desire to keep their jobs. The critical view recognizes that non-managerial employees are not powerless, they can resist control via sabotage (e.g., entering false data into the information system), non-responsiveness (e.g., refusing to react to feedback from the system), and even joking (e.g., as a psychological defense against changing their values with respect to patient care). However, the critique emphasizes the alignment between most technology theories and the interests of management, and thus contributes to the postmodern debate about silence and voice.

According to postmodern theorist Jean-François Lyotard, modernism is called into question by the effects of new technology on cognitive and social processes. This is ironic, because modernism is being challenged by what many consider to be its greatest achievement to date—the new technologies that have emerged in the period following World War II. According to this perspective, technology is at the root of radical changes in society. For instance, one of Lyotard's claims is that databases are changing the way in which knowledge is acquired, classified, distributed, and used, and these changes are bringing about radical social transformations of the same magnitude as those brought about by previous technological innovations such as modern transportation systems (e.g., train and later air travel which substantially reduced the effects of spatial distance on social relationships) and the media. Lyotard argues that "the hegemony of computers" brings a shift in emphasis from the ends of action to its means.[20] He further claims that post-industrial capitalism has shifted social values from those of truth and justice to those of efficiency—what he calls technology's cultural contribution. This value shift, Lyotard argues, implies a transition from a concern with what is true, to a concern for the usefulness or market value of knowledge.[21] Knowledge becomes a commodity rather than the hallmark of an educated mind. The difference between the modern and the postmodern, according to Lyotard, is created by the advent of the (near) perfect information that computer technology provides to society. With perfect information, there is no advantage to be gained from obtaining more information, advantage can only come from arranging data in new ways—an ability Lyotard equates with imagination.

The implication of Lyotard's argument for organization theory is that the rhetoric of efficiency that pervades modern organizations is an artifact of new technologies that leads to a redefinition of knowledge (one of the three elements of technology) and thus of technology itself. If the state of perfect information ever obtains (and there are strong arguments on both sides of that assumption), then we can anticipate another significant change: from belief in progress through learning (i.e., obtaining more information) to the adoration of imagination (i.e., the ability to organize information in new ways). One could argue we are already seeing this change in increasing pressure for innovation.

SUMMARY

In the modernist view, an organization is directly dependent on the output of certain technologies for its survival. These are the outputs that permit the organization to obtain further inputs, usually through revenues generated by sales of products and services. If this sequence of input–output is interrupted for very long, the organization will cease to exist because, without a more or less continuous stream of outputs, society will have little use for the organization and will cut off resources and/or withdraw social legitimacy.

Organizations have technologies for transforming inputs into outputs. These technologies consist of physical objects, activities and processes, and knowledge, all of which are brought to bear on raw materials, labor, and capital inputs during a transformation process. The core technology is that set of productive components most directly associated with the transformation process, for example, production and/or assembly in a manufacturing firm, or service delivery in a service organization. Of course, large, diversified organizations often have multiple core technologies, but every form of work has a technology and the technological perspective of the organization sees a system made up of all of these technologies operating together. From a modernist technological perspective, the organization can be imagined as a complex set of interacting and interdependent technologies.

Although modernist theories give us an image of technology, especially core technology, as lying inside the organization while environment is outside, these two concerns of management are closely connected in the modernist perspective. First of all, the knowledge needed to operate a technology is normally produced outside the organization's boundary and imported, except where basic research is done internally in an R & D department. Second, tools and many production processes are imported in the form of hardware, software, and skilled or educated employees. The environment contains the technological ingredients of an organization just as it holds the material resources upon which the organization depends for its survival. These are scattered about in a more or less random fashion until a portion of the environment becomes organized, that is, until resources and technologies are combined so as to provide outputs to satisfy the environment's needs or demands.

A different image of technology is provided by those who adopt the social construction of technology perspective. These theorists rely upon detailed descriptions of the social, cultural, and economic context within which resources and technological innovations become linked. Thus they provide a view of how the organization of society influences the shape of technology and its products and raise the question of how society, in its turn, is shaped by technology. The theme of society being shaped by technology is taken up in postmodern depictions of technology which are only beginning to draw the attention of organization theorists interested in technology.

KEY TERMS

core technology	mediating technology
high technology	intensive technology
service technologies	task variability
technical complexity	task analyzability
unit and small batch production	routine technology
large batch or mass production	craft technology
continuous processing	engineering technology
long-linked technology	non-routine technology

the technological imperative

routineness of work

pooled task interdependence

rules and standard procedures

sequential task interdependence

planning and scheduling

reciprocal task interdependence

mutual adjustment

teamwork

social construction of technology

stochastic

continuous

abstract

ENDNOTES

1. Granovetter (1985).
2. MacKenzie and Wajcman (1985).
3. Zeleny (1990: 17).
4. Ibid. 20.
5. Woodward (1965).
6. Thompson (1967).
7. Perrow (1967, 1986).
8. Pugh, Hickson, Hinings, MacDonald, Turner, and Lupton (1963).
9. Guttman (1944).
10. Galbraith (1973).

11. Bijker and Law (1992: 19).
12. Pinch and Bijker (1987).
13. Bijker and Law (1992: 3).
14. Weick (1990).
15. Perrow (1984).
16. Weick (1990: 17, 33).
17. See, for example, Scott (1990).
18. Zeleny (1990: 20).
19. Coombs, Knights, and Willmott (1992).
20. Lyotard (1979: 4).
21. Ibid. 51.

REFERENCES

Bijker, Wiebe E., and Law, John (1992) (eds.). *Shaping technology/Building society: Studies in sociotechnical change*. Cambridge, Mass.: MIT Press.

Coombs, Rod, Knights, David, and Willmott, Hugh (1992). Culture control and competition: Towards a conceptual framework for the study of information technology in organizations. *Organization Studies*, 13: 51–72.

Galbraith, Jay (1973). *Designing complex organizations*. Reading, Mass.: Addison-Wesley.

Granovetter, Mark (1985). Economic action and social structure: The problem of embeddedness. *American Journal of Sociology*, 91: 481–510.

Guttman, Louis (1944). A basis for scaling qualitative data. *American Sociological Review*, 9: 139–50.

Lyotard, Jean-François (1979). *The postmodern condition: A report on knowledge*. Minneapolis: University of Minnesota Press.

MacKenzie, D., and Wajcman, J. (1985) (eds.). *The social shaping of technology*. Milton Keynes: Open University Press.

Perrow, Charles (1967). A framework for comparative organizational analysis. *American Sociological Review*, 32/2: 194–208.

Perrow, Charles (1984). *Normal accidents: Living with high-risk technologies*. New York: Basic Books.

Perrow, Charles (1986). *Complex organizations: A critical essay* (3rd edition). New York: Random House.

Pinch, Trevor J., and Bijker, Wiebe E. (1987). The social construction of facts and artifacts: Or how the sociology of science and the sociology of technology might benefit each other. In Wiebe E. Bijker, Thomas P. Hughes, and Trevor Pinch (eds.), *The social construction of technological systems: New directions in the sociology and history of technology*. Cambridge, Mass.: MIT Press, 17–50.

Pugh, D. S., Hickson, D. J., Hinings, C. R., MacDonald, K. M., Turner, C., and Lupton, T. (1963). A conceptual scheme for organizational analysis. *Administrative Science Quarterly*, 8: 289–315.

Scott, W. Richard (1990). Technology and structure: An organizational-level perspective. In Paul S. Goodman, Lee S. Sproull, and Associates (eds.), *Technology and organizations*. San Francisco: Jossey-Bass, 109–143.

Thompson, James (1967). *Organizations in action*. New York: McGraw-Hill.

Weick, Karl E. (1990). Technology as equivoque: Sensemaking in New Technologies. In Paul S. Goodman, Lee S. Sproull, and Associates (eds.), *Technology and organizations*. San Francisco: Jossey-Bass, 1–44.

Woodward, Joan (1958). *Management and technology*. London: Her Majesty's Stationery Office.

Woodward, Joan (1965). *Industrial organization: Theory and practice*. London: Oxford University Press.

Zeleny, Milan (1990). High technology management. In H. Noori and R. E. Radford (eds.), *Readings and cases in the management of new technology: An operations perspective*. Englewood Cliffs, NJ: Prentice-Hall, 14–22.

FURTHER READING

Bijker, Wiebe E., Hughes, Thomas P., and Pinch, Trevor (1987) (eds.). *The social construction of technological systems: New directions in the sociology and history of technology*. Cambridge, Mass.: MIT Press.

Perrow, Charles (1984). *Normal accidents: Living with high-risk technologies*. New York: Basic Books.

Thompson, James (1967). *Organizations in action*. New York: McGraw-Hill.

Weick, Karl E. (1990). Technology as equivoque: Sensemaking in New Technologies. In Paul S. Goodman, Lee S. Sproull, and Associates (eds.), *Technology and organizations*. San Francisco: Jossey-Bass.

Woodward, Joan (1965). *Industrial organization: Theory and practice*. London: Oxford University Press.

Zeleny, Milan (1990). High technology management. In H. Noori and R. E. Radford (eds.), *Readings and cases in the management of new technology: An operations perspective*. Englewood Cliffs, NJ: Prentice-Hall, 14–22.

6 Organizational Social Structure

STRUCTURE refers to the relationships among the parts of an organized whole. As such, the concept of structure can be applied to almost anything. For example, a building is a structure of relationships between its foundation, frame, roof, and walls. The human body is also a structure; it consists of relationships between bones, organs, blood, and tissue. Organization theorists are particularly interested in two types of structure—physical and social. Physical structure refers to relationships between the physical elements of an organization such as its buildings and the geographical locations in which it conducts business. In organization theory, social structure refers to relationships among social elements including people, positions, and the organizational units to which they belong (e.g., departments, divisions). In this chapter we discuss organizations as social structures; their physical structures will be the subject of Chapter 8.

In Classical and early modernist organization theory, the relationships which form an organization's social structure were conceived as static or routinized to such an extent that change only occurred when management decreed a redesign of the organization's structure. Open systems theory brought with it ideas about organic growth and development that inspired evolutionary models of growth and change in organizational social structures. Even more dynamic views of social structure are introduced by symbolic-interpretive and postmodern perspectives including structuration theory and ideas about new organizational forms such as network structures and virtual organizations.

In this chapter we will begin with a discussion of differentiation and integration, two related ideas that many organization theorists believe explain how and why organizations take the forms that they do. From there we will move to defining organizational social structures and consider some of the elements and dimensions that comprise the core of Classical and early modernist thinking. Next we move to three dynamic theories of organizational social structure—life-cycle and open systems theories, which derive from modernist perspectives, and structuration theory, a symbolic-interpretive approach. Finally, we turn our attention to the problems of describing, analyzing, and designing organizational social structures. Here we will examine a variety of prototypical structural forms including those associated with the post-industrial organization.

SOCIAL STRUCTURE AS DIFFERENTIATION AND INTEGRATION

Organization theorists often claim that organizations form around tasks that are too large for individuals to perform by themselves. The advantage of organizations over individuals, they explain, comes from pooling different skills and abilities. If some persons take responsibility for one part of a task, while others perform other parts, much can be achieved that would be impossible otherwise. Consider the example of NASA. No one individual would have been capable of a moon landing. This extraordinary achievement was accomplished through the organized efforts not only of scientists, engineers, and astronauts, but also technicians, production workers, maintenance workers, clerical employees, and managers (not to mention organized efforts within the scientific community, the defense industry, and the United States government). Of course, the advantages of organization can be lost if differentiated tasks and workers are not well integrated, as the NASA Challenger disaster of 1986 so painfully made clear.

The concept of **differentiation** used by modernist organization theorists is similar to that of biologists. In biology, differentiation is the process by which differences in function occur, for example, among the cells of a plant or an embryo. Consider the differentiated cells that form a plant. The plant's roots, stem, and leaves each carry out different life sustaining functions: the roots draw nutrients from the soil, the stem carries the nutrients to the leaves, and the leaves conduct photosynthesis which feeds the plant and produces oxygen that is released into the environment. By analogy, you can see differentiation in the activities that organizations perform. Purchasing departments draw raw materials into the system, production departments transform these inputs into outputs, and sales departments transfer outputs to the customer and bring revenues to the firm.

As differentiation continues in an organization, it becomes harder and harder for employees to both perform their primary activities and coordinate what they are doing with the other employees of the organization. For instance, a production engineer may lose touch with purchasing agents who spend much of their time with suppliers. The strain on communication and coordination that grows out of differentiation produces pressure for **integration**. One common way to deal with integration pressures is to create a management group. However, the emergence of a management group is a further differentiation of organizational activities that will require even more integration if the organization continues to grow, thus creating a cycle of differentiation and integration. Differentiated activities can either add up to the realization of intended goals, or they can lead to chaos. The ability to integrate distinguishes chaos from organization.

Stewart Clegg, an Australian organization theorist, recently suggested that differentiation in modern organizations has gone too far, that they are over-differentiated. He claims such organizations need to de-differentiate.[1] **De-differentiation** differs from integration in that integration implies that coordination supplements differentiated activities. De-differentiation means that the organization reverses the very conditions of differentiation that created the need for integration in the first place. In de-differentiation, organizations become more integrated, but not as the result of structural elaboration for purposes of coordination. Rather in de-differentiation, integration is the result of creating an organization that requires less coordination because it is less differentiated. Since traditional approaches to organization place the role of integration in the hands of management, the de-differentiation view implies cutting back on the responsibilities of managers thus establishing self-management as a fundamental condition of organizing. This view is closely aligned with what postmodernists refer to as emancipatory interests. Emancipatory interests focus on undermining the emphasis on control that dominates modernist thinking.

An example of de-differentiation is the team concept in manufacturing in which semi-autonomous groups of workers are given responsibility for a set of tasks; they schedule their time and monitor their own performance and quality. Volvo's Kalmar Plant, where automobiles are assembled start to finish by teams of workers, offers a good example of de-differentiation in manufacturing. Another example is subcontracting, where independent organizations are contractually hired to perform and manage a portion of the organization's activities such as running the restaurants in a hotel, or the concession stands at a national park.

Such challenges to modernist links between notions of integration and management do not undermine the concepts of differentiation and integration. Instead, they suggest the continuing importance of maintaining a balance between the two. They also suggest that we can form a concept of integration that is independent of the notion of hierarchy. This makes it easier to imagine an organization in which integration and coordination are the responsibility of everyone and not just management's concern. Such a view points toward new ideas about organizations as networks of interdependent actors, a view we will

163

return to at the end of the chapter. First, let us consider the Classical and modernist perspectives and some of the history of the development of social structure as a concept within organization theory.

WHAT IS AN ORGANIZATIONAL SOCIAL STRUCTURE?

Max Weber, the famous German sociologist who first published his theory of bureaucracy in the early 1900s, conceived of organizations as social structures (bureaucracies) comprised of a hierarchy of authority, a division of labor, and formal rules and procedures.[2] Weber's conception was highly influential in forging a basic understanding of social structures in organization theory, however, this influence was not keenly felt outside Germany until his works were translated into English in the late 1940s.

Hierarchy of Authority

It may seem natural to think of organization in terms of a hierarchy. Some people believe that hierarchy is a fundamental aspect of life; their evidence is that sexual reproduction and feeding order are organized hierarchically throughout much of the animal kingdom. Organizational hierarchies are seen as an extension of these natural tendencies. To others, hierarchy is a poorly disguised effort to legitimize the unfair distribution of power that enables some individuals and groups to dominate others. Regardless of your personal view on this matter, you will probably recognize hierarchy as a common feature of most modern organizations.

According to Weber, **hierarchy** reflects the distribution of authority among organizational positions. **Authority** grants the position holder certain rights including the right to give direction to others, and the right to punish and reward. These rights are called positional powers because they belong to the position rather than to the position holder. When individuals leave their positions (e.g., through retirement, replacement, or promotion), their authority remains behind to be taken up by the next person who fills the position.

Authority empowers position holders to influence those who are responsible to them; this influence is exercised via downward communication. The hierarchy also defines formal reporting relationships that map out upward communication channels through which management expects information to flow. When each position in an organization is made subordinate to some other position (recall Fayol's scalar principle from Chapter 2), authority and vertical communication combine to permit highly placed individuals to gather information from, and to direct, control, and encourage high performance by all individuals at lower levels in the organization.

In the past, many managers believed that every member of the organization should report to only one person so that each member had one clear path through the hierarchy stretching from themselves to their boss, to their boss's boss, and all the way to the top person in the organization. Fayol called this the unity-of-command principle. Today, dual reporting relationships are more acceptable and lateral (i.e., non-hierarchical) connections are increasingly recognized for the important part they play in integrating an organization's diverse activities.

Division of Labor

If hierarchy specifies the distribution of authority, then the **division of labor** defines the distribution of responsibilities. The organization's task is to perform a set of activities for the environment. Whereas the work activities themselves are usually thought of as part of the technology, the way in which activities are divided up and assigned to different members of the organization is considered to be an element of the social structure called the division of labor.

In 1776 Scottish economist Adam Smith, one of the intellectual forefathers of modern economics, described the division of labor in a pin manufacturing firm:

One man draws out the wire, another straightens it, a third cuts it, a fourth points it, a fifth grinds it at the top for receiving the head; to make the head requires two or three distinct operations; to put it on is a peculiar business, to whiten the pins is another; it is even a trade by itself to put them into the paper; and the important business of making a pin is, in this manner, divided into about eighteen distinct operations.[3]

Although pin-making is now automated and no longer follows the division of labor observed by Smith, the principle of dividing labor remains the same as it was in Smith's time. You can find this principle at work in all organizations. Consider, for instance, the manufacture of automobiles, computers, and airplanes, or the provision of services such as banking, education, and insurance. In all of these examples the work of the organization is divided among employees, each of whom performs only a piece of the whole.

In addition to defining jobs and linking individuals to them, the division of labor concerns the ways that jobs are grouped into organizational units such as

TABLE 6.1. DIMENSIONS OF ORGANIZATIONAL SOCIAL STRUCTURE

Dimension	Typical operational measure
Size	number of employees of the organization
Administrative component	percentage of total number of employees that have administrative responsibilities
Span of control	total number of subordinates over whom a manager has authority
Specialization	number of specialities performed within an organization
Standardization	existence of procedures for regularly recurring events or activities
Formalization	extent to which rules, procedures, and communications are written down
Centralization	concentration of authority to make decisions
Complexity	vertical differentiation–number of hierarchical levels; horizontal differentiation—the number of units within the organization (e.g., departments, divisions)

departments (e.g., purchasing department, production department, marketing department) or divisions (e.g., consumer products, international sales). The term division of *labor* is a bit misleading, since it suggests that only those employees who are below the level of management are subject to this division. In most organizations, the work of managers is also divided and so the term is now used in a broader sense to indicate the division of organizational activity into all sorts of work tasks at various levels in the hierarchy.

Coordination Mechanisms

Although the hierarchy of authority makes a substantial contribution, hierarchy alone is not enough to integrate the many activities defined by the division of labor, especially as the organization grows in size and complexity or copes with high levels of uncertainty or interdependence. Numerous additional mechanisms must be devised to fill the gaps between the coordination provided by hierarchy and that which is demanded by the division of labor. Rules and procedures, schedules, and lateral communication are the most common of these mechanisms.

Rules and procedures specify how decisions should be made and how work processes are to be performed. They contribute to coordination by assuring that desired activities are carried out in an acceptable manner. For example, rules and procedures can be built into forms that workers use to make applications for resources and positions. Such forms help to ensure that decisions are made on the basis of particular types of information and that this information is retained in the corporate record. Another good place to look for rules and procedures is in policy manuals.

Schedules specify the period of time in which activities are to be accomplished. They can also be used to communicate the assignment of individuals to tasks. When activities conducted by different persons must occur in a sequence, such as in the construction of a building or the work done on an assembly line, schedules are a key element in coordination.

Communication across positions and units formed by the division of labor is essential to the coordination of organizational activities. Vertical communication is associated with the hierarchy and so has already been described as part of the social structure, but you should also consider **lateral communication**. When lateral communication within an organization becomes patterned through repetition, you will recognize it in such forms as liaison roles, committees, task forces, and project and management teams.

Dimensions of Organizational Social Structure

In the early days of modernist organization theory, around the late 1950s and early 1960s, theorists were eager to measure aspects of the social structure of organizations in the hope of finding a best way of organizing. They were looking for a means to ensure high levels of organizational performance and thought that by examining statistical relationships between characteristics of structure and performance they could arrive at a formula for success. Empirical research revealed, however, that what works for one organization may or may not work for others. These findings led to contingency theory, which claims that the degree of relationship between two variables, such as structure and performance, varies with other aspects of the organization such as its technology and environment.

In Chapter 3, I presented the distinction between mechanistic and organic organizations in relationship with the environment as an example of contingency reasoning. The contingency argument in this case is that in stable environments, mechanistic organizations will outperform organic organizations, while in rapidly changing environments the organic organization will be more successful. That is, the success of a particular form of organization, mechanistic or organic in this example, is contingent upon the nature of the environment in which it operates. As we saw in Chapter 5, similar arguments were made with respect to technology following Woodward's discovery that different social structures were related to high performance depending upon the firm's core technology type.

Social structure has been measured using a wide variety of variables (see Table 6.1). Of the Classical dimensions, three have consistently appeared in contingency arguments and are therefore particularly revealing of modernist organization theorizing today: complexity, centralization, and formalization.[4]

Structural complexity can be a response to perceived environmental complexity or it can result from differentiation in the technical core. Complexity refers to both horizontal and vertical differentiation. Horizontal differentiation is measured by counting the number of different units (e.g., departments) within the organization. Vertical differentiation is measured as the number of levels from the highest position in the organization to the lowest. Of course size is a major factor in complexity; in general, the bigger the organization the more complex it is, however, two organizations of the same size will not necessarily be equally complex.

One of the findings resulting from studies of complexity is the relationship between complexity and communication.[5] The more complex the organization in terms of both horizontal and vertical differentiation, the greater the need for communication. However, complexity is also linked to communication difficulties including failure to send or receive needed information, information distortion, and loss of information control by top management.

Centralization addresses the question of the level in the organization at which decisions are taken. In a centralized organization, final choices are made almost exclusively at high levels and unquestioning acceptance of top-level decisions is expected. As a result, there tends to be a minimum of participation from lower level members in a centralized organization. In a decentralized organization, decisions are taken by the individuals who are closest to the situation. Decentralized organizations rely on the participation of many members of the organization in decision-making processes.

One difficulty in measuring centralization results from the different kinds of decisions that are taken in organizations. For example, an organization may be highly decentralized with respect to work-related decisions, but highly centralized with respect to strategic decisions.[6] In universities, for instance, decisions about course offerings, new faculty hires, and the distribution of travel funds are taken in the academic departments, and thus you would consider them to be decentralized decisions. Decisions about university fundraising campaigns or charting new directions for university growth and development are centralized, since these are taken at the strategic level of the university president and the board of trustees.

Studies of centralization show that the amount of communication, involvement, and satisfaction tends to be higher in decentralized firms, but coordination and control are more difficult to accomplish. Centralized organizations are quicker to respond to the dictates of higher authority because of the relative efficiency of communication compared with decentralized structures. However, when centralized organizations are large, decision bottlenecks can undermine organizational performance by slowing organizational response to environmental pressure.

Formalization involves the extent to which explicit rules, regulations, policies, and procedures govern organizational activities. For example, indicators of formalization in an organization include: written policies, job descriptions, procedures manuals, organization charts, management systems such as MBO (Management by Objectives), technical systems such as PERT (program evaluation review techniques), and official lists of rules and regulations. A lack of formalization is usually referred to as informality, a term that denotes flexibility and spontaneity. Formalization tends to reduce the amount of discretion employees have in performing their work activities while increasing the sense of control management maintains over its employees. These conditions lead to the feeling of impersonality that is often associated with formalized organizations.

Studies suggest that formalization tends to discourage innovation and leads to a reduction in communication within organizations.[7] Most studies of large organizations indicate a negative relationship between formalization and centralization. In these cases, decentralized organizations are more likely to be formalized than are centralized organizations,[8] a surprising relationship that will be explained next.

Mechanistic, Organic, and Bureaucratic Organizations

One interesting application of the structural dimensions of complexity, formalization and centralization involves a comparison of mechanistic, organic, and bureaucratic forms of organization. These structural forms can be defined with respect to the three classic dimensions as shown in Table 6.2.

Mechanistic forms of organization are characterized by high levels of complexity, formalization, and centralization. In mechanistic organizations, labor is divided and subdivided into many highly specialized tasks (high complexity); workers are granted limited discretion in performing their tasks and rules and procedures are carefully defined (high formalization); and there is limited participation in decision making which tends to be conducted at the highest levels of management (high centralization).

Organic forms are characterized as the opposite of mechanistic forms.

TABLE 6.2. A COMPARISON OF MECHANISTIC, ORGANIC, AND BUREAUCRATIC ORGANIZATIONS

	Complexity	Formalization	Centralization
Organic	low	low	low
Mechanistic	high	high	high
Bureaucratic	high	high	low

Mechanistic organizations are complex, formal, and centralized, while organic organizations are relatively simple, informal, and decentralized. Compared with mechanistic organizations, employees in organic organizations, such as design firms or research labs, tend to be more generalist in their orientation (reflecting lower structural complexity); are granted greater discretion in performing their tasks (lower formalization); and decision making is pushed down to lower levels of the hierarchy (decentralization).

You may think that mechanistic and bureaucratic are two words for the same thing. Experience with bureaucracies tends to confirm this belief because the idea of an unfeeling machine fits with the images of red tape and "the runaround" that are associated with bureaucracy. Notice, however, that there is one feature of bureaucracies that distinguishes them from mechanistic organizations—the bureaucracy is *de*centralized whereas the mechanistic organization is centralized.[9] The trick to resolving the decentralization puzzle is to understand what it means to say that a bureaucracy is simultaneously highly formalized *and* decentralized. In a bureaucracy, decisions are pushed to low levels of the organization, but there are strict rules and procedures that prevent much discretion in the way that decentralized decisions are made. Thus, like mechanistic organizations, the bureaucracy remains highly controlled even though it is decentralized. Let's look at bureaucracy more closely.

BUREAUCRACY

Max Weber advanced the concept of **bureaucracy** and provided us with an elaborate definition.[10] The central characteristics of bureaucracies are shown in Table 6.3. You should understand that when Weber developed the idea of bureaucracy he saw it as an alternative to the organizational practices that were dominant during an earlier period of history. Furthermore, to really appreciate the concept of bureaucracy it is important to recognize the difference between Weber's ideal bureaucracy and the organizational reality with which we are familiar today. For Weber, bureaucracy was not the ponderous, frustrating bastion of mediocre public service that some people associate with this concept, but was a rationalized, moral alternative to the common practice of nepotism and the abuses of power that were rampant in the feudal, pre-industrial world from which the modern organization emerged.

TABLE 6.3. CHARACTERISTICS OF WEBER'S IDEAL BUREAUCRACY

- A fixed division of labor
- A clearly defined hierarchy of offices, each with its own sphere of competence
- Candidates for offices are selected on the basis of technical qualifications and are appointed rather than elected
- Officials are remunerated by fixed salaries paid in money
- The office is the primary occupation of the office holder and constitutes a career
- Promotion is granted according to seniority or achievement and is dependent upon the judgment of superiors
- Official work is to be separated from ownership of the means of administration
- A set of general rules governing the performance of offices. Strict discipline and control in the conduct of the office is expected

---

Source: Parsons (1947); Scott (1992).

Weber conceived of bureaucracy as an ideal-type. His use of the term "ideal" is probably not what you would expect. Weber used ideal in the sense of ideas rather than objects, and in his original discussion of ideal types, he makes reference to similar notions in other academic disciplines, such as ideal gases in physics, or ideal competition in economics. Notice that ideal does not equate with goodness or virtue. In Weber's sense of the term there could also be ideal crimes or ideal diseases. Ideals provide a basis for theorizing, but are not expected to exist in the world around us. In his terms, an ideal is an abstract image, something that can only be known through imagination. The image that Weber formulated was of bureaucracy as a system for turning employees of quite average ability into rational decision makers serving their clients and constituencies with impartiality and efficiency. The bureaucratic form promised reliability in decision making, merit-based selection and promotion, and the impersonal (and, therefore, fair) application of rules.

Core Concepts of Organization Theory

Since Weber's time we have learned much about the negative face of bureaucracy, its tendency to over-rationalize decision making and decision makers to the point of turning people into unfeeling and unthinking automatons. These tendencies have been satirized in Terry Gilliam's film *Brazil* and Joseph Heller's novel *Catch 22*. As was discussed in Chapter 2, Weber himself called attention to the likelihood that bureaucracy would become an "iron cage." But when organizations are large and operate routine technologies in fairly stable environments, bureaucracy apparently offers benefits enough—we continue to create and maintain bureaucracy in spite of widespread distaste for the working conditions it fosters and the levels of service it provides. Today bureaucratic features are characteristic of most governments, almost every university, the Catholic Church, and large business organizations such as CIBA-GEIGY, IBM, and General Motors.

There are several situations in which bureaucracy is decidedly inappropriate. Small organizations do not need bureaucracy. Their size makes direct supervision and centralized decision making easy and natural. Formal mechanisms of control are overkill in these situations; informal controls are cheap and since they are more satisfying for members of the organization, bureaucracy is inappropriate. Non-routine technologies and unstable environments also undermine the effectiveness of bureaucratic organization. The bureaucracy is not set up to accommodate constant changes, since change requires rewriting policies and rules and disseminating the revisions to decision makers who must then remember the new rules or constantly refer to manuals and memos. Whenever flexibility is a primary consideration in work, bureaucracy is a hindrance.

Organizations that employ large numbers of professionals will not perform well if they become overly bureaucratic. Professionals are highly trained and socialized to accept high standards of performance so that rules and procedures are redundant and often offensive to them. An organization will not get full value from its professional employees if it insists that they do only what they are told. Professionals hired for their knowledge and expertise must have the discretion to use their skills and training, or much of their value will be wasted. Such waste is inefficient from the point of view of the organization, and frustrating from the perspective of the employee. The recent professionalization of management in both private and public sectors through higher education programs (e.g., the MBA and MPA degrees) has created interesting tensions in some of the largest bureaucracies. As these newly professionalized employees carry their professional values into their organizations, bureaucratic characteristics come into conflict with professionalism and in some cases are starting to be replaced by more flexible ways of doing things (e.g., the great wave of privatization occurring in Britain and throughout Europe).

The key to understanding bureaucracy lies in recognizing why bureaucratic characteristics arise in the first place. To address this question, we need to consider dynamic models of social structure. The dynamic perspective encourages us to see bureaucracy, not so much as a type of social structure, but as a developmental stage through which organizations pass.

DYNAMIC MODELS OF SOCIAL STRUCTURE

Classical and many modernist approaches to social structure fall into the category of static rather than dynamic models, that is, they give the impression that social structure stays more or less constant over a fairly long period of time. Static models focus on defining the essential features of stable phenomena, and attempt to isolate the critical conditions necessary to predict their appearance or success. Dynamic models, on the other hand, focus on how a phenomenon changes over time and with changing circumstances.

Dynamic models of organizational social structure typically take one of two forms. One is a historical, often evolutionary, approach geared to explaining how an organization develops over a fairly long stretch of time. Evolutionary and historical perspectives often see organizational development in terms of a series or progression of static states which are described as phases or stages. The other type of dynamic model is aimed at discovering the dynamics of change as these occur in the course of everyday life in organizations. In these views, the seeming stability of social structure is undermined by a view of the numerous interactions that shape and transform social structure on a continuous basis. Evolutionary or stage models tend to stay within the boundaries of the modernist approach, while everyday interaction views are more typical of symbolic-interpretive perspectives.

The evolutionary perspective is represented by Larry Greiner's highly popular lifecycle theory that depicts organizational growth as a sequence of evolutionary periods punctuated by revolutionary events. The historical view will be illustrated using an open systems model that portrays social structure as emerging from organizational responses to environmental and technical pressures. Finally, Anthony Giddens's structuration theory and his conception of the duality of structures will offer an opportunity to examine social structure as the product of ongoing interactions.

The Organizational Lifecycle

American organization theorist Larry Greiner describes organizations as if they, like humans, have a lifecycle that moves through phases or stages of

Core Concepts of Organization Theory

development.[11] Just as a child passes through infancy and childhood to adolescence and maturity, so, according to Greiner, an organization passes through five stages that he labelled entrepreneurial, collectivity, delegation, formalization, and collaboration (see Figure 6.1). In each stage of the lifecycle the organization is dominated by a different focus, and each phase ends with a crisis that threatens organizational survival. When a crisis is successfully met, the organization passes into its next developmental stage.

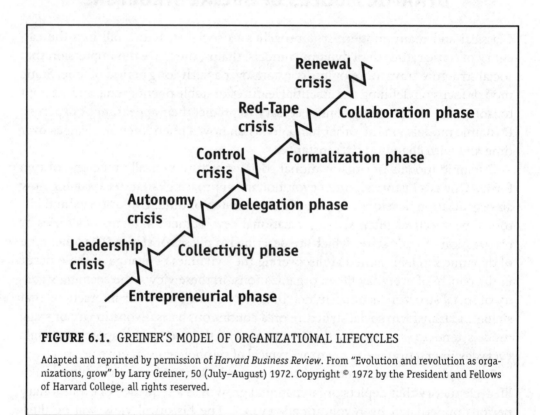

FIGURE 6.1. GREINER'S MODEL OF ORGANIZATIONAL LIFECYCLES

Adapted and reprinted by permission of *Harvard Business Review*. From "Evolution and revolution as organizations, grow" by Larry Greiner, 50 (July–August) 1972. Copyright © 1972 by the President and Fellows of Harvard College, all rights reserved.

In the **entrepreneurial phase**, the organization is embroiled in creating and selling its product. This phase usually takes place in a small setting in which every member of the organization is familiar with what the other members are doing. The entrepreneur can easily control most activities personally and this personal contact makes it easy for other employees to sense what is expected of them and to receive direct feedback and close supervision. If successful (and remember, the majority of organizations fail at this early stage), the entrepreneurial organization will find itself in need of professional management. Entrepreneurs are usually "idea people" or technical experts rather than orga-

174

nizers, and further organizational development often necessitates bringing management skills in from outside the organization, although sometimes it is developed from within.

It often takes a crisis to convince the entrepreneur that professional management is required, since the early successes that allowed the organization to survive and prosper will also give the entrepreneur the impression that things are fine the way they are. However, sooner or later the organization becomes too complex for a single individual to monitor everything that is going on. This condition can be compounded by an entrepreneur's distaste for management activities. According to Greiner, the result of this early differentiation, coupled with inadequate attention to integration, throws the organization into a **leadership crisis**. Successful resolution of the crisis places the organization in a new phase of development called the collectivity phase.

The introduction of the organization's first professional management usually brings the organization through the leadership crisis and provides it with centralized decision making and a focus on goals. The primary concern of the new management is to give the organization a sense of direction and to provide a collective sense of integration among the differentiated groups now operating within the organization. In the **collectivity phase**, concern for establishing clear goals and routines takes over the manufacturing and marketing focus of the entrepreneurial phase. In this phase the organization's complexity grows through differentiation until, once again, the organization becomes too much for the existing social structure and its management to handle. This time the crisis occurs because the decision-making process becomes overloaded—the result of too much centralization.

During the collectivity phase centralization gives the organization its sense of a clear direction because decisions are coordinated by a set of well-integrated decision makers (i.e., the new professional management). However, at some point even the most effective managers of a centralized social structure cannot keep pace with the decisions required by an ever more elaborated and differentiated organization. Thus, sooner or later, centralized decision making becomes a bottleneck for action, and decisions must be pushed down the hierarchy if the organization is to continue functioning. Greiner calls this the **crisis of autonomy**. The reason this situation produces a crisis is that most managers find it difficult to relinquish control over formerly centralized decisions. It is typical, therefore, for management to wait overlong in initiating decentralization and this hesitation is what provokes the crisis.

The solution to the autonomy crisis is delegation, and the next phase of the organizational lifecycle is described as the **delegation phase**. However, once delegation is initiated, usually via decentralization of decision making, the need for integration arises. This need grows steadily until a **crisis of control** occurs. The response to loss of control is usually to create formal rules and procedures to ensure that decisions are made in the way that management would make them if they could do so themselves. This is the point at which bureaucracy appears; Greiner calls it the formalization phase.

During the **formalization phase**, the organization continues to grow and differentiate by adding more and more complex control mechanisms in an attempt to integrate the increasingly diverse activities of the organization through planning, accounting and information systems, and formal review procedures. The tendency to control through bureaucratic means, eventually leads to what Greiner terms the **crisis of red tape**. The red-tape crisis is what has given bureaucracy a bad name. It is not, however, that bureaucracy is the villain, but rather that in this situation management overindulges and ends up with too much of a good thing. Attempts to apply formal rules and procedures in a universal and impersonal manner create an organizational environment that becomes not only ineffective, but increasingly distasteful to workers. Things will generally worsen when management's first response to the breakdown of bureaucratic controls is to implement even more controls. The problem reaches crisis proportions when employees either cannot figure out how to make the system of rules and procedures work, or when they rebel against it.

If the organization is to emerge from the red-tape crisis, it will generally proceed to a phase of development that Greiner calls the **collaboration phase**. During this phase the organization uses teamwork as a means of re-personalizing the organization by distributing the now over-differentiated tasks into more recognizable chunks and assigning shared responsibility for them to groups of individuals in ways that make work once again comprehensible. What was too complex for rule-making to regulate can be reorganized into smaller units managed from within as teams. A greater focus on trust and collaboration is often required in these circumstances.

The collaboration phase of organizational development requires a qualitative change in organizational form as well as in the integration skills and leadership styles demanded of managers. Instead of the former emphasis on controlling the organization, top management must shift its concern to constantly regenerating motivations to work and to stay organized. However, if at some point the management fails to provide regeneration, the organization will undergo a **crisis of renewal** marked by what in humans would be described as lethargy. The primary symptom of this crisis is employees and managers who suffer from burnout and other forms of psychological fatigue due to the strains associated with temporary assignments, dual authority, and continuous experimentation. According to Greiner, the crisis of renewal will either lead to a new form of organization (perhaps the sort Clegg's de-differentiation idea describes, or those of post-industrialism), or to **decline** and perhaps death.

Greiner uses his theory to emphasize the point that every stage of an organization's development contains the seeds of its next crisis. This is because the arrangements and leadership strategies that are adaptive for one stage in the life-cycle will be seen as maladaptive when the organization grows more complex. In growing organizations, old structural arrangements and leadership styles are replaced by new patterns and leaders throughout the life of an organization.

Greiner's model has been extremely popular, but his emphasis on leadership obscures some important information about how the social structure of an organization develops. A model that focuses more directly on social structural development has been offered by Daniel Katz and Robert Kahn, two American social psychologists often credited with introducing the open systems perspective into organization theory.

An Open Systems Model of the Development of Social Structures

Katz and Kahn's open system model encourages a historical view of social structure.[12] In this view, structure first develops out of technical core needs, and later from internal integration pressures, in combination with the demands from the environment. At first, a primitive organization emerges from cooperation between individuals who wish to pool their efforts to achieve a common goal, such as bringing a new product to market. This primitive organization has not actually got a structure in the technical sense of the term because the cooperative effort is more the result of individual motivation than it is an organizational achievement. However, if the primitive organization is going to survive beyond its initial project, it will develop an elaborate social structure and become an organization in the usual sense of the word. This development from primitive to fully elaborated organization will occur in several stages, each of which involves differentiation and integration. Katz and Kahn's model describes these stages.

In the first stage, activities such as purchasing and marketing are structurally differentiated from **core production tasks**. This initial differentiation is a natural extension of the primitive production process which also required procurement and disposal processes, but on such a restricted scale as to be easily accomplished by members of the production core. This stage of differentiation provides the organization with buffering capacity in the sense that it permits the production core employees to focus all their attention on transforming raw materials into

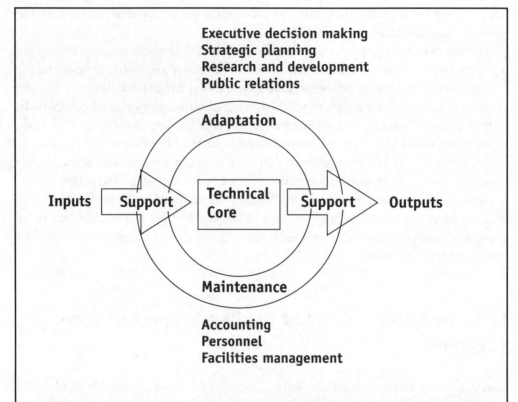

Executive decision making
Strategic planning
Research and development
Public relations

Adaptation

Inputs   Support   Technical Core   Support   Outputs

Maintenance

Accounting
Personnel
Facilities management

FIGURE 6.2. KATZ AND KAHN DESCRIBE THE DEVELOPMENT OF SOCIAL STRUCTURE IN RELATION TO THE NEEDS OF THE TECHNICAL CORE AND DEMANDS OF THE ENVIRONMENT

According to their historical view, a primitive technical core is first elaborated with support structures, then maintenance structures appear, and finally adaptive structures are added. *Based on*: Katz and Kahn (1966).

products. Meanwhile, other individuals specialize in the buffering tasks of purchasing raw materials to feed the transformation process and transferring the organization's products to its environment so that new inputs can be acquired (see Figure 6.2). Katz and Kahn call these **support activities**.

Once the initial differentiation of activities is underway, pressures to integrate begin to appear. In elaborating itself to ensure continuous input of raw material, and production and sale of output, the organization produces three different pockets of activity that can lose track of one another. The three functions of purchasing, production, and sales must be aligned, so that the correct levels of raw materials are brought into the organization and so that sales balance with scheduled production. This demands integration which is usually provided by a manager who oversees purchasing orders and production schedules while taking sales projections into account.

At this point in the development of the social structure, an organization has usually survived long enough that it requires maintenance—employees quit and must be replaced and trained, bookkeeping tasks expand to include corporate tax considerations and financial planning, expanding physical facilities require regular upkeep and modification, and the community may begin making inquiries about the organization and demands regarding its community involvement. It now becomes necessary to supplement core production, purchasing, and sales activities with **maintenance tasks** such as accounting, personnel, facilities management, and public relations.

Maintenance tasks help to preserve the organization in a steady state of readiness to perform, while the core technology actually does the performing. Because the activities of the maintenance group are not highly interdependent with those of purchasing, production, and sales, the maintenance function can be performed with considerable independence of the core technology. This represents further differentiation of the social structure of the organization which, in turn, demands more integration. The addition of managers to achieve this integration is typical, but now, with multiple managers, a new level of management emerges in the form of the manager who oversees the other managers. Thus, integration designed to overcome the ill-effects of differentiation, breeds further differentiation, including hierarchy.

If the organization survives the early stages of development described above, it will probably exist long enough to encounter some change in the environment and its demands for the organization's product. Such changes create problems for the organization, such as predicting what amounts of output will be sold and, thus, what levels of raw material need to be ordered and how much product should be produced. Mistakes in scheduling production runs will be acutely felt as both over- or undersupply of customers' demand can threaten the firm's cash flow position as well as its reputation. In order to minimize these problems, another elaboration of social structure occurs which introduces the adaptive function into the social structure.

The **adaptive function** is responsible for attending to changes in the environment and for interpreting the meaning of the changes for the rest of the organization. The earliest manifestation of the adaptive function is executive decision making, which in one form or another exists from the beginning. However, other, more specialized, adaptive functions emerge over a longer period of time, including strategic planning, economic forecasting, market research, research and development, tax planning, legal advising, and lobbying.

Structuration Theory

Organizations bring people into regular interaction with one another. Structuration theory considers these repeated interactions to be the foundation of social structure. For instance, a boss may regularly ask a subordinate for certain information and this type of exchange will become a routine feature of their relationship. Similarly, employees whose desks or offices are located side-by-side may exchange greetings and then remarks, and finally form a friendship. Such repeated interactions give you the sense that structure is solid and stable. But actually, social structures are highly dynamic and open to many small changes because they depend on the daily reproduction of the interaction patterns that constitute them. To a large extent, the degree of stability of a particular structure depends upon the extent to which interactions become a matter of habit or routine.

If interaction patterns are disrupted or changed, then the social structure is opened to change. We can see the importance of understanding the interaction view of structure in the example of a strategic reorganization. If top management decides to reorganize, their success will ultimately depend upon individuals changing their daily patterns of interaction. Without this change, old patterns of relationship will be maintained and the intended reorganization will not be achieved. Even though changes in organization charts, position titles and unit affiliations may make it seem as though a reorganization has taken place, no change will occur unless and until changes are made at the level of everyday interactions.

When interactions occur regularly, social structure becomes more apparent to us. However, non-repetitive interactions and even non-interaction among particular groups or individuals also contribute to the social structure of an organization. Non-interactions create gaps in the social structure. Because we tend to think of social structure more easily if we focus on the well-established relationships rather than their absence, the idea of social structure gives us an image of the organization as those interactions that have stabilized to the extent that we have come to expect them to recur. Nonetheless, social structure is the product of both interaction patterns and patterns of non-interaction.

In British social theorist Anthony Giddens's perspective,[13] the traditional view of social structure as a constraint on interaction is expanded by the recognition that interaction creates the structure of constraint to which it is subjected. The view is a bit like M. C. Echer's famous image of two hands drawing each other. According to the structuration view, structure is made by interacting individuals whose activities are constrained by structure even as they form the patterns that we then recognize as structure. This idea is called the duality of structure.

The **duality of structure** argument states that social structures constrain the choices that humans make about their activities, but at the same time social structures are created by the activities that they constrain. Furthermore, structures do not merely constrain. They enable interaction. Structuration theory emphasizes the minute changes and the ever-present dynamics that occur within social structures. Social structure is not seen as a fixed and immovable object, but as a delicate cooperative moment of tentative and everchanging interactivity sustained by the complicity of the individuals involved at particular places and specific moments in time.

Giddens's work promises to revolutionize conceptions of social structure in organization theory. Its primary influence comes from turning our attention away from an understanding of social structure as a system for defining and controlling interaction and social relationships, and toward interest in how the everyday practices in which organizational members participate construct the very rules of organizing that they follow. What is taken for granted as an inflexible system is really a dynamic condition whose seeming stability is the result of the unexamined assumption that it is stable. Structuration theory examines assumptions of structural stability and reveals the underlying dynamics by which the organization is sustained in a particular structural form. Giddens's theory is not fully formulated at the organizational level of analysis as yet, and only a small number of empirical studies using his perspective have been published.[14] However, it is clear that this theory will have an important influence within organization theory in the years to come.

DESCRIBING, ANALYZING, AND DESIGNING THE ORGANIZATIONAL SOCIAL STRUCTURE

Social structure cannot be avoided; if you do not design your organization around a social structure, one will emerge from the work activities and associations of people within the organization. Analyzing a social structure usually begins by determining the basis for differentiation of work activities, which also indicates the major challenges of integrating the units, positions, and people that comprise the organization.

Organization charts are frequently used by organization theorists and managers to get a quick overview of a social structure (Figure 6.3). Such charts provide a fairly clear representation of an organization's hierarchy of authority and a general idea of its division of labor. But, if it is to be a useful descriptive or analytical tool, the chart must be an up-to-date map of the actual structure rather than a history of past relationships or a reflection of stakeholders' expectations. The organization charts of some organizations do not live up to this standard for two reasons: (1) change so quickly outdates the charts that they are never accurate for very long, or (2) conflict and jealousy over relative positioning leads top management to either keep the charts a secret or not keep them at all. In these cases you will have to create your own chart from information you collect by interviewing employees and managers and observing work activity throughout the organization.

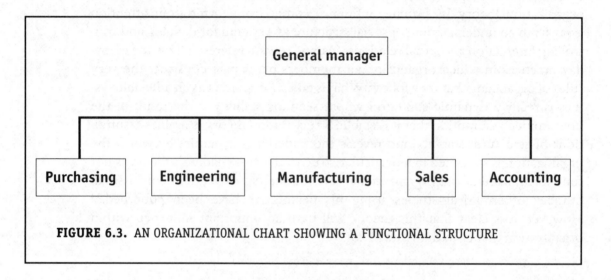

FIGURE 6.3. AN ORGANIZATIONAL CHART SHOWING A FUNCTIONAL STRUCTURE

You should be aware that the organization chart does *not* give much information about coordination mechanisms, informal relationships, or the distribution of power that flows outside of the formal hierarchy of authority. These aspects of social structure are revealed by observation and interview. Be certain to attend not only to interactions, but also to evidence that some units have little or no contact at all.

Grouping people, positions, and units in one way means that some relationships are given an advantage over others. This is because differentiation into groups within an organization sets up natural boundaries that affect communication and coordination. Within the group, communication and coordination are generally supported and encouraged by the close relationships and frequent interactions among group members, while a lack of relationships and interactions will create barriers to communication and coordination between groups.

Ideally, the function of social structure is to guide the attention of employees to the differentiated activities for which they are responsible in a manner that promotes ease of integration of all the activities of the organization. But careful analysis of social structure frequently reveals instances where this is not the case. Every social structure has conflicts and contradictions built into it which result from the practical impossibility of perfectly integrating a differentiated organization. Conflict and contradiction should not automatically be interpreted as a bad thing, however, because these features of organizations sometimes function in ways that allow an imperfect social structure to work in spite of its imperfections. We will examine these issues more thoroughly in Chapter 10 when we discuss organizational conflict and contradiction.

The concept of design as it is applied in organization theory has a tendency to give the false impression that social structures can be erected and then left alone until they need repair or replacement. Symbolic-interpretive perspectives, such as Giddens's structuration theory, mitigate such simplistic views by reminding us that social structures are in a constant state of flux.

Simple Structure

As soon as there are two people involved in an enterprise, a relationship of some sort is implied. Structure is defined by relationships, so even the simplest organizations have social structures. However, extremely small and/or highly organic (flexible, dynamic) organizations often appear to have little if any structure. These cases are classified as **simple structures**.

The simple structure is a set of completely flexible relationships that has low levels of complexity resulting from limited differentiation. The members of such an organization can easily carry the organization chart around in their heads so formalization is not required. Attention to tasks is determined by management decree or by mutual agreement and is usually open to direct and informal coordination and supervision. Simple structures are characteristic of newly formed organizations (e.g., an entrepreneurial venture) or permanently small organizations (e.g., a traditional, one-dentist dental office) but also occur within some units of larger organizations such as prototype laboratories or design teams.

Functional Structure

Organizations that grow too complex to be administered through a simple structure usually adopt the functional structure as a means of coping with the increased demands of differentiation. The **functional structure** is so called because it groups activities according to a logic of similarity in work functions produced by interdependent tasks and common goals. For instance, the functions of a typical manufacturing organization include production, sales, purchasing, personnel (or human resource management), accounting, and engineering, and may also include finance, marketing, research and development, public relations, and facilities management (Figure 6.3).

The functional structure is efficient in the sense that there is limited duplication of effort. This design is intended to maximize economies of scale from specialization. The logic of these organizations is highly transparent in that it is easy for employees to recognize the similarity between their functions and the functions served by those closest to them in the social structure. The functional structure also gives the top manager in the organization tight control in the sense that this individual is the only person whose position grants them the big picture with respect to what everyone else is doing in the organization.

The tight control that is offered by the functional structure, however, can be one of its greatest shortcomings. As the only person with a general perspective, should the top position suddenly be vacated, no other managers in the organization are well-prepared to take over. Another drawback is that the top manager can easily become overburdened by centralized decision making as the organization grows.

Multi-Divisional Structure

In developmental terms, the organization that outgrows a functional structure will often turn to the multi-divisional form as a means to alleviate overburdened centralized decision makers. The **multi-divisional structure** is essentially a set of separate functional structures that reports to a headquarters staff (see Figure 6.4). Each functional structure is responsible for managing its day-to-day internal operations, while the headquarters staff are primarily responsible for monitoring and managing the organization's relationship with its environment and for formulating strategy.

The multi-divisional form (or M-form, for short) groups people, positions, and units in one of three ways, either by similarities in production processes (or products), customer type, or geographical region of activity. For example, America's General Motors is divisionalized on the basis of its products—Chevrolet Division, Cadillac Division, etc. Banks, on the other hand, are more likely to differentiate their activities in terms of geographical regions (sections of a city or state, or by nations if the bank operates internationally). Customer-based divisions separate their activities according to the types of customer served such as consumer,

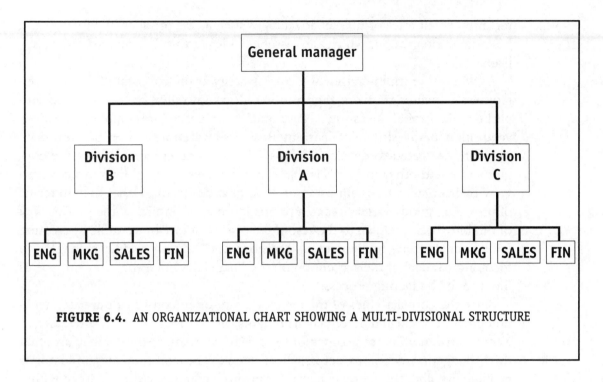

FIGURE 6.4. AN ORGANIZATIONAL CHART SHOWING A MULTI-DIVISIONAL STRUCTURE

industrial, and government. For instance, in the U.S., large defense contractors generally keep their business with the government completely separate from activities that do not involve government contracts.

When the multi-divisional form is created out of a functional structure, the first move is to construct several small functional organizations from the larger one. Each of the smaller organizations operates as a separate functional organization with one main difference, because of the interdependence between the divisions, a higher level of coordination is required that is not needed by the purely functional structure. This additional level of coordination is provided by the headquarters staff and executive level of the hierarchy. The corporate office is typically responsible for overall financial control of the divisions and the long-range strategic development of the firm, while the divisional managements have responsibility for operating decisions such as production scheduling, sales, and marketing.

Sometimes companies operate divisions in different industries rather than just divisionalizing products within an industry. Such organizations are known as **conglomerates** or holding companies. Conglomerates are usually formed by merger or acquisition of other organizations, although not all mergers and acquisitions result in conglomerates. The reasons for forming a conglomerate are generally financial, involving investment opportunities rather than concern for technical economies or market advantages such as are produced by vertical and horizontal integration, which can also be achieved through merger or acquisition.

As with other multi-divisional forms, strategy at the corporate level of a conglomerate focuses on managing resource flows into divisions which is accomplished via capital investment and budgeting procedures and by creation, acquisition, or divestment of divisions. Business-level strategy and operating decisions are delegated to divisional heads. The main difference between the conglomerate and other M-forms is that top executives of conglomerates come to view their organizations almost entirely in financial terms, rather than in terms of providing goods or services to a particular market or environment. This way of thinking trickles down to the rest of the organization, for example by creating enormous concern for budgeting decisions and causing middle managers to focus a great deal of their attention on the financial reports that they provide as input to the budgeting process.[15]

Since the core activities of the conglomerate often consist of unrelated technologies operating in different environments, all information must be reduced to a common denominator in order for top executives to make the comparisons that drive budgeting decisions across all divisions. The common denominator is profitability, and, therefore, concern for profit becomes the driving force within the organization.

Most if not all outcomes within the divisions of a conglomerate depend upon decisions concerning how profitability is to be calculated, and arguments over the calculation of profits abound. For example, when divisions are treated as profit centers, they are compared on the basis of their relative profitability, and when divisions sell products to one another, heated debates rage over transfer prices. This is because one division's loss is the other division's gain. The irony of the multi-divisional form is that, for all their emphasis on profit, M-forms in general turn out not to be as profitable as their functional equivalents.[16] A greater irony is that the financial management model developed within conglomerates has become an institutionalized feature of many multi-divisional organizations. The irony is that the M-form, which focuses so much attention on profit, is usually less profitable than structures that focus attention on other matters and that, in spite of this, institutional pressures in support of the M-form organizational structure cause managers to prefer M-form organizations.

One reason that M-form organizations are not as profitable as those having functional structures is that each division is in essence a functional structure. Instead of one sales, accounting, production, and purchasing department, the M-form organization has one of each for every division. To the extent that some of the work of these departments is redundant, M-form organizations will be more costly to operate. This redundancy can only be reduced by centralizing, however, coordination costs are high and the advantages of responsiveness to the market will be lost if the organization moves too far back toward a centralized alternative such as the functional structure. The costs of integrating multi-divisional structures are also greater. Top management must coordinate across several divisions which are often geographically separated. Increased complexity is costly in terms of loss of control, travel, and communication expenses.

In spite of the drawbacks, the M-form has several advantages to recommend it. The first of these is size. Multi-divisional organizations consistently grow larger than their functional counterparts. Size gives organizations a competitive advantage in that large organizations can have greater influence on their environment and usually occupy more central positions in their interorganizational networks than do small organizations. Thus, large size brings power and influence to the organization and its executives. Furthermore, the resources that are under the control of large organizations give them more opportunities to broaden their competitive activities both domestically and abroad.

The multi-divisional form of social structure also provides better training for future executives than does the functional structure because there are multiple individuals who operate with roughly the same perspective as that of the president of a functional structure. Individuals who spend time working at headquarters acquire broad-based experience that is unlikely to be gained within the functional form.

When they are treated as profit centers, divisions allow for a type of accountability that is not possible in a functional structure; each division can be assessed in comparison with its competitors on the basis of its performance in the marketplace, whereas the higher level of interdependence among groups in a functional structure makes this type of accountability impossible. However, you should recognize that, within each division of an M-form organization, the problems of functional accountability remain. Nonetheless, multi-divisional structures are usually able to offer enhanced responsiveness to the needs of customers because the specialization of the organization allows greater focus on the businesses each division operates. This is particularly true where divisions are operated as strategic business units (SBUs) with strategies specifically formulated for each division's domain of activity.

Matrix Structure

The matrix structure was developed with the intention of providing the best of both the functional and multi-divisional alternatives. The **matrix structure** is

Core Concepts of Organization Theory

intended to combine the efficiency of the functional structure with the flexibility and responsiveness of the divisional structure. This is accomplished by overlaying functional and divisional structures rather than allowing the logic of product, customer base, or geography to take priority over the functional logic that occurs in the divisional structure (Figure 6.5).

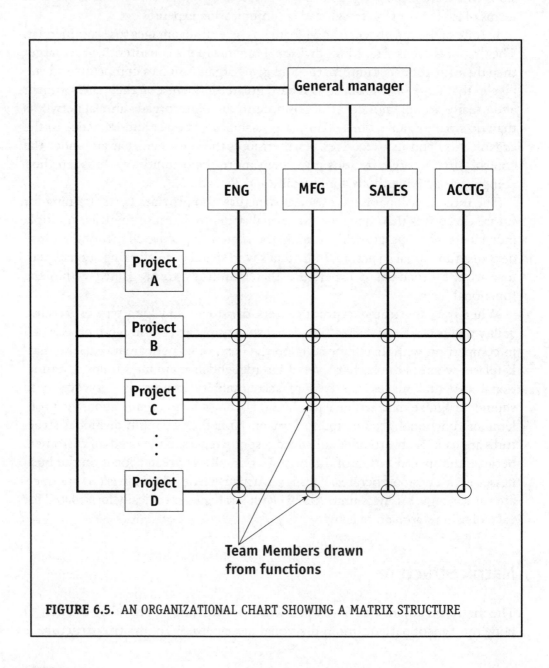

FIGURE 6.5. AN ORGANIZATIONAL CHART SHOWING A MATRIX STRUCTURE

You can think of the matrix organization as two structures, each of which is the responsibility of a different group of managers. Managers on the functional side of the matrix are responsible for allocating specialists to projects, helping them maintain their skills and acquire new ones, and monitoring their performance with respect to the standards of their specialty. Managers on the project side of the matrix structure are responsible for overseeing projects in terms of budgets, timelines, and other project specific goals, they coordinate task performance and encourage employees to minimize the time it takes the team to complete the project. Project managers are also charged with keeping project expenses beneath a preordained limit. Their battle cry is "On time and within budget!"

In the matrix organization, functionally specialized employees are assigned to one or more project teams. These assignments are often made through a process of negotiation between the functional and project managers, sometimes with input from the teams involved or potential members. Project teams are made up of a group of employees having the variety of different functional specialties required by the project. An employee assigned to a project reports to two managers—the functional chief and the project manager. Employees assigned to multiple projects may have several bosses.

The greatest difficulty in using the matrix structure lies in managing the conflict built into the dual lines of authority to which matrixed employees are subjected. Matrix employees confront the often contradictory pressures of performing difficult tasks to high quality specifications while at the same time facing pressure to perform quickly while limiting their use of resources in order to minimize costs and meet tight schedules. When employees serve on more than one project team, they will face the additional pressure of conflicting demands from multiple project leaders. You should recognize, however, that it is this same conflict that provides the primary benefit of the matrix structure, it promotes simultaneous attention to both functional standards and project demands.

By design, then, matrix employees face conflicting demands. But conflict is also built into the jobs of functional chief and project boss. At this level in the matrix, for example, conflict frequently emerges over the assignment of persons to projects. Obviously some individuals and some task assignments will be preferred to others and political maneuvering is to be expected in the process of forming project teams. Another challenge with a matrix structure is that the person responsible for the total matrix structure will need to balance the functional and project interests to be certain that one side of the matrix does not dominate the other. The result of an imbalance is to lose most of the benefits of using the matrix form, either the flexibility of the divisional structure or the efficiency of the functional form.

In spite of the considerable difficulties inherent in adapting to the pressures of a matrix structure, this form of organization has offsetting advantages to recommend it. One is enormous flexibility to take on new projects. Within functional and M-form structures, starting up a new activity generally requires a major structural adjustment such as creating a new division, whereas starting a new project is a common event within the matrix organization. Structurally, at least, starting a new project only entails finding a project manager and recruiting a team. Thus the matrix form retains the advantage of the divisional structure for flexibility in providing customer service and responding to opportunities in the environment.

Another advantage of matrix structures derives from their unique ability to maximize the value of expensive specialists. This is because the talents of specialists can be pooled for use among a wide variety of projects, some of which may be otherwise unrelated and thus likely to remain structurally unconnected in the divisional form. Although the individual specialist will have to deal with the fragmentation that this disconnectedness implies (e.g., working on two or more unrelated projects for project managers who have little concern for the specialists' competing responsibilities), from the perspective of the organization, the sharing out of specialized capabilities amounts to the considerable efficiency of the functional, relative to the multi-divisional, form. This is because where the M-form would hire potentially redundant specialists for each of its divisions, the matrix can more easily use its specialists to their full capacity.

Hybrid Structure

The structures examined above represent pure types. Organizations will not always conform to one of these. **Hybrid structures** are partly one type of structure and partly another. Hybrids may occur either because designers deliberately mix forms in an attempt to blend the advantages of two or more different types, or because the organization is changing. For example, a research and development division may move to a matrix structure, while other divisions remain functionally structured. Network structures and multinational organizations (discussed below) may also appear to be hybrids. Hybrid forms can be confusing in that the basis of relationships changes as you move from one part of the structure to another. On the other hand, the hybrid form allows the organization the flexibility to adopt the structure most appropriate to the varied needs of its different subunits.

Network Structure

A relatively new form of organization has appeared that challenges modernist notions of what an organization is and confirms some predictions made by post-modernists about the effects of fragmentation and incoherence on organizations in the post-industrial age. This new form is most often referred to as a network. The **network organization** replaces most, if not all, vertical communication and control relationships with lateral relationships. Thus the formal ties that bind the units of an organization together are replaced with a partnership among several organizations. Networks seem most likely to form when organizations face rapid technological change, shortened product lifecycles, and fragmented, specialized markets. In a network, needed assets are distributed among several network partners such that it is not a single organization within the network that produces products or services, but rather the network at large that is the producer or provider.

A network can be the result of massive **outsourcing** or collaboration between small firms whose scale of operations would not allow them to compete in international markets by themselves. Outsourcing means that many of the activities of a once complex organization are moved outside the organization's boundary. Sometimes the suppliers will be spin-off units with the original organization retaining only those activities for which it has a particular competence. All other necessary activities are purchased from other organizations. When all the task activities are outsourced, you have a **virtual organization**.

Benetton is an example of a network organization. It is comprised of hundreds of small clothing manufacturers and thousands of franchised sales outlets arrayed around a central distribution channel with a common information and control system. Many of the manufacturers within the Benetton network were spun off of the original Benetton operation, while others joined the network because their small size would otherwise have left them out of the international fashion market in which Benetton firms participate. In addition to managing the distribution channels (which are also part of the network) Benetton provides its suppliers with technical manufacturing expertise, much of the necessary equipment and sometimes capital, and handles marketing efforts for the network.

Within a network structure, partners are linked by supplier–customer relationships that resemble a free market system. That is, goods are bought and sold between network partners just as they would be on the open market. In this way competitive pressures on the supplying partners keep downward pressure on prices. Also, the use of market mechanisms to coordinate activities eliminates much of the need for the vertical hierarchy of traditional organizations and this reduces administrative overhead. These characteristics of network organizations reduce their overall costs and increase efficiency and profitability which helps keep the network competitive.

However, a simple economic relationship between network partners can lead to exploitation either by partners who have control of critical information, or by certain suppliers who are able to create and take advantage of dependencies in the larger system (i.e., charging higher prices once demand for their products is generated by the rest of the network). In these situations, one segment of the network holds the rest hostage for higher profits. This is where networks developed upon more than economic relationships have an advantage. For instance, relationships built on friendship, reputation, or shared ideology may prove more effective due to their greater ability to generate cooperation and trust.

Other advantages associated with networks are that they encourage information sharing, liberate decision making, and inspire innovation. Also, networks are capable of extremely rapid information exchange because they can process information in multiple directions at once. Rapid information exchange enables network partners to exploit opportunities before non-networked competitors become aware of them. Relative independence of decision making allows experimentation and learning, and the product of this learning can be rapidly diffused throughout the network. By enhancing the spread of information, networks provide the conditions for innovation by bringing together different logics and novel combinations of information.

However, many of the advantages networks enjoy depend upon members working voluntarily together to innovate, solve problems of mutual concern, and coordinate their activities. This demands a level of organizational teamwork that cannot be taken for granted. Networks create webs of information exchange and mutual obligation that can provide a foundation for deeper relationships, but these relationship are not automatic—they must be managed.[17] Network partners may undermine network effectiveness by pursuing self-interest and middle managers and technical specialists within network organizations may not always be enthusiastic about cooperation.[18] Probably the greatest challenge in managing network relationships is developing and maintaining an organizational identity and sense of purpose in the face of geographic diversity and loosely coupled interests and activities.

Structural Design and Organizational Logic

An organization's structural design can be used as a kind of cognitive map of how managers think about the internal differentiation and integration of their organization. In simple structures, coordination among individuals is the only structural concern of the owner/entrepreneur. If a functional structure is in use, then the top manager will spend a great deal of energy coordinating across the various functions, while functional managers will focus attention on their technical specializations and coordinating the work of individuals in their units. If product divisions are the basis of the structure, then the executive group will think about how the different divisions will best be coordinated, leaving the concern for coordinating across functions to the general managers in each division. In a matrix structure, top management will be concerned to balance functional and project interests to be certain that one side of the matrix does not dominate the other, since the result of this would be to lose the benefits of using the matrix form. Other managers in the matrix are either function or project oriented. Hybrid structures mix these concerns while network organizations distribute them throughout the network.

Understanding organizational logic in terms of structural design helps you to understand the potential for confusion, conflict, and miscommunication lodged in most complex forms of organization. Take the case of a matrix structure in which some managers and employees are thinking functionally, others divisionally, and others still are trying to think both ways at once. Or consider the hybrid or network structure in which some managers and other employees must communicate with people from other units whose structure is different from their own. Looked at from this perspective, the confusions and contradictions of everyday experience in complex organizations begin to make sense. The advantage of seeing structure in terms of different logics is that it enhances appreciation of differentiation and the correlated need for integration, and provides a way to talk about the many different points of view that comprise an organization. If a manager is to be an effective communicator, the ability to understand these different points of view is invaluable.

MULTINATIONALS AND GLOBAL ORGANIZATIONS

In these days of increasing international competition, many organizations are strategically positioning themselves to take advantage of opportunities around the world. An organization that desires to move beyond a purely domestic orientation to operate on a multinational or even a global scale will confront the need for structural adaptation.[19] This is because the new orientation will require the organization to engage in new activities which will put differentiation pressures on existing structures. A functionally structured organization that merely wants to market its products or services abroad, or wants to take advantage of low cost labor to produce products for home markets, will generally form a new department to handle the details of import and export, usually by subcontracting with experts in the markets in which the organization wants to be involved. At this stage the organization is really not international in its focus, but rather remains committed to the logic of its domestic business.

As experience with international markets accumulates, the organization will typically become aware of opportunities abroad and become more experienced in addressing the opportunities, at least in one or a few of its foreign locations. At this point many of the activities that were originally subcontracted will be brought in-house and an **international division** will be formed. Notice that the M-form structure adopted at this stage allows the organization to maintain essentially a multi-domestic orientation. That is, it acts like a firm operating domestically in several markets at once, a bit like a conglomerate does in relation to operating in several industries at the same time.

Finally, the **multinational corporation** (MNC) appears. This comes about as international sales become the main source of organizational revenues and as suppliers, manufacturers, and distributors from a variety of countries form an interdependent interorganizational network on a truly international level. No longer can the activities of the firm be separated into either domestic or international units, and the international division is replaced by an internationalized product or geographic M-form structure in which all units engage in the coordination of international activities. Of course, as with conglomerate M-forms, an organization can achieve a multinational structure either through internal growth, generally progressing through the stages described above, or through joint venture, merger, and/or acquisition.

The multinational product or geographical divisional forms confront the same drawbacks as do domestic M-form organizations. The desire to be more efficient and flexible leads to matrix structures which move MNC logics into the domain of global thinking (see Figure 6.6). In a **global matrix** there are managers of geographic regions and of products or product groups such that local units are organized both by interests in corporate effectiveness related to serving a particular region of the world *and* by interests in developing the corporation's knowledge and efficiency in regard to production across regional markets. Each of the local units can be fully operational companies in their own right, and the array of these units that comprises the MNC may be a mixture of simple, functional, divisional, matrix and/or hybrid structures.

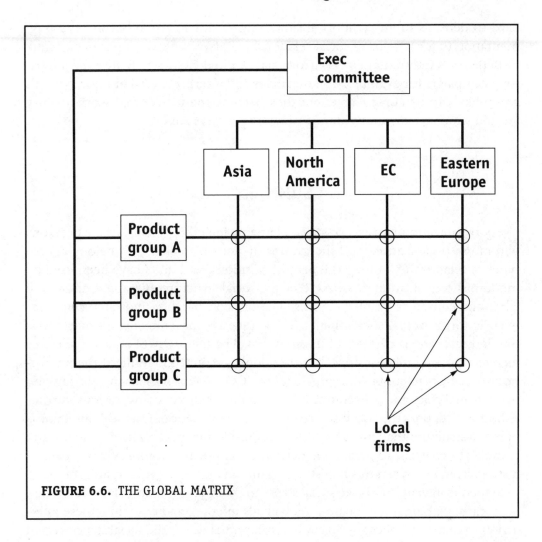

FIGURE 6.6. THE GLOBAL MATRIX

Obviously, a major drawback of this structure is its enormous, often mind-boggling complexity. Even with electronic communication and rapid transportation between most destinations, the coordination problems of the global organization stretch the concept of structure to the limits of modernist conception. As complexity increases through demands for attention to more than the two dimensions representable in this structure (e.g., regions, products), the fragmentation and incoherence about which postmodernists write becomes increasingly helpful.[20] Here, an image of fragmented organizations as networks of loosely connected interests operating without grand narratives of overarching corporate strategy overtakes the images of planning and control offered by modernist organization theory. Here, too, the importance of symbolism becomes hard to deny, as often symbols are the only means to reach beyond the fragmentation to form webs of social relationship between network partners. Think of Benetton's internationally controversial "United Colors of Benetton" advertising campaign, for example. The meanings and interpretations of these symbols are unlikely to be controllable, but they become the focus of network identity around which relationships among network partners cohere.

SUMMARY

Every organization consists of social elements including people, their positions within the organization, and the groups or units to which they belong. Three types of relationship among the people, positions, and units have been used by modernist organization theorists to define social structure: hierarchy, division of labor and coordination mechanisms. The division of labor, indicates who does what in terms of task assignments. These task assignments create expectations that indicate who is dependent upon whom. The hierarchy of authority defines formal reporting relationships, but these only account for some of the interactions necessary to support an organization. Coordination mechanisms, ranging from formal rules and procedures to spontaneous hallway conversations, further define and support the social structure of the organization. Classical dimensions of social structure that continue to interest modernist organization scholars are: complexity, centralization, and formalization. These dimensions offer a means of distinguishing between mechanistic, organic, and bureaucratic organizations.

Symbolic-interpretivists see social structure as emerging from relationships that form through human interaction. Individuals interact, and over time these interactions stabilize into recognizable relationships that define the social structure and contribute to the ways that work is accomplished. These relationships link the formal hierarchical positions into groups and the groups into departments and divisions. However, although structure serves to direct and constrain deviations from expected patterns of behavior, structuration theory reminds us that these constraints are nothing more than our willingness to do things in practiced or habitual ways. Structuration theory stresses that social structure both influences and is influenced by the everyday interactions of the members of the organization.

In addition to representing the pattern of human relationships through which organization takes place, the social structure of an organization reflects patterns of differentiation in work activities and, at least partially, addresses its mechanisms of internal integration. Analysis of social structure using the organization chart as a primary analytical tool provides a partial map of how the managers think about what the organization does. The top level of differentiation reflects top management's basic categories for goal setting, budgeting, and the development of other coordination and control mechanisms. Closer to the technical core, structural design provides information about the functional orientation of employees to their tasks, and indicates task interdependence among individuals and units directly responsible for the output of the firm. Postmodernism and network organizations challenge many of these modernist ways of looking at social structure, focusing research attention instead on processes and relationships. Symbolic-interpretive and postmodern perspectives remind us that organizations have other resources beyond the social structure to aid in the integration of differentiated activities, as you will see in the following chapters on organizational culture and physical structure.

KEY TERMS

differentiation
integration
de-differentiation
hierarchy
authority
division of labor
rules and procedures
schedules
lateral communication
structural complexity
centralization
formalization
mechanistic, organic, and
    bureaucratic forms
bureaucracy
organizational lifecycle
  entrepreneurial phase
  leadership crisis
  collectivity phase
  crisis of autonomy
  delegation phase
  crisis of control
  formalization phase

crisis of red tape
collaboration phase
crisis of renewal
decline
open systems model
  core production tasks
  support activities
  maintenance tasks
  adaptive function
duality of structure
simple structure
functional structure
multi-divisional structure
conglomerates
matrix structure
hybrid structure
network organization
outsourcing
virtual organization
international division
multinational corporation (MNC)
global matrix

Core Concepts of Organization Theory

ENDNOTES

1. Clegg (1990).
2. Weber (1946, 1947).
3. Smith (1957: 2).
4. Jablin (1988).
5. Hage, Aiken, and Marrett (1971); Bacharach and Aiken (1977).
6. Grinyer and Yasai-Ardekani (1980).
7. Hage (1974); Rousseau (1978).
8. Blau and Schoenherr (1971); Pugh et al. (1968, 1969); Mansfield (1973).
9. Perrow (1986).
10. Weber (1946, 1947).
11. Greiner (1972).
12. Katz and Kahn (1966).
13. Giddens (1979, 1984).
14. e.g., Ranson, Hinings, and Greenwood (1980); Riley (1983).
15. Tosi (1974).
16. Rumelt (1986).
17. Powell (1990: 316).
18. Doz (1988) cited by Powell (1990: 318).
19. Adler (1991).
20. Ghoshal and Bartlett (1990).

REFERENCES

Adler, Nancy J. (1991). *International dimensions of organizational behavior*. Boston: PWS-Kent.

Bacharach, Samuel B., and Aiken, Michael (1977). Communication in administrative bureaucracies. *Academy of Management Journal*, 20: 356–77.

Blau, Peter M., and Schoenherr, Richard A. (1971). *The structure of organizations*. New York: Basic Books.

Clegg, Stewart (1990). *Modern organizations: Organization studies in the postmodern world*. London: Sage.

Doz, Yves (1988). Technology partnerships between larger and smaller firms: Some critical issues. *International Studies of Management and Organization*, 17/4: 31–57.

Ghoshal, Sumantra, and Bartlett, Christopher A. (1990). The multinational corporation as an interorganizational network. *Academy of Management Review*, 15: 603–25.

Giddens, Anthony (1979). *Central problems in social theory: Action, structure and contradiction in social analysis*. Berkeley: University of California Press.

Giddens, Anthony (1984). *The constitution of society*. Berkeley: University of California Press.

Greiner, Larry (1972). Evolution and revolution as organizations grow. *Harvard Business Review*, 50: 37–46.

Grinyer, P. H., and Yasai-Ardekani, M. (1980). Dimensions of organizational structure: A critical replication. *Academy of Management Journal*, 23: 405–21.

Hage, Jerald (1974). *Communication and organizational control: Cybernetics in health and welfare settings*. New York: John Wiley.

Hage, Jerald, Aiken, Michael, and Marrett, C. B. (1971) Organization structure and communications. *American Sociological Review*, 36: 860–71.

Jablin, Fredric M. (1988). Formal organization structure. In F.M. Jablin, L. L. Putnam, K. H. Roberts, and L. W. Porter (eds.), *Handbook of organizational communication: An interdisciplinary perspective*. Newbury Park: Sage.

Katz, Daniel, and Kahn, Robert L. (1966). *The social psychology of organizations*. New York: John Wiley & Sons.

Mansfield, Roger (1973). Bureaucracy and centralization: An examination of organizational structure. *Administrative Science Quarterly*, 18: 77–88.

Parsons, Talcott (1947). *The theory of social and economic organization*. Glencoe, Ill.: Free Press.

Perrow, Charles (1986). *Complex organizations: A critical essay* (3rd edition). New York: Random House.

Powell, Walter W. (1990). Neither market nor hierarchy: Network forms of organization. *Research in Organizational Behavior*, 12: 295–336.

Pugh, D. S., Hickson, D. J., and Hinings, C. R. (1969). An empirical taxonomy of structures of work organizations. *Administrative Science Quarterly*, 14: 115–26.

Pugh, D. S., Hickson, D. J., Hinings, C. R., and Turner, C. (1968). Dimensions of organization structure. *Administrative Science Quarterly*, 13: 65–91.

Ranson, Stewart, Hinings, Robert, and Greenwood, Royston (1980). The structuring of organizational structures. *Administrative Science Quarterly*, 25: 1–17.

Riley, Patricia (1983). A structurationist account of political culture. *Administrative Science Quarterly*, 28: 414–37.

Rousseau, Denise (1978). Characteristics of departments, positions, and individuals: Contexts for attitudes and behaviors. *Administrative Science Quarterly*, 23: 521–40.

Rumelt, Richard (1986). *Strategy, structure, and economic performance*. Boston, Mass.: Harvard Business School Press (first edition, 1974).

Scott, W. Richard (1992). *Organizations: Rational, natural, and open systems* (3rd edition). Englewood Cliffs, NJ: Prentice Hall.

Smith, Adam (1957). *Selections from "The Wealth of Nations"* (ed. George J. Stigler). New York: Appleton Century Crofts (originally published in 1776).

Tosi, Henry L. (1974). The human effects of budgeting systems on management. *MSU Business Topics*, Autumn: 53–63.

Weber, Max (1946). *From Max Weber: Essays in sociology* (ed. Hans H. Gerth and C. Wright Mills). New York: Oxford University Press (translation of original published 1906–24).

Weber, Max (1947). *The theory of social and economic organization* (ed. A. H. Henderson and Talcott Parsons). Glencoe, Ill.: Free Press (translation of original published 1924).

FURTHER READING

Galbraith, Jay R. (1995). *Designing organizations: An executive briefing on strategy, structure and process*. San Francisco: Jossey-Bass.

Ghoshal, Sumantra, and Bartlett, Christopher A. (1990). The multinational corporation as an interorganizational network. *Academy of Management Review*, 15: 603–25.

Mintzberg, Henry (1979). *The structuring of organizations: A synthesis of the research*. Englewood Cliffs, NJ: Prentice-Hall.

Scott, W. Richard (1975). Organizational structure. *Annual Review of Sociology*, 1: 1–20.

7 Organizational Culture

I N many ways, the culture of an organization is borrowed from and bound up with larger cultural processes associated with the organization's environment. Every organization expresses aspects of the national, regional, industrial, occupational, and professional cultures in and through which it operates.[1] Each organization is formed, in part, through cultural processes established by a variety of environmental actors. However, the most immediate source of outside influence on the organizational culture is found *within* the organization—its employees.

Before joining an organization, employees have already been influenced by multiple cultural institutions such as family, community, nation, state, church, educational systems, and other work organizations, and these associations shape their attitudes, behavior, and identity. Employees bring these influences with them when they join an organization. Because of this, it is difficult to separate an organizational culture from the larger cultural processes that we labelled the cultural sector in our discussion of the general environment in Chapter 3.

Even though it is difficult to distinguish an organization's culture from larger cultural processes, organization theorists believe that it is necessary to try to do so. Experience with only a few different organizations shows why this is so. Think of the contrast between Apple Computer's anti-establishment employees devoted to rule-breaking innovation and IBM's white-shirted professionals committed to customer service. If you only pay attention to larger cultural forces and do not consider culture at the level of the organization, you will miss much of what makes these two companies seem distinctive. Nonetheless, most of the following discussion about what culture is applies equally well across levels of analysis including nation, society, organization, and organizational subculture. What makes a study of culture (or anything else) *organizational* is your focus of interest which defines your level of analysis, as was explained in Chapter 2.

This generality may cause you some initial discomfort, partly because I will often use examples drawn from the societal level. I do this because societal-level examples are familiar enough to most people to render them understandable, whereas organizational examples demand familiarity with the everyday life of specific organizations that most people do not have. It is important, however, that you apply these concepts to organizations with which you are familiar. The examples I will offer are designed to inspire this application to your own experience.

Beyond the levels of analysis issue, you will face another challenge in coming to grips with the organizational culture concept. This challenge arises from the symbolic-interpretive roots of the culture concept as it is used in organization theory. In the early 1980s several books on corporate culture appeared on best-seller lists in the United States. Among them the most widely known are William Ouchi's *Theory Z*, Terrence Deal and Allan Kennedy's *Corporate Cultures: The Rites and Rituals of Corporate Life*, and Tom Peters and Robert Waterman's *In Search of Excellence*. The enormous attention these books generated was no doubt linked to concern at that time to explain Japanese competitiveness in American markets, but it also offered an opportunity to symbolic-interpretive organization theorists who were frustrated by modernist theories and methods and wanted to strike out in new directions. These researchers were the first organization theorists to jump on the corporate culture bandwagon and they made liberal use of over 100 years of theory and research in cultural anthropology and folklore studies to inspire and legitimize their efforts. The result was importation of the symbolic-interpretive perspective as a new approach to organization theory.

Thus, unlike theorizing about social structure, technology, environment, and strategy, the conceptualization of organizational culture was influenced from the beginning by the symbolic-interpretive perspective. In the study of organizational culture, it is more often modernist perspectives that challenge symbolic-interpretive ideas rather than the other way around. Because of this reversal in the fortunes of symbolic-interpretivism, the study of organizational culture has a different feel. One of the most important differences that you will notice has to do with the subjectivist epistemology adopted by symbolic-interpretivists compared to the objectivist epistemology of the modernist perspective. As was explained in Chapter 2, using an objectivist approach means that you view the phenomenon of interest from the outside, as natural scientists attempt to do when they adopt the role of independent observer. The subjectivist approach of symbolic-interpretivists involves discovering how insiders experience and construct their world which involves grappling with their meanings and interpretations, rather than imposing the researcher's meanings and interpretations upon them. This is what anthropologists refer to as the **native view**, and understanding it requires empathy, which is encouraged by a subjectivist epistemology.

This chapter begins with the question: What is organizational culture? Following discussion of the ways in which culture has been defined, we will explore national influences on organizational culture via Dutch culture researcher Geert Hofstede's model of the national cultural differences he found in the international subsidiaries of IBM. Next we will examine American social psychologist Edgar Schein's theory of organizational culture which served as a departure point for many of the organizational theorists who have contributed to this field of study. Symbols and interpretation, two fundamental ideas defining the symbolic-interpretive approach, will then be examined in relation to the organizational culture concept, and ethnography, the favored method of symbolic-interpretive cultural researchers, will be described and illustrated. Two typologies of organizational subcultures and a postmodern perspective on organizational culture will be presented next. The chapter concludes with examination of some of the ways in which modernists have addressed the culture concept, with particular attention given to their concerns about whether or not culture can be managed.

WHAT IS ORGANIZATIONAL CULTURE?

Organizational culture is probably the most difficult of all organizational concepts to define. The same has been said about defining culture at the societal level.[2] As British sociologist and cultural critic Raymond Williams explains, culture originally referred to the tending of crops and animals. Its meaning was extended beyond the physical domain by the metaphoric identity of crops and animals with the human mind and soul. According to **the culture metaphor**, society tends humans via the family, the community, educational institutions, and religious practices, just as farmers tend their crops and animals via plowing, pruning, feeding, herding. Close association between culture and social progress, civilization and aesthetic achievement (i.e., music, painting, sculpture, literature, poetry, and philosophy) added a sense of superiority and elitism to culture's meaning. This elitism is reflected, for example, in distinctions such as primitive versus advanced cultures and high versus popular (pop) culture.

According to British sociologist Chris Jenks, early efforts to define culture are associated with the formation of the academic disciplines of sociology and anthropology. Both of these fields were born with emerging interest in applying the techniques of science to the study of humans. Often located in the same academic departments in their universities, sociologists and anthropologists worried a great deal over whose territory was whose and eventually worked out an agreement that sociology would study all phenomena having to do with human society, and anthropology would explain the origins and cultural development of the human species. However, the close association between the interests and physical location of sociologists and anthropologists (their offices were frequently situated along the same hallway) shows up time and again as overlap in their key ideas and it is often difficult to separate their contributions to the study of culture.

The culture concept was originally proposed as one way to answer the question: What makes us human? Early on, anthropologists were primarily concerned with explaining the differences between humans and other animals and to differentiate culture and nature (in order to provide a foundation for the human sciences that was distinguishable from that of the natural sciences on which they were modelled). Thus the notion of culture was at first a very general one, having to do with characteristics that all humans held in common. For instance, British social anthropologist E. B. Tylor defined culture as: "that complex whole which includes knowledge, belief, art, morals, law, custom, and any other capabilities and habits acquired by man as a member of society."[3] The focus on culture meant concern with symbolic representations (e.g., language) through which humans distinguished themselves from say ants or dolphins.

As anthropologists extended the idea of evolution to the concept of culture, they reasoned that if humans develop along some sort of evolutionary continuum, as other animal species seem to do, then culture is a possible explanation for the distinctiveness of human development. From this line of reasoning emerged the idea that different cultural groups or societies could be ordered according to their stage of development, from primitive on one end, to modern on the other. For researchers interested in the cultural development of humankind, one place to look for evidence was to primitive cultures who were believed to be living as advanced cultures must have done earlier in their own developmental cycles. So anthropologists went in search of culture's origins by living in primitive cultures for extended periods and documenting the various aspects of their members' lives. However, as their studies accumulated, the idea that primitive societies were socially and culturally backward became difficult to sustain. It gradually became more and more obvious that so-called primitive cultures were in some ways more sophisticated than the so-called advanced cultures from which the anthropologists had come, and that the so-called advanced cultures were barbaric in certain respects when compared to what had previously been described as primitive.

The ethnocentrism of the basic premise of cultural research became a source of great criticism directed at the field of cultural anthropology which was then accused of having conspired with colonialist governments to the great disadvantage (and in some cases the disappearance) of tribal societies. The change in attitude has refocused culture theory. Anthropologists still believe that cultures change, but not in a way that gives any of them the right to claim cultural superiority. In fact postmodern anthropologists now argue that the idea of superiority itself is embedded in cultural meaning systems and to study culture requires acknowledging preconceived notions derived from your own cultural background when approaching the study of another person's culture.

So, in the early days of anthropology, interest in culture meant an interest in understanding what is distinctively human, what separates humans from the other animals and thus what defines our similarity. As researchers pursued this interest out into the field, culture became associated with particular groups of people (e.g., primitive tribes, modern societies), and comparisons between these groups took place. This association between groups and cultures (rather than culture) caused anthropologists to talk about groups as if they *were* cultures and shifted the focus of anthropology from the general understanding of humankind as a species, to the distinctive characteristics of particular groups, and thus to human differences. This shift can be seen by comparing Tylor's 1871 definition of culture given above, with the definition offered in 1948 by American cultural anthropologist Melville Herskowitz: "a construct describing the total body of belief, behavior, knowledge, sanctions, values, and goals that make up the way of life of a people."[4] This shift of culture onto groups opens the door to the study of organization culture because, since organizations are by definition groups, the culture metaphor can be applied to organizations.

Although, for some (especially postmodernist) organization theorists, culture retains its association with the intellectual and artistic, most organization theorists have emphasized the meaning of culture as a particular way of life among a people or community. Thus, organizational culture usually refers to the way of life in an organization. A sample of the definitions that have been offered by organization theorists is provided in Table 7.1. Notice that all but one of these definitions explicitly associates the concept of culture with groups, and that they all refer to something held in common or shared among group members: meanings, assumptions, understanding, norms, values, knowledge.

The definitions in Table 7.1 should reveal to you how central the notion of sharing has been in the development of the organizational culture concept. However, when researchers go looking for these shared meanings, understanding, values, and so on, they do not find them. What they find instead are some key symbols that are widely recognized by organizational members, but which are associated with a multitude of meanings and interpretations. This puzzle is solved when you examine the concept of sharing closely. There you will discover that sharing has two contrary meanings.[5] The meaning most of us immediately

---

TABLE 7.1. SELECTED DEFINITIONS OF ORGANIZATIONAL CULTURE

Elliott Jaques (1952: 251) "The culture of the factory is its customary and traditional way of thinking and doing of things, which is shared to a greater or lesser degree by all its members, and which new members must learn, and at least partially accept, in order to be accepted into service in the firm."

Andrew Pettigrew (1979: 574) "Culture is a system of publicly and collectively accepted meanings operating for a given group at a given time. This system of terms, forms, categories, and images interprets a people's own situation to themselves."

Meryl Reis Louis (1983: 39) "Organizations [are] culture-bearing milieux, that is, [they are] distinctive social units possessed of a set of common understandings for organizing action (e.g., what we're doing together in this particular group, appropriate ways of doing in and among members of the group) and languages and other symbolic vehicles for expressing common understandings."

Caren Siehl and Joanne Martin (1984: 227) ". . . organizational culture can be thought of as the glue that holds an organization together through a sharing of patterns of meaning. The culture focuses on the values, beliefs, and expectations that members come to share."

Edgar Schein (1985: 6) "The pattern of basic assumptions that a given group has invented, discovered, or developed in learning to cope with its problems of external adaptation and internal integration, and that have worked well enough to be considered valid, and, therefore, to be taught to new members as the correct way to perceive, think, and feel in relation to these problems."

John van Maanen (1988: 3) "Culture refers to the knowledge members of a given group are thought to more or less share; knowledge of the sort that is said to inform, embed, shape, and account for the routine and not-so-routine activities of the members of the culture. . . . A culture is expressed (or constituted) only through the actions and words of its members and must be interpreted by, not given to, a fieldworker. . . . Culture is not itself visible, but is made visible only through its representation."

Harrison Trice and Janice Beyer (1993: 2) "Cultures are collective phenomena that embody people's responses to the uncertainties and chaos that are inevitable in human experience. These responses fall into two major categories. The first is the *substance* of a culture—shared, emotionally charged belief systems that we call ideologies. The second is *cultural forms*—observable entities, including actions, through which members of a culture express, affirm, and communicate the substance of their culture to one another."

---

think of has to do with common experience; when we share, we are directly involved with others in a way that emphasizes our similarity. This has been the meaning most often linked to the culture concept in organization theory. But sharing also means that we divide something into individual pieces (shares) and distribute them among ourselves, as in sharecropping. This second meaning emphasizes our separateness.

Take the example of sharing a meal with friends. We join in a communal activity when we share a meal, but, at the same time, we each eat our own separate portions of food. You might say that sharing means doing something separately together. It is a communal act accomplished by splitting something up. Just as sharing a meal does not mean that we all eat exactly the same food, sharing cultural patterns does not imply that all members have the same cultural experiences and understandings. Sharing culture means that each member participates in and contributes to the broad patterns of culture, but the contributions and experiences of individual members of the culture are not identical.

When speaking of culture as shared meaning, understanding, values, belief systems, or knowledge, keep in mind that a culture depends upon both community and diversity. It allows for similarity, but also supports and relies upon difference. As our discussion moves from theories that present culture as a unity in the first half of the chapter, to theories that focus on subcultures, and then on cultural fragmentation, notice that the idea of sharing shifts from the similarity pole (Schein's model) to the pole of differences that lie within cultures (the subculture and fragmentation views).[6] Notice how the same shift that refocused anthropology from culture in general to the culture of groups has been repeated in the shift within organizational culture studies from culture as an organizational unity, to culture as a means of explaining differences between various subgroups of the organization.

NATIONAL CULTURE DIFFERENCES WITHIN ORGANIZATIONS

The most unified understanding of organizational culture comes from the idea that organizations are manifestations of larger cultural systems. In the late 1970s Geert Hofstede examined this idea in relation to the influence of national cultures on IBM, a large multinational corporation based in the U.S., and, at the time of the study, operating in over 40 countries. Hofstede analyzed survey data concerning work-related values. He made comparisons across the international affiliates of IBM and found evidence of national cultural differences within IBM's organizational culture. In analyzing the data, Hofstede found that differences in the attitudes expressed by managers of IBM's international subsidiaries could be explained using four dimensions which he labelled: power distance, uncertainty avoidance, individualism, and masculinity (see Figures 7.1 and 7.2).

Power distance refers to the extent to which the members of a nation are willing to accept an unequal distribution of power, wealth, and prestige. Low power distance characterizes countries, like Denmark, where such inequalities are difficult to accept. For instance, the Danish Jante Law (pronounced yenta) proclaims that no individual should have more than, or stand out in any noticeable way from, other Danes. When Danes try to put themselves forward as more prestigious or powerful than others, they are quickly reprimanded by peers who remind them of the inherent equality of all Danes and thus reinforce the value for low power distance in Danish society. Another example is the exceptionally high income tax paid by the Danes which is an indicator of their unwillingness to accept an unequal distribution of wealth. Many organizations rely heavily on an unequal distribution of authority which forms a hierarchy. When such organizations attempt to impose their authority structures on subsidiaries in low power distance cultures like Denmark, difficulties generally follow.

Uncertainty avoidance involves the ways in which human societies have learned to cope with uncertainty. For instance, technology is often used to defend against uncertainties caused by nature (e.g., reinforced building structures in earthquake prone areas), while law helps us to defend against uncertainties produced by the behavior of others (e.g, laws against thievery, brutality, fraud). Religion, on the other hand, is a cultural means to help us accept uncertainties that we cannot defend against. Hofstede argues that different societies have different levels of tolerance for uncertainty, ambiguity, and unfamiliar risks, and that these differences can be defined as the degree to which members of a culture feel threatened by uncertainty, ambiguity, and risk. In low uncertainty avoidance cultures, people are more accepting of innovative ideas and eccentric or deviant behavior, whereas in high uncertainty avoidance cultures, these are resisted. Hofstede finds that uncertainty avoidance is high in Greece, Portugal, and Japan, while it is low in Singapore, Hong Kong, and Sweden.

Individualism involves the degree to which individuals in a culture are expected to act independently of other members of the society. You will find evidence of individualism, which Hofstede opposes to collectivism, in the ways in which people live together (e.g., in nuclear families, tribes, or in shifting partnerships or alone). Hofstede points out that, in some cultures, such as the U.S., individualism is seen as a source of well-being, whereas in others like Chinese or Mexican cultures, it is seen as undesirable and alienating. Relationships between members of individualistic cultures are loose and individuals are expected to take care of themselves. By contrast, in collectivist cultures, cohesive groups give individuals their sense of identity and belonging, demanding considerable loyalty in return for the sense of security that they impart.

Masculinity refers to the clear separation of gender roles in society. In highly masculine cultures, men are expected to be more assertive and women more

Core Concepts of Organization Theory

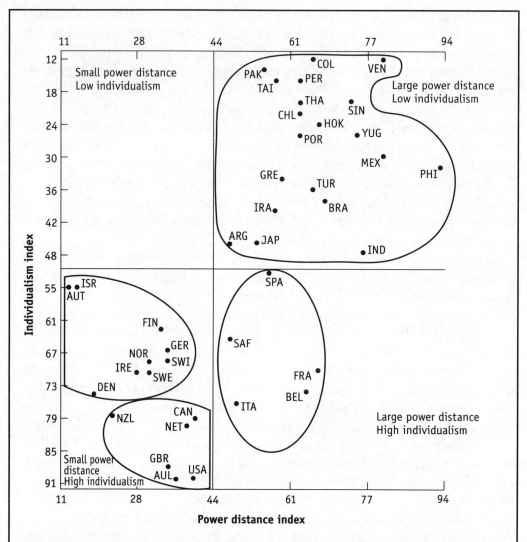

FIGURE 7.1. POSITION OF 40 COUNTRIES ON HOFSTEDE'S POWER DISTANCE AND INDIVIDUALISM DIMENSIONS (Key opposite)

Source: Hofstede, Geert (1980: 159). *Culture's Consequences: International differences in work related values.* Copyright © 1980 by Geert Hofstede. Reprinted by permission of Sage Publications.

KEY

ARG	Argentina	CHL	Chile	GER	Germany
AUL	Australia	COL	Columbia	GRE	Greece
AYT	Austria	DEN	Denmark	HOK	Hong Kong
BEL	Belgium	FIN	Finland	IND	India
BRA	Brazil	FRA	France	IRA	Iran
CAN	Canada	GBR	Great Britain	IRE	Ireland

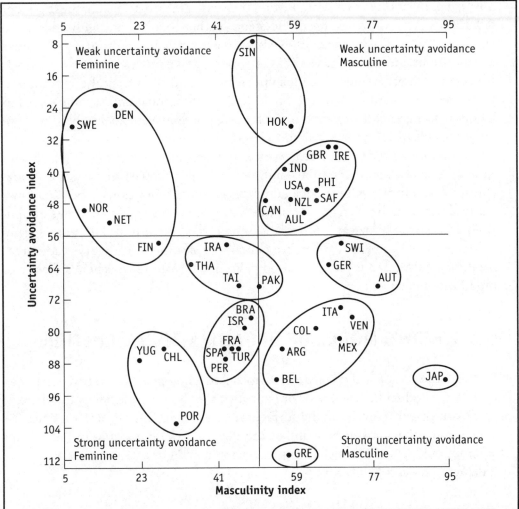

FIGURE 7.2. POSITION OF 40 COUNTRIES ON HOFSTEDE'S UNCERTAINTY AVOIDANCE AND MASCULINITY DIMENSIONS (Key opposite)

Source: Hofstede, Geert (1980: 219). *Culture's Consequences: International differences in work related values.* Copyright © 1980 by Geert Hofstede. Reprinted by permission of Sage Publications.

ISR	Israel	PER	Peru	TAI	Taiwan
ITA	Italy	PHI	Philippines	THA	Thailand
JAP	Japan	POR	portugal	TUR	Turkey
MEX	Mexico	SAF	South Africa	USA	United States
NET	Netherlands	SIN	Singapore	VEN	Venezuela
NOR	Norway	SPA	Spain	YUG	Yugoslavia
NZL	New Zealand	SWE	Sweden		
PAK	Pakistan	SWI	Switzerland		

nurturing. In cultures that score low on the masculinity dimension, these gender differences are less pronounced. Hofstede further found that highly masculine cultures tend to place more emphasis on work goals having to do with career advancement and earnings, whereas less masculine cultures favored work goals concerning interpersonal relationships, service, and the physical environment. Hofstede also found that women held fewer professional and technical jobs in highly masculine cultures such as Japan, Austria, and Venezuela, than in more feminine cultures such as Sweden, Norway, and the Netherlands.

The importance of Hofstede's work is not only that it identified specific cultural differences between nations, but Hofstede also showed that organizational culture is an entry point for societal influence on organizations. These national cultural traits can be seen as part of the web of meaning that constitutes organizational culture. In a way, Hofstede's dimensions of cultural difference supply information about some of the core beliefs and assumptions that pervade organizational cultures, a topic we will now discuss in relation to Schein's theory of organizational culture.

SCHEIN'S MODEL OF ORGANIZATIONAL CULTURE

Early in the 1980s, Edgar Schein, a social psychologist, developed what has become an influential theory of organizational culture.[7] In Schein's theory, culture exists on three levels: on the surface we find artifacts, underneath artifacts lie values and behavioral norms, and at the deepest level lies a core of beliefs and assumptions. Schein's model of culture is shown in Figure 7.3 and the three levels it depicts are described below.

Beliefs and Assumptions

According to Schein, beliefs and assumptions form the core of an organization's culture. **Assumptions** represent what members believe to be reality and thereby influence what they perceive and how they think and feel. Assumptions are taken for granted. They exist outside ordinary awareness and are, for the most part, inaccessible to consciousness. Try to imagine what a fish thinks about water and you get an idea of the level of awareness cultural members usually have of their basic assumptions. From the perspective of the members of a culture, the set of basic assumptions is truth, and what they assume or believe to be real is generally not open for discussion. This unquestioned "truth" penetrates every aspect of cultural life and colors all forms of experience that it touches.

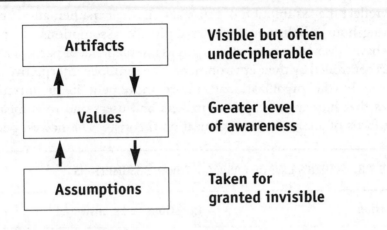

FIGURE 7.3. SCHEIN'S THREE LEVELS OF CULTURE

Adapted from *Organizational Culture and Leadership* (p. 14) by E. H. Schein. Copyright © 1985 Jossey-Bass Inc., Publishers, San Francisco. All rights reserved.

TABLE 7.2. OUR UNDERSTANDING OF "ORGANIZATIONAL MAN" EXPANDS WITH EACH NEW PERSPECTIVE IN ORGANIZATION THEORY

Perspective	Assumption	Focus/Values
Classical	Economic man	Wealth Power
Early Modern	Scientific man	Rationality Management control
Modern	Ecological man	Environment External control
Symbolic-Interpretive	Symbolic man	Interpretation Meaning
Postmodern	Aesthetic man	Creativity Freedom Responsibility

As an example, consider one type of basic assumption—the nature of human nature—and how it differs among the perspectives of organization theory (see Table 7.2). The assumption that humans are primarily concerned with wealth led classical scholars to develop ideas that focused on economic incentives. In contrast, the dominant assumption during the early days of modernism was that

Core Concepts of Organization Theory

humans are primarily rational animals, and the theories developed during this period reflect the assumption of rationality in their mathematical equations for predicting human behavior. More recently, the assumptions of open systems theory have advanced a view of humans as interdependent parts of a system and are thus controlled by their environment. The symbolic-interpretive perspective, illustrated by the organizational culture movement in organization theory, assumes that humans are symbol makers and users and thus meaning is the proper focus of attention for organization theorists. The newest perspective in

TABLE 7.3. SCHEIN'S LIST OF BASIC CULTURAL ASSUMPTIONS

Dimension	Questions to be answered
1. The organization's relationship	Does the organization perceive itself to be to its environment dominant, submissive, harmonizing, searching out of niche?
2. The nature of human activity	Is the "correct" way for humans to behave to be dominant/pro-active, harmonizing, or passive/fatalistic?
3. The nature of reality and truth	How do we define what is true and what is not true: and how is truth ultimately determined both in the physical and social world? By pragmatic test, reliance on wisdom, or social consensus?
4. The nature of time	What is our basic orientation in terms of past, present, and future, and what kinds of time units are most relevant for the conduct of daily affairs?
5. The nature of human nature	Are humans basically good, neutral, or evil, and is human nature perfectible of fixed?
6. The nature of human	What is the "correct" way for people to relationships relate to each other, to distribute power and affection? Is life competitive or cooperative? Is the best way to organize society on the basis of individualism or groupism? Is the best authority system autocratic/paternalistic or collegial/participative?
7. Homogeneity vs. diversity	Is the group best off it is highly diverse or if it is highly homogeneous, and should individuals in a group be encouraged to innovate or conform?

Adapted from *Organizational Culture and Leadership* (p. 86) by E. H. Schein. Copyright © 1985 Jossey-Bass Inc., Publishers, San Francisco. All rights reserved.

organization theory derives from the philosophy of postmodernism. One assumption of postmodernism is that human experience is fragmented. Such an assumption leads to accepting a diversity of interpretations, including those offered by Classical scholars and modernist and symbolic-interpretive organization theorists.

TABLE 7.4. SCHEIN'S EXTERNAL ADAPTATION VERSUS INTERNAL INTEGRATION TASKS

External adaptation tasks	Internal integration tasks
Developing consensus on:	Developing consensus on:
1. The core mission, functions, and primary tasks of the organization vis-à-vis its environments.	1. The common language and concep tual system to be used, including basic concepts of time and space.
2. The specific goals to be pursued by the organization.	2. The group boundaries and criteria for inclusion.
3. The basic means to be used in accomplishing the goals.	3. The criteria for the allocation of sta tus, power, and authority.
4. The criteria to be used for measuring results.	4. The criteria for intimacy, friendship, and love in different work and family settings.
5. The remedial or repair strategies if goals are not achieved.	5. The criteria for the allocation of rewards and punishments.
	6. Concepts for managing the unmanageable—ideology and religion.

The differences in the assumptions described above help to explain how organization theorists have shifted from nearly total reliance on economics and engineering, to interest in cybernetics, human biology, sociology, cultural anthropology, and, recently, semiotics and literary theory (review Figure 1-1 in the first chapter). Schein claims that assumptions have the capacity to influence what members of a culture perceive and how they think and feel. Thus, differences in the basic assumptions held by proponents of different theoretical perspectives lead to different perceptions of what is central to explanations of organization and this, in turn, produces interest in the array of basic disciplines upon which organization theory has drawn.

Culture is not a single belief or assumption, it is a set of interrelated (but not necessarily consistent) beliefs and assumptions. Schein defines seven issues that must be resolved by every culture in each historical period and claims that giving your attention to how a culture resolves each of these will help you to define its core assumptions. In addition to the nature of human nature, these issues are: the organization's relationship to its environment, the nature of reality and truth, the nature of time, the nature of human activity, the nature of human relationships, and homogeneity vs. diversity (see Table 7.3).

Schein argues that the core assumptions that resolve these issues find their way into many aspects of organizing. Schein groups these into two categories: (1) external adaptation (mission and strategy, goals, means and control systems), and (2) internal integration (common language, group boundary definition, rewards and punishments, status and power relations) (see Table 7.4). But, according to Schein, the most important influences of core assumptions from the standpoint of shaping culture are norms, values, and artifacts.

Norms and Values

Values are the social principles, goals, and standards held within a culture to have intrinsic worth. They define what the members of an organization care about, such as freedom, democracy, tradition, wealth, or loyalty. Values constitute the basis for making judgments about what is right and what is wrong, which is why they are also referred to as a moral or ethical code. Because values are used as standards for making moral judgments, they are often associated with strong emotions. Values are more conscious than basic assumptions but are not usually on the top of members' minds. Nonetheless, members of an organization are able to recognize their values fairly easily and become especially aware of them when someone tries to change their culture in some fundamental way. When values are challenged, the challenge most often comes from marginal members of the organization, such as newcomers or revolutionaries, or from outsiders (see Figure 7.4).

Norms are closely associated with values. They are the unwritten rules that allow members of a culture to know what is expected of them in a wide variety of situations. Examples of social norms typical of American culture include: do not talk in a crowded movie theater while the movie is playing, do not cut in line, and only stand up at a football game when something really exciting is going on (that is, when everybody else is standing). Business norms involve concerns such as when you should inform your boss of potential problems, what sort of clothing you should wear, and whether or not it is appropriate to display emotion in the workplace.

While values specify what is important to the members of a culture, norms establish what sorts of behavior they can expect from one another. In short,

FIGURE 7.4. CHALLENGES TO CULTURAL VALUES MOST OFTEN COME FROM MAR-
GINAL MEMBERS OF THE CULTURE SUCH AS NEWCOMERS, REVOLUTIONARIES, OR OUT-
SIDERS

In the 1960s, being marginal and challenging mainstream cultural values became
part of the youth subculture which in the U.S. was known as the "hippie" subculture within which driving a VW bus, preferably old, was a symbol of belonging.

values define what is valued, while norms make clear what it takes to be considered normal or abnormal. The link between values and norms is that the behaviors that norms sanction (that is, reward or punish) usually can be traced to
outcomes that are valued. For example, the norms about talking in movie the-
aters, cutting in line, and standing at football games might be traced to a cultural
value for courtesy to others. Norms about wearing formal business attire (e.g.,
suits and ties) and not displaying any emotion while at work may indicate a value
for self-discipline or for conformity with the American business ideal.

TABLE 7.5. ARTIFACTS OF ORGANIZATIONAL CULTURES

General category	Specific examples
physical manifestations	• art/design/logo • buildings/decor • dress/appearance • material objects • physical layout
behavioral manifestations	• ceremonies/rituals • communication patterns • traditions/customs • rewards/punishments
verbal manifestations	• anecdotes/jokes • jargon/names/nicknames • explanations • stories/myths/history • heroes/villains • metaphors

---

According to Schein's theory, the members of a culture hold values and conform to cultural norms because their underlying beliefs and assumptions nurture and support these norms and values. The norms and values, in turn, encourage activities that produce surface-level artifacts. Artifacts are further extensions or expressions of the same cultural core that maintains the values and norms.

Artifacts

You could think of **artifacts** as remains of the cultural core left strewn about on the surface of a culture, sort of like cooled lava is left lying around the earth's surface after a volcano has been active. In the same way that geologists study lava as evidence of what the earth's core is like, we can study artifacts as evidence of a culture's core. Artifacts are the visible, tangible, and audible remains of behavior grounded in cultural norms, values, and assumptions.[8] Categories of artifacts include: physical objects created by the members of a culture, verbal manifestations seen in written and spoken language, and rituals, ceremonies, and other behavioral manifestations. Table 7.5 shows several examples of each category.

Members of a culture may or may not be aware of their culture's artifacts, but the artifacts themselves can be directly observed by anyone. From the researcher's viewpoint, artifacts are the most accessible elements of culture. Even though they are highly accessible, however, remember that artifacts lie furthest from the cultural core. Their remoteness from the core indicates that they are easily misinterpreted by those who are culturally naive, including cultural researchers when they begin a new study.

How Culture Works

According to Schein, the essence of culture is its core of basic assumptions and established beliefs. This core reaches outward through the values and behavioral norms that are recognized, responded to, and maintained by members of the culture. The values and norms, in turn, influence the choices and other actions taken by cultural members. Finally, culturally guided action produces artifacts.

Schein claims that when new members are brought into a culture, they are either selected on the basis of the match between their values and those of the culture, or they are socialized to accept cultural values. Cultures change, but only when new values are brought in from outside the culture, for instance by the decree or example of top management. However, Schein emphasizes that new values will be incorporated into basic assumptions only after they have proved their worth in terms of desired organizational outcomes. Only when members of the culture can see their benefit, will new values become taken for granted and drop to the level of unconscious assumptions.

From the point of view offered by Schein's model, culture appears to be driven from the inside out—from the depths of unconscious assumptions, values, and norms to the surface where numerous artifacts can be observed. But this is not the end of the story; the arrows in Schein's model point both ways. At the same time that values and assumptions are pushing their way "up" to the level of artifacts, the artifacts are being interpreted in ways that can transform the very values and assumptions that produced them in the first place. This happens because artifacts and norms are consciously and creatively used by the members of a culture to express their identity and to formulate and pursue their purposes. To study this aspect of culture it is useful to turn from Schein's model to the symbolic tradition within organization theory.[9]

SYMBOLIC-INTERPRETIVE ORGANIZATIONAL CULTURE THEORY

Early on, symbolic-interpretive culture researchers adopted Clifford Geertz, an American cultural anthropologist, as a sort of guru. One particular quotation from his work is widely cited because it concisely and evocatively represents both the conceptual foundation of the symbolic-interpretive approach and Geertz's engaging spirit: "man is an animal suspended in webs of significance he himself has spun, I take culture to be those webs, and the analysis of it to be therefore not an experimental science in search of law but an interpretive one in search of meaning."[10]

The symbolic-interpretive approach starts from the assumption that cultures are socially constructed realities, or, in Geertz's memorable terms, "webs of significance [man] himself has spun." You will remember from Chapter 2 that socially constructed reality refers to the idea that, for groups, organizations, and societies, reality is not formed by conditions in the natural or physical world as much as it is defined through interpersonal association and agreement. For example, a family does not require biological relationships, but it does depend upon the willingness of family members to define themselves as such and to engage in certain expected behaviors. The argument is that families can be created that have no genetic basis at all, as in the case of adoptions. Yet, when genetic parents and their children cease to define one another in these terms, the family usually dissolves, even though they may still live together.[11] It is in the sense that all cultures, including families and organizations, require cooperative effort and mutual self-definition that we say they are socially constructed. Socially constructed entities exist only so long as their members regard them as existing and behave accordingly.

The symbolic-interpretive approach in organizational culture studies is concerned with describing how organizational realities are socially constructed. Humans can engage in the socially constructed aspects of organizational life because they make, use, and interpret symbols and because they are sensitive to the interpretations made by others. The use and interpretation of symbols permits the members of an organization to create and maintain their culture. It is, therefore, through observation of symbol construction and use that culture comes to be known by the symbolic-interpretive researcher. When working within the symbolic-interpretive tradition, a culture researcher searches for the key symbols of a culture and seeks out local interpretations in order to glimpse cultural meaning from the native point of view.

Although symbolic-interpretive culture researchers steep themselves in the experiences and meanings of specific members of a culture, the objective of their search is a larger perspective than that of any individual member. The perspective sought is, ideally, that of the entire system of experiences and interpretations distributed across all the culture's members. The native view is not one native's view, but a delicate amalgamation that represents the whole culture in its full complexity. To gain this perspective, culture researchers describe the ways in which the experiences and interpretations that they have collected fit together to form cultural patterns. The goal is to formulate patterns that are recognizable to cultural members, or at least to others who have been close to the culture.

Symbols

A **symbol** is anything that represents a conscious or unconscious association with some wider concept or meaning. Thus, a symbol consists of both a tangible form and the wider meaning (or meanings) with which it is associated. The dove, for example, is a commonly recognized symbol for peace (Figure 7.5). In this symbol the tangible form is the image of the bird; the meaning that extends beyond this form is peace.

The Mercedes-Benz logo is an example of a symbol associated with an organization. As a tangible form, this logo is usually a piece of metal with a distinctive shape. It is a designed artifact of a manufacturer of German automobiles. The logo signifies that a given automobile is the product of Daimler-Benz. In terms of *symbolic* meaning, however, the Mercedes logo extends well beyond both the tangible form of the artifact and its capacity to signify the maker. For instance, it is capable of symbolizing quality, luxury, and prestige. However, it can also symbolize overindulgence or the injustice of being poor. This illustrates an important point about symbols—the same symbol can support different, and even contradictory, meanings.

In the example of the Mercedes logo we see that management *can* exercise considerable control over the design and display of its artifacts, but the symbolic

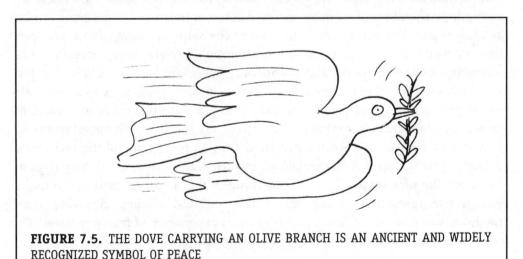

FIGURE 7.5. THE DOVE CARRYING AN OLIVE BRANCH IS AN ANCIENT AND WIDELY RECOGNIZED SYMBOL OF PEACE

messages with which artifacts become associated are far less easy to control. Many symbolic associations are unpredictable. Recognizing the difficulty of controlling symbolic meaning is important for understanding the symbolic approach to studying cultures.

Symbols come in many forms, but all of them fall into one of three broad categories: physical objects, behavioral events, and verbal expressions. Notice that these categories could easily be applied to the artifacts shown in Table 7.5. This is because there is a theoretical relationship between cultural symbols and artifacts. Cultural artifacts can become symbols, but not all artifacts do so. An artifact becomes a cultural symbol only when members of the culture attach meaning to it and use the symbol thus made to communicate meaning to others.[12] For instance, we can see that a national flag is a symbol by the responses given to it by members of the culture that it represents; in the case of the American flag, examples include saluting, waving, burning, and using it as an article of clothing. Notice, however, that an artifact can be used symbolically at one moment and not at the next (e.g., when the flag is tucked away in a drawer). What makes an artifact a symbol is its use by humans to make meaning. Notice also that recognizing that an artifact is being used as a symbol does not necessarily equate with knowing its meaning within the culture; meaning involves interpretation.

Interpretation

The symbolic-interpretive approach teaches us that symbols are inherently ambiguous; members of a culture can give different meanings to the same symbol as well as use different symbols to convey the same meaning. However, even though members may give ambiguous symbols private interpretations, their interpretations are formed under a more or less constant barrage of influence provided by other members of the culture such as bosses, gossips, newscasters, television personalities, and professors. Interpretations are not made in a vacuum, rather they, like the culture that embeds them, are socially constructed realities.

It is impossible to lay down a precise definition to capture all the nuances of meaning that the term "interpretation" evokes. The most effective way to communicate the idea is to tell you about some of the methods used by symbolic-interpretive researchers when they make cultural studies. Applying these methods will give you a direct and conscious experience of interpretation. The set of methods I will focus on is called ethnography.[13]

Ethnography: How to Make Cultural Studies of Organizations

Ethnography means cultural description, and the specific techniques that fall into the broad category of ethnographic methods are almost as varied as the definitions of culture. We will focus on ethnography produced via two general methods of data collection—observation and interviews. These methods have been chosen because culture researchers often rely upon some combination of these to produce their ethnographies. The typical organizational culture study proceeds from data collected by: (1) direct observation of artifacts and symbols and the uses to which members of a culture put them, and (2) interviews with cultural members focused on discovering their ways of experiencing and interpreting their world. Analysis and cultural description follow data collection.

Step 1—Data Collection

You cannot directly experience another person's values, assumptions, or symbolic interpretations, but you can directly experience their artifacts. Therefore, observation of artifacts and the behavior that occurs around them is a typical starting point in a study of culture. At the start of your study, artifacts will appear as isolated objects, events, or linguistic forms (e.g., stories, jokes, metaphors). Tempting as it may seem, it is unwise to interpret these first artifacts until additional evidence is collected. The best way to proceed is to examine as many artifacts as possible, making extensive notes about the artifacts and the symbolic uses to which you see them put in the daily lives of organizational members.

Through interviews you will then try to discover the interpretations that members give to the artifacts you have observed. Try to write down or tape record as much of their actual language as possible rather than putting the members' ideas into your own words. Sometime during this part of your study, you will begin to sense the degree of symbolic significance in the artifacts you have collected. Make notes about these feelings, and also jot down what caused you to believe a particular artifact was acting as a symbol within the culture. Keep notes about your hunches, feelings, and ideas in a separate **field journal** so that they do not become confused with your descriptions, which are called your **field notes**. Take care with all of the notes that you keep because they are the raw data for your analysis. Take them out from time to time and play with them as you might play with a collection of rocks or seashells.

Step 2—Phase I: Analysis

During phase I of data analysis, your data must be organized and reorganized until patterns suggesting specific norms and values (the Schein model) and symbolic themes (the symbolic approach) can be found. You will know that you have collected and analyzed enough evidence when you find that you are able to link a fair number of artifacts to several norms and values and that you can identify the convergence of some key symbols on one or more cultural themes (e.g., aggression, innocence). It is likely that you will find it useful to go back into the field during this phase of your analysis. This is because, as it progresses, your analysis will suggest additional places to look for artifacts and symbols and additional questions to ask of cultural members.

Do not force your analysis at this or any other stage of your cultural study. Instead, allow your answers to emerge from the process. Ethnographers often describe this emergence by saying that "the data speak" to them. What they mean is that you should keep reading and rereading your notes, and arranging and rearranging the artifacts and symbols you find there until you begin to feel that the data have their own order and meaning. This procedure is designed to minimize the chances that you will impose an order or a meaning onto the data based only on your own biases or strictly personal interpretations.

Step 3—Phase II: Analysis and Description

When you feel comfortable that a larger picture of the culture is emerging from the first phase of your analysis, the data, along with the emerging norms, values, and symbolic themes, are further sorted and organized. This second phase continues, along the lines of the first, until the deeper beliefs, assumptions, and symbolic patterns of meaning linking the norms, values, and themes begin to reveal themselves. This is the point at which it is appropriate to try to finalize your description of the order in your data. Do so. If you have insurmountable difficulties, go back to the data and continue processing, going all the way back to data collection if you feel the need.

A word of warning: because the deep patterns you are seeking are theoretically distant from the original observations on which your study is based, the second phase of analysis is considerably more challenging than the first. As a consequence, your level of confidence will seem to ebb away as you move from considering norms, values, and symbolic themes to trying to define beliefs, assumptions, and webs of meaning. This loss of confidence is natural. You are not alone, all ethnographers must learn to cope with this aspect of cultural analysis, as Geertz makes clear:

There is an Indian story—at least I heard it as an Indian story—about an Englishman who, having been told that the world rested on a platform which rested on the back of an elephant which rested in turn on the back of a turtle, asked (perhaps he was an ethnographer; it is the way they behave), what did the turtle rest on? Another turtle. And that turtle? "Ah, Sahib, after that it is turtles all the way down." . . . I [have never] gotten anywhere near to the bottom of anything I have ever written about . . . Cultural analysis is intrinsically incomplete. And, worse than that, the more deeply it goes the less complete it is. It is a strange science whose most telling assertions are its most tremulously based, in which to get somewhere with the matter at hand is to intensify the suspicion, both your own and that of others, that you are not quite getting it right.[14]

You cannot avoid uncertainty *and* do a successful culture study. In fact, you would not want to. Facing the uncertainties inherent in cultural description will help you come to grips with the inadequacy of a single mind attempting to understand an entire organization. Press on. Although you will probably never reach the ideal of complete clarity, you will learn a great deal about culture by trying. In the process, you may also enhance your ability to handle uncertainty.

An Example of Cultural Analysis

Illustrating the ethnographic approach to understanding organizational culture demands a rich example. Our example comes from a colorful American culture that developed around the Chicago Cubs baseball team—the Cubs fans. The analysis begins with a general description of the baseball game as a cultural event. Following this, I will describe a notorious ritual that occurs during baseball games (themselves a kind of ceremony) that take place at Wrigley Field, the Cubs' home stadium located in Chicago, Illinois.

The baseball game is a key cultural event for every baseball organization. A team's reputation hinges on how many games it can win. Winning a game depends upon scoring "runs," so the run is particularly meaningful within baseball cultures. A run requires that a player ("the batter") hit the baseball so that it comes down within the playing field ("in fair territory") but is not caught by the opposing team before it touches the ground. The ball is then considered to be "in play." When this happens, the player (now called "the runner") must run around a diamond-shaped path ("the diamond") painted in white on the playing field. During his run, the player must step on each corner of the diamond which is marked by a "base." Meanwhile, the opponents try to carry or throw the ball back and "tag" either the runner or the base that the runner is approaching, before he can make it around all the bases. Runners who cannot complete the run try to stop on one of the bases, where they will be "safe." If an opponent can tag a runner while he is between two bases, the runner is declared "out" which means he is no longer in position to score a run. If safe, he must wait for another batter from his team to hit the ball into play or for the pitcher to walk a batter or make a mistake (e.g., throw a wild pitch).

Players who cross "home plate" score a run. The most decisive way to score a run is to hit the ball "out of the park," which generally means into the seats ("grandstands" or "bleachers") where the audience sits, but can literally mean hitting the ball over the back wall. Such a hit has a special name—a "homerun" or "homer." Because of the difficulty and the advantages of hitting a homerun, this particular act is given high regard, in fact, a homerun is considered a heroic achievement for a ballplayer. For a baseball fan, the commensurate achievement is catching a homerun ball. At Wrigley Field, non-paying fans even stand outside the park in case a homer is hit over the wall, at which point there is a mad scramble to grab the ball. Baseball fans honor homerun balls they have caught by placing them on special display pedestals or in lucite cases, some even inscribe their display case with the date on which they caught the ball.

Some years ago, fans of the Chicago Cubs baseball team introduced an interesting cultural twist to the tradition of catching homerun balls: at home games, if a Cubs fan catches a homerun ball hit by the opposing team, they are expected to throw the ball back onto the field. Within baseball culture, returning a homerun ball to the field clearly communicates that the ball is worthless and, by implication, that *this* homerun was an insignificant achievement. The act is a symbolic insult thrown (along with the actual ball) at the opposing team. Within baseball cultures, harassing the opposition is a time-honored tradition. For example, catcher's banter ("Hey-batter-hey-batter-hey-batter") while the ball is being pitched is designed to interrupt the concentration of the batter as he prepares to swing. Other examples include mocking the opposing team with the ridiculing behavior of team mascots or displays of humorous messages on computerized scoreboards.

The gesture of the returned homerun ball *could* be interpreted simply as one among many forms of harassment that exist within all American baseball cultures. But there is more to this story because fans of other teams do not engage in this particular practice. Although their catchers also razz batters and they too mock the opposing team, fans of other teams keep homerun balls regardless of which team hit them (some fans spend hundreds of hours and a great deal of money attending games hoping for such an unlikely catch). Therefore, prying a Cubs fan loose from a prize like a homerun ball is a cultural achievement worthy of notice—and careful cultural analysis.

First, it should be recognized that throwing a homerun ball back is a considerable personal sacrifice for a Cubs fan, just as it would be for a fan of any other team. Second, if you watch carefully during the unfolding of several of these events, you will observe that the fan who has caught the ball does not always give it up immediately. Throwing the ball back can require prodding. This is accomplished by loud booing clearly directed at the fan. The booing continues, increasing in volume, until the ball is returned to the field, and the (now) compliant fan is rewarded with a hearty cheer. Of course, fans who are well-established members of the culture require no prodding and they gleefully throw the ball back while the runner is still trotting around the bases enjoying his moment of glory. Non-paying fans outside the stadium have even been known to throw retrieved balls back over the wall!

Another interesting twist is found on careful examination of videotapes of these events. The tapes show some fans switching a caught ball for their own, perhaps older, or non-official, ball that they then throw back onto the field in feigned compliance with the cultural norm.[15] Finally, you should know that the Cub's local tradition of throwing homerun balls back onto the field is spreading, fans of other clubs have picked up the idea and are diffusing this ritual throughout the rest of American baseball culture.

Now let us apply some culture concepts to the Cubs example. Underlying cultural assumptions and beliefs produce, among other things, a value for homerun balls, a competitive urge, and knowledge of effective ways to sanction the behavior of other members of the culture. In the case of the Cubs fans, shared cultural understandings are manifested in the norm for throwing back opponents' homerun balls. This cultural norm is reinforced by booing (negative sanction using a verbal symbol) and subsequent cheering (positive sanction using a different verbal symbol) that we see within the cultural ritual (artifact). The ritual consists of a fan first catching (a ritual Cubs fan culture holds in common with other American baseball cultures) an opponent's homerun ball (artifact about to become a physical symbol) and then throwing it back onto the field (a ritual unique to the Cubs fan culture and also a behavioral symbol of disrespect).

At this point you would probably like to draw some further conclusions about the underlying assumptions of this culture. Resist this urge! Remember, we have only considered *one* cultural event at this point and we need a great deal more information to do a credible job of analyzing the culture. Nonetheless, this illustration should give you some appreciation for the richness provided by a cultural understanding of organizations and for the requirements of doing such analyses.

ORGANIZATIONAL SUBCULTURES

In understanding the dynamics of Cubs fan culture we used information about cultural forces associated with the entire domain of American baseball and about

Core Concepts of Organization Theory

specific baseball organizations within this larger domain. This illustrates the concept of subcultures—different baseball teams and their fans comprise subcultures within American baseball culture. Two American contributors to the development of the subculture school within organization theory, John van Maanen and Stephen Barley, define subculture as:

a subset of an organization's members who interact regularly with one another, identify themselves as a distinct group within the organization, share a set of problems commonly defined to be the problems of all, and routinely take action on the basis of collective understandings unique to the group.[16]

Compare this definition of subculture with the definitions of culture shown in Table 7.1. The comparison underscores the similarity between subcultures and organizational cultures. The main difference is that, instead of seeing a culture as one unitary whole, as Schein does for example, the subculture view paints a picture of numerous small cultures (i.e., the subcultures) all existing within the same organization. Several ways to envision this are illustrated in Figure 7.6.

The seemingly minor amount of difference between the concepts of culture and subculture has a major implication. The subculture view opens up the concept of organizational culture with about the same effect as the opening of Pandora's box in Greek mythology. Once the box is opened, we must live with the chaos we have unleashed. In the case of subcultures, the chaos is an image of culture that is far more complex and contradictory than it ever appeared to be

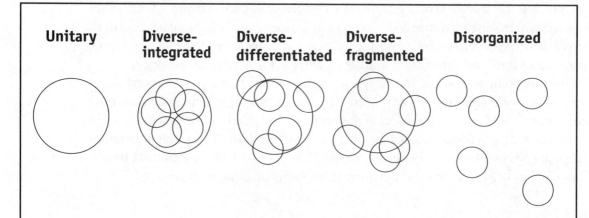

FIGURE 7.6. A CONTINUUM FOR DESCRIBING A CULTURE'S STATE OF INTEGRATION-DIFFERENTIATION

Notice how the disorganized state is similar to multiple unitary cultures.

226

within the unitary framework offered by Schein.[17] The subculture view makes us acutely aware of the many differences that distinguish multiple subcultures co-existing within a single organization.

At the organizational level, we are faced with untangling how all of the sub-cultures relate to each other and discovering how they fit together to form the larger organizational culture. This is the same situation we face when we try to understand an organizational culture in relationship to its environment. At the environmental level, the entire organizational culture can be thought of as a single subculture within an even larger cultural framework, such as a societal culture (Figure 7.7). Here an organizational subculture is seen as equivalent to a sub-sub-societal culture.

Finally, let us return to the possibilities illustrated in Figure 7.6. Consider a continuum that ranges from unity through integration, differentiation, and fragmentation to disintegration. Different organizational cultures can be placed along the continuum according to the relative degree of unity–fragmentation among their subcultures. That is, the greater the degree of fragmentation among subcultures, the closer the organizational culture will come to the end of the continuum marked "fragmented." Another way to look at this idea is to think about tracing changes in a particular culture in order to describe shifting levels of unity and fragmentation within the organization. This view allows us to see that cultures are not static, but shift and change over time.

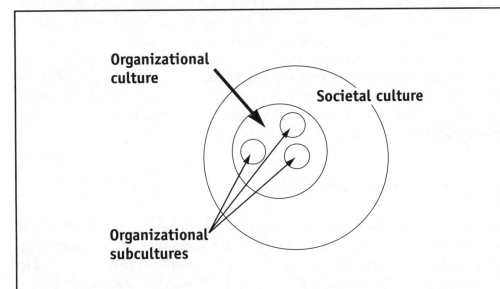

FIGURE 7.7. LEVELS OF ANALYSIS IN RELATION TO THE CONCEPT OF ORGANIZA-TIONAL CULTURE

Types of Subcultures

The **subculture** approach introduces the interesting question of what distinguishes the subcultures of an organization from one another. Subculture researchers have so far proposed two frameworks for describing these differences.

American organizational culture researchers Caren Siehl and Joanne Martin believe that subcultures are defined in relation to an organization's overall cultural patterns, especially with respect to the culture's dominant values.[18] In this view, subcultures are classified according to whether they support, deny, or simply exist alongside the dominant values of the overall culture. Enhancing subcultures support the dominant values with great enthusiasm. Countercultures defy the dominant values of the larger culture of which they are a part. Orthogonal subcultures maintain their own, independent values alongside the dominant values of the overall culture.

Another group of researchers distinguishes subcultures on the bases of occupation, work group, hierarchical level, and previous organizational affiliations.[19] For example, two occupational subcultures found in many R & D organizations are professional business managers (e.g., MBAs) and scientists (or designers). Work group subcultures are likely to be found wherever the requirements of their jobs cause people to work closely together. Project teams, branch offices, and small or physically isolated departmental units are good places to look for work group subcultures.[20] Hierarchical subcultures emphasize the distinction between different levels of management or between management and workers, the latter sometimes becoming institutionalized in union–management relations. Subcultures based on previous organizational affiliations can often be found in organizations formed by merger or acquisition, for example the innovative (former Sperry employees) and bureaucratic (former Burroughs employees) subcultures produced by the 1986 Unisys merger.[21]

Why are there Subcultures?

Van Maanen and Barley make two observations about human behavior that help to explain the occurrence of subcultures.[22] First is the interpersonal attraction explanation. Psychological studies have shown that people tend to be attracted to others they see as like themselves. This suggests that, in general, similar people will be attracted to an occupation, a job, a position in the hierarchy (management or worker), or a particular organization. To the extent that this is true, the interpersonal attraction hypothesis provides a reason for subculture differentiation along the lines of these differences. Other ways in which people are similar include age, gender, and memberships in other organizations (churches, schools, sports clubs, etc.). These similarities also contribute to subcultural differentiation in organizations.

A second explanation for subcultural differentiation involves interaction among the members of an organization. Studies of group dynamics show that when individuals regularly engage in interaction, groups are more likely to form and become cohesive. Thus, interaction patterns also explain subcultural differentiation. Task interdependence, reporting relationships, proximity, design of offices and work stations, and shared equipment or facilities (e.g., copy machines, coffee dispensers, mailboxes, break rooms) all bring certain members of an organization into contact with one another. Look for these as possible contributors to the formation of subcultures.

Of course, the forces of interpersonal attraction and opportunities to interact may combine to explain patterns of subculture formation. To see this more clearly, consider a hierarchical subculture found in many organizations: the top management team. Most members of top management are older than other members of the organization, in many firms they are all male, may have the same level of education, and surprisingly often have attended the same or similar schools (e.g., a prestigious university). Their histories within the organization will differ by their areas of expertise and their power bases, but they are probably united in their desire to promote the overall interests of the organization within its environment. Members of top management usually interact regularly and, more often than not, occupy offices located next to one another and clearly marked off from the rest of the organization. Contrast the situation of top management with that of middle-level managers. Middle managers are usually located near their subordinates and so are spatially disbursed throughout the organization leaving them relatively limited opportunities to interact with each other. Middle managers also are more likely to have goals that conflict with the goals of other managers at their level, and their age, gender composition, and educational backgrounds are usually more varied than those of the top management team.

CULTURE AS FRAGMENTATION: A POSTMODERN VIEW

American organizational culture researchers Joanne Martin and Debra Meyerson identify three distinct perspectives within the field of organizational culture studies: integration, differentiation, and fragmentation.[23] In the integration perspective, organizational culture is described as being shared by all members of the culture in an organization-wide consensus. This view is illustrated by Schein's theory of organizational culture. The differentiation perspective takes a subcultural point of view and describes how organizational unity is fractured by subcultures. Subcultures themselves, however, are depicted in much the same way as unitary cultures—as consensual, consistent, coherent, stable wholes. The **fragmentation perspective**, which embraces a postmodern view of organizational culture, looks for neither consistency nor stability. Instead it focuses on the ways in which organizational cultures are inconsistent, ambiguous, multiplicitous, and in a constant state of flux.

According to Martin, the fragmentation perspective can be defined as a postmodern critique of the differentiation perspective. The focus of the critique is on the way in which the differentiation perspective identifies subcultures using dichotomous or oppositional thinking (e.g., labor versus management, staff versus line, men versus women, blacks versus whites, smokers versus non-smokers). Says Martin, "subcultures [usually] represent ends of a dichotomy, and one of these dichotomous alternatives is viewed as having a higher status than the other." She continues:

One problem with dichotomous thinking is that it oversimplifies and misrepresents the attributes and viewpoints of members of lower status groups. When differences between groups are defined using dichotomies or other forms of oppositional thinking, the terms of these definitions are usually based on the characteristics and viewpoints of the dominant group.[24]

As an example of oppositional thinking, Martin offers some observations about racial differences in American organizations. She writes:

what it means to be black in a given organizational context has meaning only in so far as being black is seen as being not-white. Racial differences are assessed within an established hierarchical system that begins with dimensions of comparison relevant to the dominant group. Thus, not surprisingly, on these dimensions whites are seen as having more status and greater value than blacks. In this kind of oppositional thinking, attributes of the subordinated group that are unique to that group, and might be valued differently, fall outside the established hierarchy reified by the dichotomy and are ignored.[25]

In place of oppositional thinking, the fragmentation perspective offers acknowledgement of multiplicity. That is, the fragmentation perspective begins from the observation that, although there is only one way in which things may be considered the same, there are multiple ways in which they can be different. For example, there are many ways in which being black can be defined in terms that have nothing to do with the black is not-white opposition, but all of them require taking an other-than-white perspective. Doing so produces the experience of multiplicity—at least for whites. One implication of multiplicity is that identity becomes fragmented. For instance, Martin describes persons with mixed racial ancestry who get by, for example, by learning to be Indian in Mexican culture and Mexican in Anglo culture.[26]

Martin suggests that not only racial identity, but gender, occupation, hierarchical position, and many other identifying characteristics may be perceived as oppositional but are actually multiplicitous and that they all co-exist within members of organizations. Because of the variety of individual bases of identity, allegiances to subcultures may constantly shift with the issues of debate or discourse. As Martin puts it:

when two cultural members agree (or disagree) on a particular interpretation of, say, a ritual, this is likely to be a temporary and issue-specific congruence (or incongruence). It may well not reflect agreement or disagreement on other issues, at other times. Subcultures, then, are reconceptualized as fleeting, issue-specific coalitions that may or may not have a similar configuration in the future. This is not simply a failure to achieve subcultural consensus in a particular context; from the Fragmentation perspective this is the most consensus possible in any context.[27]

In this view, alliances or coalitions can never stabilize into subcultures and certainly not into unified cultures because discourse and its focal issues are always changing—hence the image of fragmentation.

CULTURE IN THE MODERNIST PERSPECTIVE

Modernists follow symbolic-interpretivists in believing that assumptions and values influence behavior through their expression in norms and expectations and communicate identity through symbols, tradition, and customs. The difference comes in the way in which knowledge about culture is used by proponents of each perspective. Symbolic-interpretivists define culture as a context for meaning making and interpretation. In their view, awareness of assumptions and values offers a framework for knowing yourself in relation to those around you. Knowledge of this relationship is what permits insight into culture, your own as well as somebody else's. Modernists, on the other hand, interpret knowledge about culture as a tool of management, and culture itself as a variable to be manipulated to enhance the likelihood of achieving desired levels of performance from others within the organization.[28]

The difference between modern and symbolic-interpretive uses of the culture concept derives, in part at least, from the epistemological departure point each takes. Whereas modernists believe in scientific detachment from the object of study (which defines an outsider's view), symbolic-interpretivists claim that cultural meaning can only be encountered and understood from within the cultural system in question. These differences come to a head in debate about whether subjective approaches can be scientific. Modernists argue against this proposition. To support their position they cite the rules of the scientific method and its requirement of scientific objectivity. Symbolic-interpretivists counter that not only is a subjectivist approach to science possible, but that the scientific objectivity claimed by modernists is an illusion. They claim that no observation of phenomena is free of the effects of the observational act, thus, there can be no such thing as an outsider's objective perspective, especially when it comes to understanding something as subjective as cultural meaning.

Symbolic-interpretivists contend that what modernists measure when they claim to study culture, usually with survey questionnaires, is simply a reflection of their own culture of academic research. This is because respondents are forced to formulate answers to survey questions in the terms set out by the survey writers rather than in their own terms. The difference is one of being sensitive to context. Symbolic-interpretivists argue that meaning is dependent on the context in which artifacts and symbols are encountered. You have, no doubt, had the experience of having your words taken out of context, for example when someone uses something you have said against you in an argument. Similarly, you have probably heard politicians make this claim in defending themselves against charges made by the press or other politicians. The act of taking a cultural symbol out of context has a similar effect on meaning. Thus, when symbolic-interpretivists talk about **contextualizing** in regard to cultural analysis, they are advocating studying artifacts and symbols in the situations and locations in which they naturally occur (e.g., via ethnographic observation), allowing organizational members to use and speak about them as they ordinarily do (e.g., via ethnographic interviewing). Their goal is to enter the cultural context of the organization and learn to understand it from the inside.

The goal of modernist research, on the other hand, is to develop generalized knowledge that can be applied across contexts. Thus, the modernist approach is *de*contextualized by definition. Modernists argue their own case by pointing out that symbolic-interpretivists are so context sensitive that, although they generate rich images of particular cultures, there is not much practical value in their efforts outside of the settings in which their images are developed. What is more, the ethnographic methods of symbolic-interpretive researchers are so time-consuming that their work is economically impractical. The modernist position is that it is better to sacrifice some contextual sensitivity than to give up cross-organizational comparisons. Be sure to notice in these arguments the traces of underlying values of the symbolic-interpretive and modernist perspectives.

Whereas symbolic-interpretivists' arguments symbolize a value for sympathetic understanding of others, the modernist argument gives evidence of values for efficiency and control.

Modernist studies generally involve looking at statistical relationships between variables representing organizational culture and performance. To quantify cultural variables requires choosing a particular dimension or dimensions of the culture construct to measure. So far, modernist cultural researchers have given the most attention to a variable they call **cultural strength**. Terrence Deal and Allan Kennedy first described cultural strength as the extent to which organizational members share core values.[29] Deal and Kennedy claim that cultural strength is indicated by the presence of many symbols and artifacts associated with core values.

Measuring cultural strength can be much more difficult than defining it. For example, one way to measure cultural strength might be to ask survey respondents about the extent to which they agree or disagree with certain value-laden statements. The variance in the responses to the statements could then be computed for all (or a statistical sample of) members of each organization to be studied and this number used to estimate the organization's cultural strength. Observations of cultural strength for numerous organizations could then be used to form a variable and compute its correlation with other measures, such as organizational performance. However, not only would it be difficult to collect the necessary data, since the cooperation of an enormous number of individuals would be required, but the quality of the measure would depend on whether or not the researchers who wrote the questionnaire correctly identified the core values of each organization and communicated them effectively in the survey items.

American researchers John Kotter and James Heskett, used a different method to measure the cultural strength of over 200 corporations.[30] They contacted financial analysts and managers of firms that were in competition with the organizations they wanted to study and asked them to rate the cultural strength of their sample firms. They formulated an average score for each firm and then correlated this measure with organizational performance measured in terms of average yearly increases in net income, average yearly return on investment, and average yearly change in stock price (i.e., market value of the firm). These researchers found that although strong culture is significantly related to organizational performance overall, when cultural values support organizational adaptation to the environment, the relationship becomes much stronger. More explicitly, culture has an important influence on organizational performance when it either helps the organization to anticipate or adapt to environmental change (positive influence on performance) or interferes with its adaptation to the environment (negative influence on performance). When cultures do not support adaptation, cultural strength can interfere with performance. Kotter and Heskett argue that this is because culture can blind organizational members to information that does not match their assumptions and because an entrenched culture can resist efforts to implement new strategies.

Organizational theorist Dan Denison follows a similar line of reasoning in his theory of the relationships between environment, strategy, and culture.[31] Based on the findings of his research, Denison claims that organizations operating in rapidly changing environments will perform best if they either value flexibility and change (Denison calls this an adaptability culture) or participation and high levels of organizational commitment (which he calls an involvement culture). In stable environments, Denison argues, successful organizations either share a vision of the future (the mission culture) or have strong values for tradition, established procedures, and conformity (a consistency culture). You will recognize Denison's approach as an extension of modernist contingency theory.

Managing Culture

The question of whether or not cultures can be managed is largely a modernist concern that has provoked a long and, at times emotional, debate among organization theorists. For those who believe that culture can be managed, culture theory holds a promise of new forms of managerial influence and control in organizations.[32] This group reasons that, if culture influences behavior via norms and values, then it should be possible to manage the norms and values of the organization in such a way that desired behaviors and other organizational performance outcomes are more or less guaranteed. Such control might come, for instance, through recruiting and hiring practices aimed at finding value-compatible employees.[33] Those who oppose the idea that culture can be managed argue that, since norms and values are grounded in deeply rooted basic assumptions and unquestioned beliefs, the possibilities for managing culture are severely limited.

One unexamined assumption within this debate is the belief that top managers are the most influential members of an organizational culture. Because of their enormous visibility to other members and because the power structure favors them, their behavior sets a standard for others and their words have great likelihood of being heard. This opportunity to influence, however, does not necessarily guarantee that the intentions of top managers will be understood or that they will be acted upon by other members of the culture. This is the heart of the culture as control debate. Those who believe culture can be used as a mechanism of control are accused by those who do not of being unrealistic about the potential to control interpretations. Others, such as some postmodernists, go further and argue about the ethics of control or the benefits of relinquishing control (e.g., to innovation, personal freedom, the democratic process).

The symbolic-interpretive approach to culture theory offers a way to carve out a middle ground in this debate. From this perspective it can be argued that managers have the potential to become powerful symbols within their organizations.[34] As symbols, managers represent the meanings that other employees associate with the organization. However, it should be recognized that the symbolic power of managers and the meanings that they represent depend upon the interpretations that other members of the culture give to them, thus, successful leadership requires adaptation to the symbolic interpretation schemes that constitute the organizational culture.[35] This argument recognizes that managers are themselves part of the culture and are, therefore, likely to be managed *by* cultural influence even while they are trying to be managers *of* the culture. In other words, managers are artifacts who would like to be symbols.

The implication, and I believe the central message of the symbolic-interpretive study of organizational culture, is that, rather than trying to manage culture through *cultural change* programs, you should consider your cultural context whenever you contemplate or carry out *organizational change*. When you attempt to change organizational culture, while it is true that something will change, generally the changes are unpredictable and sometimes undesirable (e.g., increases in employee cynicism toward cultural change programs). This does not mean that concern for culture is unwarranted. To the contrary, it is essential. But you need to give up thinking of culture as an entity and trying to understand what it *does*. Instead, think of culture as a context for meaning making and interpretation. Do not think of trying to manage culture. Other people's meanings and interpretations are highly unmanageable. Think instead about trying to culturally manage your organization, that is, manage your organization with cultural awareness of the multiplicity of meanings that will be made of you and your efforts.

SUMMARY

An organization can be viewed as a culture in its own right, as a set of subcultures, or as an artifact through which an even larger culture expresses itself. We have emphasized the first and second of these viewpoints in this chapter, since these are the perspectives from which organizational members typically think about their organization. Nonetheless, effects of larger cultures are part of the organizational environment and will, therefore, be an important part of a complete

Core Concepts of Organization Theory

organizational analysis, as Hofstede's study of the influence of national cultures indicates. The environmental context of the organization should be kept in mind as the analysis of organizational culture (or any other aspect of the organization) is pursued.

Culture involves the members of an organization in a socially constructed reality. Organizational members share this reality in the dual senses of similarity and difference. The elements upon which cultural sharing is based include artifacts, symbols, norms, values, beliefs, and assumptions (from Schein's perspective), and physical, behavioral, and linguistic symbols (from the symbolic point of view). These cultural elements are interrelated in a web of interwoven meanings—a set of core assumptions and a worldview—accessible to all members of the culture (or subculture, if that is your level of analysis). The worldview aids members in managing their activities and in making sense out of their organizational experiences. This socially constructed context, to which cultural members routinely orient their experience and activity, is what we refer to as organizational culture.

No amount of talk about culture will substitute for the direct experience of studying a culture yourself. In order to appreciate fully the power and value of the cultural perspective you will have to personally go into an organization and look for artifacts and symbols and listen to interpretations. When you rely upon others to study your culture for you, you miss the opportunity to broaden your experience of your organizations and limit the development of your symbolic potential.

KEY TERMS

native view	ethnography
the culture metaphor	field journal
assumptions	field notes
values	subculture
norms	fragmentation perspective
artifacts	contextualize
symbol	cultural strength
interpretation	

ENDNOTES

1. Phillips, Goodman, and Sackmann (1992).
2. Williams (1983).
3. Tylor (1871\1958: 1).
4. Herskowitz (1948: 625).
5. Allaire and Firsirotu (1984); Eisenberg and Riley (1988).
6. The idea that organizational culture theory can be divided into three schools of thought (integration, differentiation, fragmentation) was developed by Meyerson and Martin (1987; Martin 1992).
7. Schein (1981, 1984, 1985, 1992).
8. Gagliardi (1990).
9. Hatch (1993).
10. Geertz (1973: 5).
11. I am grateful to Kristian Kreiner, who suggested this example.
12. Ortner (1973); Hatch (1993).
13. Van Maanen (1988).
14. Geertz (1973: 28–29).
15. I am grateful to Joe Harder for alerting me to these videotaped incidents.
16. Van Maanen and Barley (1985: 38).
17. Martin (1992); Meyerson and Martin (1987).
18. Martin and Siehl (1983).
19. Van Maanan and Barley (1984); Borum and Strandgaard-Pedersen (1989).
20. Young (1989).
21. Borum and Strandgaard-Pedersen (1989); Molin and Strandgaard-Pedersen (1992).
22. Van Maanen and Barley (1984).
23. Meyerson and Martin (1987); Martin (1992).24. Martin (1992: 135–36).
25. Ibid. 136.
26. Ibid. 156, citing Anzaldua (1987: 79) and Rosaldo (1989: 216).
27. Martin (1992: 138).
28. Denison (1990).
29. Deal and Kennedy (1982).
30. Kotter and Heskett (1992).
31. Denison (1990).
32. Peters and Waterman (1982); Ouchi (1980); Kilmann, Saxton and Serpa (1986); Wilkins and Ouchi (1983).
33. Kilmann, Saxton, and Serpa (1986); O'Reilly (1989); O'Reilly, Chatman and Caldwell (1991).
34. Pfeffer (1981).
35. Hatch (1993).

REFERENCES

Allaire, Yvan, and Firsirotu, Mihaela E. (1984). Theories of organizational culture. *Organization Studies*, 5/3: 193–226.

Borum, Finn, and Strandgaard-Pedersen, Jesper (1989). Understanding the IT people, their subcultures, and the implications for management of technology. In Finn Borum and Peer Hull Kristensen (eds.), *Technological innovation and organizational change: Danish patterns of knowledge, networks, and culture*. Copenhagen: New Social Science Monographs, 219–48.

Deal, Terrence E., and Kennedy, Allan A. (1982). *Corporate cultures: The rites and rituals of corporate life*. Reading, Mass.: Addison-Wesley.

Denison, Daniel R. (1990). *Corporate culture and organizational effectiveness*. New York: John Wiley & Sons.

Eisenberg, Eric M., and Riley, Patricia (1988). Organizational symbols and sense-making. In G. M. Goldhaber and G. A. Barnett (eds.), *Handbook of Organizational Communication*. Norwood, NJ: Ablex.

Gagliardi, P. (1990). Artifacts as pathways and remains of organizational life. In P. Gagliardi (ed.), *Symbols and artifacts: Views of the corporate landscape*. Berlin: Walter de Gruyter, 3–38.

Geertz, Clifford (1973). *Interpretation of cultures*. New York: Basic Books.

Hatch, Mary Jo (1993). The dynamics of organizational culture. *Academy of Management Review*, 18/4: 657–63.

Herskowitz, Melville J. (1948). *Man and his works: The science of cultural anthropology*. New York: Alfred A. Knopf.

Hofstede, Geert (1980). *Culture's consequences: International differences in work-related values* (2nd edition). Beverly Hills, Calif.: Sage.

Jacques, Elliott (1952). *The changing culture of a factory*. New York: Dryden Press.

Jenks, Chris (1993). *Culture*. London: Routledge.

Kilmann, R., Saxton, M., and Serpa, R. (1986). *Gaining control of the corporate culture*. San Francisco: Jossey-Bass.

Kotter, John P., and Heskett, James L. (1992). *Corporate culture and performance*. New York: Free Press.

Louis, Meryl Reis (1983). Organizations as culture-bearing milieux. In L. Pondy, P. Frost, G. Morgan, and T. Dandridge (eds.), *Organizational culture*. Greenwich, Conn.: JAI Press, 39–54.

Martin, Joanne, and Siehl, Caren (1983). Organizational culture and counterculture: An uneasy symbiosis. *Organizational Dynamics*, Autumn: 52–64.

Meyerson, Debra, and Martin, Joanne (1987). Cultural change: An integration of three different views. *Journal of Management Studies*, 24: 623–47.

Molin, Jan, and Strandgaard-Pedersen, Jesper. (1992). Mergers, myths and mistakes. Paper presented to the 2nd Western Academy of Management International Conference: Leuven, Belgium, June 21–24.

O'Reilly, Charles (1989). Corporations, culture, and commitment: Motivation and social control in organizations. *California Management Review*, 31: 9–25.

O'Reilly, Charles, Chatman, Jennifer, and Caldwell, David (1991). People and organizational culture: A Q-sort approach to assessing person-organization fit. *Academy of Management Journal*, 16: 285–303.

Ortner, S. B. (1973). On key symbols. *American Anthropologist*, 75: 1338–46.

Ouchi, William (1980). Markets, bureaucracies, and clans. *Administrative Science Quarterly*, 25: 129–41.

Ouchi, William (1981). *Theory Z: How American business can meet the Japanese challenge*. Reading, Mass.: Addison-Wesley.

Peters, Thomas J., and Waterman, R. H. (1982). *In search of excellence: Lessons from America's best run companies*. New York: Harper & Row.

Pettigrew, Andrew (1979). On studying organizational culture. *Administrative Science Quarterly*, 24: 570–81.

Pfeffer, Jeffrey (1981). Management as symbolic action: The creation and maintenance of organizational paradigms. In L. L. Cummings and B. M. Staw (eds.), *Research in Organizational Behavior*, 3: 1–52.

Phillips, Margaret E., Goodman, Richard A., and Sackmann, Sonja A. (1992). Exploring the complex cultural milieu of project teams. *Pmnetwork*, VI/8: 20–26.

Schein, Edgar H. (1981). Does Japanese management style have a message for American managers? *Sloan Management Review*, 23: 55–68.

Schein, Edgar H. (1984). Coming to a new awareness of organizational culture. *Sloan Management Review*, 25: 3–16.

Schein, Edgar H. (1985). *Organizational culture and leadership*. San Francisco: Jossey-Bass.

Schein, Edgar H. (1991). What is culture? In P. Frost, L. Moore, M. Louis, C. Lundberg, and J. Martin (eds.), *Reframing organizational culture*. Newbury Park, Calif.: Sage.

Schein, Edgar H. (1992). *Organizational culture and leadership (2nd ed.ition)*. San Francisco: Jossey-Bass.

Siehl, Caren, and Martin, Joanne (1984). The role of symbolic management: How can managers effectively transmit organizational culture? In J. D. Hunt, D. Hosking, C. Schriesheim, and R. Steward (eds.), *Leaders and managers: International perspectives on managerial behavior and leadership*. New York: Pergamon, 227–39.

Trice, Harrison, and Beyer, Janice (1993). *The cultures of work organizations*. Englewood Cliffs, NJ: Prentice Hall.

Tylor, Edward Burnett (1958). *Primitive culture: Researches into the development of mythology, philosophy, religion, art and custom*. Gloucester, Mass.: Smith (first published in 1871).

Van Maanen, John (1988) *Tales of the field: On writing ehnography*. Chicago: University of Chicago Press.

Van Maanen, John, and Barley, Stephen R. (1984). Occupational communities: Culture and control in organizations. In B. M. Staw and L. L. Cummings (eds.), *Research in organizational behavior*. Greenwich, Conn.: JAI Press, vi. 287–366.

Van Maanen, John, and Barley, Stephen R. (1985). Cultural organization: Fragments of a theory. In P. J. Frost, L. F. Moore, M. R. Louis, C. C. Lundberg, and J. Martin (eds.), *Organizational culture*. Beverly Hills: Sage, 31–54.

Wilkins, Allen, and Ouchi, William (1983). Efficient cultures: Exploring the relationship between culture and organizational performance. *Administrative Science Quarterly*, 28: 468–81.

Williams, Raymond (1983). *Keywords: A vocabulary of culture and society* (revised edition). New York: Oxford University Press.

Young, Ed (1989). On naming the rose: Interests and multiple meanings as elements of organizational change. *Organizational Studies*, 10: 187–206.

FURTHER READING

Several overviews of organizational culture studies are available. I recommend the following sources.

Brown, Andrew (1995). *Organisational culture*. London: Pitman.

Martin, Joanne (1992). *Cultures in organizations: Three perspectives*. New York: Oxford University Press.

Schultz, Majken (1994). *On studying organizational cultures: Diagnosis and understanding*. Berlin: Walter de Gruyter.

Trice, Harrison M., and Beyer, Janice M. (1992). *The cultures of work organizations*. Englewood Cliffs, NJ: Prentice-Hall.

For futher background in the area of organizational symbolism, try these sources.

Eisenberg, E. M., and Riley, P. (1988). Organizational symbols and sense-making. In G. M. Goldhaber and G. A. Barnett (eds.), *Handbook of Organizational Communication*. Norwood, NJ: Ablex.

Core Concepts of Organization Theory

Gagliardi, P. (1990) (ed.). *Symbols and artifacts: Views of the corporate landscape*. Berlin: Walter de Gruyter.

Turner, Barry A. (1990) (ed.). *Organizational symbolism*. Berlin: Walter de Gruyter.

To experience some of the research that has had an influence on the field of organizational culture studies, dip into any of the following readers.

Frost, P., Moore, L., Louis, M., Lundberg, C., and Martin, J. (1985) (eds.). *Organizational culture*. Beverly Hills, Calif.: Sage.

Frost, P., Moore, L., Louis, M., Lundberg, C., and Martin, J. (1991) (eds.).*Reframing organizational culture*. Newbury Park, Calif.: Sage.

Pondy, Lou, Frost, Peter, Morgan, Gareth, and Dandridge, Tom (1983). *Organizational symbolism*. Greenwich, Conn.: JAI Press.

Smircich, Linda, and Calas, Marta (1987). Organizational culture, a critical assessment. In F. Jablin, L. Putnam, K. Roberts, and L. Porter (eds.), *The handbook of organizational communication*. Beverly Hills, Calif.: Sage, 228–63.

8 | The Physical Structure of Organizations

I
NTEREST in physical structure in organizations is generally traced to the
Hawthorne studies which were carried out at the Western Electric plant in
the U.S. in the late 1920s and early 1930s.[1] The Hawthorne researchers, led by
Harvard University professor Elton Mayo, set out to perform a series of field
experiments to determine how changes in the physical setting of work affected
worker productivity. To set up the experiment, workers were moved into an
enclosed space so that illumination levels could be more easily and precisely controlled. Once in the room together, the workers were asked to perform their normal tasks while the researchers systematically increased the illumination and
measured the workers' productivity levels. As anticipated, they found that productivity increased with illumination.

In order to check the effectiveness of the experimental manipulation, the
researchers then reduced illumination levels, expecting productivity to drop
according to the degree of reduction in available light. To everyone's surprise,
productivity continued to increase—even when the workers were operating in
near darkness. Apparently the workers had interpreted the special room, and all
the attention the researchers lavished upon them, as managerial concern for and
interest in their work. The special attention also gave the workers an elevated
social status among co-workers who were not included in the study. The
researchers concluded that the increases in productivity were due to these social
effects, and therefore they abandoned their initial hypothesis (i.e., that the physical conditions of work explained productivity) in favor of exploring the social
effects on performance.

Because of the discovery of the potency of social influences on worker productivity, the Hawthorne studies are often credited with providing the foundation for the field of human relations. But, for our purposes, it is important to recognize that these events also marginalized interest in physical structure within organization studies by making the effects of physical structure seem insignificant compared with social effects. However, as sociologist George Homans has astutely observed, the social effects registered by the Hawthorne researchers were triggered by a change in physical structure—the workers were moved to a separate space away from the surveillance of their supervisors.[2] Homans's argument is that the new physical structure symbolized management concern for these particular workers and marked their special social status. Thus, it could be claimed that physical structure set the social dynamics of the Hawthorne situation in motion.

In spite of Homans's reinterpretation of the Hawthorne study findings, the concept of physical structure was relegated to the theoretical backwaters of organization theory in the years following the Hawthorne report. Fortunately a few researchers, such as American management consultant Fred Steele and American psychologist Eric Sundstrom, kept this line of research alive. Today, organization theorists are renewing their interest in physical structure, stimulated by several rich sources coming from outside traditional organizational domains such as material culture studies in anthropology and postmodernist studies in human geography and architecture.

Modernist and symbolic-interpretive perspectives live much more peacefully together in the domain of physical structure than they do in organizational culture theory. Some modernist organization theorists argue that this is because the theoretical stakes are so low. They claim that, because it is centered in the realm of the concrete and particular rather than the abstract, physical structure has no theoretical importance at all. Symbolic-interpretivists, on the other hand, see nothing atheoretical about the concrete and particular and they cite the long tradition for studying material culture in anthropology in support of their claim to theoretical importance. Postmodernists, such as Lyotard, who stake their faith on little narratives rather than the grand narratives of modernist theory, accept the modernist argument but transform it into a reason to make physical structures the center of organizational study. They believe the little narratives of the non-abstract, concrete, and particular are precisely what should engage our attention.

In this chapter we begin by defining three basic aspects of organizational physical structures: organizational geography, layout, and design/decor. Next we consider the influences of physical structures on the behavior of their inhabitants, a perspective that derives from modernist concerns. We then turn our attention to the symbolic uses to which physical structures have been put in organizations.

The role physical structure plays in the formation of individual, group, and organizational identity will also be examined. The chapter concludes with some postmodernist ideas about physical structures and their potential influence on organization theory.

DEFINING PHYSICAL STRUCTURE

Just as relationships between the social elements of an organization define its social structure, relationships between the physical elements of an organization define its physical structure. The physical elements of organization include buildings and their locations, furniture and equipment, decoration, and even human bodies. Among these elements, the relationships of particular interest to organization theorists are: organizational geography, layout, and design and decor (Figure 8.1).

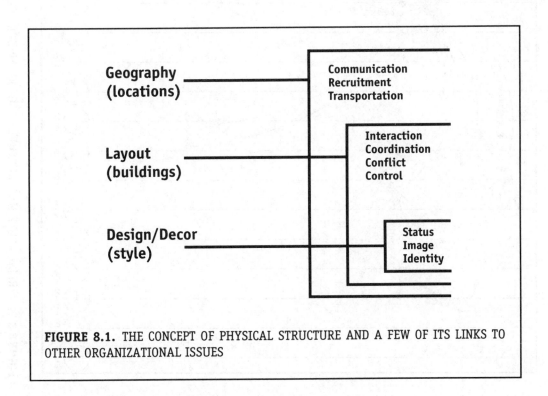

FIGURE 8.1. THE CONCEPT OF PHYSICAL STRUCTURE AND A FEW OF ITS LINKS TO OTHER ORGANIZATIONAL ISSUES

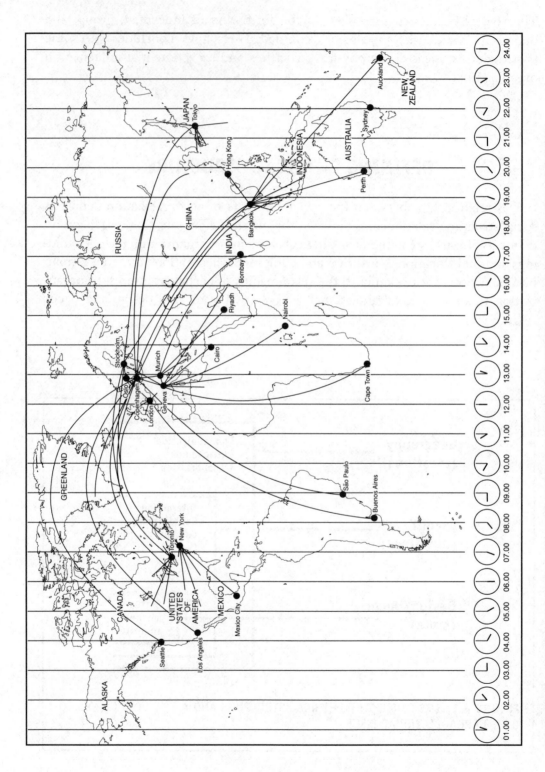

FIGURE 8.2. AIRLINE ROUTE MAP SHOWING THE GEOGRAPHICAL DISTRIBUTION OF ORGANIZATIONAL ACTIVITIES

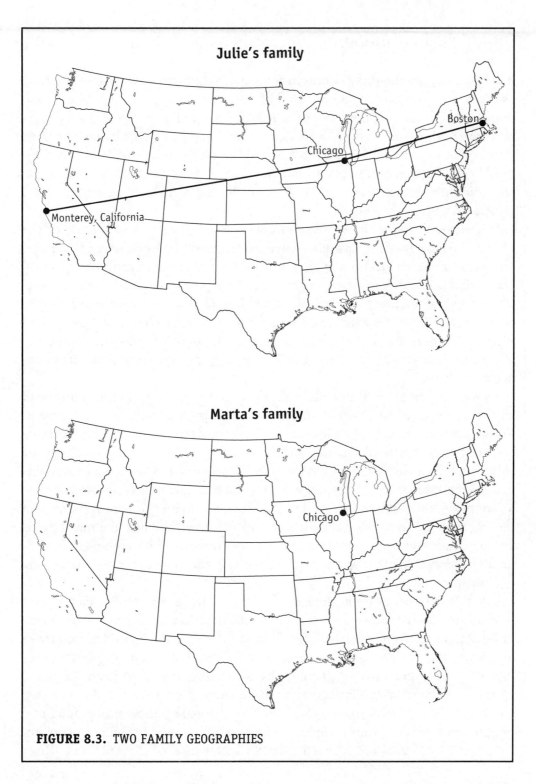

FIGURE 8.3. TWO FAMILY GEOGRAPHIES

Organizational Geography

It is becoming increasingly common for organizations to operate in more than one location. You can no doubt think of numerous examples such as multinationals, conglomerates, joint ventures, franchises, retail or fast food chains, organizations with branch offices or service centers, and firms with regional plants, distribution centers, or field sales offices. Although the importance of **organizational geography** is more obvious in cases involving multiple locations, all organizations, no matter how small or spatially self-contained, confront issues associated with geography.

Within organization theory, the concept of geography focuses attention on the spatial distribution of the locations where an organization operates and the physical features of each location. In geographical terms, an organization is a physical entity, that is, it exists in space and in time. The space occupied by an organization forms a set of interconnected locations described with reference to an ordinary map. This is easily seen in any airline route map, such as the one illustrated in Figure 8.2, where the airline's organizational geography is represented as the collection of destinations (organizational locations) and well-travelled paths connecting them.

As you can see in the airline example, the organization's geography consists of all those points on the planet where the organization conducts its business. Primary among these will be locations of headquarters facilities, plants, service centers, retail outlets, subsidiaries, and administrative offices. Depending on your reasons for performing the analysis, you might also want to include locations visited by representatives of the organization such as customers' facilities or the locations of other influential stakeholders. Such an analysis provides an image of the organization as a set of activities that extend from the internal interactions among employees to the external interactions the organization engages in with its environment. In other words, you produce a spatial map of the activities of the organization.

Consider another example. Julie is a student studying business in Chicago. Her parents are retired and live in Monterey, California, and her brother studies jazz in Boston. In terms of its spatial distribution, Julie's family is divided into three locations that reach across the continental United States. The organization of Julie's family is much more spatially disbursed than is that of her roommate, Marta, who grew up in Chicago and whose entire family lives in the area (see Figure 8.3). Julie plans to make a career in international business after graduation; her brother intends to tour Europe. Notice how these plans will alter Julie's family geography if they are realized. Marta's acceptance of a position as a loan officer in a Chicago bank, on the other hand, will not introduce as much change into the geographic configuration of her family. You can imagine that her family's geography will remain more stable for a longer period of time than will Julie's.

Spatial distribution poses both problems and opportunities for organizations. In the case of Julie's and Marta's families, different problems and opportunities include, for example, the cost of phone calls, availability for mutual support in times of crisis, coordinating across time zones, exposure to different cultural influences, and coping with change. The same is true for other organizations, each of which faces different circumstances associated with its geography.

In addition to organizational communication and information-sharing, spatial distribution relates to the logistics of supplying the organization with raw materials and delivering output to customers. Access to various modes of transportation (domestic and international airports, waterways, etc.), proximity to markets (including labor, supply, and consumer markets), and the speed and cost of communication, transportation, and travel are but a few of the logistical concerns related to spatial distribution. Additionally, locations near to influential elements of the environment (e.g., regulatory agencies, funding institutions, universities engaged in relevant basic research) offer an organization advantages in terms of managing critical environmental dependencies.

Once an organization's spatial distribution is mapped out, you can analyze its geography with respect to the physical features of each of its locations. These physical features include climate, terrain, and natural resources. Population density, industrialization, urbanization, and the presence or absence of members of different races and ethnic minorities are human features of geography that are also useful for describing the locations in which an organization operates.

The features of geographical locations can affect many aspects of doing business. Success with recruiting is just one example. Consider the features of particular geographic locations and their influence on the lifestyles of members and prospective members of the organization. The lifestyle associated with an organization's location will help to define the types of employees the organization will attract. For instance, compare the lifestyles of employees of firms operating in Paris, San Francisco, Moscow, and Tokyo, or compare any of these to the lifestyle offered by a firm located far from any large metropolitan or industrialized area. Lifestyle is just one implication of organizational geography. Other aspects of organization likely to be related to the features of organizational geography include corporate image and organizational identity, issues we will return to later in this chapter.

Layout

Layout refers to the spatial arrangement of physical objects and human activities. Within a specific building, layout involves the internal placement of objects, especially walls, large pieces of furniture and equipment, and employees. These spatial arrangements carve up and help to define the interior spaces of a building. When a particular location has more than one building, its siting, which refers to the orientation of the buildings to each other, is another feature of layout. For example, employees of large, high technology organizations are often placed in a group of buildings arranged to look like a college campus. Such campus arrangements usually consist of several buildings visually tied together by walkways and/or landscaped areas.

The assignment of people to specific locations and groups to particular spatial regions are key aspects of the internal layout of a building. For instance, office and work station assignments, and locations of shared facilities such as cafeterias, restrooms, and conference rooms, all contribute to internal layout. So does the spatial grouping of similar forms of work activity such as by project teams or by organizational function, such as R & D, sales, manufacturing, and accounting. Figure 8.4 shows a functional layout designed for a geophysics firm.

In office buildings, internal layout is often described in terms of openness, accessibility, and privacy. The most common way of making these distinctions is to contrast open with private offices. Open offices have either low partitions with no doors, or use file cabinets, bookcases, and/or living plants to visually separate areas that are otherwise accessible to anyone in the vicinity. Private offices have floor-to-ceiling walls, usually with a door to allow their occupants full enclosure when they desire privacy. Bullpen offices have the greatest degree of accessibility, as these are rooms having no physical barriers between work stations whatsoever.

Layout affects the way that individuals and groups communicate and coordinate their efforts. For instance, layout is related to the development of informal channels of communication such as grapevines and rumor mills. The most obvious example of the relationship between layout and coordination is the automated assembly line where individuals and their tools are located at fixed positions along a moving line of partly assembled products.

In the case of an assembly line, layout involves matching locations with task requirements. If layout is poorly conceived, many inefficiencies and inconveniences will be introduced into the transformation process. This physical aspect of assembly line work should help you to visualize a relationship that is common to many other types of work; whenever workers perform interdependent tasks, their ability to coordinate their activities will be affected by the layout of the work

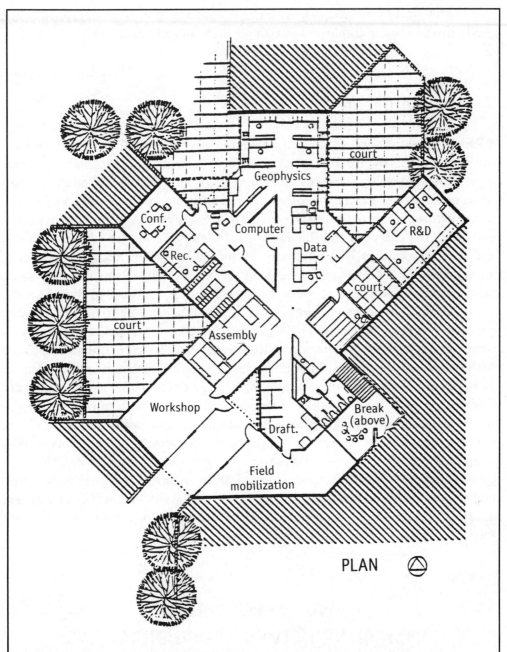

FIGURE 8.4. LAYOUT OF ACTIVITY REGIONS IN A GEOPHYSICS FIRM

Source: Doxtater, D. (1990: 121, Fig. 2), "Meaning of the Workplace: Using ideas of Ritual Space in Design". In P. Gagliardi (ed.) (1990). *Symbols and Artifacts: Views of the Corporate Landscape*. By permission of Walter de Gruyter.

spaces they occupy. Although it is easier to visualize in the case of assembly line work, this is true for employees at all levels of management as well as for technical core and other non-management level employees.

Design and Decor

When you hear the words **design and decor**, you probably think of the architectural style of an organization's facilities. Facade, landscaping, furnishings, lighting, ceiling and wall treatments, floor coverings, use of color and form, displays of art or technology, and many other details contribute to these aspects of a physical structure. When analyzing an organization's design and decor, be sure to consider both the exteriors and the interiors of the organization's factories, offices, and other workplaces. Focus not only on the architecturally designed features of an organization's built environment but also pay attention to the unplanned aspects of the appearance of buildings and other organizational facilities.

Notice that physical structures can range from being ugly to being tolerable, pleasing, beautiful, and inspiring. However, even when an organization's physical structure has nothing to recommend it aesthetically, physical elements associated with design and decor offer important clues to the organization's culture and its image to outsiders. Take the example of the organization that occupies low-rent facilities and furnishes its offices minimally and inexpensively. Such an organization may either communicate its commitment to a low-cost strategy or tell you that the organization is unaware or unconcerned about its physical appearance. Keep in mind, however, that design and decor preferences are heavily influenced by personal taste. For the purposes of organizational analysis, your personal preferences are less important than your sensitivity to the fact that organizations have aesthetic qualities that are open to the interpretations of employees and other members of the organizational community.

TWO APPROACHES TO PHYSICAL STRUCTURE IN ORGANIZATIONS: BEHAVIOR AND SYMBOLISM

Organization theorists have explored two different approaches to understanding the physical side of organizations—the behavioral and the symbolic. The behavioral approach, which derives from the modernist perspective, focuses mainly on the relationship of physical structure to interaction and other forms of activity within the organization. The symbolic approach, which derives from the symbolic-interpretive perspective, takes the view that physical structures are a rich source of symbols and an important channel for cultural expression. Those who adopt the symbolic view see the physical structure of an organization as shaping and maintaining a system of meaning that helps organizational members to define who they are and what they are doing, whereas those who take the behavioral approach see it as shaping and maintaining a system of activity directed toward the realization of goals.

The Behavioral or Modernist Approach

When you look at physical structure from the modernist perspective, you will see that it provides opportunities for and constraints upon the communication of information and ideas, and the coordination of interdependent activities. The focus of studies in this tradition has been on the relationship between the physical form an organization adopts and the behavior of individuals performing their work activities within these spaces. The basic idea is that, since humans cannot walk through walls or see through floors, their behavior is shaped by the design of their organization's physical environment.[3]

In general, the more distance separating people, the fewer will be the opportunities for direct interaction and the more time such activities will consume. While it is true that new methods of electronic communication, such as fax machines and teleconferencing, and faster modes of transportation have considerably reduced the limitations of geographical distribution on interaction capabilities, these limitations are far from being entirely overcome. Face-to-face interaction is still considered superior to all other forms of communication, and this form of interaction makes the greatest demands on spatial configuration because there are limits to how many people can be located close to one another (e.g., a traditional office has no more than two adjacent offices).[4]

One way to assess the relationship between internal layout and interaction involves measuring the distance from one employee's assigned work space to another. Many studies have shown a negative relationship between this measure of distance and the likelihood that two employees will engage in interaction, especially interaction involving face-to-face encounters.[5] That is, all other factors being equal, the more distance between the work stations of two individuals, the less likely they are to share information or to form a friendship. Separation by assignment to different floors or to different buildings decreases the likelihood of interaction even further.[6]

Keep in mind that formal reporting relationships, similar cultural backgrounds, and task interdependence are also related to information-sharing and friendship patterns in organizations. However, physical distance will usually create problems for the formation of relationships because, when potential partners are far apart, they must take the trouble to arrange their meetings. When locations are close, relationships can form through casual interactions that occur spontaneously, for instance, in the hallway or at the coffee machine.

While distance between employees has been shown to interfere with informal interaction, other physical barriers, such as movable partitions and fixed walls, have been found to be positively related to some forms of interaction. In particular, meetings, brief interruptions, confidential conversations, and working together have been found to occur significantly more often, and for longer periods of time, when employees occupy enclosed spaces.[7] However, even though modernist studies show that these forms of interaction are more likely to occur in closed than in open offices, many people continue to believe that open office settings, with few or no physical barriers, encourage interaction and communication.

One explanation for the belief that open offices encourage communication is found at the group-level of analysis. Some groups, especially innovative design teams, claim that the intimate sharing of their workspaces stimulates creativity and supports teamwork. In these cases, however, enclosure rather than openness seems the most likely causal factor, since these groups generally have some sort of boundary separating them from the rest of the organization. (We will return to the discussion of group boundaries below.) A second explanation for the link between open physical arrangements and the impression of greater (more open) communication is that the openness of a physical setting is *symbolically* associated with open communication.[8] That is, at least in some situations, open offices operate as symbols for open communication. This brings us to the important topic of the meaning of physical structures in organizations.

The Symbolic Approach

What may appear to be a fairly straightforward matter of understanding physical structure in terms of behavior becomes considerably more complicated when the symbolic aspects of physical structure are brought into focus. The study of organizational culture has taught us that managers should not overlook the importance of meanings and interpretations associated with organizational symbols and symbolic events, and many aspects of physical structure serve in this symbolic capacity. The most obvious example is found in the communicative power of architecture.

Over time, buildings come to represent their organizations and have the effect of helping people construct what they think and feel about the organization.[9] Consider impressive structures you have encountered—maybe a castle, court house, parliament building, religious temple, cathedral, or museum. Such structures serve to communicate respect for the activities and persons contained or celebrated within these buildings. Interpretations of buildings provide masterful examples of this power. For instance, Umberto Eco, semiotician and author of the popular novel *The Name of the Rose*, states: "The colonnade by Bernini in St. Peter's Square in Rome can be interpreted as an immense pair of arms, open to embrace all the faithful."[10]

Although many business organizations do not take full advantage of the communicative power of architecture, a few do. A German insurance company located in Dusseldorf provides an example. The headquarters building was shaped in a giant pyramid to symbolize hierarchy and to underline the importance of working one's way up in this organization.[11] From a higher level of analysis we might also interpret this building as a reflection of its society's ideas about success and hierarchy.

Apart from the grand scale of architectural edifices, all of us use symbolic cues provided by more mundane aspects of physical structures to define who we are and what we are doing. Think about how you instantly know by your surroundings whether you are at home or at work, in your own office or in someone else's. What is more, knowing where you are triggers specific behavioral routines.[12] For example, members of the Catholic Church know how to behave in the presence of the altar because responses such as kneeling and making the sign of the cross have been conditioned to this element of the physical structure.[13] For a member of the Catholic faith, these responses are so automatic that the mere sight of the church altar provokes the expected behavior. Because the stimulus to which the behavior has been conditioned is a symbol of the organization, this sort of conditioning is referred to as symbolic conditioning. Similar evidence of symbolic conditioning can be observed in business organizations. For instance, consider responses to the counter of a McDonald's restaurant where customers have been conditioned to queue up to receive service from employees who work behind the counter (see Figure 8.5). Other places to look for conditioned responses include outside closed doors, and in and around waiting rooms, executive offices, libraries, and conference rooms.

The importance of the idea of symbolically conditioned behavior lies in the unconscious link between physical structure and the normal routines that make up so much of daily life in organizations. For instance, the habit of responding to others in an impersonal way is typical of many business people and can become symbolically conditioned to the physical surroundings of the workplace. As a

FIGURE 8.5. FAST FOOD RESTAURANT CUSTOMERS HAVE BEEN SYMBOLICALLY CONDITIONED TO QUEUE UP FOR SERVICE

Notice how when you enter such an establishment you automatically engage in the desired behavior. What signals the appropriate response may be the other customers lined up waiting to be served, or, over time, the counter itself may act as the signal.

result, it is not uncommon to find people meeting outside office settings from time to time in order to interact with each other in more personal ways. Or consider the example of the employee who works at home but finds it necessary to dress up and say goodbye to family members before "going to work" in order to overcome the effects of symbolic conditioning to being at home, and to send a signal to family members not to interrupt work activity.

In addition to the symbolic conditioning of behavior, spatial elements (locations, buildings, color schemes) and spatial relations (geography, layout, design and decor) play a significant role in producing and shaping identity in and around organizations. Consider the symbolic importance of a Wall Street address for an investment firm operating from New York City. Or imagine the symbolic value of being assigned to a luxurious private office next to the office of a high-ranking executive. Each of these examples illustrates how physical structure communicates powerful messages about the identity of the organization and its members.

PHYSICAL STRUCTURE AND THE FORMATION OF IDENTITY

Elements of physical structure contain cues and communicate messages capable of reminding people, not only of where they are and how they should behave, but of who they are in terms of their individual, group, and organizational identity. We will discuss the relationships between physical structure and identity in terms of three issues: status, group boundaries, and corporate image.

Status and Individual Identity

Quality of furnishings, amount of floorspace, privacy, and a privileged location are consistently associated with high status for many American employees.[14] Such associations make it possible for the physical structure of an organization to communicate the pattern of its existing social hierarchy using the language of spatial distances and physical objects.

You can learn to read a great deal about the organization's status hierarchy by carefully observing **status indicators** within its physical structure. Try noting the relative size and location of spaces occupied by individuals, or assessing the style and value of furnishings and decorations (e.g., artwork and other objects on display). You will also observe differences in the accessibility of a given organization member to important members of the organization, to support facilities and equipment (e.g., copiers, fax machines, personal computers, laser printers), and to conveniences (e.g., restrooms, coffee machines, parking lots). All of these are clues to status and hierarchy in organizations.

Some organizations try to downplay status differences using the absence of traditional status markers to communicate this message. Here it is the *lack* of normal status symbols that can be observed, such as no assigned parking spaces, no executive washrooms, no differences in office size or quality of furnishings. However, in these situations it is not uncommon to find informal, often bizarre, status symbols created by the employees to fill in the gap left by the absence of traditional symbols. In one such case, the location of cheap coatracks, initially purchased because the building designers neglected to install closets, served to designate the powerful members of the organization. At first the coatracks had been made available to anyone who wanted them on a first come, first served basis. Over the course of only a few weeks, however, the coatracks migrated into the cubicles of those with the greatest status. In another case work group coffee pots became an informal indicator of status, however this time the migration was to the offices of lower status clerical employees whose offices were next to those with the greatest status.

Territorial Boundaries and Group Identity

Physical structures in organizations come to be divided into territories and these territories are then associated with the types of activities carried out within them or with the specific people assigned to the spaces. Many organizations divide their buildings according to units defined by their social structures, for example by assigning marketing to one spatial area, manufacturing to another, accounting to a third. Another way to separate activity is by project teams; this arrangement is often found in matrix structured organizations. Even when organizations do not deliberately create territories, groups may come to view themselves as linked together because of their common locations.

Territorial boundaries may be marked by a wide variety of physical elements—walls, doors, different buildings or locations, or by decorating schemes or other discriminating spatial features. Individuals contribute to this marking of territories with displays of personal belongings, signs, slogans, or other visual expressions of identification and ownership. The physical marking of territories within physical structures creates visible boundaries that become symbolically associated with the groups who occupy these spaces.

Although there has not been much empirical investigation of the phenomenon, the available evidence suggests that the physical marking of group boundaries is associated with strong **group identity** in organizations.[15] In other cases the emergence of subcultures appears to coincide with the marking of territories, such as has been observed in sociological studies of street gangs.[16] What is not known is whether boundaries give groups their strong sense of identity, or whether groups that are in the process of forming a strong identity tend to construct visible boundaries. It is possible, of course, that both forces are at work. Remember too that strong group identity can interfere with intergroup cooperation—no expressed value for strong versus weak group identity is implied by the discussion here. Sometimes group identities need to be weaker, sometimes stronger. The link with physical structure primarily gives you a way of examining existing group identities and may provide a source of inspiration concerning what to do if a change is desired.

Corporate Image and Organizational Identity

You can see some of the same forces that make territorial boundaries significant for group identity formation on a grander scale in the phenomenon of organizational identity. Where group identity forms in association with a particular place within an organization, the organization itself is associated with a more general notion of place. This is often symbolized by a particular building or other physical point of reference such as a sculpture, fountain, or main entrance. Architects and designers claim that having a visual reference point to which all members can orient themselves is a key component of establishing and maintaining an organizational identity.[17]

Organizational identity refers to members' experiences of and beliefs about the organization as a whole. Identity should be distinguished from a closely related term that is also important to the discussion—image. Organizational identity is self-focused. It refers to how the organization's members regard themselves as an organization. **Corporate image**, however, refers to impressions of the organization formed by others. Image reflects the many impressions that an organization makes on its external audiences.[18]

Notice that there are numerous possible perspectives reflected in both corporate image and organizational identity. There is, therefore, no reason to expect that either organizational identity or corporate image will be consistent or coherent within themselves. For example, an exquisite new corporate headquarters building may favorably impress investors ("they must be generating great wealth to afford such a wonderful facility"), customers ("this kind of opulence indicates real staying power"), and community leaders ("what a marvelous aesthetic complement to the community"), while simultaneously being viewed as irresponsible by union leaders ("that money could have gone into better wage packets") and environmentalists ("a little less squandering on executive perks and more environmental projects might have been possible").

Because the physical appearance of an organization is a potent medium in which to create a lasting impression, some top managers attempt to influence organizational identity and corporate image by focusing on elements of their organization's appearance. Physical elements with particular potential to represent organizational identity or to influence corporate image include: dramatic architectural features (facade, roofline, lighting effects, office interiors, decorating themes), product design, company logos, corporate literature (e.g., annual reports, brochures), and uniforms. Corporate design consultants such as the British corporate identity specialist Wally Olins claim that, when they are carefully designed to complement each other, these elements influence impressions of organizational credibility and character[19] and symbolically reinforce strategic vision.[20]

257

Core Concepts of Organization Theory

In our enthusiasm to unleash the forces of appearance, we must not forget the relationship between organizational identity and corporate image. Image and identity are intertwined in the sense that the image an organization puts forth to its environment cannot avoid contributing to the identity the organization maintains.[21] This does not mean that an image campaign will necessarily serve to control organizational identity, it is only to suggest that the two are not unrelated. Furthermore, we must be aware that mixed signals can be sent symbolically in organizations. For instance, an organization that makes claims about its innovativeness but does not provide its employees with physical symbols of innovation (e.g., the latest design tools or the newest personal computers), may find that its employees and/or its publics will question its commitment to innovation. Stories about such situations and their unfortunate consequences abound in the folklore of organizations. Finally, you should be aware that image and identity-related components of physical structure are available to other interpretive readings than those that are intended by designers or by top managers.

An excellent example of an unplanned interpretation is found on the American campus of Notre Dame University in South Bend, Indiana. Notre Dame is famous for the many championship football teams it has contributed to college athletics in the United States. Several years ago Notre Dame University built a large new library building intended to be an architectural focal point for the entire campus. To symbolize the religious heritage of this Roman Catholic institution, the building was adorned with a beautiful mosaic featuring the figure of Jesus Christ with outstretched arms raised toward heaven (see Fig. 8.6). Coincidentally, in American football when one team scores a goal, called a "touchdown," the official in charge indicates the score by raising his outstretched arms in a gesture similar to the one depicted in the mosaic. What is crystal clear in retrospect, but apparently no one foresaw during the design of the library, is the connection between these two important symbols of campus culture—Christ and football. The Notre Dame culture produced the now obvious name for the mosaic: "Touchdown Jesus."

POSTMODERNISM AND PHYSICAL STRUCTURES

Recent critiques of social theory by neo-Marxist and postmodernist geographers such as Henri Lefebvre, David Harvey, and Edward Soja, focus on the marginalization of issues of space in theories of social relations. These critics accuse social theorists including Karl Marx, Emile Durkheim, and Max Weber of ignoring space to the detriment of their theorizing about social processes and institutions.

FIGURE 8.6. NOTRE DAME LIBRARY MOSAIC

Photograph by Joseph C. Fross.

George Homans raises a similar critique against organization theorists who interpret the Hawthorne studies[22] as evidence that social aspects of organizing prevail over physical aspects.

At issue here is the relationship between physical structure and social structure. The critics from Homans through the postmodernist geographers assert that social structures and processes produce and organize built space and the effects of these built spaces then rebound back upon social relations. So interrelated are social and physical structures, claims British human geographer Derek Gregory, that "social structures cannot be practiced without spatial structures, and vice

259

versa."[23] As American postmodernist geographer Edward Soja points out, spatial forms are produced by human action.[24] Built space is a socially constructed object and it therefore shares symbolic potential with other cultural artifacts that are similarly able to carry meaning or ideological content. Because built space often appears to be a natural part of the social world, its meanings are generally taken for granted. But although social content such as power and dominance relations are naturalized in physical structures, we can learn to reflect on these meanings and control their reproduction. Postmodernists call for denaturalization of meaning and demystification of the processes by which meanings get built into (or constructed around) physical structures. Only through a figurative deconstruction of built space, they argue, can misuses and abuses by the powerful be exposed.

The Fordist assembly line is a favorite target of deconstruction for many neo-Marxists. Their deconstructions typically begin with the assertion that management ideology (e.g., factory owners' desire to control the productivity of their workers) is built into the technology by which work is organized. The mass production technology, pioneered by Henry Ford in the United States, illustrates how the ideological content of the assembly line worked to the advantage of owners and managers. The assembly line rendered at least one portion of the conflict of interest between workers and capitalists invisible because once it was installed, its physical presence precluded discussion of the right of management to organize work as a mass production process. In this way, the workers accepted the ideology of management control of the organization of work as a given, along with the seemingly ideologically neutral assembly line technology. As American economist Richard Edwards describes the situation:

Struggle between workers and bosses over the transformation of labor power into labor was no longer a simple and direct *personal* confrontation; now the conflict was mediated by the production technology itself. Workers had to oppose the pace of the *line*, not the (direct) tyranny of their bosses. The line thus established a technically based and technologically repressive mechanism that kept workers at their tasks.[25]

At this point, the physical structure of the production process organized social relations of dominance and submission within the hierarchy of owners and workers by reconstituting the status quo and suppressing resistance to it each time the machinery was turned on.

Interpretations of the effects of physical structures on social relations are not always so sinister. Postmodernist architects and their critics, for example, see in built space the possibility of reconstructing the symbolic world we inhabit in any way we choose. Postmodern architecture (re)introduces an awareness of the symbolic potential of built space and the possibility of exploiting it (for good or for evil). Heinrich Klotz, former director of the German Architecture Museum in

Frankfort, explains modernist architecture this way:

For many decades we were indifferent to the meanings of architectural forms, either because we were totally opposed to them or because we could afford to ignore them. The structural aspects of a building and the functional values in terms of cost economisation and optimisation of use were the main objects of interest. The fact that a form could mean one thing or another was not a topic for official discussions, and it remained outside the range of debatable questions for architectural theory. To consciously consider the form of architecture a vehicle of meaning was an exceptional thing to do.[26]

"But," Klotz continues, with postmodernist hindsight:

Whether architects like it or not, a building acts as a vehicle of meaning even if it is supposed to be meaningless. One way or another, it presents a visual aspect. Even the vulgar postwar functionalism that cut the characteristic features of a building to a minimum produced buildings that, as they entered one's visual field, acquired a meaning: An apparently neutral and monotonous uniformity.

Klotz then explains the "new possibilities of architectural symbolisation" that postmodern architecture offers:

In contrast to the kind of architecture that consciously renounced any symbolic effect since by its own definition in terms of functional efficiency any consideration of meaning was too much, the new trends in architecture are predominantly marked by attempts to draw attention to other contents besides the functional qualities of a building—to contents referring to nonarchitectural as well as architectural contexts.[27]

Postmodernist architectural theory thus points to the possibility of using built space to refer to organizational contexts of meaning. Not that these possibilities did not exist prior to postmodernist comment upon them, only that modernists have chosen to ignore them. Although few organization theorists have yet walked through this door,[28] it is now open to new theoretical and practical possibilities.

SUMMARY

An organization is a designed and decorated physical entity with a geography and a layout of workspaces, equipment, and employees. These physical aspects have important implications for the behavior of people who are part of the organizational community, including managers, employees, customers, suppliers, members of the local community, and others who need to interact with or within the organization. The physical shape an organization takes also has symbolic importance. The most obvious symbolic message that an organization's physical structure delivers is the impression it makes with its buildings, particularly when they are architecturally designed to make a strong visual statement. But, physical structures deliver more subtle symbolic messages as well, and interpretations of geography, layout, style, and decor can make valuable contributions to the study of organization. Both the designed and the undesigned features of an organization's physical structure can be useful clues to the culture of an organization and can help you to visualize organizational identity (e.g., status symbols, group boundaries, and corporate image) as well as provide insight into many features of organizational social structure (e.g., the relative placement of people and status symbols provides insight into hierarchy and the distribution of power) and technology (e.g., the layout of equipment and machines provide insight into work flows).

When observing the physical structures of your organization, ask yourself what sort of interactions are supported and which are discouraged by the geography and layout? What symbolic messages do inhabitants of these spaces read in the design and decor of their surroundings? How do changes in social relations (e.g., the hiring of new employees, restructuring, downsizing) affect physical structures and how do changes in physical structures (e.g., brought about by moving to a new building or co-locating a team or unit) influence social relations? What do layouts of equipment and machinery, or human traffic patterns, tell you about the technology used by the organization? How does physical structure support or challenge cultural assumptions and values, and how are these values and assumptions expressed in choices about physical structure that appear as cultural artifacts?

As you can see in the array of questions posed in the previous paragraph, the concepts of organization theory—environment, technology, social structure, organizational culture, and physical structure—overlap considerably. Return to Figure 1.2 in the first chapter and recall our discussion of the intersections of the circles. As the questions above demonstrate, you should now be able to discuss the ways in which all of the concepts of organization theory are both different and similar. The similarities expose the content of the overlaps in Figure 1.2.

As with the concepts themselves, the overlaps between concepts can be interpreted from modern, symbolic-interpretive, and postmodernist perspectives. The modern perspective suggests the possibility of integration across all of these concepts—that there is hope for one unifying theory to explain everything we know about organizations. Postmodernists would regard this modernist project as mere illusion, a grand narrative that they predict will soon collapse under its own weight. Instead, postmodernists see in the overlap of the concepts of organization theory reasons to question the boundaries we set up when we choose to think and speak in these or any other ways. What, they ask, are the possibilities awaiting us when we tear down these walls? Their vision for the future is of a democratic, interdisciplinary dialogue in which we construct new and more liberating alternatives.

Symbolic-interpretivism offers a middle ground in this debate. Symbolic-interpretivists are not convinced by modernist unification arguments because the concrete everyday world of organizations they observe provides little evidence for such a theory. They see in the interplay of similarity and differences among organization theory's concepts a world filled with the ambiguity and contradiction of symbolism. Instead of shuddering at this diversity, as modernists tend to do, they welcome the richness of interpretation that multiplicity implies. But neither do they take up the radical (op)position of the postmodernist perspective. Symbolic-interpretivists are more inclined to seek understanding of the processes of social construction, not to satisfy the need to control typical of the modernists, and not to emancipate others like the postmodernists, but rather to understand ourselves.

In the remaining chapters of the book, I will present some issues that have been longstanding interests of organization theorists and practicing managers: decision making, power and politics, conflict and contradiction, control, ideology, and organizational change. In each of these chapters the theories presented draw upon several of the key concepts examined in previous chapters. Each issue also will be examined from modern, symbolic-interpretive, and postmodernist perspectives and the nuances of meaning that each brings to the issues will be the focus of our discussions. These concluding chapters will give you the opportunity to practice combining concepts and applying them to issues and will also give you a deeper and more applicable appreciation of the three perspectives of organization theory.

KEY TERMS

organizational geography	territorial boundaries
layout	group identity
design and decor	organizational identity
status indicators	corporate image

ENDNOTES

1. Roethlisberger and Dickson (1939); Mayo (1945).
2. Homans (1950).
3. Pfeffer (1982).
4. Daft and Lengel (1984).
5. Gullahorn (1952); Wells (1965); Gerstberger and Allen (1968); Allen and Gerstberger (1973); Conrath (1973); Szilagyi & Holland (1980).
6. Festinger, Schacter, and Back (1950); Estabrook and Sommer, (1972).
7. Oldham and Brass (1979); BOSTI (1981); Oldham and Rotchford (1983); Hatch (1987).
8. Hatch (1990).
9. Urry (1991); Yanow (1993).
10. Eco (1986: 297).
11. Steele (1973); Berg and Kreiner (1990).
12. Giddens (1987).
13. Berg & Kreiner (1990).
14. Louis Harris and Associates (1978); BOSTI (1981); Konar et al. (1982).
15. Richards and Dobyns (1957); Wells (1965).
16. Whyte (1943).
17. Olins (1989).
18. Albert and Whetten (1985); Olins (1989); Berg and Kreiner (1990); Dutton and Dukerich (1991); Dutton, Dukerich and Harquail (1994).
19. Berg and Kreiner (1990).
20. Olins (1989).
21. Abratt (1989); Hatch and Schultz (forthcoming).
22. Homans (1950).
23. D. Gregory (1978: 121).
24. Soja (1989).
25. Edwards (1979: 118).
26. Klotz (1992: 235).
27. Ibid. 235–36.
28. Yanow (1993: 310).

REFERENCES

Abratt, R. (1989). A new approach to the corporate image management process. *Journal of Marketing Management*, 5/1: 63–76.

Albert, Stuart, and Whetten, David A. (1985). Organizational identity. In L. L. Cummings and B. M. Staw (eds.), *Research in Organizational Behavior*. Greenwich, Conn.: JAI Press, vii. 263–95.

Allen, T., and Gerstberger, P. (1973). A field experiment to improve communications in a product engineering department: The nonterritorial office. *Human Factors*, 15: 487–98.

Berg, Per Olof, and Kreiner, Kristian (1990). Corporate architecture: Turning physical settings into symbolic resources. In Pasquale Gagliardi (ed.), *Symbols and artifacts: Views of the corporate landscape*. Berlin: Walter de Gruyter, 41–67.

BOSTI (Buffalo Organization for Social and Technological Innovation) (1981). *The impact of office environment on productivity and quality of working life: Comprehensive findings*. Buffalo: Buffalo Organization for Social and Technological Innovation.

Conrath, C. W. (1973). Communication patterns, organizational structure, and man: Some relationships. *Human Factors*, 15: 459–70.

Daft, Richard L., and Lengel, R. H. (1984). Information richness: A new approach to managerial behavior and organization design. In Barry M. Staw and Larry L. Cummings (eds.), *Research in Organizational Behavior*. Greenwich, Conn.: JAI Press, vi. 191–233.

Doxtater, Dennis (1990). Meaning of the workplace: Using ideas of ritual space in design. In Pasquale Gagliardi (ed.), *Symbols and artifacts: Views of the corporate landscape*. Berlin: Walter de Gruyter, 107–27.

Dutton, J., and Dukerich, J. (1991). Keeping an eye on the mirror: Image and identity in organizational adaptation. *Academy of Management Journal*, 34: 517–54.

Dutton, Jane E., Dukerich, Janet M., and Harquail, Celia V. (1994). Organizational images and member identification. *Administrative Science Quarterly*, 39: 239–63.

Eco, Umberto (1986). *Travels in hyper reality*. San Diego: Harcourt Brace Jovanovich.

Edwards, Richard (1979). *Contested terrain: The transformation of the workplace in the twentieth century*. New York: Basic Books.

Estabrook, M., and Sommer, R. (1972). Social rank and acquaintanceship in two academic buildings. In W. Graham and K. H. Roberts (eds.), *Comparative studies in organizational behavior*. New York: Holt, Rhinehart & Winston, 122–28.

Festinger, Leon S., Schacter, Stanley, and Back, Kurt (1950). *Social Pressures in Informal Groups*. Stanford, Calif.: Stanford University Press.

Gerstberger, Peter G., and Allen, Thomas J. (1968). Criteria used by research and development engineers in the selection of an information source. *Journal of Applied Psychology*, 52: 272–79.

Giddens, Anthony (1985). Time, space and regionalisation. In D. Gregory and J. Urry (eds.), *Social relations and spatial structures*. New York: St. Martin's Press, 265–95.

Giddens, Anthony (1987). Structuralism, poststructuralism and the production of culture. In A. Giddens and J. Turner (eds.), *Social theory today*. Stanford, Calif.: Stanford University Press, 195–223.

Gregory, Derek (1978). *Ideology, science and human geography*. London: Hutchinson.

Gregory, Kathleen L. (1983). Native-view paradigms: Multiple cultures and culture conflicts in organizations. *Administrative Science Quarterly*, 28: 359–76.

Gullahorn, J. T. (1952). Distance and friendship as factors in the gross interaction matrix. *Sociometry*, 15: 123–34.

Hatch, Mary Jo (1987). Physical barriers, task characteristics, and interaction activity in research and development firms. *Administrative Science Quarterly*, 32: 387–99.

Hatch, Mary Jo (1990). The symbolics of office design: An empirical exploration. In Pasquale Gagliardi (ed.), *Symbols and artifacts: Views of the corporate landscape*. Berlin: Walter de Gruyter, 129–46.

Hatch, Mary Jo, and Schultz, Majken (forthcoming). Relations between organizational culture, identity and image. *European Journal of Marketing*.

Homans, George (1950). *The human group*. New York: Harcourt Brace & World.

Klotz, Heinrich (1992). Postmodern architecture. In C. Jencks (ed.), *The post-modern reader*. London: St. Martins Press, 234–48.

Konar, E., Sundstrom, E., Brady, C., Mandel, D., and Rice, R. (1982). Status markers in the office. *Environment and Behavior*, 14: 561–80.

Louis Harris and Associates, Inc. (1978). *The steelcase national study of office environments: Do they work?* Grand Rapids, Mich.: Steelcase.

Mayo, Elton (1945). *The social problems of an industrial civilization*. Boston: Graduate School of Business Administration, Harvard University.

Oldham, Greg R., and Brass, Daniel J. (1979). Employee reactions to an open-plan office: A naturally occurring quasi-experiment. *Administrative Science Quarterly*, 24: 267–84.

Oldham, Greg R., and Rotchford, Nancy L. (1983). Relationships between office characteristics and employee reactions: A study of the physical environment. *Administrative Science Quarterly*, 28: 542–56.

Core Concepts of Organization Theory

Olins, Wally (1989). *Corporate identity: Making business strategy visible through design.* London: Thames and Hudson.

Pfeffer, Jeffrey (1982). Chapter 8: Developing organization theory, Organizations as physical structures. In *Organizations and organization theory.* Boston: Pitman, 260–71.

Richards, C. B., and Dobyns, H. F. (1957). Topography and culture: The case of the changing cage. *Human Organization,* 16: 16–20.

Roethlisberger, F., and Dickson, W. (1939). *Management and the worker.* Cambridge, Mass.: Harvard University Press.

Soja, Edward W. (1989). *Postmodern geographies: The reassertion of space in critical social theory.* London: Verso.

Steele, Fred I. (1973). *Physical settings and organization development.* Reading, Mass.: Addison-Wesley.

Szilagyi, Andrew D., and Holland, Winford E. (1980). Changes in social density: Relationships with functional interaction and perceptions of job characteristics, role stress, and work satisfaction. *Journal of Applied Psychology,* 65: 28–33.

Urry, John (1991). Time and space in Giddens' social theory. In Christopher G. A. Bryant and David Jary (eds.), *Giddens' theory of structuration: A critical appreciation.* London: Routledge, 160–75.

Wells, B. (1965). The psycho-social influence of building environments: Sociometric findings in large and small office spaces. *Building Science,* 1: 153–65.

Whyte, William Foote (1943). *Street corner society.* Chicago: University of Chicago Press.

Yanow, Dvora (1993). Reading policy meanings in organization-scapes. *Journal of Architectural and Planning Research,* 10: 308–27.

FURTHER READING

Becker, Franklin D. (1981). *Workspace: Creating environments in organizations.* New York: Praeger.

Gagliardi, Pasquale (1990) (ed.). *Symbols and artifacts: Views of the corporate landscape.* Berlin: Walter de Gruyter.

Sundstrom, Eric (1986). *Work places: The psychology of the physical environment in offices and factories.* Cambridge: Cambridge University Press.

Part III
Key Issues and Themes in Organization Theory

The conversations and interests of organization theorists have ranged much more broadly than is indicated by the basic concepts and theories described in Part II. Several key themes have emerged over the years as having significance for both researchers and practitioners, including: decision making, power and politics, conflict, control, and change. Because these issues arise again and again, and cut across the perspectives of organization theory, they provide another, if more complicated, entry point to the study of this field. In Part III we will examine these key themes, continuing to trace the multiple influences of the Classical theorists and of the three perspectives of organization theory.

You will soon discover that Part III is messier than Part II. The difficulty of keeping topics and distinctions separate is more acute in Part III than it was in Part II. In a way, the circles of Figure 1.2 from Chapter 1 will begin to melt back together and new lines of demarcation will suggest themselves. It is not that the ways of thinking we developed in Part II are wrong, it is that you are now ready to move on to more complex aspects of organization theory and theorizing.

Adding to the complexity in Part III is my assumption that you now know the concepts and theories covered in Part II. In Part III I will chunk these ideas in order to allow greater scope to our discussions (recall the concept of chunking from Chapter 1). This means that you may need to go back to core concepts and theories covered in earlier chapters to refresh your memory of them. Rereading the earlier material will enrich the meanings of your concepts and will help you to build associations necessary for theorizing. I have indicated the connections I make to material from earlier chapters in the text to help you see how this process works, at least for me. But you should explore your own connections as well. This exploration is part of being a theorist. What is more, it is fun.

9 | Organizational Decision Making, Power, and Politics

T HE study of organizations as decision-making systems and as political orders introduces another metaphor into organization theory—the organization is a political arena. The political metaphor entered organization theory very early in its history but was initially suppressed by popular attitudes favoring explanations based in formal structures of authority and legitimacy. Politics was considered by many to be inappropriate in business because it undermines rationality.[1] It was not until observational studies of organizational decision making revealed undeniable evidence of political behavior in organizations that political theories of organization gained attention within organization theory. The transformation of attitudes occurred largely through the influence of American administrative and political scientists Herbert Simon and James March. March was particularly influential in organization theory, not just in provoking discussion of organizational politics, but in developing the field of organizational decision making, which was his primary interest. So far reaching was the transformation of attitude that by 1980 American sociologists Samuel Bacharach and Edward Lawler were able to state flatly that: "Survival in an organization is a political act. Corporations, universities, and voluntary associations are arenas for daily political action."[2]

In this chapter we will define decision making at the organizational level of analysis and consider theoretical challenges to the rational model including three alternative organizational decision-making processes and their implications for organization theory. These models describe how and when power and politics enters into daily organizational life. Having turned our attention to politics, we will define power in the organizational context and then explore organizational theories based in the political metaphor. The chapter ends with consideration of alternative views of power and politics grounded in feminist and critical theory.

ORGANIZATIONAL DECISION MAKING

Decisions are made throughout organizations. Issues such as new products, new technologies, pricing strategy, geographic location of facilities, restructuring, or a new emphasis on cultural values, all depend upon decision-making processes, but so do choices about which computer to purchase, or how many new employees to hire for the holiday season. Decisions of all types and magnitudes shape and form organizations, and in this sense, you can look at an organization as a locus for decision-making activity. This is the perspective of organizational decision-making theory.[3] Of course, decisions take place endlessly, so it is also possible at a given point in time to interpret an organization as the product of its decisional history.

When organization theorists speak of organizational decision-making they refer to decision making processes that occur at all levels and in all units of an organization. In most traditional organizations the decision-making process is specialized. Top management focuses on strategic decision making, middle managers emphasize decisions about internal structural arrangements and coordination among units, and lower level managers are responsible for decisions about day-to-day operational activities within their assigned units (see Figure 9.1). Meanwhile, in functional structures, decisions about marketing are made by marketing departments, accounting decisions by accounting departments, and so forth (see Figure 9.2). In divisional structures, decision making follows divisional interests and concerns (see Figure 9.3).

You can see the same specialization in the structures of traditional business school curricula in which there are separate courses for studying finance, accounting, marketing, and operations research, as well as management courses focused on the executive level (strategic management), interunit and organizational levels (organization theory), and the individual level of decision making (organizational behavior). Studies of post-industrial organization suggest that this sort of specialization is no longer effective within the fragmented and organic structures of new organizational forms like networks, joint ventures, and strate-

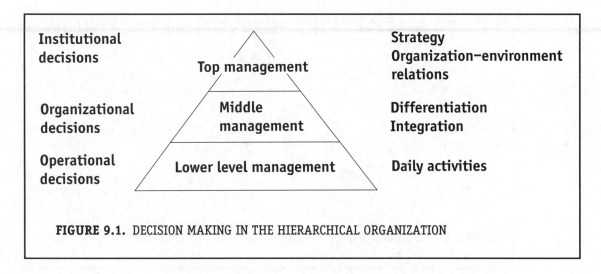

FIGURE 9.1. DECISION MAKING IN THE HIERARCHICAL ORGANIZATION

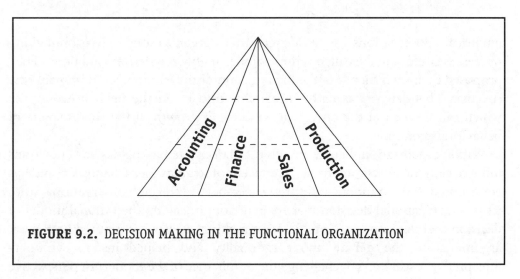

FIGURE 9.2. DECISION MAKING IN THE FUNCTIONAL ORGANIZATION

gic alliances. In response to these changes, many business schools are moving to a less functionally structured, more integrated curriculum.

The origins of organizational decision-making theory can be traced to March and Simon's book, *Organizations*, which was published in 1958. This was followed in 1963 by Richard Cyert and March's *A Behavioral Theory of the Firm* which focused on the politics of organizational decision-making processes. These books embodied a debate between organization theorists and economists concerning the social aspects of decision making. Economists traditionally built their models of the firm on the assumption of rationality in organizational decision-making processes. Simon, March, and Cyert questioned this assumption, offering

271

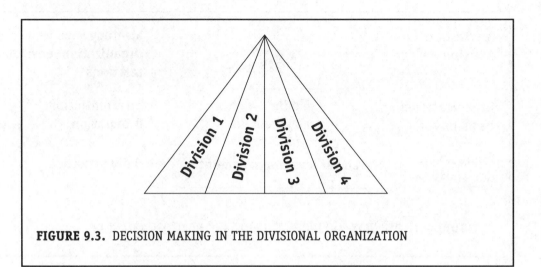

FIGURE 9.3. DECISION MAKING IN THE DIVISIONAL ORGANIZATION

empirical observations as evidence that organizational decision-making processes could only be called rational under highly restrictive conditions. They proposed their own theory of the firm to counter the economists' dominant perspective. This debate has had considerable impact on the field of economics which can be seen in the emergence and rapid growth of the subdiscipline of behavioral economics.

Within organization theory, the subject of decision making has had enormous influence on the development of the concept of strategy (see Chapters 4) and has contributed to the symbolic-interpretive perspective through observational studies of organizational decision makers in action. In calling the rational model of decision making into question, decision-making studies contributed important arguments to the debate about rationality and helped inspire symbolic-interpretive researchers to challenge the dominance of the modernist perspective in organization theory.

Bounded Rationality

Traditional economists assume that the rational model drives decision making in organizations. The rational model, you will recall from Chapter 4, begins with the definition of a problem and the collection and analysis of relevant information that serves as a frame for the decision-making activity. The next step is to generate and evaluate as many alternatives as possible, considering the likelihood of both positive and negative consequences for each option. This is followed by selection from among the alternatives on the basis of criteria that have been worked out in advance and are related to the objectives of the firm. Finally, the selected alternative is implemented. The steps of the rational decision-making process are shown as a flow chart model in Figure 9.4.

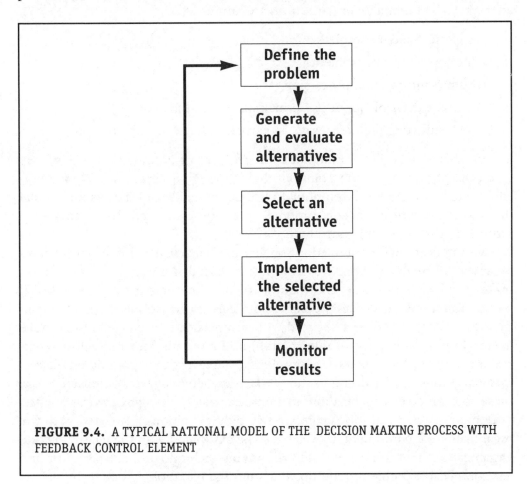

FIGURE 9.4. A TYPICAL RATIONAL MODEL OF THE DECISION MAKING PROCESS WITH FEEDBACK CONTROL ELEMENT

Nobel laureate Herbert Simon identified and questioned the assumptions of the rational model.[4] He pointed out that the rational model assumes that decision makers have knowledge of their alternatives and of the consequences of implementing those alternatives, but that real decision makers often possess incomplete and imperfect information about alternatives and consequences. Second, he suggested that the rational model ignores the internal politics of the organizational system. It assumes that there is a consistent preference ordering among decision makers (i.e., that everyone agrees about the goals of the organization), and that decision rules are known and accepted by everyone concerned.

Issues and Themes in Organization Theory

Simon pointed out, however, that real organizational decision makers often confront conflicting goals.

On the basis of his comparison of actual decision-making activities with the ideal set forth in the rational decision-making model, Simon proposed that attempts to be rational in organizations are limited by:

(1) imperfect and incomplete information;

(2) the complexity of problems;

(3) human information-processing capacity;

(4) the time available for decision-making processes;

(5) the conflicting preferences decision makers have for organizational goals.

Simon labelled this set of limitations the problem of **bounded rationality**. He chose this phrase in order to point out that, although decision makers undoubtedly try to be rational by attempting to live up to the ideal of the rational model (he said they were intendedly rational), they are prevented from being fully rational by the set of limitations noted above.

Two implications of bounded rationality are particularly important from an organization theory perspective. The first is that, in some situations, decision makers will have too little information to meet the demands of the rational model. You should relate this problem to our earlier discussions of uncertainty in Chapter 3. The difficulties associated with complexity and change both produce uncertainty (i.e., the lack of information) and interfere with rational decision making. When environments are simple and stable, organizations do not face as many decisions and the decisions they do face are generally less complicated than those confronted by organizations in complex, rapidly changing environments.

Complexity and rate of change are not only conditions associated with the organization's environment, they can also be associated with the technical core. Organizations that use simple and unchanging technologies face far fewer and less complicated problems requiring decisions than do those whose technologies are complex and/or rapidly changing. Since decision-making situations differ depending on complexity and rate of change in environments and/or technologies, it is clear to see why uncertainty is a key concern of organization theorists studying decision making as a property of organizations.

The second implication of bounded rationality derives from an understanding of conflicting goals. Under conditions favoring the rational model, interpretation is not problematic because there is agreement about the framework within which decision makers are making their choices, that is, there is consensus about goals and values. When this agreement does not exist, the decision-making problem is ambiguous because decision makers can, and usually will, evaluate alternatives in more than one way. The difference between **ambiguity** and uncertainty is that, whereas added information reduces uncertainty (since it is a lack of information that produced the condition in the first place), ambiguity is often heightened by the addition of information because the new information contributes additional points over which decision makers can disagree.

Disagreement (regardless of whether it is associated with uncertainty or ambiguity) is a critical factor establishing what sort of decision-making process will unfold in a given situation. With agreement, the conditions of the rational decision-making model are more likely to be met, than under conditions of disagreement. Disagreement, as Simon points out, has several faces. The two that decision-making theorists have focused the most attention on are: (1) disagreements about goals to pursue or problems to solve (what direction to take), and (2) disagreements about what knowledge to bring to bear on the decision-making process, in other words, about how the goals should be achieved. The first form of disagreement involves ambiguity, while the second is generally a problem of uncertainty (too little information). These two forms of agreement/disagreement provide the foundation for a two by two matrix presented by James Thompson.[5] The matrix defines four decision-making situations, each of which favors a different decision-making process as shown in Figure 9.5 and described below.

The Rational Decision-Making Process

When there is agreement about goals or about the problem being addressed, and there is agreement about how to go about achieving the goal or addressing the problem, then uncertainty and ambiguity are at a minimum and conditions are right for using the **rational model** of decision making shown in Figure 9.4. Consider the example of what engineers call systems analysis, a tool of rational decision making that uses statistical procedures, such as linear programming techniques or Pert charts, to solve complex problems. These aids help the rational model work well even where problems are enormously complex, but, as with all forms of rational decision making, they assume that needed information is either known or estimable.

Of course, when important factors are unknown, or cannot be responsibly estimated, the engineering aids to decision making fail, as do all processes based on the rational model. This does not mean that managers will cease to use them. In fact, as uncertainty or ambiguity increases, managers may find that they have even greater incentive to use these methods to provide the symbolic sense of security that is lacking in the decision process. Institutional theorists would argue

	agree	disagree
agree	**Rational model**	**Coalition method**
disagree	**Trial-and-error model**	**Garbage can model**

Above the columns: Agreement/disagreement on goals or problem definition

Left side label: **Agree/disagree on methods**

FIGURE 9.5. MATRIX SHOWING CONDITIONS FAVORING DIFFERENT DECISION-MAKING PROCESSES

Based on: Thompson and Tuden (1959) and Thompson (1967).

that this urge comes from institutionalized norms for rationality. But giving in to norms for rationality can lead you to ignore important aspects of a decision or decision-making situation that can be appreciated only if you break out of the rational frame. Breaking out of the rational decision-making process ushers in a variety of alternative decision-making methods, characterized by the three remaining cells in Figure 9.5.

The Trial-and-Error Decision-Making Process

You may encounter situations in organizational decision making in which parties to the decision are in agreement about goals and/or the nature of the issue to be resolved, but do not agree about how to achieve the goal or resolve the issue. You have faced this situation many times before; it occurs whenever you do not know how to do something. Under these conditions, uncertainty (lack of information) is high, but ambiguity (multiple interpretations of what you are trying to accomplish) is not a critical factor. Here the decision-making process will most likely take the form of **trial-and-error learning**.

Where decisions are of significant magnitude, it is common to find decision makers in this set of conditions moving cautiously, engaging in a succession of limited small decisions that can be fit together over time into a full solution or plan of action.[6] Furthermore, since finding and evaluating information on all imaginable alternatives is not possible in these circumstances (e.g., due to bounded rationality), decision makers who cannot agree on a course of action often content themselves with finding enough information to make limited comparisons between a few alternatives, most of which are mere increments to the last decision made. You can see this decision-making process at work in budgeting decisions that use the previous budget as their starting point.[7] This process is also referred to as the incremental model.

The Coalitional Model

Organizational decision-making processes are sometimes shaped by a lack of agreement about the goals to be pursued or the issues to be addressed. This situation is the natural result of organizational realities such as multiple, conflicting goals, competition over scarce resources, interdependence, and other sources of conflict and contradiction (we will examine these in Chapter 10). Under these conditions, those with the most powerful positions tend to dominate the decision-making process. However, when decision makers are aware of this tendency, they can act to manage or manipulate the decision-making process by engaging in politics.

The political process involves individuals uniting their interests and proposing alternatives that are collectively beneficial to themselves. These interest groups then take stock of their relative power position vis-a-vis other interest groups within the decision-making domain and, if their forces are not strong enough to overcome opposition, they will seek to join together with other interest groups in order to form a coalition. Usually coalition formation is based upon some behind-the-scenes negotiations that strive to give consideration to all interests in the coalition's joint position.

In cases that fit the conditions of the **coalitional model** of decision making, ambiguity is far more problematic than uncertainty. Under these conditions, decision makers do not focus primarily on a search for problem-solving information, but rather emphasize interest-accommodating alternatives. Although many people believe that the coalitional model implies that sound organizational practices have broken down, when interests are so conflicted that common goals cannot be agreed upon, interest-accommodation becomes a reasonable basis for decision-making processes. We will return to these considerations when we examine organizational politics in greater depth later in this chapter.

The Garbage Can Model

When agreement about goals (or issues) and the means to achieving them is absent, decision makers confront both uncertainty and ambiguity. Under these conditions the **garbage can model** seems to best describe the organizational decision-making process as it occurs in organizations. The model is particularly suited to situations in which the environment or technology is poorly understood, or where key actors move in and out of the decision process because other activities compete for their time and attention. The model has been named "the garbage can" to emphasize the randomness of this decision-making process. Although no organization operates in this mode all of the time, every organization will find itself in this situation some of the time. Furthermore, some organizations seem to have more than their fair share of this type of decision making. The university is a good example.

March has described universities as organized anarchies on the basis of the chaotic nature of many of their decision-making processes.[8] March and his colleagues describe the garbage can decision-making process as random streams of events that intertwine, allowing some solutions to attach themselves to problems in the presence of a random set of individuals at a random point in time. In the garbage can model, problems, solutions, participants, and choice opportunities are independent streams of events that flow into and through organizations, much like a random selection of waste gets mixed together in a garbage can. Whenever solutions, participants, and choice opportunities connect, a problem may be identified or solved. Because of the randomness of the process, however, choices may be made without solving a problem, some problems are never solved, and solutions may be proposed where no problem exists (e.g., putting personal computers in every office). Nonetheless, even in an organized anarchy, some problems are solved, even if only by chance.

The garbage can model contrasts sharply with the assumptions of the rational model of decision making. It argues against the assumption that goals can be clearly defined and that alternatives to achieving them are known in advance and can be evaluated according to whichever criteria are deemed most relevant (e.g., efficiency, cost, expected return on investment). Instead, it proposes that decision making presents an arena within which organizational members act out their conflicts and differences. This view downplays the instrumentality of decision making and presents it instead as an organizational drama within which decisions are social constructions of reality.[9]

A Dynamic View of Organizational Decision Making

All four types of decision-making processes can occur within any organization and can even occur at the same time. This can be envisioned by imagining all of the decisions being made throughout an organization viewed from the organizational level of analysis. This imaginative exercise encourages you to look at the organization as a system of decision-making processes (the modern perspective), as a culture within which decision making is a key symbolic activity (the symbolic-interpretive perspective), and as a collage of decisions that have been made in the past and exist today as a sedimented history (postmodern perspective). Regardless of the perspective taken, a dynamic view sees all of the decision processes as a means to working through uncertainty and ambiguity in the act of creating and recreating organizations.

The decision-making perspective links ambiguity and uncertainty to disagreements over goals and methods. As decision makers work through uncertainty in their methods, organizational decision-making processes shift from garbage can or trial-and-error to coalitional or rational processes. As decision makers work through ambiguity in their interpretations of goals, organizational decision-making processes shift from garbage can or coalitional to trial-and-error learning or rational processes. However, because organizations always confront or enact new sources of complexity and change and differing interpretations of these new aspects of their reality, decision makers continually experience new uncertainty and ambiguity that will push other decision-making processes away from the rational model. Thus, the use of all four modes of decision making in the organization is likely to be ongoing.

Notice, however, that this way of viewing decision making forms a grand narrative in the sense that all forms of decision making are embraced within a single contingency framework. It furthermore reinforces the ideal of rationality associated with institutional norms and thus participates in managerial hegemony. A more radical view of decision making that challenges the hegemony of the contingency framework is provided by an argument favoring irrationality in the decision-making process.

The Irrationality of Organizational Decision Making

Swedish organization theorist Nils Brunsson criticizes the decision-making school for restricting its focus to decisions, which he claims are purely cognitive phenomena. He argues that decisions themselves are not the primary concern of practicing managers, but rather action is their chief interest. Thus, Brunsson claims, research into decision-making processes stops short of the organizational issue of greatest significance. Brunsson proposes putting decisions in the context of action, but says that doing so calls the concept of decisional rationality into question. In Brunsson's words: "rational decisions do not always provide a good basis for appropriate and successful action."[10] Brunsson calls instead for **action rationality**. He claims that when action rationality is invoked, the usefulness of *irrationality* in the decision-making process becomes clear.

Brunsson's argument rests on his observation that organizational action depends upon more than a decision to act, which is purely a cognition or thought—it also depends upon motivation (i.e., a desire to contribute) and commitment (i.e., public endorsement) which in turn require positive expectations. He argues that effective organizational action depends upon the implementation of decisions. Implementation requires that those who must act have positive expectations for their actions in order to experience motivation to take the action and the commitment to involve themselves in seeing it through to a successful conclusion. But, according to Brunsson, the rational decision-making process actually undermines positive expectations, and thus dilutes motivation and destroys commitment.

Brunsson argues that the rational decision processes of alternative generation and evaluation provoke doubt and uncertainty by requiring decision makers actively to consider conflicting, contradictory, or incompatible alternatives. Focusing on conflicting, contradictory, or incompatible alternatives can paralyze action by undermining expectations of success ("maybe we should have selected a different alternative after all") which dilutes motivation and destroys commitment to implement decisional choices. Considering both the positive and negative consequences likely to unfold in each alternative adds to this uncertainty and doubt with further negative consequences for the motivation and commitment to act. Brunsson also argues that it is impractical to evaluate alternatives according to predetermined criteria, as the rational model suggests. This is because, as Simon and others who back the coalitional model have observed, objectives are often inconsistent. Under these conditions, attempts to apply previously formulated criteria are doomed because they can only generate argument and confusion among decision makers who discover that needed information is either lacking or is pointing in contradictory directions. Argument and confusion, like doubt and uncertainty, undermine expectations of success, dilute motivation, and destroy the commitment to act.

Following up on his analysis of action versus decisional rationality, Brunsson makes several counter proposals to the rational model. He proposes, that, in making a decision, organizational decision makers should:

(1) analyze few alternatives, and of these it is best if only one has a good chance of being accepted (proposing *unacceptable* alternatives reinforces the decision to accept the preferred alternative with positive consequences for expectations of success, motivation, and commitment);

(2) consider only the positive consequences of the favored alternative (this reduces doubt, bolsters expectations of success, and creates enthusiasm and commitment to the alternative);

(3) avoid formulating objectives in advance; instead reformulate the predicted consequences of the favored alternative as your decision-making criteria (this supports motivation and commitment to the selected alternative).

Brunsson refers to these steps as **decision irrationality** and claims that observation of decision makers in action indicates the validity of this model. That is, Brunsson's observations suggest that decision makers often consider few alternatives, ignore the negative consequences of favored alternatives, and define criteria for selection among alternatives in terms of the expected consequences of their favored alternative. He argues that they are justified in this seeming irrationality by the need to form positive expectations that build motivation and commitment (i.e., by achieving action rationality).

Brunsson does not completely abandon decisional rationality, but he restricts rational decision making to situations "where the benefits to be gained from motivation and commitment are slight—for instance when the actions concerned are less significant, less complicated, and geared to the short term."[11] In other words, Brunsson sees rational decision making as appropriate for small and insignificant, rather than large or important, decisions. Brunsson bases this surprising conclusion on his belief that "the two kinds of rationality [decisional and action] are difficult to pursue simultaneously, because rational decision making procedures are irrational in an action perspective."[12] If the decision is important and requires action, Brunsson argues, decisional rationality must often be sacrificed to action rationality for the sake of getting something done. If decisions that demand action are poorly founded on rationality, what foundation should they use instead? Brunsson argues that ideologies (i.e., ideas shared by all organizational members) provide an alternative. We will return to the topic of ideology in Chapter 11.

POWER AND POLITICS

The alternatives to the rational decision-making model introduced above suggest that when there is disagreement over goals or over the preferred means for pursuing goals, then the decision-making process will be open to the effects of power and politics. Thus, power and politics is likely to be part of the decision-making process in three of the four situations depicted in Figure 9.5. As American organization theorist Jeffrey Pfeffer put it: "Organizational politics involves those activities taken within organizations to acquire, develop, and use power and other resources to obtain one's preferred outcomes in a situation in which there is uncertainty or dissensus about choices."[13]

Because differing interests are built into an organization (unit differences, differences in the perspectives of different levels in the hierarchy), each decision represents but one opportunity for negotiation and re-negotiation in a never-ending stream of political maneuvering that constitutes the organization. This is the political perspective which describes organizations as fundamentally pluralistic (divided into factions, subunits, and subcultures), and suggests that political aspects of organizational decision making are closely aligned with the issues of conflict and contradiction which we will address in Chapter 10.

Political theories of organization originally focused on the relationship between power and structural arrangements (e.g., the hierarchy of authority), or on explaining how conflict situations such as contested decisions or unequal distributions of scarce resources are resolved. However, recent work in this field has emphasized the hidden aspects of power in organizations. In this section of the chapter we will explore the issues involved in defining power, especially in relation to the concept of authority.

Defining Power

Modernist organization theorists interested in the study of **power** in organizations often take their point of departure in the definition of power offered by American political scientist Robert Dahl. Dahl claimed that: "A has power over B to the extent that he can get B to do something that B would not otherwise do." A and B can be defined as any type of social actor (individual, group, or organization).[14] Dahl's definition points to an important characteristic of power, namely that all power is relationship specific (sometimes we just say that power is relational). In other words, power exists within the relationship between social actors rather than residing within the actors themselves.

Power is generally assumed to be used to attain desired outcomes. This is where the issue of self-interest enters the discussion of power and politics. Power can be, and often is, used to promote individual self-interest, but it is also used to achieve outcomes favorable to most or all members of the organization, or to society at large. Thus, the use of power is not inherently selfish or evil, only potentially so.

Power can involve the use of coercion (the threat of force), rewards (control of material resources desired by the subject), norms (the legitimacy bestowed by cultural assumptions and values), and knowledge (control of unique and needed information). American sociologist Amitai Etzioni based his typology of organizations on the different uses of power that he found to be characteristic of different types of organizations in society: coercive (prisons, mental institutions), calculative or remunerative (economic organizations such as factories and other businesses), and normative (churches, gangs, volunteer groups).[15] We might add post-industrial organizations (e.g., networks, joint ventures, strategic alliances) to Etzioni's list and characterize them as having expertise-based orientations toward power.

Organization theorists agree that there are many sources of power. One in particular—authority—stands out, however, because it is associated with hierarchy, part of the structural definition of organizations. This point of view suggests the need to distinguish other sources of power from authority, which we will do below. These other sources of power in organizations include: personal characteristics (the most influential of these is a charismatic personality), expertise, and opportunity. Opportunity occurs, for example, when executive secretaries or administrative assistants use their access to powerful persons as a source of power for themselves. Outside of authority, the sources of power do not necessarily follow the organizational hierarchy, thus, as American sociologist Melville Dalton showed, lower level participants in organizations can also enjoy significant levels of power in their work relationships.[16]

Power and Authority

Pfeffer sees organizational structure as a picture of who governs critical resources and decides important activities within the organization. He claims that, through structural arrangements, communication is prescribed, reporting requirements are made apparent, and information networks are forged. It is through this structuring of communication, relationship, and information that top management is provided the legitimate authority to use organizational power to set goals, make decisions, and direct activities.[17] In other words, authority derives from an individual's structural position in the hierarchy. Thus, one of the main differences between authority and other forms of power is that the exercise of authority is directed downward in organizations, while the exercise of other forms of power can be multidirectional.

Authority is not always easily distinguished from other forms of power. Many theorists argue that authority is power in any form that has become legitimized within the organizational setting, thus they argue that the primary difference between authority and other forms of power derives from the way power is perceived within a given relationship. Authority occurs when the development of norms and expectations make the exercise of power both accepted and expected. In this view, organizations are formed by an active distribution and redistribution of power among units and individuals, but when a particular distribution becomes accepted as a normal part of the organization's daily operations, then the power distribution crystallizes into an authority structure produced by expectations about how those in authority will behave and how others will behave towards them. Here, social construction theory argues that authority is less easily redistributed than are other forms of power because cultural forces (values and expectations) stabilize interpretations of reality among organizational members.[18]

Another important difference between authority and other forms of power is that the exercise of authority has fewer costs. Using one's non-authorized power demands an expenditure of resources such as expertise or personal attention, or by making commitments or side-payments in exchange for support on a given issue. These resources, once expended, cannot be recovered, and the influencer must replace them by developing additional expertise or opportunity, or suffer an eroded power base. The exercise of authority, however, because it is accepted and expected, has fewer costs and, in some cases, is enhanced through use.

David Knights, a British industrial sociologist and labor process theorist, makes an important distinction between relationships of authority and coercive relationships. In the following excerpt, Knights and Roberts argue that when individuals in authoritative positions resort to coercive practices, the authoritative relationship upon which organizations depend, breaks down:

By "authoritative" power we refer to those circumstances under which individuals, rather than opposing and trying to avoid attempts to supervise their actions, voluntarily accept the advice and direction of others. As opposed to coercion, the distinctive feature of authoritative power relations is that they involve, and are only maintained through a mutual recognition of each other as subjects; each recognizes his/her dependence on the others' action, as well as the others' freedom of action. It is this that makes authoritative power a moral relationship and a relationship of trust. Authority cannot be imposed or individually possessed, but always remains only a quality of the relationship *between* people, in which *both* are personally committed to, and see as legitimate, the reciprocal rights and obligations realized through their interaction. As soon as one individual seeks to elevate his/her own instrumental ends above concern for the other then mutual trust is quickly destroyed, and transformed into attempts at mutual manipulation. Interaction changes from a mutual recognition of each other as interdependent subjects, to a concern to reduce each other to known and predictable objects.[19]

Symbols of Power and Authority

Pfeffer points out that authority is often inferred from symbols that powerful members of an organization acquire through political maneuvering. These symbols include the location, size, and decor of one's office, the right to call a superior by his or her given name, or the ability to force others to call oneself by title (e.g., Sir, Madame, Doctor, or Professor). Other symbols of authority include reserved parking spaces, luxurious offices, executive dining room privileges, high salaries, and other special benefits and considerations.

Since individuals can acquire the symbols of authority without the actual authority that may be associated with them, symbols of authority produce one of the major problems with interpreting power in organizations. Thus, in some organizations the competition over status symbols may be as high, or even higher, than the competition over the actual authority that the symbols represent. The musical comedy "How to Succeed in Business Without Really Trying" satirized this phenomenon. The story is about a young man who works his way into an organization and then up the corporate ladder by systematically associating himself with the symbols of authority and success that are recognized within the organization. Although believing that symbols are all that is required for power is going too far, it is true that symbols help to establish and maintain power by supporting interpretations of who has power within the organization.

POLITICAL THEORIES OF ORGANIZATION

Political theories of organization address many issues: What determines the power of the various social actors within the organization? What are the conditions under which power is used? What strategies can one use to develop and use power? How can managers enhance their chances of having their power legitimized? Much of the research into these questions is conducted at the individual level of analysis, and many theorists have suggested how an individual manager

---

TABLE 9.1. SOME COMMON STRATEGIES FOR DEVELOPING AND USING POWER WITHIN AN ORGANIZATION

Develop power by:

Creating dependence in others
- work in areas of high uncertainty
- cultivate centrality by working in critical areas
- develop non-substitutable skills

Coping with uncertainty on behalf of others
- prevention
- forecasting
- absorption

Developing personal networks

Developing and constantly augmenting your expertise

Use power to:

Control information flows to others

Control agendas
- issue definition
- order of issues
- issue exclusion

Control decision-making criteria
- long vs. short term considerations
- return vs. risk
- choose criteria that favor your abilities and contributions

Cooptation and coalition building
- external alliances (e.g., supplier or customer relationships, interlocking boards of directors)
- internal alliances
  promote loyal subordinates
  appoint committees
  gain representation on important committees

Bring in outside experts (consultants) to bolster your position

---

can maximize his or her power relative to other actors within the organization (see, for example, Table 9.1).

By contrast, organization theorists have been more interested in dealing with power and politics at the level of units within organizations or at the level of the organization itself. Sometimes this involves nothing more than interpreting organizational theories from a political point of view. For example, population ecology and institutional theory can be interpreted as explanations for the distribution of power among organizations. Population ecology concerns the distribution of power based in coercion (physical resources), remuneration (economic resources), and knowledge (technological resources), whereas institutionalization theory concerns the distribution of power based in institutionalized expectations and social norms (social, cultural, and legal resources).

In the remainder of the chapter we will examine four political theories of organization. The first is strategic contingencies theory, a modernist theory focused on explaining how uncertainty predicts which social actors will have power in an organization. Next we will return to resource dependence theory (introduced in Chapter 3) and examine how it builds on strategic contingencies theory to offer an explanation of the links between uncertainty, power, and the hierarchy of authority. Finally, we will turn to critiques of modern approaches to studying power and politics in organizations; here we will examine Bacharach and Baratz's ideas about the hidden face of power, and then turn our attention to feminist critiques and other critical views of the use of power in organizations and conclude with discussion of the politics of gender.

Strategic Contingencies Theory

According to **strategic contingencies theory**, power derives from the ability to provide something that the organization highly values and that can only be obtained through a particular social actor, for example an unusually high level of performance, an irreplaceable skill, or a scarce and critical resource. The ability that is arguably the most valued at the interdepartmental level of analysis is the ability to protect other organizational actors from uncertainty. As Pfeffer explains:

Uncertainty coping is seen as a critical task or activity within organizations in part because organizations are viewed as social entities in which uncertainty is reduced through the use of standard operating procedures, forecasting, buffering, and other activities that permit the rationalization of organizational activity, while at the same time keeping the organization adaptive to external constraints.[20]

In his study of power among units in an organization, the French sociologist Michel Crozier noted the influence of uncertainty on power relationships in a cigarette factory that was owned and operated as a state monopoly in France. Crozier discovered that the maintenance men who repaired broken machinery had an unexpected amount of power in an organization that was otherwise completely bureaucratized and faced little uncertainty (i.e., it operated with a highly routinized technology, within a stable environment).[21] Within the cigarette factory, Crozier observed that the maintenance workers were able to exercise their power to win self-interested outcomes such as the ability to organize their own work.

Production workers in the factory were paid on a piece-rate system so that any breakdown in the machinery was a direct threat to their income stream. Management was also dependent upon the maintenance workers because plant productivity was affected by machine failures and this was critical to their own performance evaluation. Crozier's work illustrates the way in which the ability to handle a critical uncertainty confers power to units or individuals. In this case, the power was conferred on the maintenance workers who maintained their power by sharing critical information about how the machines operated with one another but with no one else. Similar findings regarding the ability to handle critical uncertainty have been reported in studies of universities where power has been found to accrue to those departments that have the highest levels of enrollment, or that produce the most grant or other outside contract income for the university.[22]

British organizational researchers David Hickson, C. R. Hinings, and their colleagues pointed out that it is not uncertainty itself that produces power, but rather the ability to cope with the sources of uncertainty that otherwise affect the organization negatively.[23] They suggest three coping strategies that partly determine whether or not uncertainty will translate into power differences: prevention (forestalling uncertainty), forecasting (providing information), and absorption (taking action after the event to prevent negative consequences for other units of the organization). Their theory further predicts that coping with uncertainty will only generate power differentials when the task of the dominating unit is central to operations of the organization and the coping activities can only be performed by the dominate unit (that is, they are non-substitutable). This theory is known as the strategic contingencies theory because it outlines the contingencies that predict which social actors within an organization will have the greatest power.

Resource Dependence Theory

Resource dependence theory extends strategic contingency theory to explanations of how the environment is linked to organizational action via political processes. According to strategic contingencies theory, environmental constraints and contingencies (such as the scarcity of critical resources) provoke uncertainty and thus produce opportunities to cope with uncertainty on behalf of the organization. The ability to cope with uncertainty can then be transformed into power internal to the organization. The distribution of environmental contingencies thus produces a distribution of opportunities to develop power which influences the power distribution within the organization.

Insofar as this environmentally contextualized power distribution becomes legitimated, environmental dependence can explain formal structures. That is, the power derived from coping with uncertainty will be transformed into positional authority by being used to gain appointments to formal positions within the hierarchy. At this point power then focuses on making decisions and taking action which reflects back on the environment as is explained, for example, by enactment theory (see Figure 9.6).

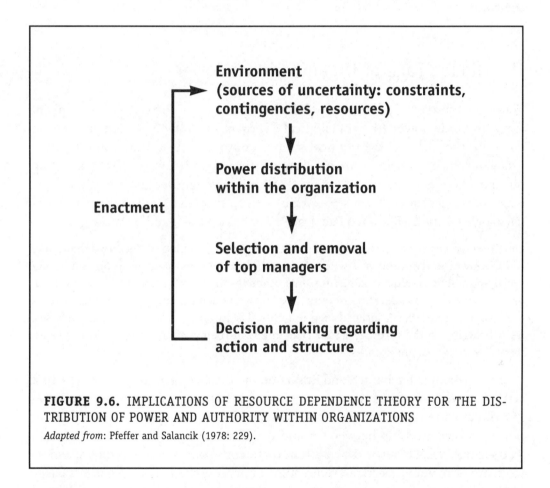

FIGURE 9.6. IMPLICATIONS OF RESOURCE DEPENDENCE THEORY FOR THE DISTRIBUTION OF POWER AND AUTHORITY WITHIN ORGANIZATIONS

Adapted from: Pfeffer and Salancik (1978: 229).

Notice that resource dependence theory argues that internal political processes occur somewhat independently of environmental contingencies because different individuals and units within the organization make different uses of opportunities to cope with uncertainty. As Pfeffer and Salancik put it, "organizations are only loosely coupled with their environments, and . . . power is one important variable intervening between environments and organizations."[24] According to resource dependence theory, the power distribution is set up as a distribution of opportunities to manage uncertainty, differentially realized by various organizational actors. The power distribution then explains the outcomes of selection and removal processes by which the power of some managers is legitimated as authority and the power of others is delegitimized. Following this, the authority structure is used to make decisions that influence subsequent action within the organization, action which then has a feedback effect on the environment.

The Hidden Face of Organizational Power

Traditional studies of power and politics in organizations focus either on explaining who holds power (the sociological approach) or how a particular decision outcome came about (the political science approach). American political scientists Peter Bacharach and Morton Baratz criticized both approaches by pointing out that there is an aspect of power that both have ignored, namely that some issues never get raised because power is used to suppress them. In their influential article entitled "The Two Faces of Power," Bacharach and Baratz argue:

Of course power is exercised when A participates in the making of decisions that affect B. But power is also exercised when A devotes his energies to creating or reinforcing social and political values and institutional practices that limit the scope of the political process to public consideration of only those issues which are comparatively innocuous to A. To the extent that A succeeds in doing this, B is prevented, for all practical purposes, from bringing to the fore any issues that might in their resolution be seriously detrimental to A's set of preferences.[25]

In this passage, Bacharach and Baratz define the **two faces of power**. The first is the face we recognize as the exercise of power to bring about desired outcomes in a direct and visible manner. This is the face presented by Dahl's definition of power as a relationship between A and B that permits influence of B's actions. The second face, however, draws attention to conscious or unconscious attempts to create or maintain barriers to the political process itself. This face is less easily observed because it is only revealed by what is *not* discussed openly, or is only revealed in an indirect way.

You should keep in mind that Bacharach and Baratz, along with the sociologists and political scientists that they address with their argument, are referring to a particular form of social organization—the community. In borrowing their ideas and applying them to business organizations you must be careful to notice the differences as well as the similarities in the theoretical domains of community and business. For our purposes, the primary difference between a community and a business organization is the considerable extent to which a stable and legitimated power structure (i.e., the hierarchy of authority) exists within the business organization, while a community is characterized more frequently in terms of shifting structures of interest. Thus, the relative amount of interest shifting assumed by Bacharach and Baratz's argument may be somewhat restricted in the business organization. This, however, makes their point about the second face of power even more important for students of business organization.

In organizations operating with a strict hierarchy, many issues are silenced by the charge of being irrelevant to the concerns of the firm, which have tended until recently to be focused heavily on profitability and efficiency. As organizations become more diverse and pluralistic, there is evidence that issues formerly defined by higher levels of authority as outside the realm of the organization's interests are being put forward as critical, for instance child care, parental leave, and social responsibility. Perhaps this indicates that in the post-industrial world, organizations are becoming more like communities. If so, this turn of events renders political theories of organization increasingly important.

The Feminist Critique of Power in Organizations and Other Critical Views

Within discussions of the political model of organization you will find the first evidence of a postmodern view emerging within organization theory. An example is the following quote from *Power in Organizations*, written by Jeffrey Pfeffer:

> The ideology of functional rationality—decision making oriented toward the improvement of efficiency or performance—provides a legitimation of formal organizations, for the general public as well as for those working within specific organizations. . . . The legitimation and justification of these concentrations of power are clearly facilitated by theories arguing that efficiency, productivity, and effectiveness are the dominant dynamics underlying the operation of organizations. . . . To maintain that organizations are less than totally interested in efficiency, effectiveness or market performance is to suggest that it is legitimate to raise questions concerning the appropriateness of the concentration of power and energy they represent and makes it possible to introduce political concerns into the issues of corporate governance. . . . The argument, then, is that the very literature of management and organizational behavior (as well, we might add, of much of economics . . .) is itself political (Edelman, 1964), and causes support to be generated and opposition to be reduced as various conceptions of organizations are created and maintained in part through their very repetition.[26]

Pfeffer foreshadows the postmodern turn toward critical and self-reflexive thinking by raising the question of whether engaging in the discourse on management and organizations is itself a political act. However, others have gone much further in the direction of postmodern appreciations of power in organizations. Radical feminists have provided some of the first forays into this territory, along with critical theorists who think along the lines presented in Anthony Giddens's structuration theory.

Feminists, drawing on the writings of Marx and especially on neo-Marxist critical theory, argue that power is used to **marginalize** the powerless. That is, those in positions of authority maintain their claims to legitimacy by using their power to suppress voices that would otherwise be raised in opposition to their claims to authority. The postmodern dictum "give voice to silence" is a counter-attack against those whose interests are served by suppression of these marginalized points of view.

Feminist views of power differ radically from those of modernists. Power in modernist terms is closely tied to issues of domination and subordination. In feminist writings and postmodern perspectives in general, power takes on a much broader signification. It continues to refer to situations of domination/submission, but also applies to willful action (e.g., any creative activity). That is, feminists recognize a new dimension of power stretched between two poles of action: action that is produced as the result of pressure from those in positions of authority, and action that is undertaken through one's own authority. In this view, power becomes, as Anthony Giddens has put it, a transformative capacity—the capacity "of agents to accomplish their will."[27]

You will recall from Chapter 6 that Giddens tried to overcome the dualism of structure and agency that is built into our ordinary ways of thinking and speaking. From this perspective, he argued, structure is implicated in power relations and power relations are implicated in structure—the two cannot be separated. Power is not itself a resource, resources are merely the media through which power is exercised. However, he also recognized that the exercise of power through resources can reproduce structures of domination. Thus, power is experienced both as transformative capacity (the power to act as seen from the perspective of actors, called agents in Giddens's theory) and as domination (the power to constrain others' actions as seen from the structural perspective). Giddens also noted that "power relations are relations of autonomy and dependence, but even the most autonomous agent is in some degree dependent, and the most dependent actor or party in a relationship retains some autonomy."[28] Just as Giddens's duality of structure presented a picture of organizations based in the tension between structure and agency, so his treatment of power presents them framed by the tension between autonomy and dependence, a view similar to that put forward in feminist theory.

The Politics of Gender in Organizations

One of the primary applications of feminist theory has been to the analysis of **gender construction** and **gender relationships** in organizations. American feminist sociologist Joan Acker defined *gender* as "patterned, socially produced, distinctions between female and male, feminine and masculine."[29] The roots of contemporary feminist theory are typically traced to the struggle over gender relations that re-emerged with great political force in the late 1960s. A departure point for much of the study of gender relations in society and organizations is the obvious yet persuasive observation that "Most of the work of ruling—making decisions, shaping policies and laws, running institutions, managing media, operating professional systems—is done by men; and most of the men who rule are served by women, in the office (secretaries) and at home (wives)."[30] American postmodern feminist, Jane Flax put it this way:

socialist feminists have employed the concept of division of labor to point out that the labor force is segmented by gender as well as by the division between owners and producers. There is a "sexual division of labor" in the organization of production. Many women are employed in occupations that are 70 percent or more female. Not coincidentally, feminists argue, these occupations are also lower paid than those requiring equivalent education and skills, but in which men predominate. These writers discuss the congruence between gender stereotypes and some of the skills and behavior required in "women's work"—for example, caring for children (elementary school teachers) or organizing and cleaning up after men (secretaries). These stereotypes make it seem natural that women do some kinds of work and not others. In turn the devaluation of the stereotypically female contributes to and reinforces a devaluation of "women's work" and the wages it can command.[31]

Although the feminist literature is large and far from homogeneous, deconstructing and overcoming this "fact of organizational life" seems to cut across the interests of feminists theorists regardless of their philosophical orientations. Within organization theory the interests of feminists have been aligned with those of Marxist and critical theorists behind the banners of marginalization, voice, and diversity (diversity will be taken up in Chapter 10). Nonetheless, there are important tensions between these groups. In particular, feminists such as Flax argue that Marxists, neo-Marxists, critical theorists, and even postmodernists are guilty of ignoring the role gender relations plays in constructing society and its organizations.

At the heart of current debate about gender is a transformation in thinking that moves from traditional oppositions that accentuate difference—male/female, closed/open, hard/soft, action/reflection—to acknowledgment of the similarities between males and females, especially in regard to the many ways in which both are "prisoners of gender."[32] Gender systems, according to Flax, generally involve relations of domination and are "an important aspect of the context within and by which a self is constituted."[33] Gender studies examine the "systematic forces that generate, maintain, and replicate gendered relations of domination."[34]

As evidence that humans define themselves and others in gender-oriented ways, Flax offers the observation that one of the first things we notice about others when we meet them is whether they are male or female. She further observes that, in the West, we signal our compliance with established patterns of gender relations through our modes of dress and ways of walking and speaking. She points out as additional evidence of our gendered identities, the considerable anxiety we experience when we cannot fit a person into a gender category.

Understanding the politics of gender involves studying the ways in which behavior and language express and maintain dominant cultural understandings of women and men and thereby structure power relationships in society in general, and in particular organizations. The study of the use of language in organizations provides a means for exposing the gendered nature of organizational relationships of power and domination. The argument put forward by feminist theorists is that language itself is gendered, that is meaning circulates around a network of images that have distinctive male and female associations.[35] American feminist organization theorist Kathy Ferguson argued that:

Rhetorical and grammatical practices organized around, for example, images of soft and hard, fluid and solid, open and closed, particular and universal, connection and distance, reception and assertion, are gendered in the sense that they ride on an already constituted and widely circulated set of understandings about appropriately feminine and masculine ways of being in the world. Individual women and men do not automatically embody or repudiate these traits, but they do inhabit a world of knowledge claims and power practices fully infused with such oppositions. Examining these gendered codes entails tracking the ways in which women and men negotiate the symbolic terrain, and the practices by which organization privileges and legitimates some encodements at the expense of others.[36]

In advocating voice among the marginalized members of society and organizations, feminist theorists encourage listening to women and taking feminist organizations as objects of study. Ferguson argues that such strategies place "women's languages and practices at the center of the analysis, privileging the world as seen from this set of vantage-points, thus problematizing the conventional equation of men with humanity."[37]

One of the implications of the study of gender relations in organizations is that, if current gender constructions lead to devaluing women's work and to keeping women out of positions of power in organizations and society, then, in the name of justice, these constructions need to be changed. Feminist organization theorists currently pursue several lines of research aimed at creating this change politically. These include:

(1) giving voice to women in order to articulate feminist viewpoints;

(2) destruction of unitary representations of experience to make way for the multiplicity of not only gender, but race and class as well;

(3) reflexivity with regard to our research and writing practices: redefining the subjects of and audiences for our research (e.g., changing these from white, male managers to women, people of color, indigenous people, those of the working-class, youth, and the aged).

SUMMARY

When politics is needed to overcome legitimate differences in preferences for goals or methods, then the coalitional model of decision making is of great value in resolving conflicts and moving organizations forward to take action. Politics loses its organizational usefulness, however, when it is applied to situations in which these conditions do not hold. This does not mean that politics will never be misapplied in organizations. A seasoned organizational politician can create conflict out of nearly any situation and will do so if the stakes are high enough. The bad feelings you may have experienced surrounding political maneuvering in organizations most likely stem from misapplication of politics within organizational decision-making processes. However, you should recognize its useful aspects as well as its dangers.

From a modernist point of view, power flows into the organization from the environment by virtue of changing environmental demands and opportunities. As power is distributed in the organization it will move through existing channels of authority, but also can upset that balance by empowering some formerly less powerful actors so that a new pattern of legitimation replaces the old one. This transformation can occur through the conscious intention of management and other members of the organization, or without much consciousness. Shifting power shows up in restructuring efforts, negotiations over resource allocations, attempts to manage the organizational culture, and changes in core technology, among many others. When the use of power is conscious in organizations, we generally see the organization or its members as engaged in political activity. When the use of power is unconscious, so far at least, it only shows up in analyses of the hidden face of power or in feminist and critical analyses.

Traditional views suggest that the political process is most effectively managed by seeking a balance between too little and too much political activity, channelling political action into situations where it will be of value, and discouraging it when conditions favor other decision-making activities. However, the postmodern feminist view should remind you to be self-reflexive about the judgments you make as to what is a useful and what is a disruptive use of political action. If managers only permit political discourse around issues that do not challenge *their* claims to authority and autonomy, then suppression of voices within the organization is likely to occur. Since suppression can affect productivity, particularly where innovation is important, even the most modern of managers will do well to reflect honestly on their motivations concerning political actions—their own and those of other members of the organization. The postmodern manager will engage in self-reflection and avoid repressive behavior on moral grounds, and should enjoy benefits to organizational innovation and creativity.

KEY TERMS

bounded rationality
ambiguity
rational model
trial-and-error learning
coalitional model
garbage can model
action rationality
decision irrationality

power
strategic contingencies theory
resource dependence theory
two faces of power
marginalization
gender construction
gender relationships

ENDNOTES

1. Burns (1961); Pettigrew (1973).
2. Bacharach and Lawler (1980: 1).
3. Cyert and March (1963).
4. Simon (1957, 1959); March and Simon (1958); see also March (1978).
5. Thompson and Tuden (1959); Thompson (1967).
6. Mintzberg, Raisinghani, and Theoret (1976).
7. Wildavsky (1979).
8. Cohen, March, and Olsen (1972).
9. Olsen (1979).
10. Brunsson (1985: 22).
11. Ibid. 26.
12. Ibid. 27.
13. Pfeffer (1981: 7).
14. Dahl (1957: 203).

15. Etzioni (1961).
16. Dalton (1959); see also Mechanic (1962).
17. Pfeffer (1978).
18. Pondy (1977).
19. Knights and Roberts (1982).
20. Pfeffer (1981: 110).
21. Crozier (1964).
22. Salancik and Pfeffer (1974); Pfeffer and Moore (1980).
23. Hickson et al. (1971).
24. Pfeffer and Salancik (1978: 229–30).
25. Bacharach and Baratz (1962: 948).
26. Pfeffer (1981: 14).
27. Giddens (1979: 256).
28. Ibid. 93.
29. Acker (1992: 250).
30. Connell (1992) commenting on the work of Canadian feminist sociologist Dorothy Smith.
31. Flax (1990: 151–52).
32. Ibid. 139.
33. Ibid. 138.
34. Ibid. 139.
35. Ferguson (1994: 90).
36. Ibid. 91.
37. Ibid. 90.

REFERENCES

Acker, Joan (1992). Gendering organizational theory. In Albert J. Mills and Peta Tanered (eds.), *Gendering organizational theory*. Newbury Park, Calif.: Sage, 248–60.

Bacharach, Samuel B., and Baratz, Morton S. (1962). The two faces of power. *American Political Science Review*, 56: 947–52.

Bacharach, Samuel B., and Lawler, Edward J. (1980). *Power and politics in organizations*. San Francisco: Jossey-Bass.

Brunsson, Nils (1985). *The irrational organization: Irrationality as a basis for organizational action and change*. Chichester: John Wiley.

Burns, Tom (1961). Micropolitics: Mechanisms of institutional change. *Administrative Science Quarterly*, 6: 257–81.

Cohen, Michael D., March, James G., and Olsen, Johan P. (1972). A garbage can model of organizational choice. *Administrative Science Quarterly*, 17: 1–25.

Connell, R. W. (1992). A sober anarchism. *Sociological Theory*, 10: 81–87.

Crozier, Michel (1964). *The bureaucratic phenomenon*. London: Tavistock.

Cyert, Richard M., and March, James G. (1963). *A behavioral theory of the firm*. Englewood Cliffs, NJ: Prentice-Hall.

Dahl, Robert A. (1957). The concept of power. *Behavioral Science*, 2: 201–15.

Dalton, Melville (1959). *Men who manage*. New York: Wiley.

Etzioni, Amatai (1961). *A comparative analysis of complex organizations*. New York: Free Press.

Ferguson, Kathy E. (1994). On bringing more theory, more voices and more politics to the study of organization. *Organization*, 1: 81–99.

Flax, Jane (1990). *Thinking fragments: Psychoanalysis, feminism and postmodernism in the contemporary West*. Berkeley: University of California Press.

Giddens, Anthony (1979). *Central problems in social theory: Action, structure and contradiction in social analysis*. Berkeley: University of California Press.

Hickson, David J., Hinings, C. R., Lee, C. A., Schneck, R. E., and Pennings, J. M. (1971). A strategic contingencies theory of intra-organizational power. *Administrative Science Quarterly*, 16: 216–29.

Knights, David, and Roberts, John (1982). The power of organization or the organization of power? *Organization Studies*, 3: 47–63.

March, James G. (1978). Bounded rationality, ambiguity, and the engineering of choice. *Bell Journal of Economics*, 9: 587–608.

March, James G., and Simon, Herbert A. (1958). *Organizations*. New York: John Wiley.

Mechanic, David (1962). Sources of power of lower participants in complex organizations. *Administrative Science Quarterly*, 7: 349–64.

Mintzberg, Henry, Raisinghani, Duru, and Theoret, Andre (1976). The structure of unstructured decision processes. *Administrative Science Quarterly*, 21: 246–75.

Olsen, Johan (1979). Choice in an organized anarchy. In J. G. March and J. P. Olsen (eds.), *Ambiguity and choice in organizations*. Bergen, Norway: Universitetsforlaget, 82–139.

Pettigrew, Andrew (1973). *The politics of organizational decision-making*. London: Tavistock.

Pfeffer, Jeffrey (1978). The micropolitics of organizations. In M. W. Meyer and Associates (eds.), *Environments and organizations*. San Francisco: Jossey-Bass, 29–50.

Pfeffer, Jeffrey (1981). *Power in organizations*. Boston: Pitman.

Pfeffer, Jeffrey, and Moore, William L. (1980). Power in university budgeting: A replication and extension. *Administrative Science Quarterly*, 25: 637–53.

Pfeffer, Jeffrey, and Salancik, Gerald R. (1978). *The external control of organizations: A resource dependence perspective*. New York: Harper & Row.

Pondy, Louis R. (1977). The other hand clapping: An information-processing approach to organizational power. In T. H. Hammer and S. B. Bacharach (eds.), *Reward systems and power distribution*. Ithaca, NY: School of Industrial and Labor Relations, Cornell University, 56–91.

Salancik, Gerald R., and Pfeffer, Jeffrey (1974). The bases and use of power in organizational decision making: The case of a university. *Administrative Science Quarterly*, 19: 453–73.

Simon, Herbert A. (1945). *Administrative behavior*. New York: Macmillan.

Simon, Herbert A. (1957). A behavioral model of rational choice. In H. A. Simon, *Models of man*. New York: John Wiley.

Simon, Herbert A. (1959). Theories of decision-making in economics and behavioral science. *American Economic Review*, 49: 253–83.

Thompson, James D. (1967). *Organizations in action*. New York: McGraw-Hill.

Thompson, James D., and Tuden, Arthur (1959). Strategies, structures and processes of organizational decision. In J. D. Thompson, P. B. Hammond, R. W. Hawkes, B. H. Junker, and A. Tuden (eds.), *Comparative studies in administration*. Pittsburgh: University of Pittsburgh Press, 195–216.

Wildavsky, Aaron (1979). *The politics of the budgeting process* (3rd edition). Boston: Little, Brown.

FURTHER READING

Allison, Graham T. (1971). *The essence of decision*. Boston: Little, Brown.

Czarniawska-Joerges, Barbara (1988). Power as an experiential concept. *Scandinavian Journal of Management*, 4: 31–44.

Emerson, R. M. (1962). Power-dependence relations. *American Sociological Review*, 27: 31–40.

French, J. R., Jr., and Raven, B. H. (1959). The bases of social power. In D. Cartwright (ed.), *Studies in social power*. Ann Arbor: University of Michigan Press, 150–67.

Kanter, Rosabeth Moss (1977). *Men and women of the corporation*. New York: Basic Books.

March, James G. (1994). *A primer on decision making: How decisions happen*. New York: Free Press.

March, James G., and Olsen, Johan P. (1976). *Ambiguity and choice in organizations*. Bergen, Norway: Universitetsforlaget.

Mills, Albert J., and Tanered, Peta (1992) (eds.). *Gendering organizational theory*. Newbury Park, Calif.: Sage.

Pfeffer, Jeffrey (1981). *Power in organizations*. Marshfield, Mass.: Pitman.

Simon, Herbert A. (1979). Rational decision making in business organizations. *American Economic Review*, 69: 493–513.

10 | Conflict and Contradiction in Organizations

THE political perspective on organizations introduced in Chapter 9 presented an image of organizations as arenas in which interests coalesce and collide within political processes that are constantly in flux. Political processes in organizations revolve around a variety of issues and concerns that can bring various groups into direct conflict with one another, for instance, conflict occurs between workers and managers, hierarchical levels, functional departments, divisions, manufacturing plants, between professionals and non-professionals, staff and line, and between bureaucrats and the clients they serve. Thus, conflict arising from the different values, issues, or concerns of various groups is one theoretical explanation for political behavior in organizations. But political behavior, in turn, is only one response to conflict in organizations. According to March and Simon, organizational conflict can result in problem solving, persuasion, and bargaining as well as politics.[1] Thus, although related to the topics of decision making, power, and politics in organization theory, the study of conflict has its own theories and traditions.

Burrell and Morgan argued that conflict and cooperation are two different assumptions upon which theories of organization have been built. Classical management theorists took the view that cooperation is necessary in organizations, or at least is a highly desirable objective. Therefore conflict, which can undermine cooperation, is a bad thing. For instance, one argument from this perspective is that, without cooperation on goals, the organization will not have direction and will fall prey to competitors who do. This logic is then used to justify the search for effective ways to reduce or resolve conflict in organizations. This approach ignores the obvious extent to which conflict is a part of all organizations. In its quest to eradicate conflict it ignores multiple goals, subcultural values, and non-rational behavior (e.g., emotion and intuition). Recognition of the persistence of conflict within organizations leads to theories that diverge from those that are cooperation-oriented. Conflict-based theories generally trace their heritage to the sociological side of Classical theory (especially to Marx), and have mainly been developed within the field of industrial relations.

Organizational conflict has most often been defined as an overt struggle between two or more groups in an organization, or between two or more organizations. It is usually centered on some state or condition that favors one social actor (e.g., group or organization) over others. Scarce resources or limited opportunities, for instance, can generate overt struggle within or between groups and organizations. Conflict is also frequently explained in terms of interference. It occurs when the activities of one social actor are perceived as interfering with the outcomes or efforts of other social actors. American social psychologists Daniel Katz and Robert Kahn, for instance, defined conflict as "a particular kind of interaction, marked by efforts at hindering, compelling, or injuring and by resistance or retaliation against those efforts."[2]

More recent work on organizational conflict, employing ethnographic methods of observation in organizational settings, challenges the modernist view that conflict is overt.[3] For instance, American organizational researchers Deborah Kolb and Linda Putnam argue that responses to conflict, such as avoidance behavior, the development of cultural norms, and emotional behavior, represent much of the reality of conflict in everyday organizational life.[4] These researchers and their colleagues bring the private, informal, and irrational aspects of organizational conflict to light in order to temper the public, formal, and rational aspects of conflict management that are emphasized in the modernist perspective. John Van Maanen, for example, described the way conflicts that were avoided in the workplace of a British police agency were handled informally over drinks at the local pub.[5] According to Van Maanen, such organizational "time outs" carry the emotion of suppressed conflict away from the organization. Feminist organizational researchers, such as Joanne Martin show how gender conflict is suppressed from view by male domination tactics that exploit female dependencies built into their subordinate positions in the authority hierarchy.[6] This work argues that conflict in organizations is much more pervasive than cooperation-oriented theorists admit, and that hidden forms of conflict are difficult to manage because they are embedded in the routine interactions of organizational members as they go about their everyday activities.

In this chapter we take a closer look at the colliding interests represented within organizations and explore theoretical explanations of conflict and contradiction in order to develop an understanding of why these phenomena occur.

First, we will trace changes in attitudes toward conflict that have accompanied the development of conflict theory. Next we will examine a theory of interunit conflict in organizations that captures the horizontal dimensions of conflict, followed by Marxist-influenced conflict models that emphasize the vertical dimension. We conclude with a discussion of organizational contradictions and their representation in the language members use to construct their organizations.

A HISTORY OF ATTITUDES TOWARD CONFLICT

Many people naturally dislike conflict, foregoing its benefits in favor of avoiding its discomforts. If you are one of those who always prefers to avoid conflict, you may find it useful to consider the historical path of the modern organization theorists whose attitudes toward conflict have swung from negative, to positive, coming to rest on a contingency model that combines these views[7].

Conflict as Dysfunctional

At first, many organization theorists regarded conflict as wholly dysfunctional because it was believed to be the antithesis of cooperation. It was generally interpreted as a sign of a defective or an incomplete social structure. Therefore, early conflict theorists proposed that the appropriate response was the creation of structural mechanisms for dealing with issues that generate conflict. Committees, task forces, liaison roles, and many other forms of coordination were recommended for this purpose.[8]

Take the example provided by American social anthropologist William Foote Whyte, who studied conflict and its relationship to the social structure of restaurants in the U.S. in the 1950s.[9] Whyte noted that in the restaurants he studied there was often conflict between waitresses and cooks. These conflicts involved many different situations, but one of the most common was conflicts over the priority given to the orders that waitresses submitted to cooks. Whyte presented an early gender theory to explain the source of conflict in this case—that the male cooks found it difficult to accept orders from female waitresses. Given the flow of work in a restaurant from customer orders to cooks' food preparation, Whyte saw the reversal of relations of dominance (i.e., who can give orders to whom) between men and women defined in the larger social structure to be problematic for the men and thus a source of continuous conflict between the themselves and the female waitresses. Whyte observed that, when restaurants are small, the manager can resolve these conflicts via direct intervention, however, when the manager's time is taken up with other matters, the amount of conflict between the two groups can reach dysfunctional levels. Whyte observed that a solution to this conflict employed by some restaurants is to erect a counter between waitresses and cooks. The use of an order spindle on which waitresses can post orders and cooks can retrieve them at their own pace was another use of physical structuring to separate conflicted parties that seemed to relieve conflict. But Whyte also observed social structural responses to conflict in the addition of food servers to pass orders to cooks and then to garnish and pass the finished food to the wait staff. This intermediary unit reduced conflict by socially as well as physically separating the wait staff from the cooks. In effect, the new unit replaced the liaison role the manager served when the restaurant was smaller.

The main shortcoming of adding an intermediary unit to the structure of the organization is that, as structural elements are added in order to eliminate conflicts, the new units provide sites for future conflicts. In the case of Whyte's restaurant study, the new group of food servers was added to eliminate conflicts between waitresses and cooks. However, the new food servers presented further opportunities for conflict with either the cooks, or the waitresses, or both. Thus, this strategy can result in endless elaboration of the organizational structure followed by endless new instances of conflict. The realization of this limitation of structural elaboration paved the way for an entirely new conceptualization of conflict. Instead of regarding conflict as something that should be, or can be, avoided, organization theorists began to recognize conflict as an organizational fact of life.

Conflict as Natural

The second phase of theorizing about organizational conflict developed around American organization theorist Lou Pondy's observation that, although conflict may be unpleasant, it is an inevitable part of organizing.[10] In Pondy's view conflict may still be regarded as dysfunctional, however, as a natural condition, conflict is unavoidable and should be accepted. This phase of study led to theoretical interest in the sources of conflict (discussed below), and a search for understanding of its fundamental conditions. The natural view of conflict helped managers confront conflicts they could not alter or avoid by suggesting that conflict is not a sign of mismanagement, but is rather an unavoidable aspect of organization.

Conflict as Functional

Pondy also proposed taking a positive attitude toward conflict. This suggestion was prompted by the realization that conflict can stimulate innovation and adaptability. This view of conflict, which formed a third variant of conflict theorizing, challenged the assumption that organizations are, or should be, cooperative systems. This assumption is implicit in both the dysfunctional and the natural views and can be traced to Chester Barnard (recall our discussion of his work in Chapter 2).

The functional view of conflict proposes that conflict is good for the organization because it leads to stimulation, adaptation, and innovation and to better decision making, largely as a result of the input of divergent opinions. Furthermore, conflict is considered to be psychologically and sociologically healthy. Conflict is psychologically healthy in that it allows for the venting of frustrations and provides a sense of participation and even exhilaration. It is sociologically healthy because it encourages opposition to the status quo and initiates conditions for social change. In addition, some theorists credit conflict with providing the conditions for democracy by acknowledging pluralism and encouraging a respect for diversity (a topic to which we will return later in this chapter). The functional perspective also warns that too little conflict can have negative consequences such as group think, poor decision making, apathy, and stagnation.

A Contingency Model of Conflict

Today modernist organization theory offers a variant of the contingency model as the best way to understand organizational conflict and to choose a response to it. This popular view proposes that there is a curvilinear relationship between conflict and organizational performance (see Figure 10.1). Both too little and too much conflict result in poor performance, whereas performance is optimized by an intermediate level of conflict. This perspective recommends that conflict be managed so as to produce the benefits of optimal stimulation of ideas and fresh points of view, and to strengthen intragroup cohesiveness while minimizing the negative effects of uncooperative behavior or open hostility between units and individuals.

It must be recognized, however, that one of the forces that solidifies group identity and enhances cohesiveness is conflict with other groups. Because of the benefits of group cohesiveness in stimulating productivity, some organizations create competition between units to maximize productivity. However, the price

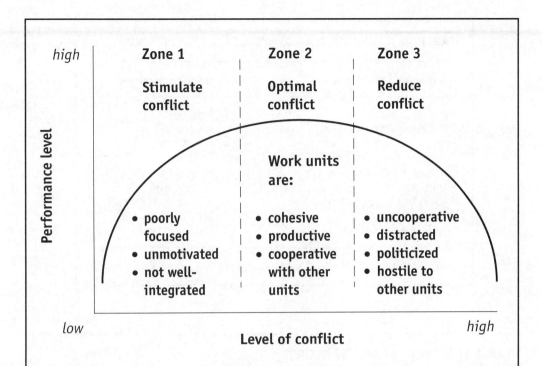

Zone 1

**Stimulate
conflict**

Zone 2

**Optimal
conflict**

Zone 3

**Reduce
conflict**

**Work units
are:**

Performance level

- poorly
  focused
- unmotivated
- not well-
  integrated

- cohesive
- productive
- cooperative
  with other
  units

- uncooperative
- distracted
- politicized
- hostile to
  other units

low

Level of conflict

high

FIGURE 10.1. THE CURVILINEAR RELATIONSHIP BETWEEN CONFLICT AND PERFOR-
MANCE IS SHOWN DIVIDED INTO THREE ZONES

Strategies for conflict management appropriate to each zone are shown above the
curve, while characteristics typical of those experiencing conflict in each zone are
described beneath the curve.

of this extra productivity can be poor cooperation and communication between
groups. In this view, there is a tradeoff between the productive influences of
interunit competition and the conflict that it can generate. Maintaining the delicate balance seems to be the course most often recommended by contingency
analysts who offer lists of ways to reduce and encourage conflict such as those
presented in Tables 10.1 and 10.2. However, to make effective use of such lists,
you must have a clear understanding of the conflict situation. This is where a
theory of conflict is helpful.

Within organization theory, research is divided between studies of horizontal
and studies of vertical forms of conflict. Horizontal conflict is so called because it
occurs in relationships that run perpendicular to hierarchical lines of authority,
while vertical conflict follows hierarchical lines. The difference can be seen in
the contrast of interunit (horizontal) conflicts between the subsidiaries of a

Issues and Themes in Organization Theory

TABLE 10.1. WAYS TO REDUCE CONFLICT IN ORGANIZATIONS

Recommended action	Implicit strategy
Physical separation	Avoidance
Increase resources	Avoidance
Repress emotions and opinions	Avoidance
Create superordinate goals	Collaboration
Emphasize similarities	Smoothing
Negotiate	Compromise
Appeal to higher authority	Hierarchical referral
Rotate jobs	Structural change
Physical proximity	Confrontation

Based on: Robbins (1974); Neilsen (1972); Pondy (1967).

TABLE 10.2. WAYS TO STIMULATE CONFLICT

- Acknowledge repressed conflict
- Role model functional conflict through open disagreement and collaborative responses
- Alter established communication channels
- Hold back information
- Overcommunicate
- Deliver deliberately ambiguous messages
- Differentiate activities or outcomes among subordinates
- Challenge the existing power structure

Based on: Robbins (1974)

---

multinational organization, and vertical conflicts between headquarters and a subsidiary (see Fgure 10.2). Another example of vertical conflict is that which occurs between management and labor; this conflict is sometimes institutionalized in union–management relations. Horizontal conflict is common among the departments of a functionally structured division or organization, between divisions or between manufacturing plants, and between the functional and project sides of a matrix organization.

While all conflict involves the use of power, not all uses of power result in overt conflict. In fact, one use of power is to suppress overt conflict, as, for example, when power is used to silence the voices of opposition. You should recognize this

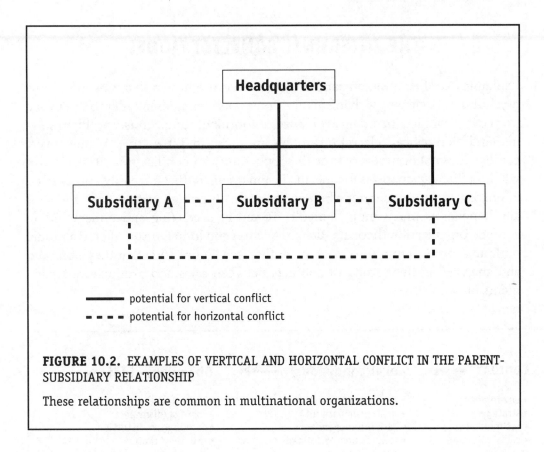

FIGURE 10.2. EXAMPLES OF VERTICAL AND HORIZONTAL CONFLICT IN THE PARENT-SUBSIDIARY RELATIONSHIP

These relationships are common in multinational organizations.

as the second face of power described in Chapter 9. In organizations, the second face of power is strongly related to authority because those who have authority are in a position to silence those who do not. But this is a purely negative interpretation of power and conflict. Power used in the positive sense of creative energy can produce innovation.

Because of the unique power dynamics built into vertical authority relationships, vertical and horizontal conflict are generally given different theoretical treatments. However, the roots of both forms of conflict can be discovered in the structural, cultural, and technological aspects of the organization and in the organization's relationship to its environment. The theoretical basis for vertical conflict will be discussed in terms of Marxist organization theory and then extended to recent concern over workforce diversity, but first we will take up the question of horizontal conflict between the units of an organization.

THE INTERUNIT CONFLICT MODEL

Explaining conflict in organizations is tricky because humans employ numerous psychological defense mechanisms and conscious strategies in order to disengage from overt conflict, including avoidance, smoothing, compromise, problem solving, and hierarchical referral (examples are given in Table 10.1).[11] Thus, overt conflict does not occur every time the opportunity for conflict presents itself. You will find that explanations for specific instances of conflict are easily constructed in retrospect, but predicting when overt conflict is going to occur before it actually happens is much more difficult. To aid in predicting and understanding conflict, organization theorists Richard Walton and John Dutton offered a model outlining some common sources of conflict (see Figure 10.3) that they observed and analyzed in their study of conflicts between sales and production departments in two firms.

Context ➡ **Local conditions** ➡ **Observable indices**

- environment
- strategy
- technology
- social structure
- culture
- physical structure

- group characteristics
- goal incompatibility
- task interdependence
- rewards and performance criteria
- common resources
- status incongruity
- jurisdictional ambiguity
- communication obstacles
- individual differences

- open hostility
- distrust/disrespect
- information distortion
- 'we–they' rhetoric
- lack of cooperation
- avoid interaction

FIGURE 10.3. A MODEL SHOWING THE POSSIBLE SOURCES OF INTERDEPARTMENTAL CONFLICT

Conflict is seen to be embedded in local conditions which are even more deeply rooted in the environment and organizational context.

Based on: Walton and Dutton (1969).

At first, you will understand Figure 10.3 best if you read it backwards, that is, from right to left. Begin by thinking of a specific occurrence of conflict in your experience. Use the model to help you identify the immediate or local conditions associated with this instance. You will find the local conditions of your instance of conflict in the events preceding its occurrence. But to grasp the deeper sources of conflict, it is necessary to examine many instances of conflict in the context of their local conditions. When you have studied enough examples, you will begin to see a deeper pattern in the wider social environment involving the aspects of organization you have studied in this textbook: environment, strategy, technology, social structure, culture, and physical structure. First, we will look at the local conditions described by Walton and Dutton, and then turn our attention to the deeper patterns of conflict that lie within the organization and its environment.

Local Conditions for Interunit Conflict

Walton and Dutton begin with what they call the observable indices of conflict shown on the right side of Figure 10.3.[12] Observable indices represent what you are likely to see or experience in a conflict situation. They can range from open hostility to complete avoidance of interaction. In between these extremes lie expressions of distrust and disrespect, information distortion, frequent use of "we–they" rhetoric, and lack of assistance or cooperation. Walton and Dutton trace these observable behaviors to nine local conditions within the organization.

Group characteristics resulting from differentiation

Differentiation and integration pressures are always in conflict within an organization and are inherent in the processes of organizing. The conflict is set up when the organization first begins to differentiate its activities in response to both internal and external pressures, for instance, to achieve economies of scale, to buffer the organization's technical core against threats, and to span its boundaries to monitor the environment for opportunities. All these pressures lead to differentiation which, in turn, creates the need for integration to help the organization coordinate its differentiated units and activities in order to realize the potential of different members to contribute to the organization's overall goals.

Differentiation pressures produce distinguishable units within an organization (departments, divisions, etc.). Each unit of an organization performs a different task and/or copes with a different segment of the environment. These differences in task and orientation manifest in characteristics that are considered to be conditions for conflict between units. Thus, each unit faces the opportunity to develop its own identity and subculture within the organization producing conditions ripe for multiple perspectives and interests to emerge and collide. When the differentiated units are expected to coordinate their activities and share resources and opportunities, the potential for conflict is confirmed. If the organization adds layers of management or additional units to bridge relations between conflicted parties, then the opportunities for conflict begin to multiply.

Earlier in this chapter you saw this set of conditions in Whyte's example of the relations between waitresses and cooks. In the restaurants Whyte studied, these groups were marked by differences in their flexibility, their time horizons, and the type of result for which they were held accountable. Wait persons must follow a strict routine in order to be efficient enough to give adequate attention to all of their customers, while cooks must be flexible so they can adapt to the unpredictable flow of customer orders coming into the kitchen. Wait persons generally keep track of time in terms of the stages of a meal, whereas cooks think in terms of shifts (e.g., lunch, dinner). Wait persons are accountable to the customer for their efficiency, accuracy in taking and communicating orders, and their demeanor, while cooks are evaluated on the merits of their culinary achievement. Differences such as these define the unique characteristics of units within an organization that make communication and coordination between them difficult and thus contribute to interunit conflict.

Operative-level goal incompatibility

Goals and strategies defined at the highest levels of an organization must be translated and divided between the units and positions of the organization so that a variety of activities will ultimately be performed to achieve them. Once the goals have been translated to the operative level, however, it is often the case that tradeoffs are revealed. For instance, marketing departments typically state their goals in terms of sales to customers which are enhanced by responsiveness to customer demands for services, such as fast delivery or customized product designs. A traditional manufacturing unit, on the other hand, will usually specify its goals in terms of efficiency of production which is best served by standardizing the product line and producing economically determined lot sizes at a steady rate regardless of the flow of customer orders. While both efficiency in production and service to the customer contribute to the overall performance of the firm, at the level of interunit relations between these two departments there is plenty of room for disagreement and hostility to develop as each group pursues its key objectives and thereby interferes with the goal-directed behavior of the other unit.[13]

Task interdependence

As James Thompson explained (see Chapter 5), there are at least three different forms of task interdependence and each implies different opportunities for conflict. Pooled task interdependence demands very little in the way of interaction in order for the interdependent units to perform their tasks. The limited need for interaction translates into few opportunities for direct conflict, as each unit pursues its own goals and interests more or less independently of the others.

Reciprocal task interdependence, on the other hand, demands almost continuous interaction and therefore offers unlimited opportunities for conflict. However, the opportunities for conflict are moderated by the mutuality of this type of dependence. Each group relies upon the other to achieve its objectives so that open conflict hinders both parties simultaneously. As a result, reciprocal task interdependence does not always lead to high levels of conflict, although it can produce periods of non-conflicted interaction punctuated by periods of intense conflict. That is, when reciprocal interdependence breaks down, there is usually rapid escalation on both sides so that the situation reaches crisis proportions in a hurry. Contrast this with situations of sequential task interdependence where one unit is dependent on another but the dependency is not reciprocated. The independent unit has little incentive to respond to the interests and demands of the dependent unit and this sets up the conditions for chronic conflict between them.

Notice how clear the links between power and conflict become when task interdependence is considered. Pooled task interdependence involves few if any power considerations, whereas reciprocal task interdependence is a case of balanced power relationships (at least with respect to task achievement) as neither side can perform without the support of the other. Finally, sequential task interdependence involves asymmetrical power relationships and is generally associated with great latent conflict.

Rewards and performance criteria

When performance criteria and rewards emphasize the distinct performance of separate units, they downplay the combined performance of the entire organization and lead units to ignore the value of cooperation. Consider the problem of giving exams to multiple sections of students taking the same course in a given semester. One way to assure that students in earlier sections will not give the questions to students in later sections is to inform them that all examinations will be graded on the same standard and that if students in later sections get the exam questions and improve their own scores it will be at the expense of students who did not have this advantage. Notice how the creation of a conflict of interests between students leads to elimination of cooperation between them. Also be aware that while this strategy may increase fairness in the grading system, such strategies may be counterproductive from the viewpoint of encouraging information-sharing and the formation of cooperative study groups which can benefit all students and the classes they attend.

Issues and Themes in Organization Theory

Common resources

Dependence on a common pool of scarce resources will often provoke conflict. The resources can include, for example, operating funds or capital allocations, physical space, shared equipment such as copying machines or computer terminals, and centralized staff services (administrative, computer, or other technical support). Also, because the acquisition of resources can indicate power, additional pressure to compete for scarce resources adds to the conflict potential of these situations.

Status incongruity

Conflict can occur whenever two groups have significantly different statuses within the organization yet are asked to coordinate their activities. The imbalance of status is not problematic as long as higher status groups influence lower status groups, however, if lower status groups must initiate activities or otherwise directly influence higher status groups, then conflict is more likely to occur than it would without the incongruity. Conflicts of this sort were observed by Whyte in his study of the relations between waitresses and cooks where the waitresses initiated activity for the cooks by giving them customer orders.[14] Similar conflicts were observed where engineers directed a higher status research group to do routine testing.[15] In both cases the inversion of the status hierarchy led to breakdowns in interunit cooperation.

Jurisdictional ambiguities

Jurisdictional ambiguities occur when there is unclear delineation of responsibility. This condition produces conflict when credit or blame is at stake. Situations in which it is unclear which groups or units are deserving of credit or blame present an opportunity for the groups to come into conflict as each tries to take credit from, or throw blame on, the other. A lost order in a busy restaurant kitchen is a problem that triggers this sort of conflict when wait staff and cooks each can claim that the other is at fault. As Whyte showed, the addition of food servers who handle the interface between wait staff and cooks eases this conflict if the servers are given the added responsibility of tracking all orders.

Communication obstacles

When units speak different languages they are less likely to agree on issues of mutual concern and more likely to assume that the lack of agreement is due to intransigence and self-interest by the other party, than to understand it as the result of the two parties looking at things in incommensurable ways. Take the example of doctors and administrators in hospitals. Their conflicts can often be traced, at least in part, to the different ways in which they communicate. For instance, doctors are trained to focus on cure rates for medical techniques and practices, while administrators emphasize costs and return on investments in expensive facilities and equipment.

Individual differences

Not all people get along with each other. There are many reasons for interpersonal conflict including personality differences such as with respect to authoritarianism and sociability, differences in self-esteem, or socioeconomic background. However, it is far too common for managers to attribute instances of conflict within the organization to individual differences, or simply to blame one party or the other (i.e., to take sides) without considering other important factors. Generally speaking, this approach is not likely to be effective since the vast majority of conflicts in organizations are not simply the result of interpersonal differences, but rather are associated with conditions at the group or organizational level of analysis. In fact, many people who truly have personality conflicts with others routinely work together in organizations everywhere. Thus, individual differences rarely provide a complete explanation of conflict in organizations.

Environment and Organization as Contexts for Interunit Conflict

As mentioned before, it is possible to discover deeper patterns that relate observable conflict to conditions in the environment, and to other aspects of organizing we have studied in this book. When you grasp the pattern, it becomes much easier to put conflict in its proper perspective, even when those around you are caught in the grip of negative emotions. This distance should help you to transform negative energy to more useful ends. In situations in which an increase in conflict is desired, this understanding will also guide you through the risky process of stimulating conflict to enhance creativity, innovation, or productivity.

Environment

The principle of isomorphism suggests that organizations attempt to match the complexity of their environments. This generally leads to internal differentiation in the form of both vertical and horizontal structural complexity. Furthermore, as they adapt to changing conditions, uncertainty is produced within the organization. As some groups develop greater capacities for coping with the uncertainty, this can lead to changes within the organizational power structure. Thus, complexity and change in the environment of an organization can contribute to the local conditions of conflict reviewed above.

Strategy

A growth strategy for an organization leads to increases in size and differentiation within an organization with effects similar to those just related to environmental complexity and change, including an increase in internal complexity and changes in the existing power structure. Downsizing contributes to conflict by creating the perception of shrinking resources which provokes competition over what remains to be divided. When jobs are on the line, competition becomes fierce. Thus, strategies that effect organizational size in either a positive or a negative direction contribute to local conditions for conflict.

Technology

The organization's tasks are defined in large measure by its choice of technology, and changes in technology mean changes in the tasks assigned to units and individuals. Since the assignment of tasks influences the amount and type of interdependence between units of the organization, technologies set up conditions for organizational conflict.

Social structure

The creation and maintenance of a hierarchy of authority defines the basis for vertical conflict in the organization, while the division of labor separates the organization in a way that presents opportunities for horizontal conflict. Thus, choices about social structure lay a foundation for the conflicts that will emerge in day-to-day interactions. Furthermore, coordination mechanisms produce additional divisions within the organization that can also be the locus of conflict.

Organizational culture

Subcultures may develop on the basis of divergence from dominant values in the organization as was discussed in Chapter 7. Divergent values may be interpreted as independent of the dominant culture in which case they are less likely to contribute to conflict, or they may diverge in opposition to dominant values, in which case they are more likely to contribute to conflict. Similarly, divergence in basic assumptions between groups can help to explain the conflicts that occur in organizations. For instance, the assumption that science is a communal activity that requires the sharing of research findings within the scientific community brings research and development scientists into conflict with corporate legal departments who believe that protecting the patent rights of the company depends upon *not* sharing research findings.

Physical structure

Differentiation of groups, communicated through differences in the quality or style of physical settings, can feed feelings of superiority or inferiority among work units. These conditions can contribute directly to local conditions for conflict or may increase sensitivity to the conflicts inherent in other contextual factors. In addition, physical proximity contributes to conflict when it makes individuals and groups more accessible to one another.

Using the Interunit Conflict Model

Once you have grasped the pattern of conflict (now try reading Figure 10.3 from left to right), you can use the model to help you visualize the organization and its environment as a context for conflict. Environment, strategy, technology, social structure, culture, and physical structure all combine to create the set of local conditions that provide a context for conflict throughout the organization. This perspective gives you the theoretical foundation needed to appreciate theories of organization that are not dependent upon the assumption of cooperation. Conflict-oriented theories of organization often take their point of departure in the work of Karl Marx. We now turn our attention to this approach.

MARXIST THEORIES OF ORGANIZATIONAL CONFLICT

Marx is seen as the father of conflict theory because of the central role conflict played in his theory of capital. It was Marx's opinion that the economic conflicts of capitalism drove relations in society and that these social relationships were fundamentally unstable, leading to the replacement of one dominant group by another in each successive stage of social history. In his writings, Marx offered a general explanation for organizational conflict based on his concepts of social contradiction, class struggle, and control.

Marx saw capitalism as a phase in the development of human relations that was preceded historically by slavery and feudalism. In the words of Marx, and his close friend and coauthor Friedrich Engels, the conflict between bourgeoisie (capitalists) and proletariat (workers) is revealed as follows:

The history of all hitherto existing society is the history of class struggles. . . . Freeman and slave, patrician and plebeian, lord and serf, guildmaster and journeyman, in a word, oppressor and oppressed, stood in constant opposition to one another, carried on an uninterrupted, now hidden, now open fight, a fight that each time ended, either in a revolutionary reconstitution of society at large, or in the common ruin of the contending classes. . . . The modern bourgeois society that has sprouted from the ruins of feudal society has not done away with class antagonisms. It has but established new classes, new conditions of oppression, new forms of struggle in place of the old ones.[16]

Marx argued that class conflict was the reason for the historical revolutions that transformed slavery into feudalism, and feudalism into capitalism. Each period in history, however, was clearly marked by its own specific tensions between oppressors and oppressed. For Marx, the central contradiction of capitalist societies lay in the inherent conflict between owners who desire to maximize their profit, and workers seeking higher wages. The contradiction rests in the difference between the use value and the exchange value of labor.

The **use value of labor** refers to what owners must pay to procure the labor of workers, while the **exchange value of labor** is reflected in revenues received from the sale of products or services produced with that labor. Where the exchange value of labor is higher than its use value there is surplus value, or profit. Because **surplus value** is defined by the difference between use and exchange value, the interests of workers and owners are perpetually in conflict. The disagreement arises over what proportion of surplus value belongs to the owners of capital as opposed to the workers. Thus, you can understand the importance that Marx placed on the distinction between those members of a society who own the means of production (the capitalists/bourgeoisie) and those who rely upon them to earn a living (the workers/proletariat). According to Marx, capitalist societies are destined to be internally divided by ownership of the means of production, and he goes on to argue that this foundation of economic contradiction forms the base upon which all other aspects of capitalist society, including organizations, are built.[17]

Marx argued that competition aggravates the conflict inherent in capitalist relations of production (i.e., between owners and workers) because it creates constant downward pressure on prices. The downward pressure on prices in turn restricts the amount of profit available and this fans the flames of conflict as each side struggles even harder for their share of a shrinking pie. Marx's contribution is his observation that contradictions within the social system are a force for change that ultimately leads to the replacement of one form of domination with another (i.e., slavery is replaced by feudalism, feudalism by capitalism) and that these forces shape conflict within organizations.

Of course, Marx also idealistically predicted that communism would overthrow capitalism and would thus resolve class conflict forever through the shared ownership of capital among all members of society. Although his prediction appears now to have been in error, we remain indebted to Marx for uncovering the critical role of contradiction in social systems and pointing the way to more dynamic appreciations of social organization. We will briefly consider two applications of Marxist thought to organizations: the deskilling of labor and stratification theory, which is also known as internal labor market analysis. These ideas will be supplemented by consideration of diversity as a source of organizational conflict and innovation. In the final section of this chapter we will turn to the important question of contradiction and its implications for organization theory.

The Deskilling Hypothesis

Drawing on Marx's historical method, some organization theorists equate the appearance of vertical conflict in organizations with the evolution of work organizations from their traditional craft-based to their modern industrial forms. In craft organizations, the hierarchy of authority can be described as task-continuous.[18] That is, each level upward in the hierarchy from apprentice to journeyman to master involves greater mastery and more experience of production methods, along with ownership and control of the means of production (the tools or other equipment for doing the work). Individuals advance in their careers, moving from apprentice, to journeyman, to master in a continuous progression that is the common experience of all members of the trade, and is, to a certain extent, shared across trades as well. In the modern industrial organization this continuity is destroyed. One can no longer (or can only rarely) move from the bottom of the hierarchy to the top. You are either a worker or a manager, and this condition is, for the most part, unchangeable. In other words, the hierarchy is task-discontinuous. According to Marxist theorists, this evolution in the nature of hierarchy occurred when owner/managers took control of the knowledge of production methods away from workers.

American sociologist Harry Braverman calls this the **deskilling** hypothesis.[19] Braverman suggests that the owners of the means of production (capitalists) systematically fragment work activities through differentiation usually carried out in the name of rationality (e.g., justified by claimed increases in efficiency). This differentiation continues until workers can no longer understand the work they are involved in doing. At this point the work is so simplified that very little training is required and it becomes easy to replace workers. In this way the workers' bargaining power is diminished. This allows owners to drive down the price of labor thereby maximizing their profits. It also exploits and degrades workers and contributes to their alienation.

Of course some skilled work remains. Crozier's maintenance workers, whom you met in Chapter 9, were skilled laborers whose power derived from their being the only organizational members who knew how to keep the production line operating.[20] Because it was necessary for someone to understand the overall workings of the machines, and because the maintenance workers carefully guarded this knowledge, it was not possible to deskill all of the work in the factory. Thus, the need for some skilled work within the organization permits certain workers to maintain a relative degree of power over others. However, these internal differences in power among workers can also support the interests of the capitalists because rifts between the workers undermine their will to organize (i.e., unionize) against the owners, or lead to the formation of separate craft-based unions, thus subverting their collective influence in the struggle against domination. From the workers' point of view, this dilemma is captured by the slogan: "united we stand, divided we fall."

Stratification Theory and Labor Market Analysis

Stratification theorists focus on the inequitable distribution of high paying, powerful, and prestigious positions in modern organizations. Citing numerous studies that demonstrate an extreme disproportion of white males in positions of power and authority in capitalistic societies, these researchers seek explanations for the exclusion of women, ethnic minorities, and youth (the elderly are sometimes considered as well). Within modernist organization theory, the stratification issue is addressed through analyses of internal labor markets.

American labor economists Peter Doeringer and Michael Piore proposed the dual labor market model, which suggests that the market for labor is composed of two different sectors: the primary and the secondary.[21] They observe that high wages and good career opportunities are provided within the primary sector, while the secondary sector is marked by lower wages and by poor conditions of employment (e.g., no job security, limited or no benefits). Doeringer and Piore argue that the reason for the discrepancy in opportunities between the primary and secondary sectors is that, to remain competitive, employers must have a steady supply of qualified workers who can maintain the firm's technological advantage in the marketplace. This means that they must pay top wages and provide substantial benefits to employees who have the desired skills and education. Employers then attempt to offset the costs of maintaining this highly skilled and motivated workforce by employing non-skilled workers to perform less central tasks for less pay and poorer working conditions. The link to stratification theory is that adult, white males tend to dominate the primary sector thus receiving high pay, job security, and career prospects. Meanwhile women, ethnic minorities, and youth are overrepresented in the low status secondary sector where pay is low and there is little job security.

Critics of dual labor market theory charge that in considering only the economic and technological reasons for the stratification of labor markets, the theory ignores important conditions in the cultural, social, physical, legal, and political segments of the general environment. It therefore cannot explain why women, ethnic minorities, and youth are underrepresented in the primary sector because economic and technological reasons do not account for these outcomes. Based on empirical evidence, claims of unequal treatment suggest that the divisions that Marx observed between capitalists and workers are not the only bases of class conflict, as Marx argued. Conflict must also be explained along gender, race, ethnicity, and age-related lines which form the bases for different classes of employees in contemporary work organizations. This thinking, often inspired by feminist theory, is found in research into the effects of diversity on organizations.

Organizational Diversity

One of the most promising sources of innovation being predicted for the future is the growing **diversity** in the workforce. As national and trade barriers are reduced, mobility increases and more multinational organizations are formed, a greater racial and ethnic mix is predicted to appear within organizations. Furthermore, greater numbers of women are part of the workforce than ever before as the result of more equal educational opportunities, growing career aspirations among women, felt needs in families for dual incomes, or the demands of single parenthood. Based on these trends, some herald diversity as a blessing that will take the shape of innovation, creativity, and improved decision making resulting from the variety of ideas and perspectives a diverse population represents.

Although diversity is only beginning to receive attention from organizational researchers,[22] its theoretical links to creativity and innovation flow from functional attitudes toward conflict in organizations. That is, the potential benefits diversity offers organizations derive from the importation of greater levels and more varieties of conflict. One can also expect on the basis of conflict theory, however, that these blessings will be balanced by overt struggles over power and domination as well as further developments in the hidden dimensions of conflict described by Kolb, Putnam, and their colleagues. The demographic changes in the composition of the workforce indicate that the numbers of organizational members who participate in the heretofore dominant white, male subculture of business are increasing rapidly. This generates conditions ripe for the airing of differences and expression of conflict and hostility as, along with these changes, the domination of the traditional white, male point of view comes to be questioned and more non-white, non-male voices are heard.

Because diversity is a relatively untheorized area of study, it provides a good place to try out your theorizing skills. To get the process started, think about how diversity might link to other concepts or theories we have studied in this book. For instance, you might observe the coincidence of diversity and predictions concerning the post-industrial age. Is it an accident that flatter hierarchies and more flexible forms of organizing are predicted at the same time that diversity in organizations is growing? Using population ecology, you might argue that diversity occurs first at the level of organizational populations which are becoming increasingly global. If organizations are to be isomorphic with the global environment, then the diversity of their multinational contexts will need to be repeated in structural and cultural diversity internal to the organization. Traditional organizations have been fairly unidimensional (hierarchical structures of domination prevailed over all other forms of differentiation). You might want to argue that the new more fluid, flexible, and less hierarchical forms are an adaptation to diversity in the globalized environments in which these organizations operate.

Or you might try a cultural approach. Given that diversity is often linked to cultural differences, one could anticipate on the basis of organizational culture theory that a more diverse workforce will bring along culturally rich contexts never before invoked in organizations and inspire new meanings and interpretations that will lead to both greater creativity and higher levels of conflict. Some of these differences are likely to form the foundations of subcultures within organizations, and others will undoubtedly provoke the development of new organizational values and assumptions capable of communicating across these subcultural differences.

See what theories of diversity you can imagine using the concepts and theories you have learned in your study of organization theory. When you can do this, you might try bringing in ideas from some of your other studies, say in accounting, finance, marketing, and strategy. Then you could try ideas from your studies of the natural sciences, the humanities, and the arts. This, in a nutshell, is what organization theorists do when they theorize. Of course it takes some practice, but you have to start somewhere.

ORGANIZATIONAL CONTRADICTIONS

Marxists and neo-Marxists alike argue against the assumption that rationality is the guiding force in organizations, claiming instead that power and domination are the most basic forces at work in these domains. They claim that rationality is an ideological tool rather than a tool of reason. That is, rationality is not based in an objective standard developed by disinterested observers of the organizational scene, as those who promote rationality claim. Instead, rational argument is a technique of persuasion founded on criteria designed to protect the interests of the powerful. Since rational argument must always have a set of criteria to use as a standard for making judgments, and since any particular criteria will always serve the interests of one group better than others, criteria are fundamentally conflictual. Thus, for example, rational arguments supporting the need for authority and the division of labor are used to extract surplus value from work relations.[23] Insofar as the disadvantaged workers believe in the doctrine of rationality, they will not question their own subordination. Only when they become conscious of the ideological nature of rationality will the system come under pressure to change. Meanwhile, without conscious pressure, the rationally-oriented organization itself remains fundamentally contradictory.

In formal logic, contradiction has the connotation of falsity. That is, a contradiction proposes that something is both the case and not the case at the same time and is, therefore, logically impossible. In social science, however, **contradiction** indicates an opposition occurring within a social structure, such as when two groups have contradictory desires (e.g., workers want higher wages while managers want lower costs; marketing departments want responsiveness to customer demands while manufacturing wants high levels of worker productivity and quality). Marxist social scientists assume that organizations are constituted by such oppositions. American sociologist J. Kenneth Benson, who takes a social constructionist approach, puts Marx's ideas about contradiction into organizational terms:

The organizational totality . . . is characterized by ruptures, breaks, and inconsistencies in the social fabric. To these we apply the general term "contradiction," while recognizing that such rifts may be of many different types. Many theorists see the organization as a reasonably coherent, integrated system, rationally articulated or functionally adjusted. This view, of course, is an abstraction. If one looks at the organization concretely and pays attention to its multiple levels and varied relations to the larger society, contradictions become an obvious and important feature of organizational life.[24]

Benson describes two types of contradiction that appear in organizations. The first type involves the social construction of a differentiated organization. The organization enacts a complex environment and then isomorphically matches its internal arrangements to reflect the perceived environmental array of conditions and exchange partners. This isomorphism creates a pattern of differences among organizational subunits that promote different views of the organization itself. These different views are fed by organizational reward and control structures that reinforce the differences between units. Then, when the units interact, they confront their constructed differences which can provoke conflict. The fact that organizational units both create and maintain the difficulties with which they struggle is the first form of contradiction Benson identifies.

The second source of contradiction involves ongoing processes of social construction that take place in all the different units of the organization and which continually present alternatives to the existing socially constructed reality. That is, since social construction is an ongoing process, any existing pattern in the system is maintained by daily interchanges among organizational members. Change occurs in the same fashion. That is, each and every day all the units of an organization participate in the social construction of the reality that they take to be their organization. Their activities each day produce the realities that then either add up to the way they constructed them the day before, or to some different arrangement.

However, because the constructions are taken as more solid than they actually are, expectations of stability bring change into conflict with previously established social constructions. Thus, human memory tends to reconstruct yesterday's organization even as today's activities strive to construct tomorrow's. Benson considers this to be an indication of the organization's fundamentally contradictory nature. He gives examples of this in terms of the ways in which new budgeting procedures or the introduction of computers into the workplace may stand in contradiction to the ways in which the organization was previously constructed by the daily activities of its members. Thus, he concludes that the structure that is constructed by one set of organizational practices comes to resist its own further development, creating the second type of organizational contradiction.

My own studies of humor in a management team offer examples of contradiction in organizations.[25] Observing senior staff meetings of the inventory management unit of a large mainframe computer company, I found extensive use of spontaneous humor throughout the 18-month long period of my study. The managers treated many issues with humor, which interested me because of the close alignment between humor and contradiction (humor theorists claim that it is the multiplicity and frequent inconsistency of meanings contained in humorous remarks that gives us the experience we express through laughter). Looking closely at the words constituting the managers' humorous remarks allowed me to identify and describe organizational contradictions exposed or constructed by their humor. For instance, in one case the managers were discussing how the manufacturing plants they served were always trying to cut their own deals with corporate suppliers to ensure timely delivery of scarce and critical parts (at the time, these were mainly computer memory chips called DRAMS). Their deal cutting allowed the plants to go around the centralized purchasing function while still enjoying the benefits of lower prices created by the centralized purchasing contract negotiations that the management team provided. This created awkward situations for the team I studied because their shipping schedules to plants who had not gone around them were disrupted by the short supply of parts the marauders siphoned off. The General Manager reported on a recent occurrence of this activity to his management team to which the Purchasing manager responded, in a sarcastic tone, that this was a terrific example of teamwork. Analysis of this ironic remark and the situations to which it related exposed the contradiction the managers experienced between the corporate ideal of teamwork and what seemed to them to be the opportunistic behavior of the manufacturing plants. This contradiction was rooted in the opposition set up by the different needs and objectives of the units involved (the inventory managers and the plants they were mandated to serve) as well as in a recently inaugurated corporate-wide culture change program emphasizing the value of teamwork. This example shows the relationship between horizontal (interunit) conflict and organizational contradictions experienced by a group of middle managers. Symbolic-interpretive studies like this one reveal the extent to which everyday life in organizations is infused with experiences of contradiction and give specific examples of the circumstances under which contradictions occur.

SUMMARY

Organizational-level conflict is frequently defined in opposition to cooperation, reflecting cases in which the negative manifestations of conflict undermine cooperation by destroying trust and closing channels of communication. However, in its positive behavioral manifestations, conflict can provide the benefits of innovation and teamwork and can thereby encourage future cooperative acts and build value for diversity. Thus, conflict and cooperation are only opposed when conflict is defined as destructive, when its constructive aspects are in focus, conflict and cooperation are seen as complementary processes.[26]

In this chapter, the study of conflict in organizations via conflict-based theories was contrasted with cooperation-based views of organizational conflict. A historical look at the changes in attitudes toward conflict charts a course which moves away from modernist notions of organizational conflict as dysfunctional, to Marxist inspired, postmodern views of conflict and contradiction as the driving force for innovation and change in organizations. A model that describes the contexts of conflict between units in organizations provided a foundation for linking the conflict construct to basic organization theory concepts of the environment, strategy, technology, social structure, culture, and physical structure.

KEY TERMS

organizational conflict   deskilling
use value of labor   diversity
exchange value of labor   contradiction
surplus value

ENDNOTES

1. March and Simon (1958).
2. Katz and Kahn (1978: 615).
3. Kolb and Bartunek (1992).
4. Kolb and Putnam (1992).
5. Van Maanen (1992).
6. Martin (1990); see also Gutek (1985); Nicholson (1986); and Gherardi (1995).
7. Robbins (1974).
8. Galbraith (1977).
9. Whyte (1949).
10. Pondy (1967, 1969).
11. Blake and Mouton (1964); Burke (1969, 1970); Shepard (1964).
12. Walton and Dutton (1969).
13. Dutton and Walton (1966).
14. Whyte (1949).
15. Seiler (1963).
16. Marx and Engels (1996: 3-4).
17. Marx's critics make some strong arguments against this point. They claim that Marx's view that economics determines political, cultural, and social aspects of society is too simplistic. The widely accepted systems theory perspective, for example, makes the counterargument that economic, political, cultural, and social conditions are equally deterministic of society even as society is deterministic of them, that is, each part of a system effects all the others. One element cannot be put forward as a base upon which the others are built, as Marx did.
18. Offe (1976) cited in Clegg and Dunkerley (1980).
19. Braverman (1974); see also Burawoy (1982); and Edwards (1979).
20. Crozier (1964); see additional discussion in Chapter 9.
21. Doeringer and Piore (1971).
22. *Academy of Management Review*, Special Topic Forum on Diversity within and among Organizations, 21: 2 (1996).
23. Edwards (1979).
24. Benson (1977).
25. Hatch (1993); see also Hatch (forthcoming); Hatch and Ehrlich (1993); and Filby and Willmott (1988).
26. Robbins (1974) was the first conflict theorist to make this observation.

REFERENCES

Benson, J. Kenneth (1977). Organizations: A dialectical view. *Administrative Science Quarterly*, 22: 1–21.

Blake, Robert R. and Mouton, Jane S. (1964). *Managerial grid*. Houston: Gulf.

Braverman, Harry (1974). *Labour and monopoly capital: The degradation of work in the twentieth century*. New York: Monthly Review Press.

Burawoy, Michael (1982). Introduction: The resurgence of Marxism in American sociology. In M. Burawoy and T. Skocpol (eds.), *Marxist inquiries: Studies of labor, class and states*. Supplement to the *American Journal of Sociology*, 88: S1–S30.

Burke, Ronald J. (1969). Methods of resolving interpersonal conflict. *Personnel Administration*, July: 48–55.

Burke, Ronald J. (1970). Methods of resolving superior–subordinate conflict: The constructive use of subordinate differences and disagreements. *Organizational Behavior and Human Performance*, July: 393–411.

Clegg, Stewart, and Dunkerley, David (1980). *Organization, class and control*. London: Routledge & Kegan Paul.

Crozier, Michel (1964). *The bureaucratic phenomenon*. London: Tavistock.

Doeringer, Peter B., and Piore, Michael J. (1971). *Internal labor markets and manpower analysis*. Lexington, Mass.: Heath.

Dutton, John M., and Walton, Richard E. (1966). Interdepartmental conflict and cooperation: Two contrasting studies. *Human Organization*, 25: 207–20.

Edwards, Richard (1979). *Contested terrain: The transformation of the workplace in the twentieth century*. New York: Basic Books.

Filby, Ivan, and Willmott, Hugh (1988). Ideologies and contradictions in a public relations department: The seduction and impotence of living myth. *Organization Studies*, 9: 335–49.

Galbraith, Jay (1977). *Organization design*. Reading, Mass.: Addison-Wesley.

Gherardi, Silvia (1995). *Gender, symbolism and organizational cultures*. London: Sage.

Gutek, Barbara (1985). *Sex and the workplace: The impact of sexual behavior and harassment on women, men, and organizations*. San Francisco: Jossey-Bass.

Hatch, Mary Jo (1993). Ironic humor and the social construction of contradiction in a management team. Academy of Management *Best Papers Proceedings*: 374–78.

Hatch, Mary Jo (forthcoming). Irony and the social construction of contradiction in the humor of a management team. *Organization Science*.

Hatch, Mary Jo, and Ehrlich, Sanford B. (1993). Spontaneous humor as an indicator of paradox and ambiguity in organizations. *Organizational Studies*, 14/4: 539–60.

Katz, Daniel, and Kahn, Robert L. (1978). *The social psychology of organizations* (2nd edition). New York: John Wiley & Sons.

Kolb, Deborah M., and Bartunek, Jean M. (1992) (eds.). *Hidden conflict in organizations: Uncovering behind-the-scenes disputes*. Newbury Park, Calif.: Sage.

Kolb, Deborah M., and Putnam, Linda L. (1992). The dialectics of disputing. In D. M. Kolb and J. M. Bartunek (eds.), *Hidden conflict in organizations: Uncovering behind-the-scenes disputes*. Newbury Park, Calif.: Sage, 1–31.

March, James G., and Simon, Herbert A. (1958). *Organizations*. New York: John Wiley.

Martin, Joanne (1990). Deconstructing organizational taboos: The suppression of gender conflict in organizations. *Organization Science*, 1: 339–59.

Marx, Karl, and Engels, Friedrich (1996). *The communist manifesto* (trans. Samuel Moore in 1888). London: Orion, Phoenix (originally published in 1848 in German and 1888 in English translation).

Neilsen, Eric H. (1972). Understanding and managing conflict. In J. W. Lorsch and P. R. Lawrence (eds.), *Managing group and intergroup relations*. Homewood, Ill.: Irwin and Dorsey.

325

Issues and Themes in Organization Theory

Nicholson, Linda (1986). *Gender and history*. New York: Columbia University Press.

Offe, C. (1976). *Industry and inequality* (trans. J. Wickham). London: Edward Arnold.

Pondy, Louis R. (1967). Organizational conflict: Concepts and models. *Administrative Science Quarterly*, 12: 296–320.

Pondy, Louis R. (1969). Varieties of organizational conflict. *Administrative Science Quarterly*, 14: 499–505.

Robbins, Stephen P. (1974). *Managing organizational conflict: A nontraditional approach*. Englewood Cliffs, NJ: Prentice-Hall.

Seiler, J. A. (1963). Diagnosing interdepartmental conflict. *Harvard Business Review*, 41: 121–32.

Shepard, Herbert A. (1964). Responses to situations of competition and conflict. In R. L. Kahn and E. Boulding (eds.), *Power and conflict in organizations*. New York: Basic Books, 127–35.

Van Maanen, John (1992). Drinking our troubles away: Managing conflict in a British police agency. In D. M. Kolb and J. M. Bartunek (eds.), *Hidden conflict in organizations: Uncovering behind-the-scenes disputes*. Newbury Park, Calif.: Sage, 32–62.

Walton, Richard E., and Dutton, John M. (1969). The management of interdepartmental conflict. *Administrative Science Quarterly*, 14: 73–84.

Whyte, William F. (1949). The social structure of the restaurant. *American Journal of Sociology*, 54: 302–10.

FURTHER READING

Bottomore, T. B., and Rubel, M. (1961). *Karl Marx: Selected readings in sociology and social philosophy*, London: D. A. Watts.

Braverman, Harry (1974). *Labour and monopoly capital: The degradation of work in the twentieth century*. New York: Monthly Review Press.

Chambliss, William J. (1973) (ed.). *Sociological readings in the conflict perspective*. Reading, Mass.: Addison-Wesley.

Clegg, Stewart, and Dunkerley, David (1980). *Organization, class and control*. London: Routledge & Kegan Paul.

Edwards, Richard (1979). *Contested terrain: The transformation of the workplace in the twentieth century*. New York: Basic Books.

Kahn, Robert L., and Boulding, Elise (1964) (eds.). *Power and conflict in organizations*. New York: Basic Books.

Kolb, Deborah M., and Bartunek, Jean M. (1992) (eds.). *Hidden conflict in organizations: Uncovering behind-the-scenes disputes*. Newbury Park, Calif.: Sage.

Lorsch, Jay W., and Lawrence, Paul R. (1972) (eds.). *Managing group and intergroup relations*. Homewood, Ill.: Irwin and Dorsey.

McCann, Joseph, and Galbraith, Jay R. (1981). Interdepartmental relationships. In Paul C. Nystrom and William H. Starbuck (eds.), *Handbook of organizational design*. New York: Oxford University Press, ii. 60–84.

326

11 | Control and Ideology in Organizations

I N the Classical period, Fayol listed control as one of the functions of the manager, along with planning, organizing, staffing, and leading. Today, concern with organizational control is a large part of the fields of finance, accounting, and management information systems as well as organization theory. Within modernist organization theory, organizational control is defined as a mechanism of strategy implementation. This view is criticized by postmodernists as a legitimating device disguising the influences of managerial power and politics. As you will see below, it is also possible to conceive of control as one function of organizational culture, although this modernist view is challenged by symbolic-interpretivism. The control perspective is further challenged by the critique of control as an ideology, a position clarified by consideration of the relationship between control and autonomy in different types of organizations.

MODERNIST THEORIES OF CONTROL

American sociologist Arnold Tannenbaum summarized the modernist view of organizational control when he stated that:

Organization implies control. A social organization is an ordered arrangement of individual human interactions. Control processes help circumscribe idiosyncratic behaviors and keep them conformant to the rational plan of the organization. Organizations require a certain amount of conformity as well as the integration of diverse activities. It is the function of control to bring about conformance to organizational requirements

327

and achievement of the ultimate purposes of the organization. The coordination and order created out of the diverse interests and potentially diffuse behaviors of members is largely a function of control.[1]

Modernist control theories start with the assumption that different individuals have different reasons for participating in organizations. Thus, organizations constantly face the problem of making certain that divergent interests do not interfere with organizational strategies and goals. This provides the rationale for control: because organizations are composed of individuals with divergent interests, managers must exercise control. Modern control theories focus on mechanisms for controlling behavior in order to ensure that self-interest is minimized and organizational interests are served by the activities occurring within, and on behalf of, the organization.

This section of the chapter will present three modernist theories of control in organizations. The control concept can be applied to the individual, unit, or organizational level, and is often applied to all three, so be careful with levels of analysis as you think through these theories. The first theory deals with performance evaluation and feedback. This approach has much in common with the cybernetic model of General Systems Theory (described in Chapter 2). The second theory, known as agency theory, developed out of recent work in behavioral economics and accounting. This view focuses on controlling the behavior of managers via contracts designed to encourage managers to serve the interests of organizational owners (e.g., shareholders) rather than their own. The third theory contrasts markets, bureaucracies, and clans as alternate forms of organizational control, and raises the issue of using culture as a control mechanism, which returns us to the debate about managing culture, which we took up in Chapter 7.

Performance Evaluation and Feedback—The Cybernetic Model of Control

The **cybernetic system** offers a dynamic model of the control process as it is conceived from a modernist point of view. In cybernetics, the current state of a system is compared to the desired state and any discrepancy between the two triggers an adjustment. Take the example of a thermostat. The thermostat is designed to recognize a difference between the ambient temperature in a room and the temperature that has been established as the standard, it reacts by turning a heating/cooling unit on or off, depending on the direction of the difference. According to the cybernetic metaphor, organizational control processes, like thermostats, are designed to recognize differences between current and desired levels of performance and to trigger adjustments when discrepancies are noticed.

You might think about organizational control processes as an addendum to the rational model of strategy and goals presented in Chapter 4 (reproduced in Figure 11.1). In the strategy model the environment provides the context within which strategy is formulated. Goals, which are interrelated with strategy, are cascaded throughout the levels of the hierarchy until every organizational member has an understanding of their part in the overall strategic plan. Individual-level goals, which have been defined in the context of unit- and organization-level goals, are then set into motion as activities that will result in the desired output of the organization, assuming, of course, that the strategy and goals have been well conceived and clearly communicated.

Notice that strategy and goals only serve to point the organization in a particular direction. It is the actions that occur throughout the organization that will implement and realize the strategy. Thus, strategists are dependent upon other organizational members to act in ways that produce strategic objectives (as opposed to pursuing self-interests). To help assure that these actions occur, managers set up control systems to monitor and make adjustments along the way to realizing their strategy. In this view, control systems mesh with the organizational goal system, supporting and encouraging individuals and units to move in directions defined by the strategy.

To begin developing the cybernetic model, focus your attention on the link

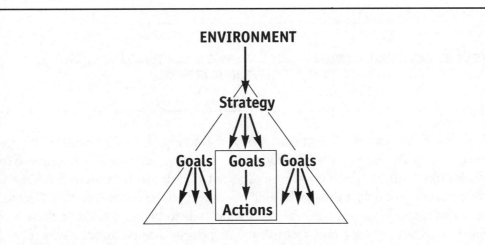

FIGURE 11.1. BASIC MODEL OF STRATEGY AND GOALS IN RELATION TO THE TASK ACTIVITIES OF ORGANIZATIONAL MEMBERS

between goals and actions shown inside the box in Figure 11.1. The setting of targets or standards of acceptable behavior in relation to goals is the first step in developing a cybernetic control system. This is followed by measuring and monitoring compliance with the targets and standards, and giving feedback. Feedback is based on a comparison between the actual performance and the set standard, and is communicated in such a way as to trigger adjustments when a deviation occurs. Figure 11.2 shows this more detailed view of the control processes that fit inside the boxed portion of Figure 11.1.

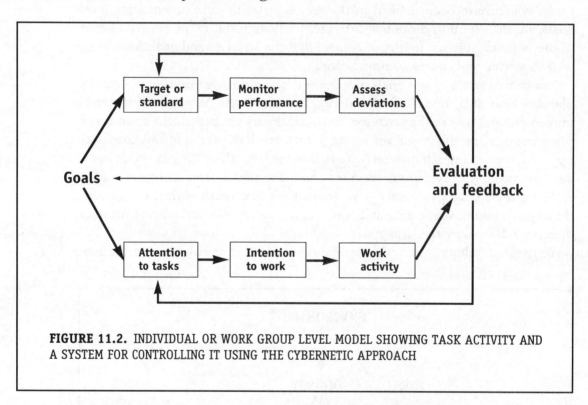

FIGURE 11.2. INDIVIDUAL OR WORK GROUP LEVEL MODEL SHOWING TASK ACTIVITY AND A SYSTEM FOR CONTROLLING IT USING THE CYBERNETIC APPROACH

Because the system is designed to bring task activity into alignment with organizational goals, the focus of a performance evaluation and feedback system is on work tasks. This demands two things. First of all it depends upon understanding the technology used by those who will be subject to the control system. Second, organizational goals must be specific to the task to be controlled. If these two conditions are not met, task control will be poorly defined and the control system will be hampered by ambiguity (i.e., lack of a clear focus). Once goals and tasks have been defined, targets or standards can be developed to encourage the activities that lead to goal realization. Two ways to accomplish this are output and behavioral control.

Output control focuses on the result of task activity and depends upon the measurement of these results. Output control can be developed at the level of individual or work-group tasks. If used at the individual level, outputs must be identified with individuals. Piece-rate systems are a good example of individual-level output control. In a piece-rate system employees are paid for the number of products they produce or steps in a process they complete in a given period of time. Quality can also be the focus of output control. Counting the number of rejects that an individual produces would be an example of an individual-level output measure that is focused on quality. When applied to a group, output is defined as a collective result of the work of the entire group, for example, the number of products assembled by a team. In situations where individual efforts cannot be clearly determined, such as with teamwork, you may find a control system that has only a group-level focus. If outputs can be easily measured and identified with either the individual or group to be controlled, then output control is possible. If output control is used, the desired amount of output (e.g., number of pieces produced or rejects accepted) becomes the **target** for the control system.

When outputs are not easily measured at any level, for instance in teaching (where the output is new learning) or customer service (where the output is customer satisfaction), **behavioral control** can often be used. Behavioral control depends upon knowing which behaviors yield desired performance levels. For example, teaching is evaluated using behavioral indicators such as demonstrated knowledge or enthusiasm for the subject matter. When indicators such as these are known, behavioral control is possible. In behavioral control systems, the behaviors identified with high performance become **standards** against which individuals can be evaluated.

Once targets or standards are set, then means for measuring performance relative to them must be found. In the case of teaching, behavioral measures may be developed using student evaluation forms, files documenting the accolades and complaints directed at particular teachers, and/or evaluations conducted by peers. With output control, a system for recording output is developed. In the case of researchers, for example, the curriculum vita contains a record of all accomplishments such as published papers or patents received. In both output and behavioral cases, the performance of the individual is compared to established targets and/or set standards, and any deviation from the desired level of performance is used as a basis for **feedback** and possible corrective action.

Deviations between standards and performance can be corrected by a number of actions. First, the goal or its measure can be adjusted if it is determined that the difference is the result of an error in the control system. Second, the individual or group can change their performance by altering their behavior or output level.

Third, workers can be replaced if it is determined that they cannot function as required by the system.

There are a number of problems that frustrate the design and implementation of performance evaluation systems. Foremost among these is ambiguity. **Ambiguity** renders some organizational activities extremely difficult to measure using either behavioral or output measures. Creativity and innovation are good examples. Here, outputs are notoriously hard to measure because recognizing the creative or innovative solution, idea, or design often takes a long time. Behaviors are equally hard to identify because the definition of appropriate behavior changes with each new customer, product, problem, or situation. Years of study have produced little progress toward the control of creativity and innovation, and its occurrence is often considered a matter of inspiration.

In cases where outputs are hard to define and where there is ambiguity concerning appropriate behavior, uncertainty can lead managers to use control systems inappropriately. That is, the uncertainty of not being able to control output or behavior can ironically lead to an even stronger desire for these controls. For instance, in a research and development laboratory, everyone generally acknowledges that time spent in the lab is less important than non-observables such as inspiration or creativity. Nonetheless, time in the lab may be used to evaluate performance because it is the only objective measure available. The result of such an approach is to underemphasize what really matters. By emphasizing the wrong aspects of work behavior, control systems can discourage the very performance that is desired.

Another problem with performance evaluation systems is their tendency to produce negative reactions among those who are subject to control. There is an inclination, for instance, to find ways to satisfy the requirements of the system without satisfying its intent. The subjects of control can achieve this by focusing only on what is measured and ignoring the goals underlying the measurement system. No set of measures can capture all aspects of strategies and goals equally well, and if measures become the focus of activity, then other aspects of performance will suffer. This is the problem of **goal displacement**. As a student, you may have experienced goal displacement as the dilemma that occurs when grades become so important that what you learn takes on secondary significance. This is called goal displacement because the secondary goal of getting high grades displaces the primary goal of learning.

There are many strategies for evading control in organizations. Among them are rigid bureaucratic behavior, impression management, and cheating. **Rigid bureaucratic behavior** takes the form of pursuing measures rather than goals, or of applying rules so rigorously that the system cannot function. Work slowdowns based on strict adherence to standard operating procedures provide an example of the rigid application of rules. **Impression management** involves looking good rather than being good and can become particularly problematic when ambiguous behavioral controls are in place. Although differences between looking good and performing at or above standard will usually emerge over time, in the short run they may create perceived inequities that undermine confidence in and respect for the system of control. This might occur, for instance, when a manager rewards a brown-noser more generously than workers who consistently do more or better work. **Cheating** is most likely to occur when you use output control. Falsification of records and invalid data reporting are examples of cheating.

Unit-level controls generally depend upon the translation of unit goals into financial targets, called budgets, which determine the amount of resource inputs the units will have available to do their work. Budgets let managers know what resources will be available for meeting established goals during a given time period. Performance during the budget period is monitored by comparing actual to budgeted costs. In many organizations, statistical reports tailored to the performance of specific units are used to provide feedback of this information to the units, who then use it for self-adjustment. Reports focus on information such as output volumes, quality control data, and other unit-level results (Figure 11.3).

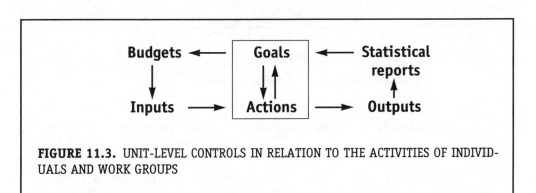

FIGURE 11.3. UNIT-LEVEL CONTROLS IN RELATION TO THE ACTIVITIES OF INDIVIDUALS AND WORK GROUPS

Two types of information are available as feedback at the organization level of the control system. One type of **organization-level control** is produced by evaluation processes ongoing at the unit and individual levels described above. Cumulative assessments of individual- and unit-level performance are used to form judgments about how well the organization is doing and in what areas it could improve. This type of feedback is represented in Figure 11.4 as arrows from outputs to statistical reports and from reports to strategy. This is the type of reporting that typically forms the focus of an organization's accounting system.

The other type of organizational-level control comes from the environment.

For instance, if the organization is a publicly traded firm, then share price will reflect the environment's opinion of the organization. If the organization operates in a competitive market, then market share can be another measure of performance. Feedback of this sort (shown in Figure 11.4 as the arrow from the environment to strategy) can be used to adjust the firm's strategy if it is not matching expectations or desires. The realigned strategy then forms the basis for a new round of goal setting, budgeting, and reporting in order to influence unit- and individual-level activities responsible for producing the organization's results.

All three levels of feedback (individual/group, unit, and organization) contribute to a system of controls that reach all areas within the organization and serve to unite them in service to the organizational strategy. Figure 11.4 shows how these levels, ideally at least, work together to coordinate strategy and activity throughout the organization.

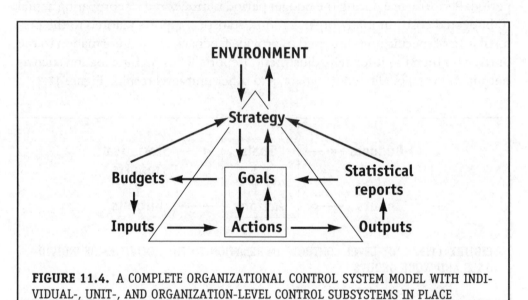

FIGURE 11.4. A COMPLETE ORGANIZATIONAL CONTROL SYSTEM MODEL WITH INDI-VIDUAL-, UNIT-, AND ORGANIZATION-LEVEL CONTROL SUBSYSTEMS IN PLACE

Agency Theory: Contracts, Rewards, and Uncertainty

In **agency theory**, the control problem for the organization is seen from the viewpoint of its owners (investors) and external stakeholders (such as underwriters, creditors, and potential investors).[2] The relationship between owners (called **principals**) and managers (called **agents**) is the central concern of the theory. The managers are called agents to indicate that they should be acting on the principals' interests rather than their own when they make decisions on behalf of the principal. The **agency problem** involves the risk that agents will serve their own interests rather than those of the principals. Agency theory focuses on ways of controlling the self-serving behavior of agents to assure that the interests of the principals are protected. Although agency theorists explain the agency problem in terms of the relationship between the owners of a firm and the managers they hire to act on their behalf, the theory can be generalized to the relationship between lower levels of management and their subordinates.

In agency theory the problem of divergent interests is addressed with contracts written to bring the self-interests of agents into alignment with the interests of their principals. **Contracts** specify measures and promise rewards such that agents will serve their own interests when they fulfill the demands of the contract. This is done by offering rewards that agents find desirable, and basing these rewards on the performance of activities that serve the interests of the principals. Thus, the problem of divergent interests between principals and agents is handled by a contract through which principals delegate work to their agents for an agreed price.

Principals contract agents to act on their behalf because they cannot or do not want to be continuously present to protect their own interests. However, because they are not present, they are open to **opportunism** by agents who do not perform their duties in a fully responsible fashion. In other words, agency theory assumes that agents cannot always be relied upon to perform as agreed; they may shirk (i.e., avoid their duties, work, responsibilities). In agency theory this dilemma is explained in terms of information.

The ability of principals to know whether their agents are shirking depends upon the information that is available to the principals. Complete information means that principals know whether or not their agents are performing to the specifications of the contract. Direct observation, where possible, provides complete information, but takes so much time that principals might as well operate the organization themselves. Furthermore, direct observation may be impossible, since management involves many non-observable aspects. Incomplete information means that agents may or may not be caught shirking, so they face the temptation to shirk. If incomplete information occurs, then the principals risk being taken advantage of. American organization theorist Kathleen Eisenhardt explains the two options principals face in the situation of incomplete information:

The principal can purchase information about the agent's behaviors and reward those behaviors. This requires the purchase of surveillance mechanisms such as cost accounting measures, budgeting systems, or additional layers of management. Alternatively, the principal can reward the agent based on outcomes (e.g., profitability). Such outcomes are surrogate measures for behaviors. However, in this option, the agent is penalized or rewarded for outcomes partially outside his/her control. In other words, good outcomes can occur despite poor efforts and poor outcomes can occur despite good efforts. While this scheme encourages effort on the part of the agent, it does so at the price of shifting some of the risk of the firm to the agent. The optimal choice between the two options rests upon the trade-off between the cost of measuring behavior, and the costs of measuring outcomes and transferring risk to the agent.[3]

From the perspective of agency theory, the issue of whether to choose behavior or outcome controls is a question of the costs associated with collecting the information required to minimize the chances that agents will shirk. Behavioral control requires either the use of added layers of management to perform surveillance activities, or the development of information systems such as cost accounting, budgeting, and formal reporting. If technology is non-routine, management and information systems are more difficult to develop and more costly to use. Furthermore, as more layers of management are added, the potential for shirking increases. As behavioral control becomes less feasible, output control becomes more attractive. Output control is least costly when output is readily measured (e.g., number of units shipped), however, if outputs are difficult to measure (e.g., morale and quality are as important as production quantities), output control becomes less attractive. Output can also become problematic when organizations face uncertain futures.

The risk of prosperity versus bankruptcy must be borne by someone, and the owners typically assume this risk, since they are the ones who will profit the most from prosperity and lose the most from bankruptcy. However, when outcome controls are used, agents assume some risk. This is because outcomes are a function of employee behaviors *and* conditions in the environment and/or uncertainties associated with technology. For example, competitor actions, changes in government regulations, bad weather, or chance events such as unforeseeable machine failure can all lead to poor performance outcomes that are outside the control of the employees whose rewards depend upon organizational outcomes. Because rewards are based on outcomes, employees assume the risks associated with the environment and technology, as well as the risks associated with their own performance levels. In other words, agents only partly determine the outcomes of their organization, technology and environment are also partly responsible. Since outcome controls hold agents accountable for unforeseen circumstances, outcome measures force them to assume some of the associated risk. In these circumstances, agents may demand a premium to compensate them for sharing risk with the principals.

Eisenhardt suggests that there are a variety of control strategies available to organizations. The first is to design a simple, routine job so that behaviors can be easily observed, and to reward based upon behaviors. The second control strategy is to design a more complex, interesting job and invest in information systems (e.g., budgeting systems, audits, or additional layers of management) in order to gain knowledge about behaviors, and to reward based on these behaviors. The third alternative is to design more complex, interesting jobs, but use a much simpler evaluation scheme (e.g., profitability, revenues), and reward based upon the results of the evaluation. In this strategy, higher, but riskier rewards are substituted for measures, and precise job design.[4] Finally, Eisenhardt describes a fourth option that moves away from the emphasis on performance evaluation and focuses instead on eliminating the divergent interests that give rise to the need for performance evaluation in the first place. This is the idea of using selection, training, and socialization as alternatives to cybernetic control systems, an idea that was described by organization theorist William Ouchi in his theory of markets, bureaucracies, and clans.

Markets, Bureaucracies, and Clans

Like other modernist organization theorists, Ouchi defines the problem of control as the problem of "achieving cooperation among individuals who hold partially divergent objectives."[5] He argues that there are three distinguishable sources of control used to solve this problem in organizations: markets, bureaucracies, and clans (see Table 11.1).

Market control takes place through competition. When organizations participate in free markets, prices and profits can be used to evaluate and control their

TABLE 11.1. CHARACTERISTICS OF MARKET, BUREAUCRACY, AND CLAN CONTROL

Source	Mechanisms	Assumptions	Forms	Examples	Focus
Market	Prices Profit	Competition Economic exchange	Output control	Outputs schedules Budgets	Results
Bureaucracy	Rules Surveillance	Legitimate authority Hierarchy	Behavioral control	Auditing Direct supervision	Actions
Clan	Commitment Socialization	Established traditions Trust	Ceremonial or symbolic control	Training Indoctrination Certification	Values Attitudes

Based on: Ouchi (1979, 1980).

Issues and Themes in Organization Theory

performance. In competition, prices are taken as indicators of economic performance because it is assumed that comparison of prices and profits among a group of competitors in a free market permits evaluation of their relative efficiency. For instance, those organizations whose costs are the lowest can presumably afford to charge the lowest prices and can therefore compete most effectively. Alternatively, organizations that consistently provide products or services of greater value (e.g., higher quality, greater utility) than their competitors can charge a premium. Both conditions contribute to an organization's revenues. In either case, the organization's performance will be reflected in the prices that its products or services receive on the market, which in turn affects its revenues and profits. In this way, the market controls the organization because poor profits force the organization to improve or suffer the consequences (e.g., decline and death).

Market control can also be used at the unit level by creating **profit centers**, within the divisions of a multi-divisional organization. This form of market control simulates a market within the organization by allowing units to make economic exchanges. This happens, for instance, when one division sells its product to another. In this internal market, **transfer prices** permit the accounting system to compute profits for units in much the same way as it does for the entire organization. In some cases real competition is introduced by allowing divisions to purchase inputs from outside suppliers when internal sources are not competitively priced, or to sell outputs to external customers when these customers offer a better price than do internal customers.

When units within an organization operate as profit centers, top management can compare the performance of each of its divisions just as stockholders do when they look at the relative performance of organizations traded on the stockmarket. Top management then tries to invest in its various divisions in such a way that the returns on the total portfolio of businesses the organization operates will be maximized. In this way, organizations use markets to control their divisions and divisions compete for the highest levels of profitability.

A market control strategy is only effective when the organization or unit produces products or services that can be defined and priced, and when competition (simulated or real) for these outputs makes prices meaningful. Without competition, prices cannot indicate internal efficiency because there is no comparison possible with other firms or units. When there is no competition, and hence no market, prices generally become inflated just as they would in any other monopolistic situation. When competition is not present, or cannot be effectively simulated, another mechanism of control must be found. As Ouchi puts it, when markets fail, organizations generally turn to bureaucracy.

Bureaucracies rely on a combination of rules, procedures, documentation, and surveillance to achieve control. The focus of bureaucratic systems is on the standardization of behavior. Rather than rewarding units for responding to market forces, the bureaucracy rewards individuals for compliance with established rules and regulations. **Bureaucratic control** depends upon the existence of a legitimatized hierarchy of authority to administer the bureaucratic mechanisms.

In bureaucratic control systems, the basic mechanisms of control involve close supervision and direction of subordinates by their superiors. The rules generally describe processes to be completed or standards of output and quality to be met. Supervisors and managers assess the extent to which rules and procedures are followed. The difference between a rule and the pricing mechanism of a market control system is that a price involves comparing the value of an output produced by various buyers or sellers, whereas a rule is a more or less arbitrary standard. The pricing mechanism does not require intervention, whereas with rules, a manager must set standards, observe performance, and evaluate it in order to determine if performance is satisfactory. This management function is expensive, thus market control is more efficient than bureaucratic control. Nonetheless, since conditions for prices are not met within many organizations, bureaucracy offers an important and widely used alternative.

You may be inclined to associate bureaucratic control with public sector and not-for-profit organizations because these types of organizations do not normally face competition. However, many public sector and non-profit organizations find ways of incorporating market control mechanisms into their operations. For example, the idea of school choice establishes competition among schools within a community. The reason for such moves is the greater efficiency associated with market control mechanisms. Of course, the question that must be addressed is what is the value of an efficient education? Is efficiency the proper criterion by which to judge our schools?

When environments are complex and rapidly changing, and uncertainty and ambiguity are consequently high, bureaucracy will not meet the control needs of the organization. Likewise, when surveillance is difficult due to limited understanding of the behaviors that produce outputs, behavioral forms of control are not suitable. If results are hard to identify, or if they occur infrequently, then output control will not be effective either. In these circumstances, rational means of control by market or bureaucratic mechanisms will not succeed, and the organization must rely upon its social system to limit fragmentation of objectives and chaos. Ouchi argues that clans provide control in these circumstances (see Figure 11.5).

Cultural values, norms, and expectations provide the primary mechanisms of control to organizations that use **clan control**. Such systems require socialization of new members because clan control mechanisms are so subtle that newcomers will not always notice them. Once socialized, however, members internalize

Knowledge of the transformation process

	perfect	*imperfect*
high	**Behaviour or outcome control**	**Outcome control**
low	**Behaviour control**	**Clan control**

(row labels under **Ability to measure outputs**)

FIGURE 11.5. CONDITIONS DETERMINING THE MEASUREMENT OF BEHAVIOR AND OUTPUT

Based on: Ouchi (1979).

control because they are committed to the objectives and practices of the organization. Clan control depends upon implicit understanding of the values and beliefs that guide the behavior of its members. This implicit understanding helps to direct and coordinate the activities of the organization. The norms and values of the organization define the limits of proper behavior and justify sanctioning any behavior that is not deemed suitable within the system. It also represents a fairly high level of commitment to the system on the part of members who frequently have to sacrifice some or all of their self-interest to become socialized members of the clan.

Organizations with large numbers of professionals are particularly good examples of clan control because professionals are highly socialized to the norms and expectations of their profession, and their professional commitment, and concern for their reputation within the profession, helps to control their behavior.

However, professional commitment can diverge from the interests of the organization, and when it does, most professionals will abandon the organization's interests in order to remain true to the interests of their profession.

Clan controlled organizations often develop a strategy of selecting and promoting those whose values reflect the established values of top management. Once this is accomplished, monitoring will be largely unnecessary because personal values will lead employees to do what the organization desires and expects without the costs associated with bureaucratic control mechanisms. However, do not overlook the potentially harmful effects that this control strategy can have, such as increasing the potential for group think (i.e., failing to challenge one anothers' ideas and ending up following a precarious path) and constraining innovation. These effects are more likely to occur when only those employees who see things pretty much the same way top managers do are promoted.

Ouchi observes that all organizations are a combination of the three control strategies he outlines, but that each organization favors one strategy over the others. Ouchi uses this tendency to characterize organizational differences. He then suggests that the type of control an organization prefers predicts the extent to which it will require highly developed social systems or well-developed information systems. He states that clan controlled organizations require the most highly developed social systems (i.e., cultural systems) while market controlled organizations require the least, with bureaucracies falling in between. With respect to information systems, Ouchi claims that the opposite relationship holds—market controlled organizations demand the most highly evolved information systems for tracking prices and profits, while clan controlled organizations require much less of this sort of activity. Again, bureaucracies fall into the middle range. Of course, all organizations will have both social and informational systems, but the extent of their reliance upon and development of these systems will vary with the type of control system they favor.

With his ideas about clans, Ouchi introduces the idea of using organizational cultures as control systems. In doing so he highlights the debate between symbolic-interpretive and modernist researchers over the possibility of managing culture. Postmodern organization theorists also join this debate by examining the implications of culture management (control) practices from a critical perspective.

CONTROL, POWER, AND IDEOLOGY IN ORGANIZATIONS

With his clan control hypothesis, Ouchi suggests that, since culture influences behavior via norms, values, expectations, and beliefs, managers can control behavior by controlling these aspects of culture. Symbolic-interpretive theorists raise objections to this claim (described in Chapter 7). They argue that, while culture controls, it cannot *be* controlled in the way that Ouchi implies. Neo-Marxist and postmodern organization theorists raise a different objection based on the moral implications of using organizational culture to dominate others.

A Symbolic-Interpretive View of Culture as Control

In his representation of clan control, Ouchi relies on a conceptualization of culture that depicts organizations as homogeneous entities based on a level of consensus that is rarely, if ever, observed (recall our discussion of culture as sharing, in Chapter 7). When it is observed, this consensus tends to be found at the highest levels of management where, after many promotions, those managers who most fully support the company line tend to accumulate. Thus, if culture is a controlling force, its clearest application is at higher rather than lower hierarchical levels. This analysis suggests that culture does exercise control in the ways that Ouchi suggests, however, the ability of top management to use culture to control lower level members is suspect, since it is top managers who are most completely controlled by their culture. According to the symbolic-interpretive view, it is culture that controls management, rather than the other way around. Thus, symbolic-interpretivists would argue that, as a modernist control strategy, clan control leaves something to be desired.

Marxist Readings of Control

Unlike symbolic-interpretivists, neo-Marxist and postmodern organization theorists accept the clan control hypothesis as stated. They assume, along with Ouchi, that managers can exercise influence over the assumptions, values, and beliefs that organizational members share and that they can thereby control behavior. Instead of questioning the assumption that clan control is possible, these theorists attack it on moral grounds. The basis of their criticism is the similarity between the mechanisms of clan control and an idea that Karl Marx labelled **false con-**

sciousness. Marx argued that consciousness is a product of social structure and the relations of domination and oppression that exist within it. False consciousness occurs when one group within a social structure, such as workers, participates in their own exploitation by recognizing the legitimacy of their oppressors' right to dominate them. In other words, the oppressed socially construct their own oppression by treating their oppressors with deference. Because the workers' beliefs serve their oppressors' interests rather than their own, their state of mind is referred to as *false* consciousness.

False consciousness is related to two similar ideas that are central to understanding neo-Marxist organization theory—hegemony and ideology. **Hegemony** refers to the power that one social group exercises over another which, in traditional Marxist discourse, would be the multiple forms of power by which the bourgeoisie controlled the proletariat. In organization theory, the power relationship of interest is that of managers over other members of the organization. Hegemony is achieved via cultural domination or ideology. **Ideology** is a system of ideas that legitimates the domination of one group over another. Cultural domination refers to a process of engineering consensus by developing symbolic forms and institutions that communicate and support ideological beliefs. It is this engineered consensus that gives rise to false consciousness and forms the focus of vigorous critiques of culture change programs, total quality management, business process re-engineering, and other popular managerial initiatives that use the rhetoric of participation to enlist the support of workers.[6]

When these ideas are applied, for instance, to Ouchi's theory, clan control is portrayed as an ideology engineered to support the hegemony of managers. The ideology is accepted and practiced by non-managers who, by so doing, engage in false consciousness, forsaking their own interests to pursue the interests of their managers. (Compare this view to that expressed by Tannenbaum in the quotation at the beginning of this chapter.) Thus, neo-Marxists accept Ouchi's assertion that, as clans, organizations control and are controlled via culture, but they equate the concept of culture with ideology. They then reinterpret the dynamics of clan control as a struggle for power and domination. British organizational communication theorist Dennis Mumby describes this viewpoint:

shared meaning structures do not arise spontaneously and consensually, but are produced through the system of vested interests that characterize all organizations. Such interests provide a grounding for ideological meaning formations which, in turn, are the medium and product of organizational practices. It is this system which tells a member what is good, true, and possible (and their opposites) in an organization. Hegemony operates in such a context when the social reality that is produced is framed by the dominant interests.[7]

Issues and Themes in Organization Theory

Postmodern organization theorists argue that it is not possible to avoid the effects of power and domination in human social interaction, but that it is possible and useful to become more conscious of their effects and to acknowledge and begin to draw upon the aspects of human experience that are suppressed by these forces. According to Barbara Czarniawska-Joerges, in the case of control, what is driven out and needs to be recovered is **autonomy**. Czarniawska-Joerges, a Swedish organization theorist of Polish origins, points out that there is a simultaneous need for both autonomy and control in organizations:

[Autonomy] offers organizations flexibility and creativity, which are essential for adaptation to changing environments. . . . Without autonomy, organizations become rigid and obsolete. [On the other hand,] Control of others offers organizations predictability, which is necessary to produce standardized outputs and to coordinate actions. . . . Without control, organization is invaded by chaos and deadly entropy.[8]

Predictability allows organizations to produce standardized outputs and to coordinate their activities. Processes of standardization and coordination help to regulate work activities so that results are aligned with organizational strategies and goals. However, when managers lose sight of the need for autonomy, organizations suffer from a lack of innovation.

Ideological Control or the Ideology of Control

Although the concept was discussed by Marx and Weber, for many years ideology was ignored by modernist organization theorists who found it an inappropriate, if not distasteful, subject. Czarniawska-Joerges characterizes the modernist viewpoint:

Ideology is something that ought not to be found in business and administrative organizations, which are by definition nonideological. Ideology's place is in political and religious organizations. Everywhere else it is a dangerous aberration and should be eliminated, in order to make room for science.[9]

Recently, however, the concept of ideology has been taken up by organizational scholars and applied to managerial practices. Kenneth Thompson interprets organizational ideology from a social constructionist perspective, describing it as a distorted social construction of reality that supports an existing organizational order.[10] In this case, ideology retains its negative connotation. However, others have been more neutral, such as Reinhard Bendix who described managerial ideologies as: "all ideas which are espoused by or for those who exercise authority in economic enterprises, and which seek to explain and justify that authority."[11] Still others, along with Czarniawska-Joerges, see positive aspects of ideology:

[Ideology] is a medium through which people make history as conscious actors, be it in an organizational or in a national context. . . . In that sense, ideologies should be seen . . . as important vehicles for change and not, as in conventional definitions, as the barriers to change . . . an organizational ideology is a set (system) of ideas describing the organization-relevant reality, projecting a desired state of affairs, and indicating possible ways of reaching the desired state.[12]

In her book called *Ideological Control in Nonideological Organizations*, Czarniawska-Joerges presents a theory of ideological control as a natural development of organizational control from coercive to calculative to ideological forms. She builds her ideas on a typology of organizations developed by sociologist Amitai Etzioni (see Table 11.2). Etzioni distinguished business organizations (and bureaucracies, which he lumps together with businesses), from totalizing institutions (e.g., prisons and asylums), and also from ideological organizations (e.g., political parties, churches) that handle the political and religious affairs of society.

TABLE 11.2. TYPOLOGY OF ORGANIZATIONS AND THEIR CONTROL MECHANISMS

Type of organization	Target of control	Basis of involvement	Prototypical organizations	Means of control	Examples from business practice
Totalizing	Physical body	Coercive	Prisons Asylums	Force Threats Sanctions	Layoffs
Economic	Behavior	Calculative	Businesses Bureaucracies	Incentives Supervision Rules Technology	Piece-rate pay Promotion ladders Commission
Ideological	World view	Identification	Political Religious	Attractive goals Persuasion Sense of belonging Uncertainty reduction	Vision management Propaganda

Based on: Etzioni (1975); Czarniawska-Joerges (1988).

Etzioni claimed that the three types of organization each depend upon a different basis of involvement on the part of its members. In totalizing organizations, membership rests on **coercion**, that is, members are forced to participate (e.g., the orientation of prisoners of war toward their captors). Economic organizations, by contrast, depend upon **calculative involvement** (e.g., the orientation of sales agents or merchants toward their customers, or economically motivated employees toward their employers). In economic organizations membership is negotiated on the basis of individual self-interest calculated as a balance between the individuals' investments of time, energy, or talent, and the rewards or payments offered by the organization. In ideological organizations, involvement rests upon a sense of **identification** (e.g., the orientation of loyal followers toward their leader). Members maintain their involvement with the ideological organization because they believe in its purposes, feel a sense of personal satisfaction, and enjoy enhancement of their self-esteem as a result of their involvement.

Czarniawska-Joerges argues that Etzioni's three types can all be applied to business and administrative organizations. For instance, the practice of laying off workers is a threat of force that approaches the sort of coercive involvement practiced routinely in totalizing institutions. Under threat of layoff or redundancy, most organizational members will work harder and comply with management wishes more stringently than they will when the threat is removed. Similarly, the practice of vision management can be interpreted as an ideological propaganda technique and, when used by business and administrative organizations, these organizations become ideological. For instance, a standard practice in the insurance industry is to require new sales agents to study and pass an examination about the history and value of the industry to society. These activities focus on the belief that insurance is a tremendous benefit to society because it allows those who participate to share the costs of disaster. Such training programs can be seen as ideological tools.

If you compare and contrast Tables 11.1 and 11.2, you will notice that Ouchi's scheme separates market controlled organizations from bureaucracies, whereas Etzioni did not make this distinction. Etzioni, on the other hand, considered coercive organizing practices not represented in Ouchi's scheme. The two typologies, however, come together with regard to the notion of clan or ideological control, which the two boxes suggest are similar concepts. Furthermore, Ouchi and Czarniawska-Joerges agree that this category applies, at least in part, to all organizations.

The ideas about ideology in organizations can be extended to further suggest that control itself is an ideology. That is, one of the ways in which hegemony is maintained in organizations is through structures of control that support the dominance of top managers. Thus, the belief that control is essential to the success of organizations (the modern view expressed by Tannenbaum at the beginning of this chapter) legitimates the right of the powerful to dominate. This belief can be characterized as an ideology—the **ideology of control**. Reinterpreting all of organization theory through the lens of idealogy is one of the projects critical postmodern organization theorists set themselves.

SUMMARY

This chapter presents three modernist theories of control in organizations. The cybernetic model of control, an application of systems theory, outlines how control of organizational activities can be achieved through setting standards, monitoring activities and/or outcomes, and feeding back results. Agency theory focuses on the tendency of agents to shirk their responsibilities by subverting the control systems that make performance evaluation possible. This theory introduces the issue of information reliability in the execution of contracts and controls. Ouchi's comparison of market, bureaucracy, and clan control suggested that culture might be considered as an alternate means to control behavior through application of norms and values rather than traditional bureaucratic controls like rules and procedures, or the market mechanism of price and to feminist revisions of the meaning of power.

The modernist assumption that management has the right, or even the ability, to control culture is questioned from both the symbolic-interpretive and postmodern perspectives. Ethnographic observation in organizations suggests that culture is not as easily manipulated as the clan hypothesis suggests. Marxist critiques claim that workers conspire in their own oppression (control), and neo-Marxist views lead to the redefinition of control as ideology. Ideological control relates to Etzioni's notions of links between types of compliance and organizational forms, an idea that Czarniawska-Joerges develops into an appreciation for both control and autonomy—a contradictory position with links to the postmodern perspective.

KEY TERMS

cybernetic system

output control

target

behavioral control

standards

feedback

ambiguity

goal displacement

rigid bureaucratic behavior

impression management

cheating

unit-level controls

organization-level control

agency theory

principals

agents

agency problem

contracts

opportunism

market control

Issues and Themes in Organization Theory

profit centers	ideology
transfer prices	autonomy
bureaucratic control	coercion
clan control	calculative involvement
false consciousness	identification
hegemony	ideology of control

ENDNOTES

1. Tannenbaum (1968: 3).
2. Alchian and Demsetz (1972); Williamson (1975); Jensen and Meckling (1976).
3. Eisenhardt (1985: 136-37).
4. Eisenhardt (1985: 147-48).
5. Ouchi (1979: 845); see also Ouchi and McGuire (1975).
6. Filby and Willmott (1988); Meek (1988); Van Maanen and Kunda (1989).
7. Mumby (1988: 90).
8. Czarniawska-Joerges (1988: 2–3).
9. Ibid. 6.
10. Thompson (1980).
11. Bendix (1970: 529).
12. Czarniawska-Joerges (1988: 7).

REFERENCES

Alchian, A. A., and Demsetz, H. (1972). Production, information costs and economic organization. *American Economic Review*, 62: 777–95.

Bendix, R. (1970). The impact of ideas on organizational structure. In O. Grusky and B. A. Miller (eds.), *The sociology of organizations*. New York: Free Press.

Czarniawska-Joerges, Barbara (1988). *Ideological control in nonideological organizations*. New York: Praeger.

Eisenhardt, Kathleen M. (1985). Control: Organizational and economic approaches. *Management Science*, 31: 134–49.

Etzioni, Amitai (1961; revised 1975). *A comparative analysis of complex organizations*. New York: Free Press.

Etzioni, Amitai (1965). Organizational control structures. In J. March (ed.), *Handbook of organizations*. Chicago: Rand McNally, 650–77.

Filby, Ivan, and Willmott, Hugh (1988). Ideologies and contradictions in a public relations department. *Organization Studies*, 9: 335–51.

Jensen, M. C., and Meckling, W. H. (1976). Theory of the firm: Managerial behavior, agency costs and ownership structure. *Journal of Financial Economics*, 3: 305–60.

Lawler, Edward, and Rhode, John (1976). *Information and control in organizations*. Pacific Palisades, Calif.: Goodyear.

Meek, V. L. (1988). Organization culture: Origins and weaknesses. *Organization Studies*, 9: 453–73.

Mumby, Dennis K. (1988). *Communication and power in organizations: Discourse, ideology and domination*. Norwood, NJ: Ablex.

Ouchi, William G. (1979). A conceptual framework for the design of organizational control mechanisms. *Management Science*, 25: 833–48.

Ouchi, William G. (1980). Markets, bureaucracies, and clans. *Administrative Science Quarterly*, 25:129–41.

Ouchi, William G., and McGuire, Maryann (1975). Organizational control: Two functions. *Administrative Science Quarterly*, 20: 559–69.

Tannenbaum, Arnold S. (1968). *Control in organizations*. New York: McGraw-Hill.

Thompson, Kenneth (1980). Organizations as constructors of social reality (I). In Graeme Salaman and Kenneth Thompson (eds.), *Control and ideology in organizations*. Milton Keynes, England: The Open University Press, 216–37.

Van Maanen, John, and Kunda, Gideon (1989). Real feelings: Emotional expression and organizational culture. In Barry Staw and Larry Cummings (eds.), *Research in Organizational Behavior*, 11: 43–103.

Williamson, Oliver E. (1975). *Markets and hierarchies*. New York: Free Press.

FURTHER READING

Dore, Ron (1973). *Japanese factory, British factory: The origins of national diversity in industrial relations*. Berkeley: University of California Press.

Etzioni, Amitai (1961; revised 1975). *A comparative analysis of complex organizations*. New York: Free Press.

Granovetter, Mark (1985). Economic action and social structure. *American Journal of Sociology*, 91: 481–510.

Lawler, Edward, and Rhode, John (1976). *Information and control in organizations*. Pacific Palisades, Calif.: Goodyear.

Ouchi, William G. (1980). Markets, bureaucracies and clans. *Administrative Science Quarterly*, 25: 129–41.

Ross, S. (1973). The economic theory of agency: The principal's problem. *American Economic Review*, 63: 134–39.

Therborn, G. (1980). *The ideology of power and the power of ideology*. London: Verso.

Thompson, Kenneth (1980). Organizations as constructors of social reality (I). In Graeme Salaman and Kenneth Thompson (eds.), *Control and ideology in organizations*. Milton Keynes, England: The Open University Press, 216–37.

Williamson, Oliver E. (1975). *Markets and hierarchies*. New York: Free Press.

12 Organizational Change and Learning

THE topic of organizational change has a rich and varied history. It is the domain of the entire discipline of organizational development and has featured prominently in discussions of organizational behavior and organization theory throughout their respective histories. In this chapter I will not attempt to review all of the work that relates to this complex topic, but instead will select a few models of organizational change that are built specifically upon the central concepts and themes of organization theory explored in this book. This strategy will allow you to see how organization theorists draw upon the breadth of their discipline to construct theory in relation to a particular topic. This should also encourage you to complete the move from theory to theorizing that I described in Chapter 1 and set as our objective in Part III.

In a way, everything we have studied in this book contributes to the theory of organizational change. To see this, go back over the material covered in each of the preceding chapters with an eye toward the ways in which they help you to understand how, when and why organizations change. Notice in particular those theories that describe the dynamic or processual aspects of organizing. They mark a shift from theories rooted in assumptions about the stability of organizations that were typical of Classical management and early modernist writing. Classical management theorists and early modernists nearly always focused on how to stabilize, routinize, and rationalize organizational knowledge about effective organizational performance. In stability-oriented frameworks such as these, changes were seen as the intended result of doing more of a good thing—more routine, more structure, more rationality. A change-centered perspective, however, has gradually swept away the dominance of stability-centered views, and all three perspectives of organization theory now embrace more dynamic ideas that celebrate organizational processes.

Widespread interest in the topic of change fits with current debate about post-industrial society. As we saw in Chapter 2, many organization theorists think that recent economic, technical, social, and cultural changes will lead to new forms of organizing, such as global and network structures (described in Chapter 6). American organizational change experts Rosabeth Moss Kanter, Barry Stein, and Todd Jick agree and gave a typical description of this vision of our organizational future:

more flexible organizations, adaptable to change, with relatively few levels of formal hierarchy and loose boundaries among functions and units, sensitive and responsive to the environment, concerned with stakeholders of all sorts—employees, communities, customers, suppliers, and shareholders. These organizations, empower people to take action and be entrepreneurial, reward them for contributions, and help them gain in skill and "employability." Overall, these are global organizations characterized by internal and external relationships, including joint ventures, alliances, consortia, and partnerships.[1]

Modernists explain the need for new organizational forms in terms of environmental change and these views are rooted in predictions of continuous, rapid change in products, markets, technology, and society. To keep up, organizations will have to be built for change, and organization theorists will need dynamic models to describe and explain them. When environments were more often stable and simple, organizations could be less adaptable and more hierarchical. Under these conditions, static models were adequate. But static models either do not account for change, or consider it only in terms of comparisons between two static states (e.g., before and after a change). As change speeds up, organization theorists realize that these static models are inadequate. It is not that they are wrong, only that something more is needed.

A scene in the movie *Star Wars* provides a vivid image of the need to shift from static to dynamic models. In this scene the Millennium Falcon, Han Solo's spaceship, is about to make the jump to light speed. The image on the screen shows us what Han, the pilot, sees out the front window of his ship. First we see a collection of distinct points of light, presumably stars, but the instant the ship reaches light speed velocity, the lights melt into linear traces past which we seem to move extremely rapidly. This image symbolizes for me the qualitative leap to dynamic views of organization that is implied by descriptions like the one quoted above. Although static representations can still tell us where the stars are, we must adjust our senses to travelling at such high speeds. New means of navigating this territory need to be found because at the new speed we will run into objects before we can see them. It may still be the same territory, but we see things differently when we move so fast. These differences in the way we see things affect our interpretations of organizations and environments and demand models that keep pace with our new perspectives—dynamic models.

In a sense, all symbolic-interpretive research in organization theory is based on a dynamic model because social construction processes concern aspects of everyday life that either reproduce existing structures and circumstances, or lead to their alteration. In symbolic-interpretive perspectives, organizations are not seen as static entities, but rather as dynamic processes in a constant state of change. Similarly, postmodern views of fragmentation and chaos reject visions of stability in favor of the paradox of stability/change in organizations. Thus, as organization theory continues to develop in directions defined by symbolic-interpretive and postmodern research, it replaces the notion of organization with that of organizing—a shift that Weick called for years ago when he first proposed enactment theory.[2]

Do not think, however, that modernism is left out of the discussion of organizational change. On the contrary, with evolutionary and developmental models such as population ecology (see Chapter 3) and organizational lifecycle theories (see Chapter 6), contemporary modernist theories have become much more change sensitive and dynamic. Furthermore, recent developments within systems theory are introducing ideas about self-reproducing and self-referential systems to organization theory that are contributing a new metaphor—the learning organization. This metaphor challenges former modernist models of organizational change that assumed organizations adapt to external pressures; instead it suggests that organizations create their own, internal dynamics which are described as processes of organizational learning.

Ironically, learning models introduce a new view of organizational change by reintroducing agency. Change theory began with modernist models of **planned change** in which a change agent (usually a person or group with authority, e.g., CEO, MD, top management team, or outside consultant) introduced change to the organization in a deliberate way. This model gave way to theories of emergent change which tended to locate the agency for change in the environment and thus outside of the organization's direct control. The learning model reintroduces organizational agency, but in a diffuse way. In learning, organizations once again are seen to define their own change processes, but not in the direct, controlling, and top-down ways described by advocates of planned change. Theories of organizational learning describe more democratic processes and bring modernist views very close to postmodern thinking in their reliance on pluralism, diversity and freedom.

As a reference point we begin this chapter with a look at an early model of planned organizational change—Kurt Lewin's unfreezing–change–refreezing model. A contemporary modernist alternative, called the Big Three model, provides an example of dynamic and evolutionary thinking about change within the mainstream modernist perspective. Two symbolic-interpretive models of organizational change framed by culture theory are presented next, followed by an illustration of postmodern approaches to organizational change which deconstruct planned organizational change as rhetoric and reconstruct organizational change processes as discourse. The concluding section takes up the topic of organizational learning and traces its development from cybernetic models to applications of postmodern literary theory to organizations.

LEWIN'S MODEL: UNFREEZING, CHANGE, REFREEZING

In the 1950s, social psychologist Kurt Lewin developed a theory of social change that defined social institutions as a balance of forces, some driving and the others restraining change.[3] In Lewin's model, stability was not defined merely by the forces opposing change, it was a stalemate between forces for and against it. Lewin's was more a theory of stability than of change, however, because he defined change as transient instability interrupting an otherwise stable equilibrium. Lewin, who once said "there is nothing so practical as a good theory," described the implications of his theory in terms of normative advice about how to bring about change in organizations. According to his model, change involves three separate activities: unfreezing, change or movement, and refreezing as shown in Figure 12.1.

Unfreezing unbalances the equilibrium that sustains organizational stability. According to Lewin, the destabilizing of present behavioral patterns works to overcome resistance to change. Locating and then taking advantage of existing stress or dissatisfaction within the current system is one strategy to bring about unfreezing. However, unfreezing can occur by either producing additional forces for change or by reducing resistance, for example through education concerning the need for change. Once unfreezing has occurred, the **change** stage involves influencing the direction of movement in the now unbalanced system. Strategies for influencing the direction of change include training new behavioral patterns, altering reporting relationships and reward systems, and introducing different styles of management (e.g., replacing an authoritarian with a participative management style). Change continues until a new balance between driving and

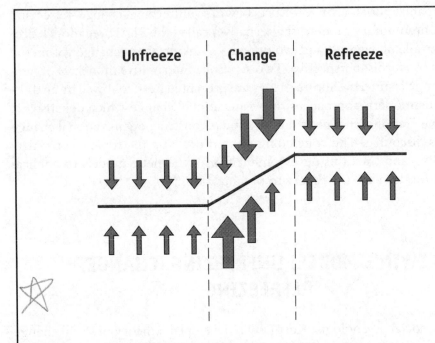

FIGURE 12.1. LEWIN'S MODEL OF ORGANIZATIONAL CHANGE

Change results from disturbances in the force field sustaining organizational stability. Whenever forces favoring change are greater than forces resisting it, the organization will "move" from one state to another. In planned change, movement can be induced via unfreezing the old equilibrium and then refreezing around a new one.

Based on: Lewin (1951, 1958).

restraining forces is achieved. **Refreezing** occurs when new behavioral patterns stabilize or become institutionalized. An example of a refreezing strategy would be establishing new recruiting policies to assure that new recruits share the organizational culture and will work well within the new structure and reward systems as well as with the new managerial style.

A large proportion of the case studies and theoretical discussions of organizational change that comprise the field of organization development are formulated in the tradition Lewin's model helped to establish. The discipline of organization development provides well-documented illustrations of the unfreezing/change/refreezing processes. To give just one example, American organization development specialists Leonard Goodstein and Warner Burke applied Lewin's model to analyze changes undertaken at British Airways (BA) during the early 1980s.[4]

354

Goodstein and Burke claimed that the changes at BA in the 1980s were a response to two environmental changes in combination with poor corporate performance. The environmental changes involved Thatcher's opposition to public ownership of business and deregulation of international air traffic with consequent air fare competition among airlines. Facing privatization and fare wars, BA's challenge was complicated by its lack of profitability in the years before the privatization decision was taken. For instance, in 1982 they lost nearly $900 million (USD) requiring large government subsidies which furthered the Thatcher government's resolve to privatize BA. As the noose tightened, BA recognized the need for radical change which was undertaken over the five-year period from 1982 to 1987. Goodstein and Burke reported that during this period, BA went from government ownership and a bureaucratic and command culture with huge losses and a decreasing market share, to a privately owned company with a service-oriented and market-driven culture with profits of over $400 million (USD) and an increasing market share.

Goodstein and Burke identified many different elements in BA's change effort. First of all, BA reduced the size of its workforce from 59,000 to 37,000. Second, an industrialist became chairman of the board and a new CEO with a marketing background was named. These men differed considerably from their predecessors, many of whom had been retired Royal Air Force officers. Goodstein and Burke argued that the effect of these new appointments was to signal an imminent change in values at BA. Third, training programs were initiated to help "line workers and managers understand the service nature of the airline industry."[5] According to Goodstein and Burke, the combination of workforce reductions, new top management, and training programs accomplished unfreezing which allowed BA top managers to introduce change.

Movement was accomplished through management training programs, changes in structure and reward systems, a new, more user friendly management information system, and team building. Management training programs helped BA move to a participative management style that emphasized employee commitment and involvement. Two elements of the unfreezing stage (cross-functional, cross-level teams used to plan the change effort plus reductions in middle management) had signalled a participative management style, which was symbolically reinforced during the change stage by the introduction of the new user friendly computer system, profit sharing, and a bottom-up budgeting process. During this phase, the CEO also became a symbol of participation by engaging in question and answer sessions during training programs. Goodstein and Burke claimed that it was also in this phase that BA made a critical identity change from a transportation to a service company. The core idea of emotional labor was a key part of the new service identity and involved developing emotional support systems for the service workers to offset the burnout that they often experience.

Refreezing in BA's case was accomplished via orientation programs for new employees at all levels, establishment of a policy of promoting people who symbolized the new corporate values, and education programs for executives and managers called "Top Flight Academies." In addition, performance appraisal and compensation systems were developed around the principle of rewarding customer service and employee development.

New uniforms, refurbished aircraft, and a new logo with the motto "We fly to serve," communicated BA's new identity. Continued use of teamwork and data feedback to management helped BA maintain its new participative management style. Of course, as Goodstein and Burke pointed out, moving from a known but undesirable state, to a desired but unknown future state, involved a transition period of disorganization and lowered effectiveness during which, they claimed, courageous and committed leadership offset anger, uncertainty, and fear.

THE BIG THREE MODEL OF CHANGE

Kanter, Stein, and Jick called Lewin's model the "organization as ice cube" view of change and criticized it for being a "quaintly linear and static conception" that simplifies "an extraordinarily complex process into a child's formula."[6] They claimed that change is both "ubiquitous and multidirectional" and thus Lewin's model does not come close to the level of complexity needed to address the phenomenon of organizational change. According to Kanter and her colleagues:

organizations have great power to shape behavior, not so much by *forcing* it as by *encouraging* it. Organizations always make some things easier and some things harder, thus making the former more likely and the latter less likely. This is the work not simply of "culture"—something in people's heads—but rather of the formal aspects of the organization, such as its distribution of roles and responsibilities, people's authority to commit resources, existing budget procedures, the physical or geographical arrangement of its space and facilities, differences in information access and availability, and reward and recognition systems. This sort of "character" is rooted in the organization's structure, systems, and culture—elements that embody the momentum of the organization by "acting on" its members, thereby enabling the organization to maintain a recognizable presence over time.[7]

Kanter and her colleagues claimed that Lewin's model sees organizations changing only with applications of concentrated effort and only in one direction at a time. In their theory, on the other hand, change is multidirectional and more or less continuous. What appears on the surface as stability, is simply unnoticed or unchallenged change:

Apparent "stability" occurs when resources are abundant and easily obtained; competitors are few and competition is geographically confined by protected markets; technologies are standard and understood; individual and group ambition is constrained (people accept what they have); disasters or system failures are few or are accepted fatalistically; commitments are clear and acceptable to stakeholders; and interests are adequately aligned.[8]

Kanter and her colleagues argued that when conceptions of organization do not fit the conditions of apparent stability, a new understanding of organization and its management is needed (be sure to notice the similarity with Burns and Stalker's mechanistic versus organic argument described in Chapter 4). For instance, rather than planning and directing change, as in Lewin's model, the manager's job within new organizations is to respond to, harness, and provoke change. For new organizations, Kanter and her colleagues put forward their own Big Three model.

The Big Three model demonstrates how a variety of key concepts and theories produced by organization theorists can be combined to form an integrated explanation of organizational change. In this sense, Kanter and her colleagues present a grand narrative that spans theories of organization–environment relations (Chapter 3), social structure (Chapter 6), organizational culture (Chapter 7), and physical structure (Chapter 8). What is intriguing about the Big Three model is that it builds upon evolutionary models as a basis for a theory of organizational change. In contrast to Lewin's model, there is no single agent of change in the Big Three model. Here change is embedded in the processes of organizing that are sustained by a multitude of forces.

Kanter and her colleagues defined organizations as "bundles of activity" that change when activities shift or as new units and individuals are included. They claim that influence over activity sets and change itself occurs at all three levels of analysis specified by organization theory—environment, organization, and individual. At the environmental level, the authors identify **macroevolutionary forces for change** that come from the behavior of *other* organizations. These forces are described by population ecology, resource dependence, and institutional theory and are combined in ways compatible with both contingency theory and systems theory. That is, changes in the population of organizations that compete for scarce or munificent resources with varying amounts of uncertainty and differing pressures for conformity to societal expectations create an environment favoring change in organizational activity systems. At the organizational level, **microevolutionary forces for change** are brought about by progress

357

through the organizational lifecycle with implications drawn from an organization's size and age and associated problems of growth or decline. At the individual level, **political forces for change** that stem from struggles for power and control influence activity sets as well. At this level the organization is seen as a battleground on which multiple stakeholders shape organizational activities around their self-interests.

Macroevolutionary, microevolutionary, and political forces for change each take different forms within the organization. At the environmental level, change in organizational identity reflects new organization–environment relationships while microevolutionary movement through the lifecycle appears as changes in the coordination of activities. Changes in the distribution of control and power among various individuals and coalitions is the form taken by political movement. Identity changes can occur in terms of an organization's asset base and markets, its customer and supplier relations, or in terms of its sources of capital. An organization's identity changes, for example, along with changes in the businesses it operates, the products it offers, or the types of investors it attracts. Coordination changes involve restructuring the organization or reorganizing technological work flows (e.g., through business process re-engineering). Changes in control involve changes in the dominant coalition or in who owns and governs the organization. Control changes occur in the most notable way during a merger or takeover.

While Kanter and her colleagues present a theory of change that is considerably more complex than Lewin's, it is not clear that theirs is as dynamic as they claim. For one thing, they present only a framework for combining other theories and a framework is itself a level one (i.e., non-dynamic) system. Another reason may be that these researchers focus on broad patterns of organizational change, rather than on change at the level of ordinary, everyday life in organizations. Although they incorporate lifecycle and population ecology theories, even more dynamic views are offered by symbolic-interpretive and postmodern perspectives.

CULTURAL CHANGE IN ORGANIZATIONS

Studies of organizational culture generally describe the social processes that sustain meaning in organizational settings. Modernist culture researchers tend to view cultures as stabilizing forces within the organization and to use the concept of culture as an explanation for resistance to change. Many symbolic-interpretivists, however, view culture in a more dynamic way. Some of these theorists have offered theoretical models to explain how organizational cultures change.

Italian organizational theorist and organization development consultant Pasquale Gagliardi offers a theory of the relationship between culture and strategy that he uses to explain both how culture affects change and how change affects culture. My own model of the dynamics of organizational culture describes four processes of cultural change and the symbolic role of management within these processes.

Culture and Strategy

Gagliardi began with Schein's notion of assumptions and values as the core of an organizational culture and then argued that every organization's primary strategy is to protect the organizational identity that these assumptions and values create and maintain (see Figure 12.2). In service to the primary strategy, Gagliardi argued, organizations develop and implement a range of secondary strategies. These secondary strategies can be either instrumental or expressive. He explained the difference this way:

Instrumental strategies permit the proper management of external problems of adaptation and internal problems of integration, both of which result from efforts to realize the primary strategy. Such strategies are mainly operational in nature (i.e., they tend towards the attainment of specific, measurable objectives). . . . Expressive strategies operate in the symbolic field and seek to protect the stability and coherence of shared meanings. These strategies may also be oriented towards either the internal or external environment of the organization. In the former case, they enable group members to maintain a lively awareness of their collective identity, while in the latter case they enable the organization to offer a recognizable identity to the outside world.[9]

Of course secondary strategies can be both expressive and instrumental. For example, an advertising campaign can be designed to present the organizational identity to its external audiences at the same time that it helps to sell the company's products. Similarly, a move to an open plan office may reflect a strategy to improve communication efficiency and to symbolize a reduction in the importance of hierarchical position. Changes in behavior, technology, symbols, and structures occur through implementation of secondary strategies. In Gagliardi's view, strategy is grounded in and limited by cultural assumptions and values.

How then, does change ever occur? Gagliardi traced three types of change. One type, which he calls **apparent change**, occurs within culture, but without changing it. That is, new problems are confronted by choosing from the range of strategies permitted by assumptions, values, and the primary strategy. Implementation of these secondary strategies produces changes at the level of cultural artifacts, but these cultural changes are superficial, the organization only

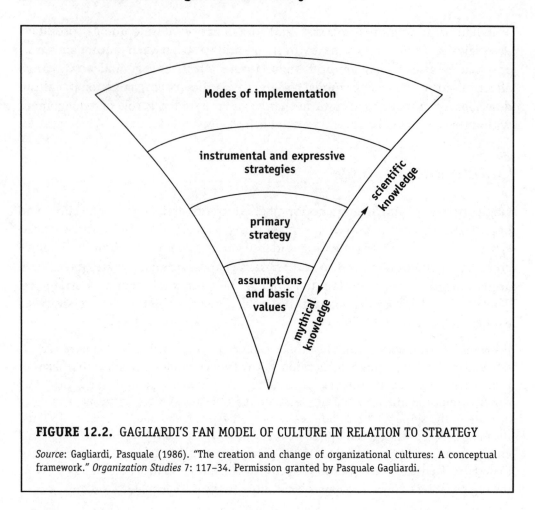

FIGURE 12.2. GAGLIARDI'S FAN MODEL OF CULTURE IN RELATION TO STRATEGY

Source: Gagliardi, Pasquale (1986). "The creation and change of organizational cultures: A conceptual framework." *Organization Studies* 7: 117–34. Permission granted by Pasquale Gagliardi.

adapts within the confines of its existing identity. In this type of change, Gagliardi claimed, the organizational culture changes (but only superficially) in order to stay the same (i.e., preserve its sense of identity).

In **revolutionary change**, however, a strategy incompatible with cultural assumptions and values is imposed upon the organization, usually through the entry of outsiders who destroy old symbols and create new ones. This can occur, for example, when the beloved founder of an organization dies, or when a company is merged or taken over from the outside. But in these cases, Gagliardi argued, it is "more correct to say that the old firm dies and that a new firm, which has little in common with the first, was born."[10]

Cultural incrementalism, Gagliardi's third type of change, is the only type that reaches the deep level of cultural values and assumptions. In this case, a strategy that implies different, but not incompatible, values stretches the organizational culture to include new values alongside its old ones (see Figure 12.3). As Schein argued, if the new strategy meets with success, then the change it brings about will be incorporated into the organization's taken-for-granted assumptions. Gagliardi adds that this transformation of values and assumptions is more likely if the success is celebrated with storytelling and myth making. These symbolic efforts are important because they establish the change within the symbolic field of the organizational culture.

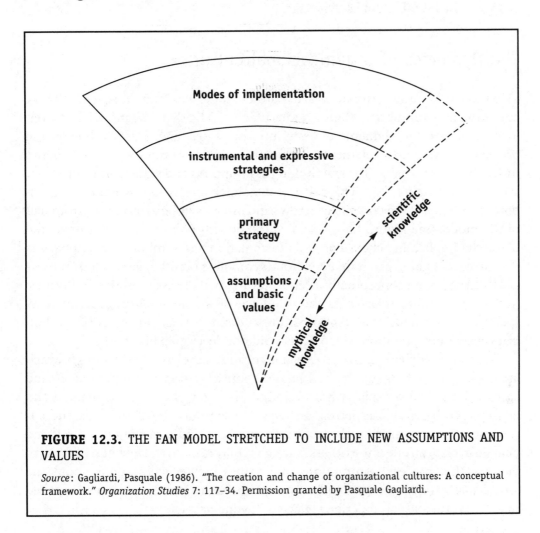

FIGURE 12.3. THE FAN MODEL STRETCHED TO INCLUDE NEW ASSUMPTIONS AND VALUES

Source: Gagliardi, Pasquale (1986). "The creation and change of organizational cultures: A conceptual framework." *Organization Studies* 7: 117–34. Permission granted by Pasquale Gagliardi.

Gagliardi's model separated culture and strategy and suggested that different strategic moves have different effects on organizational cultures. When strategies align with organizational assumptions and values, cultures do not change. When strategies are in conflict with assumptions and values, culture is either overthrown and is replaced or destroyed, or the strategy is resisted and never implemented. When strategies are different but not incompatible with assumptions and values, the culture is expanded by the new assumptions and values implicit in the new strategy. What Gagliardi's model does not explain is *how* strategies, or strategists for that matter, are actually absorbed within or act upon the organizational culture. To be more specific about the processes by which the outcomes Gagliardi described come about, consider another model of cultural change, which I call cultural dynamics.

The Dynamics of Organizational Culture

Like Gagliardi's model, the cultural dynamics model was built on Schein's theory of culture as assumptions, values, and artifacts.[11] The dynamic model, however, focuses not on the elements of assumptions, values, and artifacts, but on the processes linking these elements. These processes were represented in Schein's model by the two pairs of arrows linking assumptions and values, and values and artifacts (see Figure 7.3). The cultural dynamics model flips Schein's diagram onto its side, splits the two sets of arrows and inserts symbols into the bottom half of the model (see Figure 12.4). Flipping the diagram on its side overthrows the hierarchy implicit in Schein's original formulation and symbolically emphasizes that artifacts (which can have enormous symbolic potential) are no less important to an adequate conceptualization of culture than are assumptions and values. Inserting symbols underscores the influence of the symbolic-interpretive perspective on our understanding of culture and emphasizes processes of symbolization and interpretation which Schein did not develop in his theory.

The cultural dynamics model explains culture as the processes through which artifacts and symbols are created in the context of organizational values and assumptions. It also explains how values and assumptions are maintained and altered by using and interpreting artifacts and symbols. In other words, there is mutual influence among artifacts, values, symbols, and assumptions such that a change in one can affect the others (though it may not). In the first half of the artifact creation process, assumptions and values create expectations about the world that produce images and visions to guide action. This process is called **manifestation** and it is described in the following passage:

Consider the assumption that humans are lazy. According to the cultural dynamics perspective, this assumption produces expectations of laziness, which lead to perceptions of lazy acts. These perceptions, in combination with other manifesting assumptions, color thoughts and feelings about these acts. For instance, in an organization that assumes that success depends upon sustained effort, laziness is likely to be considered in a negative

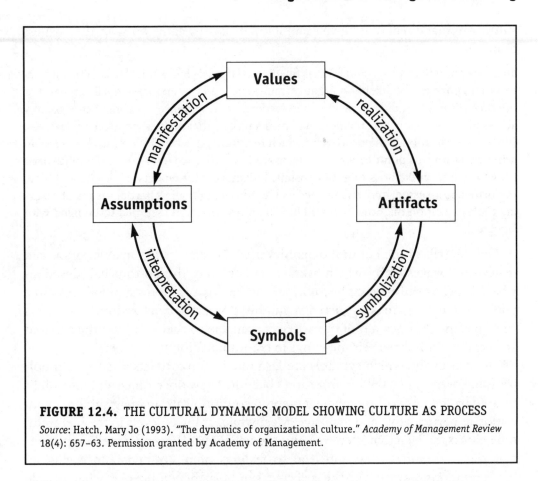

FIGURE 12.4. THE CULTURAL DYNAMICS MODEL SHOWING CULTURE AS PROCESS

Source: Hatch, Mary Jo (1993). "The dynamics of organizational culture." *Academy of Management Review* 18(4): 657–63. Permission granted by Academy of Management.

light, and perceptions of laziness along with negative thoughts and feelings about it can easily develop into a value for controlling laziness. Meanwhile the laziness assumption also works to inhibit expectations of industrious acts (because humans are lazy, why would they act in this way?), and perceptions, thoughts, and feelings about these acts will be constrained. This inhibition suppresses a value for autonomy (because giving lazy people autonomy will almost certainly lead to little or no effort being exerted), which further supports the value for control by eliminating a potentially competing force from the value set. That is, although autonomy would be compatible with an assumption that organizational success depends upon effort, the laziness assumption interferes with an effort / autonomy value set and supports an effort / control value set.[12]

Once culture influences action by manifesting images and values, culturally influenced action produces artifacts (e.g., physical objects, events, verbal statements, and texts). The production of artifacts is referred to as the **realization** process because it is by this process that images grounded in assumptions and

363

values are made real (e.g., given tangible forms). To carry on with the laziness example:

an assumption that the organization is filled with laggards contributes to a value for control that enhances the likelihood that certain social and material forms will appear. For instance, time clocks, daily productivity reports, performance meetings, and visually accessible offices are acceptable ideas in a culture that values controlling laziness. Proactive realization is the process by which manifest expectations are made tangible in artifacts. From this point of view, artifacts are left in the wake of culturally influenced activity. Thus, time clocks might be installed, daily activity reports requested and filed, performance assessed, and visually accessible offices built, all as partial means of realizing the expectation of "how it should be" in an organization assumed to be filled with laggards.[13]

The top half of the cultural dynamics model describes the manifestation and realization processes by which artifacts are created, the bottom half describes what happens once artifacts become part of the organization's symbolic resource pool for meaning making activity. In this domain, organizational members choose some (but not all) of the artifacts available to them and use the selected artifacts to symbolize their meanings in communication with others.

The process by which symbols are fashioned from artifacts is called **symbolization**. For example, the organization's beautiful new open office building might be used by members of top management to communicate an image of the organization as participative and inclusive. Meanwhile, at lower levels in the hierarchy, time clocks, daily activity reports, and the behavior of managers tell employees that they are not trusted and lead to feelings of resentment and exclusion. Interpretations invested in the selected symbols then influence what people believe and assume about the organization. However, the **interpretation** process works in two directions. It uses assumptions to help determine the meaning of symbols, but allows symbols to either maintain or challenge existing assumptions. Maintenance of assumptions occurs when interpretations support what is already expected, but interpretations sometimes run counter to expectations.

The possibility of cultural change comes when assumptions are symbolically challenged within the interpretation process. For instance, in a culture that assumes laziness, the appearance of an obviously hardworking individual challenges the basic assumption and brings the possibility of new meaning into the culture. Of course, it may happen that the symbol of the hardworking individual is simply reinterpreted to fit into existing assumptions, for instance by making an excuse for the aberration ("his twin daughters are ready for college and he really needs a promotion so he is kissing up to the boss"). But change is also possible, and when it occurs it is by the mechanism of confrontation with symbols that do not fit the assumed reality. For example, suppose the same hardworking individual wins the lottery and keeps on working. In this case, the assumption of laziness is opened a little, and now people start to assume that at least some workers have initiative. This leads to a desire to distinguish lazy and hardworking individuals and perhaps to a new employee selection process that changes the artifact pool . . . and so on, round and round the model.

The processes described by the cultural dynamics model are ongoing. Active attempts by managers to change organizations would therefore also be described as a part of these processes. Attempts to introduce change intentionally usually begin in the domain of realization and symbolization when management introduces a new idea through language or other artifacts (don't forget that physical objects and behavioral manifestations are also powerful communicators) which then may be symbolized and interpreted by those who are expected to carry the change forward. If the symbols made are in alignment with existing organizational assumptions and values, change should be relatively easy but not very deep (this is Gagliardi's notion of apparent change).

However, change in line with existing assumptions and values may not be what management wants. Some change may involve introducing "foreign" ideas into the system. Cultural processes of absorption then come into play, and change initiators must recognize that their sense of control over the process will be diminished as others confront the new artifacts, make symbols with them, and find their own interpretations of the meaning of the change and intent of the change agent. Working through processes of symbolization and interpretation with employees in open dialogue can aid both managers and other employees as they confront and cope with new problems and opportunities. However, if managers attempt to control interpretations (e.g., via rhetoric), they are quite likely to be interpreted as propagandists and to meet either with direct challenges or indirect resistance (depending on norms for confrontation in the organization and the society at large). The message to leaders is, you have more symbolic power than you realize, but less control (over interpretations) than you probably desire.

The message of the cultural dynamics model would not fit comfortably in the Classical or even the modernist perspective in which management control of organizations is presumed necessary and desirable. The cultural dynamics model places the manager within the organizational culture. It suggests that leadership power lies in the sensitivity of the manager to his or her own symbolic meaning and this symbolic meaning shifts and changes in relation to a symbolic world constituted by the interpretive acts of others. Leaders have tremendous influence within organizations, but their ability to mobilize this influence effectively depends on their knowledge of, and perceived alignment with, the culture.

The prescription for organizational change based in the cultural dynamics model would have to be: manager change thyself. As a symbol operating within cultural processes, managers only create change when the interpretations others give to them (and to their words and actions) produce changes in assumptions, values, and/or artifacts. This involves being symbolized, which means that the manager's acts, words, and/or person must be selected from the pool of artifacts by those whose interpretations will produce change. How managers formulate their words and deeds and display themselves will have an influence on the choices that others make as they engage in the cultural processes of symbolization and interpretation. Symbolically aware managers have a much better chance of using themselves effectively as symbols than do those who are symbolically unconscious. However, with this insight, we have reached a postmodern question in change management: Who has the right to change whom and with what responsibilities?

ORGANIZATIONAL CHANGE AND THE POSTMODERN PERSPECTIVE

Postmodernists often begin their analyses with deconstruction. In deconstruction, assumptions underlying arguments are revealed and overturned. The overturning of assumptions opens a space for previously unconsidered alternatives and in this way resembles Lewin's unfreezing stage of organizational change. The difference is that, in a postmodern approach, the alternatives are left open to multiple interpretations and uses rather than shut down again or refrozen. Used in this way, the postmodern perspective is a means to overcoming domination by one perspective or idea, and postmodernism advocates the use of knowledge to emancipate rather than to control. Of course, freedom demands responsibility; another postmodern message is that we carry the burdens of the choices that we make regardless of whether we admit or deny these responsibilities. Postmodernist critiques are designed to make denial uncomfortable, if not impossible, and to render consideration of alternative ways of knowing a matter of public discourse.

To apply postmodernist thinking to the problem of organizational change, let us begin with a favorite target of postmodernist criticism, the modernist position. Resource dependence and population ecology theories suggest that organizational change begins with change in the environment. In the modernist perspective the environment overpowers the organization by changing the conditions for survival and only those organizations that adapt will continue to receive resources. Institutional theory operates with similar logic, only according to this symbolic-interpretive theory the changes are normative in nature and the entire system is a political and socially constructed reality rather than the economic and technological reality of the modernist perspective. The introduction of social constructionism, however, alters advice for practitioners. In the symbolic-interpretive perspective, the environment is enacted by social constructions which then influence organizational practices even among those who remain staunchly unaware of enactment processes.

The postmodern perspective suggests pushing the social constructionist viewpoint one step further. In a socially constructed world, responsibility for environmental and organizational conditions lies with those who do the constructing. Social constructionism does not locate power in the individual, but in the social collectivity. We cannot, as individuals, choose a different reality and impose it on others, the others must participate as well. This suggests at least two competing scenarios for organizational change.

First, organizational change can be a vehicle of domination for those who conspire to enact the world for others (with or without conscious awareness of their intent). Here there is a danger of totalitarianism because complicity between modernist organization theorists and managers maintains the hegemony of management, for example, by making hierarchy appear natural and necessary. In this scenario, population ecology and institutional theory are rhetorical devices for convincing the naive and unaware that they really have no choice. Of course, less powerful members bear responsibility too. For example, by not participating, individuals allow others to determine conditions for them, and by not resisting once those conditions are in place, non-participants help to sustain the status quo with attitudes of alienation and helplessness. So, ironically, the dominated participate in their own domination through non-participation. They, too, are responsible.

An alternative use of social constructionism is to create a democracy of enactment in which the process is made open and available to all via public discourse about it. However, postmodernists do not argue that power relations disappear, only that we face an opportunity to see them also as forces of freedom, creativity, and possibility, rather than strictly as forces of domination, constraint, and control. French philosopher Michel Foucault put it this way:

to say there cannot be a society without power relations is not to say either that those which are established are necessary, or, in any case, that power constitutes a fatality at the heart of societies, such that it cannot be undermined. Instead, I would say that the analysis, elaboration, and bringing into question of power relations . . . is a permanent political task inherent in all social relations.[14]

What Foucault says of societies and power, many postmodern organization theorists believe about organizations—that we can learn to use power in new, more critical, ways such that we create opportunities for freedom and innovation rather than simply for further domination. (Notice that domination does not disappear from the list of potential outcomes, even though enthusiasts of this scenario have tended to downplay this aspect of its potential.)

We can use the latest fashions in management circles—culture change programs, total quality management, business process re-engineering, employee empowerment, to name only a few—to see these two scenarios more clearly. Many of these new management initiatives are built on theoretical links between power, autonomy, and creativity, however, in the hands of some managers, they are transformed into tools of domination. This occurs as managers use the rhetoric of participation to persuade employees to join up, but then subvert the process by insinuating or imposing their own desires on them. This is captured by the ironic paraphrase, "I empower you *to do what I say.*" When employees shrug their shoulders and reply, "It is just more of the same," they give up their creative power in equal measure to what management has tried to deny them. Neither managers nor employees are blameless—it isn't management domination any more than it is employee resistance to change that explains why more organizations do not reach empowerment, total quality, or any of the other promised lands. If anything, the reason is mutual fear based on lack of respect and trust.

But programs based on these new ideas present opportunities for the kind of change postmodernism claims is possible, even if we rarely make the choice to pursue them to these ends. One idea for achieving innovation rather than domination is discourse. If the organization is constructed from language (that is, if we talk it into existence, and talk it out of, as well as into, changing), then creating discourse within organizations offers more opportunities for organizing and thus for reorganizing—or change.

Discourse

Discourse, or **dialogue**, builds on belief in the powers of collective thought—that human minds in interaction are capable of transcending individual limitations and empowering new ideas. The topic of dialogue was presented by American systems theorist and management consultant Peter Senge in his popular book *The Fifth Discipline*. Drawing on conversations with quantum theoretical physicist David Bohm, also an influential systems thinker, Senge claims that:

In dialogue, a group explores complex difficult issues from many points of view. Individuals suspend their assumptions but they communicate their assumptions freely.

The result is a free exploration that brings to the surface the full depth of people's experience and thought, and yet can move beyond their individual views.[15]

He further claimed that:

In dialogue people become observers of their own thinking. . . . What they observe is that their thinking is active. For example, when a conflict surfaces in a dialogue people are likely to realize that there is a tension, but the tension arises, literally, from our thoughts. People will say, "It is our thoughts and the way we hold on to them that are in conflict, not us." Once people see the participatory nature of their thought, they begin to separate themselves from their thought. They begin to take a more creative, less reactive, stance toward their thought.[16]

Thus Senge defined two closely related themes that are influencing contemporary thinking about organizational change—learning and reflexivity (i.e., observers of their own thinking). Ironically, he also reintroduces the notion of human agency into the discussion of organizational change. This is ironic in that human agency was jettisoned when the planned change view was supplanted by the emergent, process-based approach to organizational change theory. However, learning and reflexivity do not abandon process, instead they juxtapose the process orientation and the notion of agency creating what might be thought of as a postmodern collage.

ORGANIZATIONAL LEARNING

Along with ideas about discourse and dialogue, Senge has been a passionate promoter of the concept of the learning organization. In Senge's view, the **learning organization** defines our organizational future:

As the world becomes more interconnected and business becomes more complex and dynamic, work must become more "learningful." It is no longer sufficient to have one person learning for the organization, a Ford or a Sloan or a Watson. It's just not possible any longer to "figure it out" from the top, and have everyone else following the orders of the "grand strategist." The organizations that will truly excel in the future will be the organizations that discover how to tap people's commitment and capacity to learn at *all* levels in an organization.[17]

American organization theorists Barbara Leavitt and James March[18] claimed that experience curves provide evidence that organizations learn. (Whether they do or not, the experience or learning curve has become a powerful symbol for organizational learning.) Experience curves demonstrate and trace the path of the negative relationship between production costs and the quantity of an item manufactured. For example, as more of a particular aircraft are built, the cost of producing one of them falls, indicating that something about producing the aircraft has been learned even though no one may be able to say exactly what that learning was. In the field of strategy, this type of learning is being touted as a competency by American strategy theorist Jay Barney who declared that an organization's unique and tacit knowledge is an important part of its competitive advantage. Barney claimed that the tacit has competitive value because it is non-replicable by the firm's competitors and he concluded that organizational culture embodies much of this advantage.[19]

Leavitt and March proposed that organizations learn in ways that are explained by other organizing processes. For instance, they learn through direct experience when they engage in trial-and-error decision making (discussed in Chapter 9), and indirectly from the experience of other organizations, such as through imitation, as explained by institutional theory (see Chapter 3). Furthermore, organizations communicate their learning through stories and symbols and behavioral norms and expectations, thus learning is also bound up with cultural processes (see Chapter 7 and Gagliardi's and Hatch's models presented earlier in this chapter). Leavitt and March also point out that there are many difficulties along the learning path which they describe as superstitious learning, the ambiguity of success, and competency traps.

Superstitious learning, the ambiguity of success and competency traps can cause organizations to learn the wrong things. **Superstitious learning** occurs when the connections between actions and outcomes are incorrectly specified, for example, when promotions are taken to indicate high levels of performance but in fact are given because the promoted individuals most duplicate the characteristics of existing leaders (e.g., white, male, domineering). This misattribution leads to superstitious learning when the promoted individuals develop self-confidence in their performance leading them to overestimate their ability to make sound decisions for the organization.

Learning failures also occur due to the **ambiguity of success**. It is often difficult to know when organizational success has occurred because the indicators of success are constantly modified (the target keeps moving), and levels of aspiration toward particular indicators also shift over time. In addition, claiming organizational success can be a political act, and counterclaims that view outcomes more negatively create uncertainty about what organizations have actually achieved. When success is difficult to pinpoint, it is tough to learn on the basis of what has worked in the past.

Competency traps can lead to improvements in procedures that have limited or no competitive advantage. Such traps occur when the organization makes improvements in one or more of its frequently used procedures such that the procedure results in a series of successful outcomes thereby reinforcing its use and reducing motivation to search for better procedures. If competitors are meanwhile developing better procedures, the organization can be caught in a competency trap created by its own learning process.

Within organization theory, the idea of organizational learning is generally linked to the open systems movement which imported cybernetic theory into the modernist perspective. The idea of feedback control systems (examined in Chapter 11) has fascinated managers and many organization theorists since the 1960s. Views of organizations as self-correcting systems form the basis of much routinization of organizational activity and underlie common business practices such as management information systems, financial accounting controls (e.g., budgets), and performance evaluations. But organizations today face increasing pressures to innovate and innovation lies in exceptions, not routines. The very foundations of traditional management are shaken by demands to alter the hegemony of control built into traditional hierarchical structures. The notion of organizational learning presents such a challenge to current management practice and the learning organization is the image offered to help management face its dilemma.

There are at least two theoretical directions from which the concept of organization learning can be approached. The modernist, following the path of natural science, develops the notion of cybernetic systems, adding a reflexive loop which allows the system self-awareness—it can learn to learn. American psychologists Chris Argyris and Donald Schon have paved the way for this stream of theorizing about organizational learning with their notion of double-loop learning which challenges earlier single-loop notions. Following further along this path are recent ideas built upon the work of Chilean systems theorists Humberto Maturana and Francisco Varela's autopoietic systems theory.

The alternate path, laid by postmodernists, lies not along the route of the sciences, but rather the arts. Beginning from an understanding of organizations as socially constructed and embedded in language, some postmodernists turn to linguistics and literary theory for insights into the more symbolic aspects of social as opposed to physical systems. Interestingly, although they certainly see things differently, there is a resonance between what they are finding to be important and the concepts of reflexivity and discourse put forward by their modernist counterparts.

Single- and Double-Loop Learning in Organizations

Single-loop learning involves learning from the consequences of previous behavior. In this model learning results from feedback generated by a process of observing the consequences of action and using this knowledge to adjust subsequent action in order to avoid similar mistakes in the future and develop successful patterns of behavior. The single-loop learning process is exemplified by a thermostat that detects when it is too hot or too cold and adjusts by turning the heat on or off. The use of budgets is an organizational practice designed to formalize single-loop learning. The budget is an ideal or target for capital expenditures to which comparison of actual results can be made. When there is a deviation from the target or ideal, the budgeting process will highlight this so that corrective action can be taken. In this way the budgeting process acts as a thermostat controlling unit spending.

According to Argyris, single-loop learning solves presenting problems but ignores issues of why the problems arose in the first place. Although this form of learning can appear intelligent in that single-loop systems can operate on their own (for instance, to keep the temperature of a room or building stable over long periods of time and across extreme variations in external temperatures), the system cannot under any circumstances establish its own standards of appropriate behavior. A system outside the thermostat must decide for the thermostat what temperature it should achieve. If the "wrong" temperature is set, the thermostat goes merrily on regulating for an undesired result. Similarly, budgeting tends to produce stable spending over long periods of time regardless of variations in the conditions of operation of the firm. If the wrong targets are set the system is helpless to alter them.

Double-loop learning involves systems that can monitor and correct behavior *and* determine what appropriate behavior is. This last part—determining appropriate behavior—involves a value judgment and thus moves the question of learning outside of the domain of the single-loop model (and into the domain of subjective appreciations of organizations such as are offered by symbolic-interpretive and postmodern perspectives). Double-loop learning requires that the system question its own underlying assumptions and values and risk fundamentally changing the terms of its own organizing. It is in this sense that double-loop learning is associated with the idea of a self-organizing system. In double-loop learning the system learns to learn and thus becomes intelligent enough to define its own fundamental operating criteria, its behavior, and thus itself.

Double-loop learning, once strictly the domain of strategists and top managers, is increasingly being seen as taking place, or needing to take place, throughout organizations as they hire professionals and skilled technicians to help them adapt to the increasing rates of change they perceive as necessary to their survival. As double-loop learning diffuses, organizational stability is replaced by chaos and new organizational orders emerge from the internal dynamics of the organization rather than at the behest of top management.

Autopoiesis: The Self-Reproduction and Self-Reference of Systems

A relatively new development in systems theory, contributed by Maturana and Varela, has begun to influence the thinking of some modernist organization theorists. Maturana and Varela proposed a theory that argues that external environments cannot influence systems because anything that influences a system is by definition a part of that system. That is, knowledge of a system is wholly contained within that system and can only be appreciated from within it. While taking a fundamentally objectivist point of departure, this line of modernist thinking leads invariably to subjectivist conclusions that have powerful implications not only for our understanding of systems, but our relationship to ourselves, our organizations, and our theorizing efforts. If knowledge can only be determined internally, then where can we find an objective point of observation? All systems, including ourselves, are systems of self-reference and therefore all knowledge is self-knowledge. Everything we claim to do in the name of developing knowledge about the world around us, we really do in an effort to know (and reproduce) ourselves.

According to German social systems theorist Niklas Luhmann, **reflexivity** amounts to the application of a process to itself. Luhmann claims that, because all social processes are based in or carried by communicative processes, achieving reflexivity in social systems requires communication about communication.[20] In addition to communication about communication, Luhmann also points to observation of observation and the application of power to the powerful. "One can speak of reflexivity," Luhmann declared, "whenever a process functions as a self to which the operation of reference belonging to it refers."[21]

In **autopoiesis**, reproduction can only be self-referential. That is, "action systems must always reproduce actions, not cells, macromolecules, ideas, and so forth."[22] Likewise, "meaning systems are completely closed to the extent that only meaning can refer to meaning and that only meaning can change meaning."[23] Thus, the self-referential nature of systems, while implying a closed system with respect to communication or meaning (communication or meaning is never determined outside the system, but always within it), does not negate the idea that systems are open to their environments. As Luhmann explained:

structures and processes that employ meaning can include system boundaries and environments, which take on meaning within the processes of a self-referential system (not in themselves!), so that such systems can operate internally with the difference between system and environment. For all internal operations, meaning enables an ongoing reference to the system itself and to a more or less elaborated environment; the choice of the main focus of orientation can thereby be held open and left to the connecting operations that reproduce meaning through internal and external references.[24]

Luhmann claims that reflexive processes have the capacity to change structures (notice that similar claims were made in regard to double-loop learning) and he predicts that they will develop whenever a great need for structural change exists. Luhmann offers several examples of social processes which have become reflexive including education, economic exchange, and power relations:

The educational process has become reflexive because only educated educators can carry it out; "born educators" (fathers and mothers) can no longer satisfy the demands. Relations of exchange are a further case. As soon as money plays a role, exchange relations become reflexive. In the form of money one exchanges the possibility of exchange. In exchanging money, one communicates about exchange processes, whether one wants to or not, and not just in general (by mentioning them!) but precisely and in conformity with the process in that one exchanges them. . . . Not least, one must think of power relations. Power is reflexive to the extent that it is applied to power, that is, concentrates precisely and exactly on directing others' means of power. This can occur from above but also, and much more subtly, from below. The same holds generally for influence.[25]

Applied to organizations, these ideas suggest a view that comes very close to Weick's notion of enacting an environment and to symbolic-interpretive understandings of the social construction of reality. In virtually annihilating the difference between objective and subjective viewpoints they also align with views being expressed within postmodern theory. While the implications of this line of argument are only beginning to appear in organization theory, look to topics such as organizational identity (see Chapter 8 and Gagliardi's model in this chapter), discourse (discussed in the last section), and reflexivity as key concepts bearing on these ideas.

Knowledge, Language, Discourse, Reflexivity

Weick claims that most conceptualizations of organizational learning, including both single- and double-loop learning models, are extensions of psychological models built upon stimulus-response theory. Thus learning is most often defined as: same stimulus (or situation), different response. Weick counters, however, that what you are most likely to observe in most organizations is the opposite of this sort of learning. What you will see instead is better described as: different stimulus, same response. This leads to the question of whether organizations learn or whether they suppress learning. Weick uses this jolt to our senses to suggest that perhaps the study of organizational learning would benefit from a nontraditional approach that runs counter to the stimulus-response model of traditional psychology which emphasizes action and its outcomes. If learning is a process—and nearly everyone agrees that it is—then perhaps this process isn't located in action, but rather in the domains of knowledge, language, and interpretation.

Weick's reasoning turns attention to processes of organizational construction captured in language. Postmodern organization theorists are just beginning to look at the ways in which talk and text produce and reproduce organizations, although organization communication theorists have taken this approach for some time. Within organization theory, one of the longest traditions of looking at language traces to the study of myths, metaphors, and stories pioneered by organizational culture researchers.[26] However, it has only been recently that researchers interested in these phenomena have taken a fully process-oriented view. For instance, David Boje has conducted studies of storytelling in organizations and Barbara Czarniawska-Joerges proposed narrating as an organizational construction process.[27] Much work in this area has so far been directed reflexively at questions of epistemology in organization theory, particularly important is work questioning the role of the researcher as an objective observer that challenges the hegemony of the modernist position and work that develops alternative writing styles.[28] This research is introducing new types of discourse into the field and paving the way for its own self-organizing. One new discourse, for instance, involves the topic of aesthetics in organizations.[29] However, as these views are in the early stages of development, I leave this discussion for my next edition . . .

SUMMARY

Although it might seem tempting to regard the different perspectives in organization theory as progressively more attuned to dynamic points of view and thus to organizational change, this would be too simplistic. As systems theorists work their way up Boulding's hierarchy (see Chapter 2), modernist organization theorists become more and more sensitized to change dynamics. Right now, modernist perspectives are struggling hard to escape their static past by emphasizing stage models and evolutionary theories. Applications of self-referential systems theory such as autopoietics promise to bring even more insights about organizational change within the modernist perspective.

Symbolic-interpretivists, with their firm commitment to social constructionism and emergent phenomena, have little in the way of a static tradition to overcome. However, their descriptive methodologies and focus on the concrete and particular make it difficult to generalize their results across situations and settings, at least in traditional, scientific ways. Where symbolic-interpretivist research has an advantage is in offering a narrative form of knowledge which focuses on small-scale changes that make up everyday life in organizations. Change in the symbolic-interpretive perspective involves changing words, activities, physical objects, and material landscapes as well as guiding images and framing individual and organizational identities. It sensitizes you to the symbolic dimensions of organizational experience including the emotional and aesthetic responses that also constitute organizational life.

Postmodern perspectives challenge existing orders and inspire thoughts about alternative realities while raising ethical questions and heightening consciousness through self-reflexivity. This perspective does not theorize change, it attempts to provoke it. It locates change in subjectivity and thus advocates organizational change via personal transformation.

You should now be sophisticated enough in your appreciation of the three perspectives of organization theory to recognize the points of contact as well as the differences between them. The topic of organizational change is a good one for underscoring the fragility and temporality of all thoughts about organizations and organization theory. Perspectives, their multiple interpretations and their interpreters shift and change, and so do we and our organizations bringing new ideas and hope as well as new forms of domination and regret—but always offering opportunities to learn. I hope that this book has increased your learning capacity and will inspire you in future to think, speak, and act more broadly and wisely than you might otherwise have done.

KEY TERMS

planned change
unfreeze—change—refreeze
macroevolutionary, micro-
    evolutionary, and political
    forces for change
apparent change
revolutionary change
cultural incrementalism
manifestation
realization
symbolization

interpretation
dialogue
learning organization
superstitious learning
ambiguity of success
competency traps
single-loop learning
double-loop learning
reflexivity
autopoiesis

ENDNOTES

1. Kanter, Stein, and Jick (1992:3).
2. Weick (1979 [1969]).
3. Lewin (1951, 1958).
4. Goodstein and Burke (1991).
5. Ibid. 12.
6. Kanter, Stein, and Jick (1992: 10).
7. Ibid. 11.
8. Ibid. 14.
9. Gagliardi (1986: 125).
10. Ibid. 130.
11. Hatch (1993).
12. Ibid. 663.
13. Ibid. 667.
14. Foucault (1983: 223).
15. Senge (1990: 241).
16. Ibid. 242.
17. Ibid. 4.
18. Leavitt and March (1988); see also March and Olsen (1975).
19. Barney (1986).
20. Luhmann (1995: 450).
21. Ibid. 443.
22. Ibid. 35.
23. Ibid. 37.
24. Ibid.
25. Ibid. 453.
26. Martin (1982); Martin, Feldman, Hatch, and Sitkin (1983); Wilkins (1983).
27. Boje (1991); Czarniawska-Joerges (1993; forthcoming); Boyce (1995).
28. Van Maanen (1988, 1995); Hatch (forthcoming).
29. Witkin (1990); Strati (1992); *Organization*, Special issue on Aesthetics and Organization, 3: 2 (1996).

REFERENCES

Argyris, Chris (1982). *Reasoning, learning and action*. San Francisco: Jossey-Bass.

Argyris, Chris (1990). *Overcoming organizational defenses: Facilitating organizational learning*. Boston: Allyn and Bacon.

Argyris, Chris, and Schon, Donald A. (1978). *Organizational learning: A theory of action perspective*. Reading, Mass.: Addison-Wesley.

Barney, Jay B. (1986). Organizational culture: Can it be a source of sustained competitive advantage? *Academy of Management Review*, 11: 656–65.

Boje, David M. (1991). The storytelling organization: A study of story performance in an office-supply firm. *Administrative Science Quarterly*, 36: 106–26.

Boyce, Mary E. (1995). Collective centering and collective sense-making in the stories and storytelling of one organization. *Organization Studies*, 16: 107–37.

Czarniawska-Joerges, Barbara (1993). Narratives of individual and organizational identities. *Communication Yearbook*, 17: 193–221.

Czarniawska-Joerges, Barbara (forthcoming). *Narrating the organization: Dramas of institutional identities*. Chicago: University of Chicago Press.

Foucault, Michel (1983). The subject and power. In H. L. Dreyfus and P. Rabinow (eds.), *Michel Foucault: Beyond structuralism and hermeneutics* (2nd edition). Chicago: University of Chicago Press.

Issues and Themes in Organization Theory

Gagliardi, Pasquale (1986). The creation and change of organizational cultures: A conceptual framework. *Organization Studies*, 7: 117–34.

Goodstein, Leonard D., and Burke, W. Warner (1991). Creating successful organization change. *Organizational Dynamics*, Spring: 5–17.

Hatch, Mary Jo (1993). The dynamics of organizational culture. *Academy of Management Review*, 18/4: 657–63.

Hatch, Mary Jo (forthcoming). The role of the researcher: An analysis of narrative position in organization theory. *Journal of Management Inquiry*.

Kanter, Rosabeth Moss, Stein, Barry A., and Jick, Todd D. (1992). *The challenge of organizational change: How companies experience it and leaders guide it*. New York: Free Press.

Leavitt, Barbara, and March, James G. (1988). Organizational learning. *Annual Review of Sociology*, 14: 319–40.

Lewin, Kurt (1951). *Field theory in social science*. New York: Harper & Row.

Lewin, Kurt (1958). Group decisions and social change. In E. E. Maccobby, T. M. Newcomb, and E. L. Hartley (eds.), *Readings in social psychology*. New York: Holt, Rinehart & Winston, 197–21.

Luhmann, Niklas (1995). *Social systems* (trans. J. Bednarz, Jr. with D. Baecker). Stanford, Calif.: Stanford University Press (originally published in German in 1984).

March, James G., and Olsen, Johan P. (1975). The uncertainty of the past: Organizational learning under ambiguity. *European Journal of Political Research*, 3: 147–71.

Martin, Joanne (1982). Stories and scripts in organizational settings. In A. H. Hastorf and A. M. Isen (eds.), *Cognitive social psychology*. New York: Elsevier-North Holland, 255–305.

Martin, Joanne, Feldman, Martha, Hatch, Mary Jo, and Sitkin, Sim B. (1983). The uniqueness paradox in organizational stories. *Administrative Science Quarterly*, 28: 438–53.

Maturana, Humberto, and Varela, Francisco (1980). *Autopoiesis and cognition: The realization of the living*. London: Reidl.

Senge, Peter M. (1990). *The fifth discipline: The art and practice of the learning organization*. London: Century.

Strati, Antonio (1992). Aesthetic understanding of organizational life. *Academy of Management Review*, 17: 568–81.

Strati, Antonio (1995). Aesthetics and organizations without walls. *Studies in Culture, Organizations and Societies*, 1: 83–105.

Van Maanen, John (1988). *Tales of the field: On writing ethnography*. Chicago: University of Chicago Press.

Van Maanen, John (1995). Style as theory. *Organization Science*, 6: 133–43.

Weick, Karl (1979 [1969]). *The social psychology of organizing*. Reading, Mass.: Addison-Wesley.

Weick, Karl (1991). The nontraditional quality of organizational learning. *Organization Science*, 2: 116–24.

Wilkins, Alan (1983). Organizational stories as symbols which control the organization. In P. Frost, L. Moore, M. Louis, C. Lundberg, and J. Martin (eds.), *Organizational culture*. Beverly Hills, Calif.: Sage, 81–91.

Witkin, Robert W. (1990). The aesthetic imperative of a rational-technical machinery: A study in organizational control through the design of artifacts. In P. Gagliardi (ed.), *Symbols and artifacts: Views of the corporate landscape*. Berlin: Walter de Gruyter, 325–38.

FURTHER READING

Bate, Paul (1995). *Strategies for cultural change*. Oxford: Butterworth-Heinemann.

Kanter, Rosabeth Moss, Stein, Barry A., and Jick, Todd D. (1992). *The challenge of organizational change: How companies experience it and leaders guide it*. New York: Free Press.

Index

Index

Index

Index